FreeHand® 10
f/x & Design

Ron Rockwell

CORIOLIS

President and CEO
Roland Elgey

Publisher
Steve Sayre

Associate Publisher
Katherine R. Hartlove

Acquisitions Editor
Alisha Blomker

Product Marketing Manager
Patricia Davenport

Project Editor
Jennifer Ashley

Technical Reviewer
Mary Rich

Production Coordinator
Meg E. Turecek

Cover Designer
April E. Nielsen

Layout Designer
April E. Nielsen

CD-ROM Developer
Chris Nusbaum

FreeHand® 10 f/x & Design

The Coriolis Group, LLC
14455 N. Hayden Road
Suite 220
Scottsdale, Arizona 85260

(480)483-0192
FAX (480)483-0193
www.coriolis.com

Library of Congress Cataloging-In-Publication Data
Rockwell, Ron.
    FreeHand 10 f/x & design / by Ron Rockwell.
        p.   cm
    Includes index.
    ISBN 1-58880-164-0
    1. Computer graphics.   2. FreeHand (Computer file).   3. Web sites--Design.
I. Title: FreeHand 10 f/x and design.   II. Title.
T385 .R5793   2001
006.6'869--dc21

2001047425
CIP

 **CORIOLIS**

Printed in the United States of America
10 9 8 7 6 5 4 3 2 1

A Note from Coriolis

Thank you for choosing this book from The Coriolis Group. Our graphics team strives to meet the needs of creative professionals such as yourself with our three distinctive series: *Visual Insight*, *f/x & Design*, and *In Depth*. We'd love to hear how we're doing in our quest to provide you with information on the latest and most innovative technologies in graphic design, 3D animation, and Web design. Do our books teach you what you want to know? Are the examples illustrative enough? Are there other topics you'd like to see us address?

Please contact us at the address below with your thoughts on this or any of our other books. Should you have any technical questions or concerns about this book, you can contact the Coriolis support team at techsupport@coriolis.com; be sure to include this book's title and ISBN, as well as your name, email address, or phone number.

Thank you for your interest in Coriolis books. We look forward to hearing from you.

Coriolis Creative Professionals Press
The Coriolis Group
14455 N. Hayden Road, Suite 220
Scottsdale, AZ 85260

Email: **cpp@coriolis.com**

Phone: (480) 483-0192
Toll free: (800) 410-0192

Visit our Web site at **creative.coriolis.com** *to find the latest information about our current and upcoming graphics books.*

Other Titles for the Creative Professional

Dreamweaver® 4 Visual Insight
By Greg Holden, Scott Willis

Dreamweaver® 4 f/x & Design
By Laurie Ulrich

Fireworks® 4 f/x & Design
By Joyce J. Evans

Flash™ 5 Visual Insight
By Sherry London, Dan London

Flash™ 5 f/x & Design
By Bill Sanders

Flash™ 5 Cartoons and Games f/x & Design
By Bill Turner, James Robertson, Richard Bazley

Flash™ ActionScript f/x & Design
By Bill Sanders

Integrating Flash™, Fireworks® and FreeHand® f/x & Design
By Joyce J. Evans

Deciphering Web Design
By David Robison

Photoshop® 6 In Depth
By David Xenakis, Benjamin Levisay

Dedicated to Hal Thomas,
who taught me how to draw.
The world misses you.
—Ron Rockwell

❧

About the Author

Ron Rockwell is an experienced graphic designer and illustrator with a wide range of styles and techniques well suited to the variety of clients he has had over the years. His clients include ministers, camera manufacturers, toy makers, oil companies, aerosol manufacturers, publishers, refrigerator manufacturers, the U.S. Navy, the state of Hawaii, computer manufacturers, television networks, and dozens of others.

Ron got his training on the job, at a commercial printing shop, where he learned all facets of printing, graphic design, production, and illustration. His illustrative skills were honed on drawing boards covered with vellum, ink, and eraser crumbs. After working at the print shop for several years, he became a freelance one-man shop, and added photography and screen printing to his list of talents.

When he got his first Macintosh computer in 1985, his professional world changed immensely. The arrival of FreeHand in 1988 meant an entirely new way to draw, and FreeHand became his program of choice. Even in those days of black-and-white 9-inch screens, he produced full-color labels and brochures with FreeHand.

Times and computers have changed, and so has FreeHand.

Ron and his wife, Yvonne, live in the Pocono Mountains of Pennsylvania. He has been employed as a graphic designer for a manufacturing company in Nevada for several years, but he is a compulsive worker and has many freelance accounts reaching from California to Massachusetts—and very little free time. Ron and Yvonne operate Nidus Corp., a graphic design/illustration/photography/Web development/original music/candlemaking business from **www.nidus-corp.com**. He is a member of the National Association of Photoshop Professionals and the Graphic Artists Guild. In 1999 he won the People's Choice Award for Infographics at Macromedia's UCON '99 in San Francisco.

In 2000, he received a patent for a light box that attaches to a computer monitor. You can see it in action at **www.nidus-corp.com/illuminox.html**. The light box is used by service bureaus and production artists who retouch or manipulate transparencies and slides that have been scanned.

FreeHand has remained the one program that is involved in virtually every job he does, although he is prolific in Flash, Dreamweaver, Fireworks, InDesign, PageMaker, and Photoshop. This latest release of FreeHand brings together the advanced type-handling characteristics, drawing tools, Web development features, and user-friendliness we have grown to expect from FreeHand.

Acknowledgments

Writing a book is not as easy as one might think. It would be impossible without the help and hard work of many people. I could not have completed it without the undying support of my wife, Yvonne. She went far beyond normal concessions and compromises in order to help me through. My father, Norman Rockwell (no, not *that* one), couldn't have been more of a champion, and my stepmom, Marian, was a great cheerleader.

My acquisitions editor, Alisha Blomker, is my new best friend. She pushed, prodded, and sweet-talked me through the entire project. It certainly wouldn't have happened without her. Jennifer Ashley rode hard on me as project editor and made me tow the line. She also taught me a few things about writing that I either didn't know or had forgotten. My knuckles still smart from the ruler whacks. Because this is my first book, my copy editor, Mary Swistara, and technical editor, Mary Rich, had more than their share of work to do. The production coordinator Meg Turecek, layout and cover designer April Nielsen, and Color Studio designer Carla Schuder worked behind the scenes to make the printed book possible.

Keith Hutchinson was extremely helpful in getting answers for me from his super Macromedia engineering staff in Richardson, Texas. Ian Kelleigh was a constant inspiration with his extremely helpful—and free—tip-filled Web site. Juan Valdez and his coffee-harvesting brethren kept me company through many late nights and early mornings, as did Sid, Boone, and Snickers. But, no one was there more than my old teacher and friend, Hal Thomas. Thank you all from the bottom of my system folder.

—*Ron Rockwell*

Contents at a Glance

Part I   **Introducing Macromedia FreeHand**

Chapter 1   Introduction to FreeHand   3

Chapter 2   What's New in FreeHand 10?   17

Part II   **Drawing a Straight Line without a Ruler**

Chapter 3   Path Operations   33

Chapter 4   Getting Colorful   55

Chapter 5   Creating Gradients and Blends   73

Chapter 6   Symbols, Hoses, and Libraries   99

Chapter 7   Vector-Based Brushes   121

Part III   **Keeping Perspective**

Chapter 8   A Matter of Perspective   143

Chapter 9   Distorting the Truth   179

Part IV   **Moving Beyond Drawing**

Chapter 10   Text and Printing   209

Chapter 11   Drawing for the Web   253

Part V   **Tricks of the Trade**

Chapter 12   The Kitchen Sink   293

Table of Contents

Foreword by Ian Kelleigh xix

Introduction xxi

Part I   Introducing Macromedia FreeHand

Chapter 1   Introduction to FreeHand 3

What's So Hot about FreeHand?   4
    Keyboard Shortcuts   4
    Customizing the Toolbar   6
    Desktop Size   7
Multiple Pages   8
Getting around the Desktop   9
    Viewing Pages   9
    Custom Views   10
    Types of Toolbars   10
A New Document   11
Grids   11
Master Pages   11
Guidelines   12
    The Zero Point   12
Setting Up Your Own Default Page   13
    In the Panels   13
    On the Document   13
    Saving Time, Money, and Your Default Page   14
    The Difference between Default Pages and Templates   14

Chapter 2   What's New in FreeHand 10? 17

New Toys and Tools   18
Brush Stroke   18
Contour Gradients   19
Navigation Panel   20
Library Panel   21
Master Pages   22
Pen Tool Features   22

Smart Cursor Pointers   24

Enhanced Tools Panel   25

Color Boxes   26

Editing Symbols   26

File Info Dialog Box (International Press Telecommunications
Council Protocol)   27

Integration with Flash   27

Print Area   28

Unsaved Document Indicator   28

Working Conditions in OS X   28

Part II   **Drawing a Straight Line without a Ruler**

Chapter 3   **Path Operations** **33**

Paths: Vectors Show the Way   34

FreeHand Xtras   35

Add Points   35

Union   36

Punch   36

Divide   37

Intersect   37

Path Modifying Xtras   38

Expand Stroke   38

Inset Path   38

Roughen   39

Add Points   39

Simplify   39

Reverse Direction   40

Correct Direction   40

Fractalize   40

Getting to Work   41

Project: The Hacksaw Project   41

Creating the Document   42

Drawing the Frame   42

The Blade   43

Drawing the Handle   45

Finishing Touches   47

Project: Drawing Hands That Look Human   49

Modifying an Image with the Pen Tool   50

Creating a Brush and Ink Technique   51

Chapter 4   **Getting Colorful** **55**

Introduction to Color   56

CMYK Colors   56

Spot Colors   57

RGB Color Explained   58

HLS Color Creation   59

Web-Safe Colors   60

Creating Color in FreeHand 60
  Choosing Colors 60
  Custom Library 61
  Decisions, Decisions: How to Choose 61
  Creating Colors 62
  A Lighter Shade of Pale—or Any Other Color 63
  Project: The Car Library 63
    Primary Color List 63
  Project: The New Car Drawing 65
    The Car's Body 67
    Details 68
    The Wheels and Tires 68
    But I Wanted a Blue One... 69

Chapter 5 Creating Gradients and Blends.......................73
FreeHand Vector Alchemy 74
The Blend Xtra 74
The Gradient Fill 76
  Project: Drawing with Blends 77
    The Cube 77
    The Cone 78
    The Sphere 79
  Project: Drawing with Gradient Fills 81
    The Cube 81
    The Cone 81
    The Sphere 82
The Contour Gradient 82
  Project: Drawing with Contour Gradients 83
    The Leaves 83
    The Petals 84
    The Stem 85
  Project: Drawing with the Whole Toolkit 86
    The Cube 86
    The Cone 89
    The Sphere 89
  Project: The Power Saw 90
    The Line Drawing 90
    Creating the Labels 91
    Creating the Color Fills 92
    The Foot and Other Details 95

Chapter 6 Symbols, Hoses, and Libraries.......................99
Symbolism in FreeHand? 100
  Adding Symbols to Your Library 100
  Modifying Symbols 100
  Replacing, Deleting, and Grouping Symbols in the Library 101
Why Use Symbols? 101
  Quick Document Modifications Using Symbols 101
  Exporting and Importing Symbols 102

Unkinking the Graphic Hose   102
  Project: Pass the Peas, Please   103
    The Pod   103
    The Peas   104
    Final Details   106
  Project: The Cherry Job   107
    The Cherries   108
    The Stems   109
  Project: More Vegetables   111
    Setting Up the Document   111
    Drawing the Stalk   112
    Bud Symbols   112
    Hosing Down Your Artwork   114
  Project: The Coffee Bag   116
    Setting Up the Document   116
    Building the Bag   116
    Making It Real   119
    Finishing Touches   119

Chapter 7   Vector-Based Brushes **121**
The Brush Feature Explained   122
  Why Use a Brush Instead of Clones or Symbols?   122
  Brush Feature vs. Graphic Hose   122
  Altering Your Brushes   123
  Working with the Brush Feature   123
  Project: The Glass Tab Brush   124
    The Basic Shape   124
    Creating the Brushes   127
    Proof It All Works   127
  Project: The Decorative Border   129
    The Basic Shapes   129
    Creating the Brush   131
    Applying the Brush   132
    Putting It All into Perspective   133
    The Type   134
  Project: Creating Organic Brushes   135
  Project: Okay, One More Brush Project   136
  Project: The Eagle   137
    Finishing Touches   139

Part III   Keeping Perspective

Chapter 8   A Matter of Perspective **143**
Getting Three for the Price of Two   144
Methods of Projection   144
  Multiview Projection   145
  Axonometric Projection   146

Project: The Jewel Case   148
   Put a Lid on It   150
   It's a Snap!   151
   The Bottom of the Case   153
   The Floor   154
   Putting It All Together   155
The Perspective Grid   156
  What Is the Perspective Grid?   156
  Applying an Object to the Grid   157
  Putting the Grid to Work   158
  Project: Let's Do Lunch   161
   The Plate   161
   Slicing the Bread   163
  Project: Setting the Table   164
   Making the Sandwich   166
   Getting Crusty   166
   Meat and Lettuce   167
   Finishing Touches   168
  Project: Mom's Diner Sign   169
   Rendering the Sign   172
   Finishing Touches   173
   One More Thing   176

Chapter 9   Distorting the Truth **179**
Lies, Lies, Lies   180
  3D Drawing in the Good Old Days   180
  3D for the Web   181
The 3D Rotation Xtra   182
Working with the 3D Rotation Xtra   182
  Rotate—What Rotates, and How?   182
  Easy Mode 3D Rotation Exercise   184
  Expert Mode 3D Rotation Exercise   184
  Project: The Solar Paddle Wheel   185
Envelope Manipulation   187
  The Envelope Feature Explained   187
  Distorting with the Envelope   188
  Envelopes and Text   188
  Project: Flat Distortions   190
   The Book Cover   190
   Adding Depth and Dimension   193
Wrap an Envelope around a Cylinder   196
  Project: The Aerosol Can   198
   Top Rim   201
   Bottom Rim   202
   Drawing the Sprayhead   204
   Future Aerosol Projects   206

Part IV   Moving Beyond Drawing

Chapter 10   Text and Printing 209

I'm Talking Text and Type   210
Text Editor   210
Keystroking Text Directly onto the Page   213
    The Text Block   213
Just Run a Tab, Billy   213
Text Characteristics   216
Getting the Runaround   217
Oh, No, a Run-in!   218
Stuck in a Rut? Attached to a Path?   218
    One More Thing…   222
    Project: The Newsletter   222
        The Front Page   223
        Page Two   231
Tables and FreeHand   232
    Project: Beef on the Table   234
        The Sidebar   236
        Clip Here   237
Duplicate Pages, Templates, and Master Pages   238
    Duplicate Pages   239
    Templates   239
    Master Pages   240
    Using a Master Page   242
All the Trappings for a Perfect Print Job   243
    Project: The Cat Tasties Package   245
        Photos inside Type Characters   246
        The Star Logo   248
        Star Trapping   249
        Text on a Path   249
        Side and End Panel Layout   250
        Back Panel Layout   251
        Wrapping It Up   251

Chapter 11   Drawing for the Web 253

FreeHand for Web Production?   254
Layers or Tables?   254
More Files Than Visiting Day at San Quentin   255
The Navigation Panel   255
A Flashier Program   255
Publishing HTML Pages   256
    Layers vs. Tables   256
    A Couple More Warnings   257
    The HTML File   258
    Editing HTML Settings   258

Project: Getting Your Feet Wet in the Web   258
   Page 1   258
   Page 2   260
Project: Caution: Explosive Web Site   262
   Setting Up the Pages   263
   Publishing to HTML   269
Animation: Watch Out, Walt!   270
  Quick Animation   271
  What About Flashy Movies?   273
  Assigning Actions   274
  Getting Your Work into Flash   275
  The Movie Settings Panel   276
  Testing the Movie   277
  Project: Rude Cows: The Movie   278
   Setting Up the Page   279
   The Fly   280
   Add Mouse Overs   280
   A Little Background   282
   Covering Your Tracks   284
   Mist-ifying Behaviors   285
   Finishing Up   288
   The End   289

Part V   Tricks of the Trade

Chapter 12   The Kitchen Sink **293**
The Variety of Drawing in FreeHand   294
  Project: Line at the Coffee Pot   294
  Project: The Espresso Drawing with Stylized Brush Strokes   297
   Stylizing the Linework   298
   Coloring the Drawing   300
  Project: Let's Be Photorealistic   302
   Making the Cup 3D   305
   The Cup Body   307
   The Handle   308
   The Rim   309
   The Inside Wall   309
   The Espresso Pot   311
   Coffee Comes in Two Flavors   312
   Bursting Bubbles   314
   The Pour   314
   The Finishing Touches   315
  Project: The Bottomless Cup of Espresso—
  Make Mine SWF Flavored   316

Index **319**

Foreword

A Letter from Ian Kelleigh, "The FreeHand Source"

Become a FreeHand Power User!

When Ron Rockwell first introduced himself and talked to me about writing this book, I was excited to work with a fellow devotee and fresh new author in the FreeHand community. After reading what he has written in the following pages, I am happy to say he has proven to me that he not only knows his stuff . . . he knows it well. This book is awesome!

In *FreeHand 10 f/x & Design*, Ron does a wonderful job of explaining the features in the latest version of FreeHand. He delivers his lessons in a straightforward, no-nonsense manner, and includes plenty of screenshots illustrating his techniques. Instead of the "do this and this happens" method, which has become rampant with many 3rd-party books, Ron takes the time to explain *why* you are doing something as you do it. This book covers everything—from cool projects highlighting the new features in FreeHand 10 (Contour gradients, Brushes, and Master Pages) to tips that can even be used in FreeHand versions 7 through 9.

Ron starts with the basics by showing you how powerful FreeHand's customization can be, such as setting up your Toolbars, keyboard shortcuts, and your own Default pages. Then, through some seriously nifty projects (check out that 3D stuff!), he takes you into the meat of the program and teaches you how to get a better feel for the variety of tools found in FreeHand. I found the tips and sidebars to be very helpful. Make sure you pay special attention as Ron points out some of the quirks you may find in FreeHand (don't worry, there aren't *that* many).

Ron peppers the lessons with humor (which is something we all need once in a while) and his own real-world experiences with FreeHand. He is now passing those lessons learned onto you before you make the same mistakes. This book definitely fills in all the gaps, and answers many questions you may have after reading the manual (you do read the manual right?).

I highly recommend this book for experts and beginners alike. Even I learned a few things—and I've been using FreeHand since version 1.

This book isn't just about creating special effects; it will teach you the basics of illustration, comping Web sites, creating interactive Flash movies, mimicking 3D objects in a 2D environment, and even creating isometric drawings.

No one can learn FreeHand in a day, but with *FreeHand 10 f/x & Design* you will have the perfect tool to help you on your way. And you'll have a lot of fun getting there.

Thanks Ron!

—Ian Kelleigh
www.FreeHandSource.com

Introduction

Why Work in FreeHand?

I'll start this book by climbing far out on a limb and say that Macromedia FreeHand is arguably the most all-round graphics program available. The program has been primarily a 2D drawing program since it was developed in the late 1980s, but it has evolved into something more robust. In the latest version of FreeHand, you can set type, make multiple-page layouts (on a huge 22-foot by 22-foot desktop), and create Web graphics, Web pages, and Flash movies. Plus, you can typeset better tables than any page layout program. And I'm only scratching the surface! Other illustration programs have a bell or whistle here and there that FreeHand lacks, but overall, FreeHand—and version 10 in particular—packs the biggest power punch of them all.

Who This Book Is For

I make the assumption that the reader is more than familiar with their computer, whether it is a Macintosh or Windows-based machine, and at least a working knowledge of Macromedia FreeHand, Adobe Illustrator, or CorelDRAW. In other words, readers should consider themselves intermediate to advanced computer artists. New versions of software products are released every year or so, and right now is a great time to get acquainted with FreeHand as an upgrade or as a brand-new program. If I've done my job, by the time you're through with the book you'll be a FreeHand convert!

Artists who have been using FreeHand will be comfortable with the projects in this book, and Illustrator artists should feel right at home. The differences between the two products grow less important with every release of either product. People using Flash or Fireworks will find FreeHand terms and tools familiar due to the Macromedia Common Interface. Although the book was written on a Mac, and most of the screen shots are from that platform, the technical editing was done on a Windows-based machine, and other than a different label on a key or button, the two platforms differ very little. All keystrokes are written with Mac keys first, followed by a slash and the Windows equivalent key. Folders and menu items are separated by pipes; i.e., FreeHand| English|Symbols or Modify|Symbol|Release Instance.

Getting Started

The book is loosely organized from easy to more complicated features and projects within chapters, and from the basic to the complex from chapter to chapter. The projects were designed to use as many of FreeHand's tools as possible so the reader can better grasp the program. Also remember that a project considered complex by one user may be simple in the hands of another artist, due to each artist's different level of exposure to the program. So it's not necessary to start at the beginning and work your way through. Thumb through the chapters and find a project that interests you and get to work. Then go on and find another project.

A book must start somewhere, and this one starts with an introduction to FreeHand (Chapter 1), followed by a chapter explaining the new features in version 10, including Brushes, Master Pages, Symbols, SWF export, and a little about Macintosh OS X issues (Chapter 2).

Chapter 3 will familiarize you with the program's main drawing instruments—the Pen and Bezigon tools—and some essential Xtras that increase speed and efficiency in your work. The main project is a line drawing of a hand holding a hacksaw that you might see as clip art for a hardware manufacturer.

The many ways color is handled in FreeHand is covered in Chapter 4. The feature project will teach you how to create accurate posterized color graphics.

Chapter 5 will teach you the difference between gradient fills and Blends. You'll draw a project using Blends, and then do the same project again using different types of gradients: linear, radial, and contour. You'll color a flower project later in the chapter completely with the new contour gradient feature. The chapter ends with a colorful saber-saw drawing project that uses a combination of lines, basic fills, blends, and gradients.

Chapter 6 is a study in food. You'll create and use symbols and the Graphic Hose Xtra to draw peas, cherries, a head of broccoli, and a bag of coffee beans. You can see final color images of these projects in the Color Studio section of the book.

You will do some brushing up with the projects in Chapter 7—the thrust of this chapter is the creation of custom brushes, and how they can be used. Projects include impasto style brushes, plastic or glass tab brushes, an eagle, and a screaming jet airplane.

When you open Chapter 8, you'll gain a new perspective on drawing. You'll get an overview of the various types of perspective drawing plus a specific project for isometric drawing. The chapter finishes with an extensive description of the Perspective Grid and how it functions, then you'll build—of all things—a bologna sandwich on the grid! In the last Chapter 8 project, you'll use the Perspective Grid to construct a sign for a roadside diner.

Chapter 9 removes the mystery of the 3D Rotation Xtra and has a great project that will increase your understanding of the tool. You'll also find out how to distort text and other graphics using the Envelope feature. The Envelope will be used to make a paperback book and an aerosol can.

In Chapter 10 you will discover the powerful text-handling attributes of FreeHand while you make an imaginary newsletter. You'll learn the finer points of Master Pages, creating tables, multiple column layouts, inline graphics, text on paths, and text runarounds. This chapter will make a believer out of you—FreeHand is one very powerful layout program. Once you get your newsletter out, you'll find yourself making a label for a box of cat treats.

All you Webmasters and Flashers will come alive when you get to Chapter 11. You'll start out learning the basics of graphic WYSIWYU (What You See Is What You Upload) HTML page layout in FreeHand, including buttons and links. The new Navigation panel will be explained so you can create a five-page Web site for firecrackers and a (questionably) humorous movie about a product for cows.

Chapter 12 contains projects designed to utilize most of the information you've learned throughout the book, and as a catch-all for features and tools that didn't find their way into earlier chapters. The main project is a photorealistic rendering of espresso being poured into a demitasse cup.

What Is Necessary to Get the Most from This Book?

Other than a desire to learn how to draw and work in FreeHand, you'll need the following equipment:

- PowerPC Macintosh processor or newer (G3 or G4) running OS 8.6 or later, including OS X (FreeHand 10 is the first drawing program to operate natively in OS X).

- Intel Pentium 133MHz processor or newer for Windows 98, NT4, 2000, ME, or later.

- A CD-ROM player to access the files on the included CD-ROM.

- Both Mac and Windows platforms will need a minimum of 64MB of RAM.

- Minimum of 70MB free disk space.

- A color monitor capable of 800×600, 256-color display (1024×768, millions of colors recommended).

- Adobe Type Manager Version 4 or later with Type 1 fonts (recommended).

- Netscape Navigator or Microsoft Internet Explorer, both version 4 or later recommended.

- PostScript Level 2-compatible printer or higher.

One more very important resource you should keep in mind comes from all the helpful people who hang out in the FreeHand Forum. You can subscribe at **news://forums.macromedia.com/freehand.** There you'll find FreeHand professional users, novices, and Macromedia employees all willing to help you.

The CD-ROM

In addition to a free 30-day, fully functional trial of Macromedia FreeHand 10 and Flash 5, the CD-ROM that accompanies this book has all the files necessary to complete the various projects. There are symbols, brushes, photos, and partially completed projects to flatten any learning curve you may experience. There are means to add page numbering to your documents (Mac only), and a library of 147 new PANTONE colors. An isometric grid and scale, and a group of common electronic graphic symbols used in electronic schematic drawing are included as symbols. To top off the list, there is a portfolio of hand photos to be used in your own work.

So Let's Get Started!

FreeHand 10 is the accumulation of more than a dozen years of enhanced and enriched drawing power. This book will teach you things you didn't know FreeHand could do. Hopefully, by the time you're finished, I'll have changed the way you think while you're working, so you'll make the most of your time. I've made a decent living with this program since it was first released, and my plan is to pass on everything I know about it within the limits of time and these few pages. I'm an illustrator first and a writer second. With the capable help of my great editors I think we've put together a book that will be easy to get through—and you'll get a lot out of it in the process. If you have any questions along the way, please email me at **rockwell@nidus-corp.com.**

Part I

Introducing Macromedia Freehand

Chapter 1

Introduction to FreeHand

*FreeHand opens a user-friendly world of creativity through
its flexible use of multiple pages, floating panels, and
customizable menus and keyboard shortcuts.*

What's So Hot about FreeHand?

FreeHand allows you to be very creative from the first time you start the program. The default menus and toolbars are more than enough to get you going, but FreeHand's customizing features let you create a program that works the way you want it to, not the way a group of engineers decided it should.

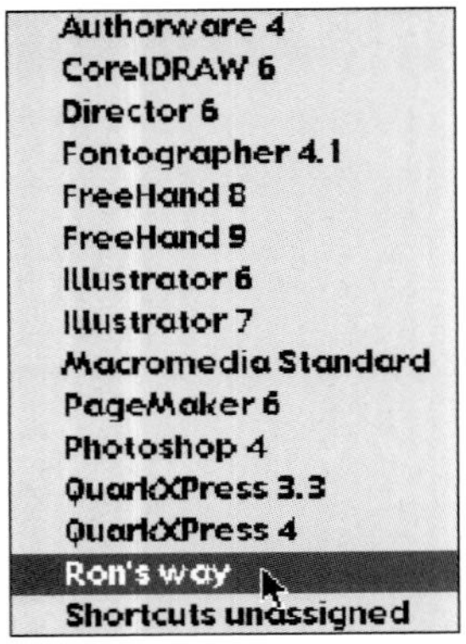

Keyboard Shortcuts

Take keyboard shortcuts, for instance. Say a third of your work is done in Adobe Photoshop. Instead of learning and memorizing a brand-new set of shortcuts for tools, you can simply go to Edit|Keyboard Shortcuts and select Photoshop from the list. From that moment on, you can switch back and forth between the two programs and use the same keyboard shortcuts in each.

As you can see in Figure 1.1, FreeHand provides keyboard shortcuts from 13 competitive programs, including CorelDRAW, Adobe Illustrator, Macromedia Director, and QuarkXPress. If you share your computer with other artists, each can have a distinct set of shortcuts, enabling all of you to work efficiently and comfortably.

I've created keyboard shortcuts for most of the tools I use regularly. This allows me to work effectively and quickly, using my right hand on the trackball and my left hand to click keys so I can change tools whenever necessary. I also type on a Dvorak keyboard, which has a layout that differs significantly from the standard QWERTY keyboard that most people use. Because of the odd arrangement of keys, I have an absolute need for custom shortcuts or I'm seriously hampered while I work.

Your custom shortcuts can be named and saved. That means you can switch between computers if necessary, and just by clicking on your set of shortcuts, you can work as fast on someone else's machine as you do on your own. And here's a cool trick: you can retrieve your saved-and-named custom keyboard shortcuts from the Settings folder inside the FreeHand application folder and copy that file to a floppy, or transfer it over your network, or even email it to another computer. That way, you won't have to try to remember all the shortcuts you use.

Setting Up a Custom Shortcut

It's so easy to create custom keyboard shortcuts in FreeHand that you can get carried away. Soon, you won't be able to touch a key without something happening on your screen. But the main reason for creating them is convenience—yours.

I guess I'm basically lazy, but I don't like to use two hands for a shortcut—two or three fingers on two hands is something I have to look at the keyboard for—and function keys are located far from the standard keys, so using one of them diverts my attention from the drawing I'm working on. For instance, the default shortcut for the Scale tool is F10. I don't know about your keyboard, but on mine, F10 is a long way from where my left hand rests on the modifier keys.

Figure 1.1

Macromedia wants you to be comfortable with these competitive and complementary program shortcuts in the Keyboard Shortcuts window.

Likewise my PowerBook function keys are so tiny I know I'd have a hard time finding one of them. With that in mind, I'll show you how to customize a default shortcut to make it a little more user-friendly. Don't worry about ruining anything. You'll be modifying an existing keyboard shortcut set and saving it as your own.

1. Start by opening the Customize Shortcuts dialog box, Edit|Keyboard Shortcuts.

2. The Commands window on the left lists the main headings in your menu, plus a catch-all called Other. Scroll to Other, and click the triangle.

3. There are eight headings under Other; next to last is Tools. Click its triangle (the + icon on a PC).

4. Scroll down until you see Scale, then click it.

5. The panel on the right has a Keyboard Shortcuts Setting drop-down menu, a text window for a new shortcut key, a button concerning conflicting shortcuts, and the shortcut that is currently active. In this case, it says F10. Highlight F10, and click the Remove button.

6. Click the Press New Shortcut Key text field, and click any modifier keys you'd like with any other key that's comfortable. For me, it's Shift+Cmd/Ctl+S. (Okay, it contradicts my earlier statement about two or three fingers, but the keys are all close together, easy to hit, and *S* stands for *Scale* in my book.)

7. After you click Assign, you may be greeted with a note: Currently Assigned To. If you have Go To Conflict On Assign selected, you'll be taken to that feature's shortcut window where you can either change it or make the decision to change your new key combination. If you are intimidated by change, you can always click the Reset button instead of clicking OK. You will be returned to the default for the particular keyboard setting.

8. Assuming there was no conflict, or you were able to come to an agreement with yourself, click the OK button. Save the new set of shortcuts with a name that won't offend the next user. The shortcut will now appear as a tooltip (if you have them selected in Preferences). Menu commands will show the shortcut on the right side of the menu.

Because I know you're going to go nuts with this, you'll be struck dumb when you decide to use one of your shortcuts and can't remember it. If need be, you can print a copy of the shortcuts by opening the Keyboard Shortcuts panel again and clicking the Print button—then again, you may want to think about it. It's about 23 pages long.

Customizing the Toolbar

Customizing FreeHand doesn't have to stop with the keyboard, though. You can also change the Main toolbar to suit the way you work. Depending on your monitor resolution, the default toolbar consists of two or three rows of buttons across the top of your screen. Some of the tools are the standard tools you find in almost every program for opening new and existing documents, saving, printing, and more. Other buttons control the visibility of panels, links for Web use, and several Xtras. Figure 1.2 shows the default toolbar arrangements for Windows, Macintosh System 9.1, and Macintosh OS X.

Figure 1.2

See what you're missing? FreeHand's default toolbar arrangement as it appears in Windows (top), Macintosh System 9.1 (middle), and Macintosh OS X (bottom).

Everything works the same way, but they look slightly different on the various platforms. Figure 1.3 shows the way I've moved tools around so I can find them on Mac OS X. Besides the layout being more functional than the default, the eye candy of the new Macintosh Aqua interface is very pleasing to work with. But then, I've always been a sucker for bright, shiny things.

Figure 1.3

My custom toolbar arrangement in Mac OS X.

The default toolbar has several buttons for functions that I prefer to access with keyboard shortcuts. There are also quite a few tools in the basic FreeHand arsenal that I don't use often. Not that there is anything wrong with these tools, but in the way I work—that is, with the types of jobs I generally produce—I don't need them. So, I simply go to Windows|Toolbars|Customize, remove any tools I won't be using from my toolbar, and replace them with other tools that I will want to use. That toolbar arrangement becomes the default on my machine and will be accessed by anyone using my particular installation of FreeHand.

Xtra, Xtra, Read All about It!

What the heck is an Xtra, anyway? Well, Xtras are plug-in software extensions that are scattered throughout FreeHand. You'll find them in toolbars, menus, and panels. There are several included free with FreeHand, and third parties create them as freeware, shareware, and pay-through-the-noseware. There are several at Ian Kelleigh's site, The FreeHand Source, at **www.FreeHandSource.com**. Xtras can be as simple as expanding a path, creating a blend, or naming colors in your document. They can also open up windows to create hyperlinks, or create transparency. Some are can't-do-without, and others are I-don't-get-it, depending on the type of work you do and how you do it. Several Xtras are explained in detail in Chapter 3.

Desktop Size

At 18.5 feet square (that's 222 inches, 1,332 picas, or 15,984 points, or 22,555.2 Kyus for those of you who think on a smaller scale), FreeHand boasts the largest desktop of any program. (It's also about half again as large as the studio I work in.) With its multiple-page layout feature, you can put together a fairly large book totally within FreeHand. Certainly, creating a 500-page book in FreeHand may not be the best idea you ever had, but you can certainly use all that space to handle most of your projects.

Graphics on the Desktop

The desktop is primarily used to place pages, but you can also store graphics there until they're needed. I actually do quite a bit of work on the desktop because it's not cluttered with other page elements. However, keep in mind that even though graphics you've used in FreeHand—TIFFs, JPEGs, and so on—will not print if placed on the desktop, unless they're overlapping the bleed margins, they *will* add to the overall file size.

In other words, if you're tracing a 16MB TIFF for a drawing and move it off the page and onto the desktop your file will be 16MB larger than if you deleted it. Those graphics also will go along with the image if you choose to export the drawing, and that can come as quite a surprise sometimes. Once, I was working on a drawing that involved a large TIFF I had traced. I had duplicated my page several times in the course of the job, and at the end I used the Page tool to delete the pages I no longer needed. Unfortunately, I overlooked the TIFF that was about 3 feet away from my final page. So, when I exported my drawing as an EPS and then opened it in Photoshop, I discovered that it was almost 4 feet wide and several hundred megabytes in size.

That only had to happen once. And you cannot avoid it by simply clicking the Fit All button in the toolbar; this will display only your pages, not loose graphics on the desktop. A simple failsafe when exporting is to select everything you want to export, and click the Selected Objects Only option in the Export dialog box.

Exporting with Room to Spare

When you use the Export command in the File menu, FreeHand draws an imaginary box around the extreme elements of the drawing, not your designated page size. This creates an extremely tight crop when you open the exported document in another program. If you want a little room around your art, draw a rectangle that encompasses your drawing with fill and stroke set to none. That shape will determine the resulting crop.

Multiple Pages

As illustrators and designers, most of our projects—brochures or catalogs—aren't usually more than a few pages long. This makes FreeHand a prime candidate for all-around production. Personally, because I'm illustratively inclined, I find it easier to do a layout entirely in FreeHand instead of using Adobe InDesign, PageMaker, or QuarkXPress. If I need to tweak a drawing, a map, or a stylized headline, it's quicker and easier for me to just make that change on original art as I'm working on the rest of the project. I don't have to switch gears mentally, and my jobs run smoother. I also don't have to worry about EPS (encapsulated PostScript) files, any fonts in those EPS files, or sizing issues.

As I mentioned earlier, in FreeHand you can have as many pages as you like in your document (up to that 18.5-square-foot limit and the amount of RAM you have dedicated to FreeHand). That's useful in many ways. You can create several versions of an ad, Web page, or drawing all in one document. You can have the core elements of the document on the first page and by duplicating the page, make minor adjustments or major changes without having to import core elements each time. It's then a simple matter to print the entire document and compare the different versions.

The one inconvenience with the multiple-pages feature is that even though you may have pages of any size (down to 1-inch square), FreeHand will only print pages the size and orientation of the first page in the sequence. For instance, say you have two versions of a letter-size document, but page one is vertical and page two is horizontal. Simply clicking the Print button would give you two vertical pages, and you'd have to reprint the second page. You'll need to do a little planning before printing, but that's a small price to pay considering that other programs would have you opening and printing several documents to accomplish the same task. Figure 1.4 shows how a multiple-page layout might look in the Document Inspector. In this case, I created page 1 as a letter-size page, then made three duplicates. The pages were numbered sequentially by FreeHand from left to right, but as they were modified to horizontal, changed size to 5.5×8.5, made tabloid, and then moved together, FreeHand renumbered them. Notice that the program wasn't even consistent with the numbering. Consider yourself warned when it comes to printing individual pages.

The Numbers Game

FreeHand has a funny habit of renumbering pages in the document layout windows as you make duplicates or shift pages around the desktop. When you put page numbers on your documents, then add or duplicate pages, the page numbers you have defined may or may not agree with those assigned by FreeHand. If you only have a few pages, it's not a big deal, but it can come as a surprise when you go to print. Whenever you will only be printing one page, select something on that page, take note of the page number in the bottom of the document window, and put that page number in the Print dialog box.

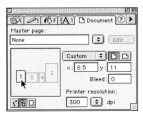 

Figure 1.4
The Document panel in the Object Inspector panel (left: Mac 9.1; right: Mac OS X).

Getting around the Desktop

With all those pages, navigation around the desktop might seem to be a night-mare, but Macromedia has given us several ways to get around the document. First, there's the new Hand tool in the Toolbox, although frankly I prefer the tried-and-true Spacebar+Click to drag my image around the screen. Second, you can go to the Object Inspector|Document tab and see your entire docu-ment in one of three preview modes (see Figure 1.5). The smallest view shows the entire 222-square-inch desktop in a space not much larger than a postage stamp, so it's pretty hard to do a lot of work within it. There is a second, larger version that's useful, but it only can show about six letter-size pages at a time. The third and largest view shows a letter-size page and edges of two or three other pages at most. Clicking on any of the pages—which happen to be num-bered in the window (but not on your document pages)—will fit that page in your window. It's normal to use any and all of the Navigator window views while working on multiple-page projects.

  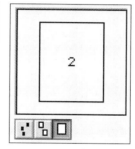

Figure 1.5
Small, medium, and large document view windows.

Viewing Pages

Three buttons useful to have in your top toolbar (shown in Figure 1.6) give you extremely broad page views. These Fit buttons can be moved to appear in any order anywhere on your toolbar:

Figure 1.6
The Fit buttons (from left to right): Fit Selection, Fit Page, and Fit All.

- *Fit Selection*—Fills the window with whatever you have selected.

- *Fit Page*—Fills the document window with the page you're working on. If you resize your document window, the page will be enlarged or reduced when you click the button again.

- *Fit All*—Shows all the pages in your document. Depending on how you have your pages laid out, this might or might not be useful. If you have 10 pages set side-by-side, then your window will display all 10 windows stretching across the monitor. However, if you set it up as two rows of 5 pages, with one row directly above the other, you'll still be viewing all 10 pages, but they'll be twice the size.

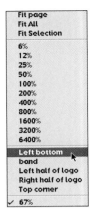

Figure 1.7

There are several default magnifications in the View window, and you can add your own custom views. The percentage at the bottom of the list is the current view of the page scaled to fit the document window.

Custom Views

By far the most useful way to view your document is by using the Custom Views feature in the View menu. Imagine that you are creating a logo consisting of a stylized lowercase letter *i*. At various times, you might be working on just the dot, just the base of the letter, or the entire letterform at once. Put the working part of your drawing in the window, then create and name a Custom View for it. As you work, you can immediately have a particular portion of your drawing filling the screen by going to the View|Custom View menu (see Figure 1.7), or by using the pop-up menu at the bottom-left of the window.

Types of Toolbars

FreeHand comes with panels. Lots of panels. Most can be tabbed, grouped, or docked, and a majority can be customized as well.

Tools Panel

The Tools Panel is where most of the action occurs, because it contains the Select tool, Direct Select tool, Pen, Ellipse, Rectangle, Line, Knife, Scale, Skew, and other basic drawing tools. FreeHand 10 added a color box for Stroke and Fill, as well. Your manual and Online Help sections describe the use of these tools fully. The Tools Panel can be modified with a mouse click+drag to be horizontal or vertical, and contain either a single or double row of buttons.

Top Toolbar

The top of your screen is where you'll find one-click solutions for dozens of routine operations. Click a button to save, another to print, another to undo or redo. Then click buttons to manipulate type, objects, lines, colors, links, and layers. Best of all, the toolbar is fully customizable, and you can add or delete buttons from the rack until you feel comfortable with it. Separate modules reside in the rack that can be moved from row to row, and those modules may be removed from the rack and made to float.

Floating Panels

Floating panels can be moved where you want them, and—if you've selected the preference for it—they'll return to where you left them the next time you open the program. I feel consistency is the key to getting a job done quickly, and I don't like to search for tools, so once I find a spot for panels, that's usually where they stay. Double-click the panel's title bar, click the Zoom box (Macintosh) or Minimize box (Windows) to hide a floating panel. Or drag it back into a toolbar. Again, Macromedia makes it easy to work your way.

Panels can snap to each other or to the extreme edges of the borders. The Windows version also allows snapping to the edge of the application.

Panels with tabs can also be customized. You can tear a tab from one panel and place it in another panel. Or you can leave it as a standalone panel. Don't get too carried away with panel stacking, however; it's more convenient to work with color when you have the Swatches panel *and* the Mixing Well open at the same time. Keeping them both in the same panel means you have to switch back and forth, and that's neither intuitive nor efficient.

Panels may also be docked to each other to save space or reduce clutter. Even people using two monitors gain further control over their environment by docking panels. To dock panels, hold down the Control key as you move the panels together horizontally or vertically. You can then move all of them with a single mouse movement, or undock them by holding down the Control key and dragging the panel by its frame.

A New Document

Every time FreeHand opens, you're faced with a blank page. At that point, you have a few tasks to do: select your unit of measurement, create your page size, input a bleed range, and decide whether to work within a grid or from guidelines. A pop-up menu on the center-left of the bottom of your document window lists the unit of measurement currently being applied. You can select inches, picas, points, centimeters, millimeters, metric inches, and Kyus. Changing that selection changes the units in every other menu or panel in that document. In the Object Inspector, click the Document tab and select a page from the default page sizes, or create a custom size by entering measurements in the X and Y boxes. Bleed area—the amount of ink you want printed outside the trim area—also can be entered here.

Grids

Grids can be applied to your document by clicking View|Grid|Show. You can change the size of the grid through View|Grid|Edit Grid. In that menu, you can make the grid any size, using the units of measurement currently selected for the document. There's also a checkbox marked Relative that will align elements to the same relative place within the grid layout—you aren't restricted to alignment on the grid. (Rules are made to be broken, aren't they?)

Master Pages

Changes are part of the job. If you've been involved in the graphic arts business for any time at all, you've noticed that it seems as though every time the client sees the job, they want to make a change. In FreeHand, making changes to your setup are as easy as deciding to make them. Any modification in measurement units, grid size, and so on ripple through the document. Unless it's strictly an illustration, I rarely finish a job without changing the units for some reason. One caveat, however—if you have multiple pages and decide to change the size of the pages, you must change *each* of the pages individually, *unless* you have created a Master Page.

For instance, suppose you have a letter-sized brochure, and in mid-course it's decided to cut the size to 8×10 inches. You happen to be working on page 1 and make the size change in the Object Inspector|Document panel. When you switch to page 2, it's still set at 8.5×11. You must repeat the change or your pages will not match. Some users may criticize this feature, but think of the other side of the coin: you have an 8.5×11 brochure, and the client wants you to make a Web page utilizing the same basic graphics. You can duplicate the pages and change their measurements to something in the range of 540×400 pixels and just manipulate the graphics until they fit, leaving the brochure complete and intact. Playing devil's advocate, you could just as easily do a Save As, and resize both pages (individually, again), but I like the advantage of having all my graphics within reach.

If you *have* created a Master Page and you decide to change the size of the printed piece, then it's an easy matter to make those changes in the Edit Master Pages portion of the Document panel in the Object Inspector. If you have more than one page size or shape, you can always set up separate Master Pages to make document changes a snap. As a rule, if you are going to have multiple pages with common attributes in your document, you should make a Master Page right off the bat.

Guidelines

If you prefer to work with guidelines, they're simply dragged out from the Rulers at the top and left of the document window. (If there are no rulers visible, choose View|Page Rulers to pop them into view.) If you are working with specific angles or shapes, it's easy to create guidelines that are not just vertical and horizontal lines. If you need a 60-degree margin on a page, just draw your line—be generous and draw it to go off both edges of the page—and while the line is still selected, click the Guides layer in the Layers Panel. The line will become a guideline, and you can move it around your document just as you would any other guideline. The guideline even gains the attribute of snapping to make your drawing more precise. You'll use the guidelines feature in later chapters.

The Zero Point

The Zero Point is quite often overlooked. By default, zero is the absolute bottom-left corner of your document. But feel free to click the cursor in the intersection between the horizontal and vertical rulers and drag the Zero Point anywhere on your page. (This moves the Zero Point only on the page you're working on.) Moving the Zero Point simplifies accuracy greatly, and it's rare that I do a drawing without doing so. However, keep in mind that you've moved the Zero Point when you print with Tiling turned On, because wherever you have placed the Zero Point will become the bottom-left corner of your printed sheet. I'll warn you now—you only forget when you're rushing to finish a job, so it's best to learn the lesson early. Just double-click the intersection area to reset the Zero Point to its original position.

Setting Up Your Own Default Page

So, now that you've gone through all those changes in page size, bleed, grids, guidelines, units of measurement, font selection, line weight and fill, plus color swatches, through all those panels and menus—why would you ever want to do it again? For each and every job? By setting up your own default page, you only have to do it once. I'll show you how. To begin, open a new document in FreeHand.

In the Panels

Set up your defaults in the panels:

1. In the Units Of Measure box at the bottom of the application window, select your preference for measurements.

2. Open the Object Inspector panel, if it's not already open, and click the Document tab. Set the page size and bleed size.

3. Click the Stroke panel and make adjustments to strokes, such as weight or color.

4. Click the Fills panel, and adjust settings as to color and type of fill.

5. In the Type panel, select a font, size, and leading, plus paragraph attributes that are important to your day-to-day work.

6. Open the Color Swatches panel, and add pertinent colors. Make them Spot or CMYK or RGB as necessary.

7. If you usually create a layer for photos or type, or graphic elements, you could add those layers now in the Layers panel, and adjust their hierarchy and visibility.

On the Document

Set up your defaults on the document:

1. Drag guidelines for the center of the page, and the margins for live matter.

2. Adjust the Zero Point, if necessary.

3. If there is a section of the page that will usually need a close-up view, such as a date or publication name/number, set the type correctly, and create a Custom View from the Views menu.

4. If you like working with a grid, set it up using View|Grid|Edit Grid, and change the setting to Show.

5. If there are recurring graphic elements—logo, frames, a block of boilerplate copy—place it as you would in a real job.

Saving Time, Money, and Your Default Page

Now save the settings you have created:

1. Go to File|Save As, and choose FreeHand Template in the Save As Format menu on a Mac, or Type in Windows (ft10 will be appended to the name in Windows). Save it to the English folder inside the FreeHand 10 folder as seen in Figure 1.8.

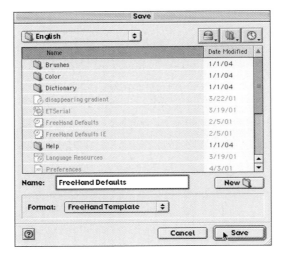

Figure 1.8
Save your customized page in the FreeHand|English folder as a FreeHand Template (don't look for the disappearing gradient file—I can't find it either…).

2. Quit the program and restart FreeHand. You'll be pleasantly presented with a document all set up with everything you need or want.

Five or 10 minutes of your time spent thoughtfully assessing the way you work—and applying it to your own default page—will save you dozens and dozens of hours over a year.

The Difference between Default Pages and Templates

Simply put, there is none. New paragraph.

Okay, there *is* a difference, but it's very slight—it depends on what you've named the page and where it's located. A Default page should be constructed for your daily routine work. That page is what will start every time you click the FreeHand application icon. If you have a set of projects that you will be working on, go through the same steps you did for a Default page, but export it as a FreeHand Template, with a name suggestive of its use. You can have dozens of FreeHand Templates on your hard drive (in any folder you wish), just waiting for the next look-alike job to come along. Double-click the one you want to start FreeHand and open that template, and then smile at all the time and money you've saved—or earned—by using good sense and doing your homework in advance.

Moving On

This chapter showed you that FreeHand is easily and quickly customizable to fit every artist's and designer's needs and styles. You've seen that the desktop is a monster, that you can place graphics on it until you're ready for them, and that you can fill that huge desktop with more than 500 letter-size pages. You now know that FreeHand's multiple-page feature is tamed by the ease with which you can navigate around the desktop using the Navigator panel, toolbar buttons, and Custom Views. Panels abound in FreeHand, and you've learned that you can dock them, snap them, slip them into toolbars, and make them disappear and reappear at will. You've also learned how to set up a new document as a default document that contains all the custom items you use on a regular basis—page size, bleed area, units of measurement, guidelines and grids, prime font selection, line weight and color, fill color, and a color pallet. And, you've learned why and how to set up custom templates for other work. Now let's get down to work—and start having fun.

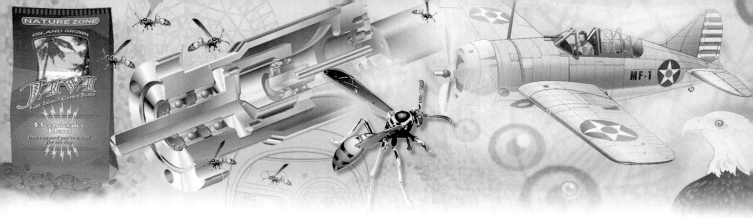

Chapter 2

What's New in FreeHand 10?

FreeHand 10 brings new features to an already feature-rich program. This chapter reveals what's new and what's changed in the world of FreeHand.

New Toys and Tools

The major change in FreeHand is its compatibility with OS X, the new Macintosh operating system. FreeHand is the first drawing program to run under OS X, Windows, and Classic Mac. Creating it required a lot of engineers going through hundreds of thousands of lines of code in order to make everything compatible on all three platforms. With such an undertaking, the road has been a little rocky, but it's a road worth traveling. While the Apple team was making final adjustments to OS X, the Macromedia team was fine-tuning the code to fit the new adjustments. That situation created the possibility that one change would cause a bug somewhere else—squash that bug, and another popped up. As Apple and Macromedia continue to work together, I am quite sure that minor annoyances we have with either software will be eliminated.

Some of the new features build on previous FreeHand attributes, but others are brand new. All updated and new features came from user requests, and most bring FreeHand closer to the Web. A few changes are cosmetic, but many are much more than skin deep. I'll discuss them in this chapter in no apparent order; each gets more fully described in a project environment in later chapters.

Brush Stroke

As an illustrator, I think the Brush feature is the most important new feature in FreeHand 10. The basic premise is that you can take any element in a document—even text—and turn it into a brush stroke that can be applied to any path. Creating a brush is as simple as selecting an object and choosing Create Brush from the Modify menu, which brings up the dialog box shown in Figure 2.1.

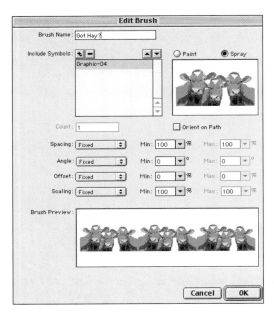

Figure 2.1
The Edit Brush dialog box.

The application to the path can be altered in several ways, as you can see in Figure 2.1. The first two choices are to either paint or spray the brush. Painting will stretch the graphic from one end point to the other end point of a path. Choosing to spray will place iterations of the graphic along the path. The brush can be set to follow the path by checking the Orient On Path button or, if it is not checked, the brush will show the orientation it had when it was created.

The next four options, Spacing, Angle, Offset, and Scaling, can each be set to be Fixed, Random, or Variable. You can change the amount of space between iterations in the Spacing menu. Choosing a number less than 100% allows overlapping, which creates a smoother curve transition. The Angle option allows you to rotate the brush as it travels along the path. Offset has the same effect as Baseline Shift in typesetting, so the brush can have a stepped effect if you desire. Scaling controls the height of the brush. If you select Spray, the brush will have proportionately enlarged or reduced versions of the brush on the path. However you choose to paint the brush, the height will be reduced or enlarged, but the entire graphic you've turned into a brush will extend the length of the path. Results vary.

You can also stack brushes in the Edit box. Click the plus sign in the Include Symbols menu, and all the symbols in the current document's Library will appear. When you choose one, it is applied directly on top of the graphic already in the brush. The Brush feature is covered in Chapter 7.

Contour Gradients

A couple of older versions of Adobe Illustrator have offered the Gradient Mesh tool. However, Gradient Mesh art must be rasterized before it can be printed. To many people working with these drawing programs occasionally, or for fun, that's no big deal. But for professional artists, it's a major factor. Rasterizing means the art is going to turn into a bitmap, and *that's* a big deal. Vector art can be scaled up or down without suffering jaggies or loss of data. Rastered art, or bitmaps, are suited to be reproduced at one size only. Reduce it or enlarge it, and you've disrupted the integrity of the artwork. Edges that were made up of dots in the first place are now jumbled or so jagged as to make the drawing useless.

So what's the big deal? Just do the art the size you want it, and raster it to fit the page or poster it will be printed on and forget it. Sure, that will work until the new guy at the agency decides to use your file at a different size or in a different document. If someone wants to enlarge my EPS file, they can do it and I don't have to worry about a frantic phone call from the printer. When I want bitmapped artwork, I'll continue using Adobe Photoshop, but for vector illustrations, FreeHand is the best choice.

But what does FreeHand's Contour gradient do, you ask? Well, think of it as a basic gradient fill coming from all directions instead of just one. Or you could think of it as a Radial gradient fill that isn't round. As a basic gradient fill, it accepts all the colors you wish to place in the color ramp, and while it's working like a radial fill, it is following the contours of the perimeter of the closed path. You would get the same results if you made a clone of the closed path and reduced it or used the Inset Path Xtra to make it smaller, while changing the color. See Figure 2.2 for a comparison between the Contour gradient and a run-of-the-mill Blend.

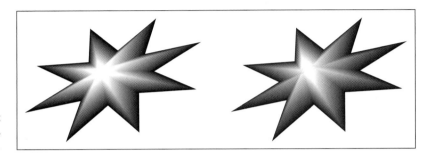

Figure 2.2
A standard Blend (left), and the Contour gradient (right).

If you create a Blend between two similar objects placed on top of each other, it will look the same as a Contour gradient. The difference is that with the Contour gradient, you control the size of the inner cloned shape with a slider; and its placement within the larger shape, just as you do the center point in a Radial gradient fill. The Contour gradient is a healthy addition to the gradient fills panel and is discussed fully in Chapter 5.

Navigation Panel

With Macromedia's strong positioning in the Web community, it's logical that FreeHand is led, or brought kicking and screaming, into Web activities. The Navigation panel is the feature doing the leading. When you select an object on your page, you can input a URL or select a page from within the current document in the Link drop-down menu, located immediately to the right of the Link field, as seen in Figure 2.3. You can also select every instance of a link in your document by using the Search button, which is located next to the Link drop-down menu button.

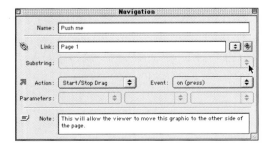

Figure 2.3
The Navigation panel gets you on the way to the Web.

If you select a string—a line of text—that you want linked, that line of text will show up in the Substring window. In the Action menu are several Flash Actions, including GoTo, Play, Stop, Full Screen, Start/Stop Drag, and Print. The Print feature allows you to select a portion of the HTML page or Flash movie that you want to let a viewer print. The Event menu lists various mouse/cursor actions, and a Frame Event. Depending on the Flash Action you've chosen, various parameters are made available to you. A note area at the bottom will jog your memory in a few days when you've lost track of what you had in mind, or will let the next person working on the job better understand what you're up to. The Navigation panel is pushed to the limits in Chapter 11.

Library Panel

I must confess that prior to this book, I didn't have much to do with symbols unless I was working in Macromedia Flash. Since then, I have been endowed with a Master of Symbols degree. The Library panel was known as the Symbols panel in previous versions of FreeHand, but the name was changed to bring it in line with the Library panels used in Flash and Fireworks. The Library shown in Figure 2.4 contains graphic elements, text, brushes, and a Master Page that can be set up with common elements used for recurring jobs. All these items may be exported for transfer to another document or computer.

Figure 2.4
The Library panel can contain many often-used elements.

Using the Library panel, you can group elements together in group folders and delete items you no longer need. Importing a Library is as simple as going to the triangle menu and selecting Import. From there, you can select individual elements of existing Libraries, or entire Libraries. The panel expands to show how many times the element has been used and the date it was placed, making it easy to know when a symbol was modified last and how many will be subject to change should you decide to change them. The Library is used constantly throughout this book—and my daily work.

Master Pages

Ahh, FreeHand finally includes Master Pages. It's about time. After all, the pasteboard and document have room for more than 500 letter-size pages. A Master Page feature is long overdue. Okay, right off the bat, no provisions for automatic page numbering exist, and that's a huge negative in the world of print. That said, including Master Pages is a major improvement.

What does FreeHand's Master Page do? I'm glad you asked. It serves a purpose somewhere between a Template before you open a document and a Duplicate Page action within a document. If you have a job that has a basic layout with constant fonts, graphic elements, columns, placement of key elements, and so on—even page numbers—then the construction of a Master Page is certainly worth the effort. The Master Page can be created as part of your Default FreeHand page, but in the Library so you can use it if you need it—or just ignore it. A Template, on the other hand, will open and be ready to go with everything as you left it (but it can also have other Master Pages in its Library). However, you will have to search out that Template before you open it. That may or may not take time, depending on where it's filed. In contrast, if you have a document open and you choose to duplicate the page, you get an exact copy of the document, which may be useful as a snapshot of work to a certain point, or as a jumping-off point for a new section in your publication. The duplicate is not transferable to another document, other than the standard Copy, Paste, Save As, etc., actions.

I have a few caveats regarding Master Pages. A page with a Master Page as-signed to it is called a Child page, and you cannot change anything on the Child page without releasing it from its master. Once you release it, you've lost all control from the Master Page, and the result becomes just another docu-ment. When you release the Child page, everything is in one group, so it must be ungrouped before continuing. If you have attached a URL to an object, or used Run Around Selection on an object to create a text runaround in the Master Page, those features will have no effect on the Child page. The Child page must be released in order for those features to function again (and again, you no longer have the control of the Master Page).

The main reason to use a Master Page, then, would be to use it for slide presen-tations where a constant background is necessary, or if you know you will want to make global changes within the job. The Master Page is covered thor-oughly in Chapter 10.

Pen Tool Features

The new Pen tool has created quite a fuss in the longtime FreeHand user com-munity. The tool no longer works the way it has for the last dozen years or so. A decision was made to bring the FreeHand Pen tool in line with the pen tools in Flash, Fireworks, and Illustrator. That decision may stand or not. I'm one of a number who hope we can have our old Pen back.

At any rate, the new and improved Pen tool works too; it just works differently. I've gotten used to it, and it has some nice features that I appreciate. In no particular order, here's a list of what the new tool does. (The Bezigon tool has the same attributes, plus its own list of tricks.)

- *Pen tool with no "smart cursor" icons*—Your next mouse click will begin a path.

- *Pen tool with open circle*—Indicates that you will close a path with the next mouse click.

- *Pen tool with carat*—Present point: will retract the handle that would control the curve of the next path segment with the next mouse click. A double-click will not remove the handle extending back to the previous point. Existing point within a path: retracts both control handles with the next mouse click.

- *Pen tool with plus sign*—Your next mouse click will place a point on a path. Sometimes. It also shows up when you are about to place a point very close to the currently selected path. If you want to add a point in the middle of your existing path, the cursor must be directly on the path. Otherwise, the cursor remains the same, but you extend the path. To keep the former from happening, hold down the Shift key as you click. These occurrences happen consistently, so practice a bit to get the hang of it and learn what it's going to mean to your way of working.

- *Pen tool with minus sign*—Your next mouse click will withdraw both control handles of a point in the middle of a path if handles are present. It will delete the point under your cursor if there are no control handles. Whatever controls the points on either side of this point had on the curved segment will now control the path. Note that you will not see the control handles until you click the mouse (corner points have no handles).

- *Pen tool with slash*—When you see this cursor, the next mouse click will make the end point of an existing path live. The next click after that will continue the path.

- *Pen tool with "X"*—You will begin a new path with this cursor.

- *Pen tool with button-hole (circle with horizontal lines on each side)*—This cursor is telling you that your next click of the mouse will connect to an end path—the current path's, or another unselected path. If the path is closed, the mouse click will delete the *last* section of the existing closed path, creating an open path consisting of your new path and the existing path. FreeHand old-timers, be careful—the tool works differently now. It takes a few hours of working with the Pen tool before you see how it reacts and how you will necessarily need to change your work habits.

In addition, if a point is selected in the middle of a path, and you have the Pen tool selected, the next click of your mouse will add a segment from the end point of that path to your mouse location. That may or may not be what you had planned. If you select the Show Solid Points option in Preferences, the active point on a path is a larger (5 pixels square) indicator than the 3-pixel open squares that make up the rest of the points. With the option deselected, the active point is a 5-pixel open square, and the other points are 3-point filled squares.

Smart Cursor Pointers

The Smart Cursor shows up in all sorts of places. First, assume that you have Snap To Guides and Snap To Points selected in the View menu. Bringing certain tool tips near a horizontal or vertical guideline will cause the cursor to change to an arrow cursor with a triangle and line, which indicates that you can select and move the guideline.

The following tools gain Smart Cursor status and can move the guideline:

- Pointer (direct selection tool)
- Text tool
- Line tool
- Pencil tool
- Rectangle tool
- Ellipse tool
- Polygon tool
- Spiral tool
- Scale tool
- Rotate tool
- Reflect tool
- Skew tool
- Knife tool

Each of these tools will also display a Snap To Guide Smart Cursor when they near a line or graphic object that you have placed on the Guides layer. That cursor is the Pointer with an open circle—the same cursor that indicates you are closing a path if you are using the Pen or Bezigon tool. It is the same cursor, but with different meanings according to the tool you have selected.

When these tools come close to a point (whether the path is selected or not), the Snap To Point Smart Cursor (the Pointer with a black square) indicates that your mouse click will be located exactly at the point you are near. Yes, this happens with the Text tool as well. The upper-left corner of the text box will be located at the point that caused the cursor to change. Skewing, rotation, and reflection will occur with that point as the point of origin.

Several Xtras also gain Smart Cursor status: 3D Rotation, Mirror, Shadow, Fisheye Lens, and Arc. The Snap To Guide can actually get in the way here, because you cannot place your insertion point directly on the guideline; the tool is set to move the guide. However, it is very useful when used with the Snap To Point feature. Placing points of origin is literally a snap.

The Arc and Spiral Xtras and the rest of the drawing tools in the list have the added benefit of placing the end point of a path exactly on an existing path. The Smart Cursor (Pointer and black square) will appear as you near the existing point.

The Pen and Bezigon tools have their own sets of Smart Cursors, but they cannot be used to move a guideline. The guide can be moved by holding down the Cmd/Ctl key. As long as the key is depressed, the Pointer tool will be selected.

These tools cannot select the guideline and do not become Smart Cursors:

- White Pointer (subselect tool)
- Page tool
- Lasso tool
- Eyedropper tool
- Perspective tool
- Freeform tool
- Trace tool
- Hand tool
- Zoom tool

Enhanced Tools Panel

Also in the "me-too" class of additions are the Subselect tool, the Hand (grabber) tool, and icons that match those in Fireworks. The Subselect tool will make Illustrator users comfortable. Longtime FreeHand users will probably delete it from the Tools panel along with the Hand tool. We are used to using the Opt/ Alt key to subselect and the spacebar to grab and move the page. But, that's what makes FreeHand so great—the customizability. If you want a function on your screen all the time, you can place it in a menu or toolbar or panel. Don't want it? Drag it off.

New icons for Freeform, Zoom, and Line tools match the icons in Fireworks. This is purely cosmetic and will have no effect on your work at all—unless you can't find the tool because it looks different.

Color Boxes

For artists working with two monitors, it's a definite plus, because it can cut down on the travel time of the mouse to the Color Swatch panel, which is usually on the other monitor. The color boxes are at the very bottom of the main Tools panel. If None is selected for either stroke or fill, a red slash through the color well appears. The slash is replaced with the actual color when one is chosen. Click and hold the color well, and a box opens with the currently selected color palette showing. You have choices of color libraries to choose from—the Swatches panel, or Web Safe colors, plus the Apple Color Picker or the Windows System Color, depending on your platform. When you run the cursor over a color in the box, its name or numeric color breakdown appears in the top of the window as shown in Figure 2.5. This is a welcome addition.

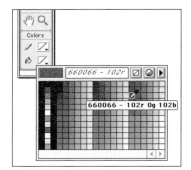

Figure 2.5
The new Colors panel in the main Tools panel.

Editing Symbols

If you need to edit or update a symbol, it's easy to accomplish. Simply double-click the symbol's icon in the Library panel or select it on the page and go to Modify|Symbol|Edit Symbol. The symbol will open in its own window, and you may make any changes you wish to it. When you close the window, every instance of the symbol throughout the document will reflect the changes you made. This applies even if you have taken a symbol and placed it in a custom brush. That makes it a pretty nice addition to the program. An "Auto-update" option is checked as default so the changes happen "live." If you turn this off (in the symbol editing window), you won't see changes take effect until you close the edit window or switch FreeHand documents. Once you make the changes in the edit window, they will occur, but this option allows you to see the changes happen dynamically, or not.

File Info Dialog Box (International Press Telecommunications Council Protocol)

This feature applies chiefly to artists working in the newspaper industry. A panel, shown in Figure 2.6, allows artists to apply pertinent data to their artwork. The International Press Telecommunications Council Protocol is described as the industry-standard file information for cataloging files destined for news media. Clicking the Filename button brings the document's name into the Object Name window.

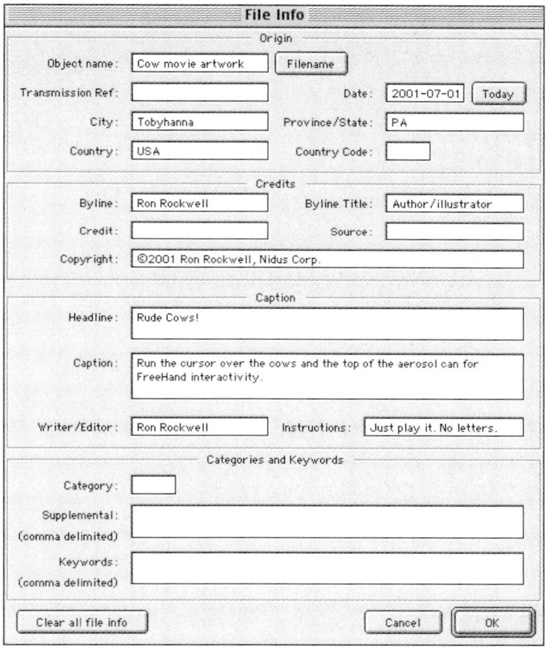

Figure 2.6
The IPTC header support window.

Integration with Flash

The assignment of FreeHand as a Web contribution tool as well as being the preeminent vector drawing program for print has put the Macromedia engineers down in Richardson, Texas, to work making it easier to get things to the Web from FreeHand. To their credit, it works. You can make an animation in FreeHand with a minimal learning curve. You can also create an entire Web page and save it as HTML, ready for placement on the server. Both of those tasks are possible, but the results are not what you would get from Flash or Dreamweaver. But why would anyone expect them to be? FreeHand is a vector drawing program. The fact that its output can go onto the Web is gratifying, but I wouldn't want to create a 20- or 30-page Web site in FreeHand. That's asking a little too much of the program. But, you can ask it to make quick, punchy HTML pages or Flash animations to show for approval, or to use as a guideline for further production. Without worrying about keyframes, rollovers, and code, you can stick to your knitting, so to speak. Put out the message instead of the medium. Chapter 11 is devoted to Web production, and there's a short movie project in Chapter 12.

You can also export FreeHand graphics as vector graphics for the Web, using the SWF format. Flash Actions can be added to objects for export directly to the Web or to be fleshed out more fully in Flash. (Would that then be Flashed out?) When your movie production is complete, you can test it within FreeHand, and view it in Flash Player. There's even a Controller panel that's basically identical to the one in Flash. Flash artists will be extremely comfortable with FreeHand 10.

Print Area

The Print Area Feature allows you to encompass a single print area from the entire pasteboard. If you use the Page tool to place your pages together in readers' spreads, you can select each pair of pages and print them on the same sheet of paper. If you are equipped to print the pages at full size, do so, but if you aren't, you can choose Fit On Paper and FreeHand will reduce the pages to fit your paper size. You can use the Print Area feature to drag a selection that covers all the pages in your document for use as a storyboard. Or you can select a section out of the middle of an oversized page for printing. Another welcome addition.

Unsaved Document Indicator

I think this one is like the Hand tool and the Subselect tool—I can't understand the reasoning for adding it, but I can tell you what it does. It places an asterisk after the document name at the top of your document window when you need to save. I'm accustomed to looking at the Save disk icon in the menu bar. When I need to save, the Save icon is in color. When I've saved, it's grayed out.

Working Conditions in OS X

I'm a Mac person. I have been since 1985. To that point, be aware that this book has no screenshots from a Windows computer. But it's largely immaterial anymore which platform we work on. I have added Windows keystrokes and commands in the text where necessary, and Windows users should be able to follow along just fine.

I like to stay on the bleeding edge of things, so I put OS X on my computer the day after it was released. I'd love to say that working FreeHand 10 on OS X made a huge difference from working on Classic Mac OS. But I can't. Problems still exist and need to be worked out between the Mac OS and FreeHand. I'm confident that they will be, but as for a huge improvement of any kind—there isn't one on my machine. I did notice that when making animations (using the Animate|Release To Layers Xtra), processing was much faster on OS X than on OS 9.1.

However, the Aqua graphics are beautiful in OS X. Icons and menus are easy to look at. Living up to its advertising, the very few times that FreeHand crashed, the Mac OS kept on going, even the Classic applications that were running. Moving windows and panels across the screen is smooth and easy. The interface is very slick and glossy.

There are a few things to contend with, however. I like to extend my windows as much as possible—right down to the bottom of the screen. That causes a slight bit of confusion occasionally when I attempt to change the view, or the units of measure, or anything in the bottom of the document window. That's because the Dock pops up with any hover time at all. It's easy enough to move the cursor a half-inch away and try again, but it does affect your speed. A simple solution would be to leave a little air at the bottom of the window, but old habits die hard.

You only have to make one installation of FreeHand. If you have OS X on, it will install fine; if you have the machine running System 9.1 when you install, it will still install without a problem. When you start FreeHand 10, it will open in whichever operating system you're using. If you have OS X chosen as your startup disk, FreeHand will open in OS X. If you are set to open on OS 9.1, then you'll open without all the eye candy and glitter. At this time, because not that many applications are available for OS X, it makes more sense, to me at least, to stay operating on OS 9.1.

I've heard that FreeHand 10 was "rebuilt from the ground up" for OS X. But most of the minor bugs that are reported come from parts of the application that have been around for many years. I have a G3 PowerBook that is set to start up on OS X, and FreeHand operates flawlessly within that system. FreeHand also works great on my G4/450 machine on OS 9.1. Given my druthers, I'd work on OS X exclusively.

Moving On

There were certainly additions to my favorite program in version 10. Some were needed for a long time; others seemed to come out of nowhere. I imagine something was added for everyone. The new Web implementation will save ad agencies hundreds of hours. The Contour gradient will add another level to realistic rendering. The Brush feature is absolutely super! It can be used for many things other than artistic brush strokes—mark my words, it will become one of your favorite features after working with it a few hours. The Master Pages would have been better with automatic page numbering, but there's always FreeHand 10.5 or 11.

All in all, FreeHand was a great program in version 9, and version 10 has cranked up the volume just a bit. In the next few chapters you'll learn—or at least be exposed to the education of—just how loud you can turn up the volume. Chapter 3 will get you started with path operations, where you can try out the new Pen tool firsthand. Good luck!

Part II

Drawing a Straight Line without a Ruler

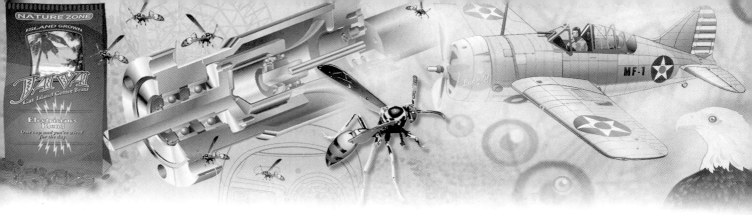

Chapter 3
Path Operations

This chapter will get you in the habit of planning ahead so you can use FreeHand's full complement of tools, features, and tricks. In it, you will learn how to do a real-world clip art project.

Paths: Vectors Show the Way

FreeHand's drawing tools are designed to create paths. Paths can be open or closed, stroked or not. Although this book is intended for intermediate to advanced users, it may have readers who are learning about FreeHand for the first time. So, for the uninitiated, a path is a line that starts at one point and ends at another point somewhere down the line (pun intended), with many or no other points in between. The line can be made to change direction every time you place a point. It can be made to go in a straight path, a curved path, or a connecting path where a straight path meets a curved path. If the path wraps around so the last point in the path lands on the first point, it becomes a closed path. Paths with more than three points may be filled with a color, texture, or PostScript pattern. I will discuss various fills in Chapter 4.

The drawing tools in FreeHand just create the path. If you want to see the path—or its effect—it must be stroked. The Object Inspector|Stroke panel has a list of line weights, and you can add more in the Edit|Preferences dialog box. During my early days with Rapidograph and Leroy pens, I liked to use a 2.5-point line for heavier outlines. It only took a few seconds to add that line weight to my Stroke panel as shown in Figure 3.1.

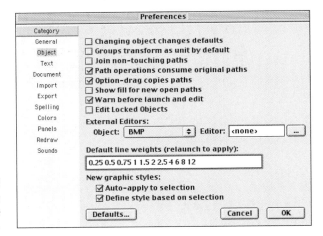

Figure 3.1

Default line weights can be modified in the Preferences panel.

But the line explanation doesn't stop there. (I felt a pun about the end of the line coming, but I managed to suppress it.) The ends of an open path have to stop somehow. The path also must suffer sharp corners sometimes. The juncture where a path changes directions abruptly—such as a square corner—is called a Join. (This Join has absolutely nothing to do with the Join Xtra that connects two paths, or creates compound paths.) FreeHand has three options for end caps and joins, as shown in Figures 3.2, 3.3, and 3.4.

The various end caps and joins that may be applied to paths can be changed as your drawings require. A particular choice of cap and join will look quite different when the line weight is changed, so what works in one part of a

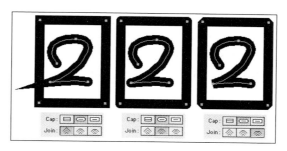

Figure 3.2

The butt Cap stops flush at end points; look in the corners for the differences in joins.

Figure 3.3

The round Cap has a circle the same diameter as the line weight surrounding the end points. Note that it still can have mitered or beveled joins.

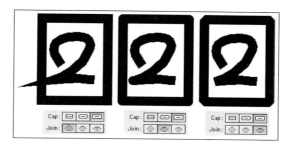

Figure 3.4

The square Cap stops half the stroke past the end points—the point is in the middle of a square equal to the line weight.

drawing may not work at all in another. Keep flexible, and feel free to make changes that improve the appearance of the drawing.

FreeHand Xtras

Once a path has been drawn and the stroke, cap, color, and join set, you can make further adjustments to the line using FreeHand Xtras. A couple dozen Xtras are bundled with FreeHand, and more are available from individuals and through commercial sources (see Figure 3.5). You will find that you will use some Xtras on a regular basis, while others you won't be able to think of any use for. It's all a matter of what you do and how you work. In this chapter, you will see how some Xtras make drawings go quickly and add a little style to them. (A complete explanation of all the bundled Xtras is available in the online help section of the program. I'll only explore a few here.)

Add Points

As you place points on your FreeHand page, the program creates a path between the points, using mathematical formulas (*Bézier* curves). The program doesn't need to add points to make the curve any tighter or wider, or the path more straight. But, if you decide for some reason that you need more points on

Line Weights in the Stroke Panel

The line weight that shows up when you open the Stroke panel will be in the unit of measurement you have set in your Default document. Clicking on the pop-up menu gives you a selection of line weights in points. You might think it would be quicker to just type a number in the dialog box instead of scrolling through the list. Keep in mind your default settings, though. If you have them set for inches, and you want to make your line 1-point wide, you'll be pretty surprised if you just type in a "1" and start to draw. Your line will be an inch wide.

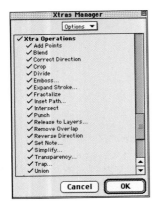

Figure 3.5
You can deselect any Xtras you don't want available in your toolbars by clicking the checkmark in the Xtras Manager window. All Xtras are accessible in button forms that can be added to your toolbars.

your path, you have a few different ways to proceed. First, it's easy to select the Pen tool, and click it along a selected path to add points. It's even easier to select your path and click Add Points Xtra. Doing this will place a point between every two points on your path. Click it again and the points double, and so on. You'd only use this option if you wanted points spaced regularly along the line, however. The main limitation to this process is that it places a point midway between any two previously placed points. Unless your points are equally spaced in the first place, the additional points will not be equally spaced.

Union

Union is part of a group of four Xtras—the others are Punch, Divide, and Intersect—that are extremely useful with overlapping closed shapes. The toolbar button icons are self-explanatory as to their functions, but I'll give you a brief description of how and why you would use them.

If you draw any two or more closed paths and call on the Union function, the entire array of shapes will combine to create one single shape with the fill and stroke of the shape on the bottom. It makes no difference how, or in what order, you select the shapes; the bottommost shape will be dominant. This tool is useful for combining ellipses and rectangles to make cylinders; adding one shape to another to make a more economical blend; or creating a combination shape that can be used for shadow effects. Where shapes overlap, the overlapping lines will be discarded. Shapes that do not overlap become a composite path. Figure 3.6 shows how Union affects these shapes.

Figure 3.6
Here you have three shapes: rectangle in the back with a solid fill, circle in the middle with a gradient fill, and starburst with a gray fill on top. The Union Xtra combines the shapes into one single shape with the bottommost object's fill and stroke.

Punch

This Xtra uses the topmost object as a cookie cutter on all the shapes below it. Any part of the top shape that does not overlap other shapes is discarded (see Figure 3.7). Punch can be used to make the background show in a hole through several shapes—with a single mouse click.

Figure 3.7
Using the shapes from Figure 3.6, you can remove one shape from another using Punch.

Divide

Take the same grouping of shapes and use Divide for exactly the opposite result that Union gives you. Each overlapping shape will become a shape of its own that is mortised exactly with its neighboring shapes. This Xtra is similar to Punch, but all the overlapping lines are retained as closed paths. Use Divide to create transparent effects without using the Lens fills, by adjusting color values in the fills, as shown in Figure 3.8. Be aware, though, that if you have gradient fills, each new shape will take on the characteristics of the shape it came from—each will have its own center point and complete gradient. To make the gradient into a composite path (and retain the original appearance), hold down the Opt/Alt key. If a lower shape is cut in half, or significantly truncated, the center point of that object will change, therefore modifying the range of the gradient whether you have made a composite path out of it or not.

Figure 3.8
Use Divide to create perfectly interlocking pieces of previously overlapping shapes. This drawing has seven distinct shapes that can each be manipulated.

Intersect

No matter how many closed shapes you pile on top of each other, the Intersect function will discard everything that is not common to all the shapes, as shown in Figure 3.9. Holding down the Opt/Alt key while clicking Intersect

Figure 3.9

The Intersect Xtra cuts everything down to the common denominator. This shape shares real estate with all three overlapping shapes. Everything else has been discarded.

Figure 3.10

Using the Option key on a Macintosh results in a transparent fill being added without modifying the rest of the drawing. The three original shapes are still intact, but there are two new transparent-fill shapes above them.

Hungry Paths

In the Preferences window (Edit|Preferences|Object), there is an option labeled Path Operations Consume Original Paths. If this is selected, overlapping lines will be discarded when using Xtras. The Shift+ Opt/Alt keys toggle the feature off if you have it selected.

brings up a Transparency dialog box. When you select your percentage of transparency, the topmost shape will have separate cutout shapes as it overlaps the shapes below. Each new shape will have a transparent tone applied. Figure 3.10 shows how it works, using the Opt/Alt key; the shapes below the Intersect shapes are still intact.

Path Modifying Xtras

I've just discussed four basic Xtras that are used with closed paths. Quite a few more Xtras work with paths, including Expand Path, Inset Path, Roughen, Add Points, Simplify, Reverse Direction, Correct Direction, and Fractalize. Most are self-explanatory, but here's a brief explanation of how each functions. All may be operated from the toolbar, through the Xtras menu, or from your own custom keyboard shortcut.

Expand Stroke

Expand Stroke is one of the more useful Xtras. It changes the path from a line to a closed shape at a line weight, cap and join, and miter limit of your choosing. A single dialog box appears where you make your changes. You can stroke and fill the object as you would any other shape. Some of its uses are to give the line a gradient fill, or make a neon effect by cloning and expanding a path, or to create a more organic line by adjusting the points on either side of the path.

Inset Path

While the name of this tool is Inset, you can just as easily "outset" the path. For obvious reasons, this tool only works on closed paths. Its dialog box lets you choose the amount of inset (or outset by inserting a negative number in the box), the join and miter limit, the number of steps involved in the inset-ting, and how those steps are applied: Uniform, Farther, or Nearer. This tool can be used to create several incrementally smaller iterations of the same shape with a single click of the mouse. I use it often to create blend shapes by first cloning the original shape, then using Inset Path to make a smaller shape. By giving each of them a different fill and blending them, you can get some very nice three-dimensional shading effects.

Roughen

This Xtra works on selected open or closed paths. I have it as part of my main toolbar, but you can find it at Windows|Toolbars|Xtra Tools. Clicking the mouse and dragging adds random points to the path. The amount and direction of the dragging determines the amount of distortion. Every time you click the mouse, more points are added. Used grossly, Roughen is good for abstract shapes. If you want to make your work look as if it didn't come off a computer, use Roughen very slightly, then use Expand Stroke, and modify some of the points. The result is an organic line that looks as if it were drawn with a brush and ink. Double-click the button to input the number of points per inch, and choose whether to have rough or smooth deformations. Rough creates sharp, angular points along the path by adding corner points, and Smooth adds curve points with control handles.

Add Points

Add Points will place a point (as discussed previously) between every two points on the path. Aside from the obvious use of adding points to modify the path, the tool can be used to divide a line equally. This tool is not something that you will use every day, but it's nice to know it is available.

Simplify

As the title would imply, this Xtra removes points from a path. Double-click the button to input the amount of simplification. Simplify does not work as an "Undo" if you've used other Xtras to add points. An easy way to see how it works is to use the Bezigon tool to create a complicated, curvy shape. Then go back and add points to the line. FreeHand will automatically create the correct Bézier control handles for new and old points to keep the path the same. Clicking on the Simplify Xtra removes points that are not necessary to create the same path. Once the path gets to a certain level, clicking it will have no effect because it's as simple as it can be.

Simplify can be useful when you use the Trace tool. Quite often the Trace tool will add many more points than are necessary. Simplify removes a lot of them, but always watch the line being modified, because Simplify may distort the path until it looks nothing like the object you've traced.

Rocks in the Inset Paths

Try not to get tripped up when using the Inset Path and Expand Path Xtras. Depending on the complexity of the new path, points will be added or deleted. If the new shape is all you wanted in the first place, it's nothing to be concerned with, but if you plan on creating a blend, those extra points can really raise havoc. It's been my experience that sometimes the situation is easily remedied by clicking matching points on the two paths, but at other times the blending will only look correct when you have the same amount of points on each path.

Reverse Direction

As its name implies, this tool simply reverses the direction of the path. I use this Xtra on two types of occasions. The first is when I've drawn a line, say from top to bottom, then a few minutes or a day later I draw another line that I'm going to blend with the first line. Accidentally, I draw it from bottom to top. When I create the blend, I'm blasted with a big X-shape instead of the blend I was expecting. To fix my mistake quickly, I hold down the Opt/Alt key and click one of the two lines and then click the Reverse Direction button. The blend will now be what I had expected to see. The second reason to use it concerns the Bézier corner handles. Sometimes I will draw a path and then decide to go back to the beginning of it to work more. When I add points, this makes no difference, but if I Opt/Alt+click a point to retract the corner handle for the next section of the line, it will retract the handle controlling the *last* point instead. You can get out of the mess by doing a quick undo, and clicking the Reverse Direction button. Then your points and corner handles will behave themselves.

Correct Direction

I'm one of those unfortunate souls that has trouble with left and right; you have to point or I'll go the wrong way. You can't point in a drawing program, so FreeHand created Correct Direction for use in compound path creation. What does this mean? Well, you set the direction of a path as you draw—either clockwise (left to right), or counterclockwise (right to left). The regular geometric shape tools, Rectangle, Ellipse, and Polygon, are always created in a clockwise direction; everything else is up to the artist. A compound path requires paths to be going in opposite directions in order for an even/odd fill to occur, and the Object inspector has a checkbox for that purpose. If you have it unchecked, your compound path will not appear as you wish. Clicking on Correct Direction will reverse the direction of one of the paths, and you'll get the correct effect.

Fractalize

I swear, I can't figure out why FreeHand included this Xtra. I don't get into abstract or "happy accident" artwork, so Fractalize just doesn't do much for me. It's right up there with the Randomize Named Colors Xtra—sorry, Macromedia, I don't get it. Both can be used to create interesting(?) patterns for backgrounds or textile design, however.

Fractalize works by creating squares along a path. For example, create a circle and click the Fractalize Xtra. The circle turns into a square by adding a right-angled corner point between each point on the path. Click it again, and the square becomes a fat "X" shape because a point has been added between each existing point, at a 45-degree intersection. After 10 clicks, the circle that started with 4 points now is a lacy octagonal shape with hundreds of intricate squares consisting of 4,097 points! Use Fractalize sparingly—it really eats up RAM.

Getting to Work

After all that dry reading about paths, fills, strokes, shapes, and Xtras, this might be a good time to put all that knowledge to use.

Your client has asked you for a black-and-white line drawing of a hand holding a hacksaw. Fortunately, he has a photo of the hacksaw, so you will trace the hacksaw and trace a second photo for the hand. The complete drawing is on this book's CD-ROM, but you should try to draw everything from scratch.

The Hacksaw Project

This project is a line art drawing of a hand tool. By *line art* I mean that there is no tone in the drawing. No shading, no color, no tints. Only lines. There's nothing to stop you from adding color or tonality to it, but just for instruction's sake, I'm sticking to plain old line art. It's a style that has put bread and butter on many tables for many years, so it's nothing to snub. For this project, you'll use a photo on the CD-ROM called Hacksaw.tif in the Chapter 3 folder. You will use the following FreeHand features and tools:

- Pen tool
- Ellipse tool
- Bézier curves (corner handles on points)
- Expand Stroke
- Add Points
- Join
- Split
- Clone
- Union
- Paste Inside
- Layers
- Custom Views

For the hacksaw, you'll draw the frame first, and use the Expand Stroke Xtra. Then you will create the blade, make teeth by using the Add Points Xtra, and Clone and Join several small sections into the final blade edge. Next, you'll trace the handle and make a compound path for the finger hole. Then you'll make the frame tail piece, and finish by adding the rivets, grip details, and other items. Be sure to save your work often—there are two kinds of artists: Those who have started over, and those who will.

Laying It On

Four shapes or icons appear to the left of the Picture name in the Layers panel. The check mark indicates whether the layer is visible. Click it, and the check mark and photo disappear. Click the empty space, and they reappear. The next shape is a circle that shows if the layer is in Preview or Keyline mode. Preview has a solid circle, Keyline shows a small X. The next icon is a padlock. If it's open, you may select, modify, and otherwise work on that layer. If you click the padlock and lock it, nothing on the layer can be selected. The layer remains visible, but all your clicking and dragging will not affect it in the least. The square next to the layer name is blue by default and indicates the color of the paths and points as you place them. To change the color for different layers, drag a new color onto the square from your Color Mixer or Swatches.

Creating the Document

Begin by opening the FreeHand document named Project 3-1 in your Chapter 3 folder on the CD-ROM.

> **Note:** In order to avoid moving the photo around as you work, it makes sense to lock the layer. However, be aware that you cannot use the Eyedropper tool on a locked layer.

1. With no tool or objects selected, set the line weight to 1 point. Import Hacksaw.tif.

2. Select New Layer from the Layers|Options panel. Name it Picture. Click and drag the Picture layer below the Guides and Foreground layers.

3. Place the photo on the Picture layer (by clicking Picture), and click the padlock icon.

Drawing the Frame

You'll start the drawing by creating the frame. You'll use the Expand Stroke Xtra to cut your drawing time. To keep your later refinements to a minimum, try to place your points as close to the center of the frame as you can. This isn't rocket science, but it will make your job easier if you plan ahead a bit.

1. Select the Pen tool and click the very bottom-left of the saw frame. Place another point just as the frame starts to turn to the right. While keeping the mouse down, drag the control handle up to the middle of the horizontal run of the frame.

2. Click another point just past where the frame has rotated to horizontal.

3. Place the last point at the edge of the handle. Your screen should look something like Figure 3.11.

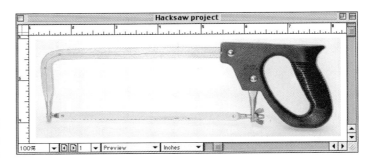

Figure 3.11
Start by running a line through the middle of the frame.

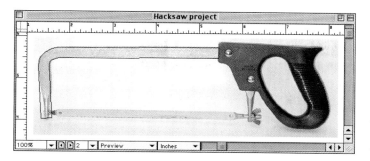

4. Keep the path selected and click the Expand Stroke button. Enter "18" with a butt cap and square join. The path should outline the frame pretty closely (see Figure 3.12).

5. Save your file. Name it My Hacksaw and place it in a new folder on your hard drive.

6. Add a point between the two points at the bottom end of the frame. Then hold down the Opt/Alt key and drag handles about halfway to either point.

7. Click one of the outer points, hold down the Shift key, and click the other outer point. Drag the points upward until they meet the place where the frame starts to angle inward.

8. Deselect everything. Click the right point you just moved. Drag a corner handle down. Move the handle until the path conforms to the frame. (Don't worry about how it fits at the very bottom—you'll catch that in a minute.) Drag a handle from the left point to conform to the bottom of the frame.

9. Fit the curvature of the path to the frame by adjusting each of the points and handles as necessary, as in Figure 3.13. Save the file.

> **What to Do When the Frame Turns Black**
>
> Don't have a heart attack! The frame turned black because you were using a black stroke. The Expand Stroke feature gives the resulting closed path the same stroke it had before the conversion *and* the same color fill. Give the shape a fill of None in the Color panel or the Color Well in the toolbar.

> **Note:** If you hold the Cmd/Ctl key down, the cursor toggles into the pointer, and you can move the point and its handles to a new location. If your original line went pretty much down the center of the frame, there won't be much adjusting to do.

Figure 3.13
The frame is finished.

The Blade

Now you'll create the blade:

1. Create a new Layer and name it Blade.

What Do You Do When the Handle Adjusts the Wrong Path?

Irritating, huh? Just swing the point to the side for a second, and drag another handle down. This one will modify the curve of the bottom of the path. Now drag that upper corner handle back onto the point. Another way to get rid of the extraneous corner handle is to go to the Object Inspector, and below the Handles: label, click the right button. That will suck the handle back into the point. If your nicely curved line goes straight, you've clicked the wrong retract button. Just select Undo, and click the other button.

Note: If the path doesn't outline the blade closely, select Undo, and adjust the amount you enter in the Expand Stroke window by a point either way until you're satisfied with the fit. It will end up with four points, and corner handles extending from all of them.

2. With the Pointer selected, change the line weight to 0.5 point. (A 1-point line would be too coarse to show the teeth in the blade.)

3. Using the Line tool, begin a line at the left hole in the blade (I know there must be a technical term for that hole and peg arrangement, but it escapes me). Hold the Shift key down and drag the line over to the right hole.

4. Use Expand Stroke again, enter "13", and give it a round cap. (The join is immaterial because there are no corners on this path.) It should look like Figure 3.14.

Figure 3.14

The Expand Path feature outlines your blade pretty precisely, saving drawing time and effort.

5. Click the bottom two points and then click the Split button in your toolbar, or select Modify|Split. Click outside the drawing. Save.

6. Select the line you just split from the blade shape, and click the Add Points Xtra. Zoom in to the left end of the line, to about 1600% or so. Keep clicking Add Points until you have a whole lot of points—a dozen clicks or more.

7. Starting with the second point in the path, click every other point on the path. If you have a lot of time on your hands, you can go all the way along the path. I don't have that much free time, so I selected about 10 points, as shown in Figure 3.15.

Figure 3.15

The toothless blade is about to get some dental work.

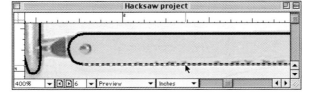

8. Use the arrows on your keyboard, and click down once and left twice (see Cursor Distance Sidebar). This should give you the approximation of the saw blade (see Figure 3.16).

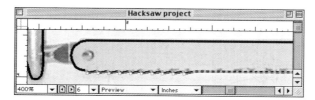

Figure 3.16
Pretty sharp, huh?

9. Deselect the blade. Click the first point in the path that begins the horizontal run to the right, and click the Split button. Discard the straight line. Select the tooth group you've just drawn, and Edit|Clone it.

10. Hold down the Shift key and drag the teeth to the right until the end points line up. Shift+click the original teeth, and click the Join button or Modify|Join command. You should have a line that looks like Figure 3.17.

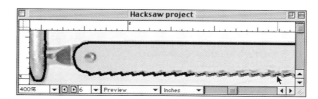

Figure 3.17
Twice as sharp.

11. Clone that path, Shift+drag again until the end points line up again, Join, and repeat until you meet the other end of the blade. Select the point that comes closest to the last point in the upper part of the blade. Click Split. Select the saw tooth path and the upper blade path, and click Join. Save.

Drawing the Handle

Start by clicking the Page button (View|Fit To Page).

1. Use the Zoom tool to drag a box that outlines only the handle. Click View|Custom|New, and name the view Handle. Create a new layer in the Layers panel and name it Handle.

Cursor Distance

The amount an object moves when you click a keyboard arrow depends on the settings you've given it in the Modify|Cursor Distance panel. First take note of what Unit Of Measurement you have selected in the bottom of your application window, because that is the unit of measurement you will be entering. While working in this chapter, set it to Points. The Cursor Distance panel has two input fields, one for an Arrow Key Distance, and the other for a Shift+Arrow Key Distance. For this project, enter "1" in the first field, and "10" in the last. When you have an object selected and click a keyboard arrow, the object will move 1 point. Hold down the Shift key and click an arrow to make the object move 10 points. Depending on the degree of accuracy you need, you can change these values. It's just as easy to have an arrow click-move an object an eighth of an inch—or a foot—if you desire. Feel free to change these values as needs dictate. I lowered the Arrow Key Distance to 0.001 points and it still works! But that's an awful lot of clicking for most of the adjustments you might need to make.

Where to Start a Path

It's always a minor challenge to figure out where to start a path. From experience, I know that the last point you place is the most important point. Look for a straight run—when the last point will follow a path without a curve, because if your last run in the path is a curve, you have to drag a corner handle out. Placing an end point and dragging a handle is no big deal, but when it connects with the beginning point, your handle extension will affect the next (first) section of the path. In other words, you'll get a curve on both sides of the line, and that's probably not what you had in mind. You can always retract the errant handle, but it's easier to avoid the situation in the first place.

2. With the Pointer selected, change the line weight back to 1 point.

3. Place your first point at the top left corner of the handle, on the vertical face, just before it starts to curve to the top. Click and drag that first handle out halfway to the top.

4. Click the second point on the top surface, and drag to the right until the path curve matches the handle. Continue down the path.

5. The next run has a slight downward curve to it, so when you place the point at the far right end of the handle, continue to drag the corner handle up and to the right just a bit until the path meets the curve you need. To retract the overextended handle, click the point.

6. Click a point at the bottom of that radiused corner, and drag the handle until the path fits. Click another point where the curve changes direction again. Drag the corner handle again to fit.

7. Continue around the handle until you meet the first point. Your drawing should look like Figure 3.18. Save.

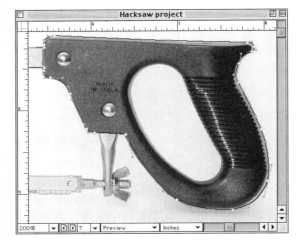

Figure 3.18
Outline the handle with the Pen tool. The Picture layer has been moved beneath the background/ foreground line in the Layers panel, causing it to be grayed out.

Drawing Circles

Circle drawing often baffles people because it seems so hard to get the circle in the right place. You can either draw from the center of the circle or not, and then drag it into place, but if it's not the right size, you'll have to adjust it, and then it will be in the wrong place again. This can be frustrating.

Here's a simpler method: Drag a vertical guideline out to meet the left edge of the top circle. Drop a horizontal line to the top of the circle. Select the Ellipse tool and place your cursor on the junction of the two guidelines. Hold down the Shift key and drag down and to the right until the circle fits.

To make life easier (in the directional sense of compound paths), I make it a habit to usually draw the outside of a shape in a clockwise manner, and inner shapes counterclockwise. That's because the paths must be traveling in opposite directions for the compound path to be created. You have a choice: draw in different directions, or change the direction of the path later.

8. There are no straight runs in the hole—but if you look closely, you'll see two circles. That gives you the opportunity to either draw two circles and combine them with another curved shape, or you can trace the hole with the Pen tool.

9. To give the handle a fill later, you'll make a compound path out of it. Using the Ellipse tool with the Shift key held down, draw a circle that fits the top of the hole, and draw another circle at the bottom of the hole.

10. Draw the bottom circle that fits as shown in Figure 3.19. Save.

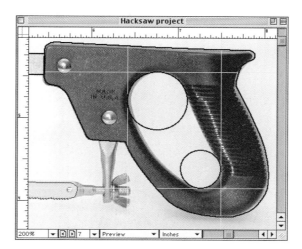

Figure 3.19
Draw easy circles in the right place the first time using the techniques I explained under "Drawing Circles."

11. Now, deselect both circles, and place a new point with the Pen tool on the upper circle where its tangent leaves or meets the handle hole. Click another point across the circle at the other tangent.

12. Place another point on the right tangent of the bottom circle, and drag a handle down and to the right until the path fits the inside of the handle.

13. Click the next point across the circle, pretty much toward the bottom. Save. Click Reverse Direction.

14. Okay, now select the shape you just drew, and both circles. Click the Union Xtra, and the hole is finished. Shift+select the outside path of the handle, and click the Join button (see Figure 3.20).

Finishing Touches

Now you can finish the base of the frame.

1. Click the Frame layer to keep everything concerned with the frame on the same layer. Start the path at the top right corner, and place your next point at the bottom right. Drag the handle to make the path fit, then slide the bottom corner handle up until the path fits the slight curve.

Dragging to Fit a Curve

You could drag out a corner handle to fit the left curve of the hole, but that probably won't work. Why? Well, remember what I said about starting a path at the end of a straight run? In this case, the amount of "drag" you have to apply will cause the next section of path to extend past the circle. That will cause you to have to adjust or retract the handles. So, instead of clicking directly on the first point, click just below that point, drag the corner handle out to fit, and then move the point on top of the first point. Minor adjustment of the corner handle will be necessary, but it seems quicker than the retract handles routine because I'm keeping the mouse right on the work instead of navigating all over the monitors.

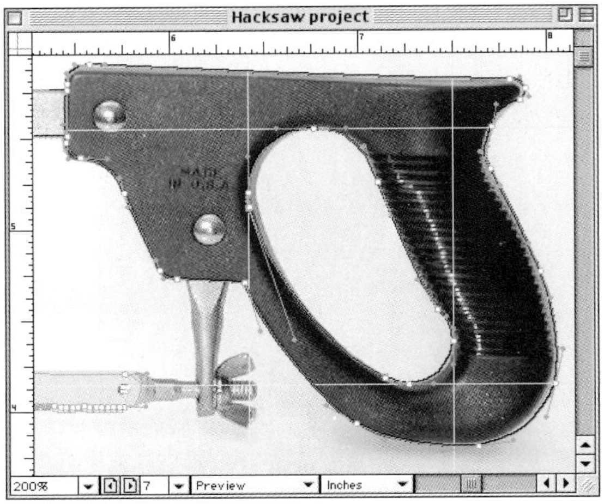

Figure 3.20
The finished handle is a compound path.

> **This Tip Is a Drag**
>
> When you're dragging corner handles out, it's easy to know if you've gone too far with your drag: if the handle extends past the next point, then your curve will also extend past that point. You'll end up with a hump in the line (see the "Overextended Handles" sidebar).

> **Note:** The threads on the connector aren't necessary for this lesson; however, if you feel inclined, you can add them.

2. Add a point to the left bottom corner, and one more at the top, Opt/Alt+dragging the corner handle out for the curve. This time click the point to retract the corner handle. Click the first point.
3. Continue with the Pen tool until you've finished the wing nut and blade tail connector.
4. In the Views window at the bottom-left of your application window, select Handle, then click the Handle layer. Using the same method for circle alignment that you applied in the handle hole (guidelines at top and side), draw one of the rivets in the handle. Click the Handle layer to place your art there.
5. Draw the piece that connects the left end of the frame to the blade. Click the Blade layer. Draw the hole/connector in the saw blade in the same manner as the handle rivets, and Copy the circle to the Clipboard.
6. Scroll to the left until you see the left end of the blade. Paste the circle (Cmd/Ctl+V), and drag it into place.
7. Clone it, and drag the clone to the other rivet. Draw a horizontal line with the Line tool where the grips start that goes from well inside the hole to well outside the handle.

Overextended Handles

To see the perfect amount of handle extension, select the Ellipse tool and drag while holding the Shift key down to constrain the ellipse to a circle. Ungroup it, and with the Pointer, drag a selection box around it. Notice how far the handles extend from each point. That's what you should attempt when you're drawing perfectly radiused corners and dragging corner handles. If you experiment by dragging the handles farther or closer to their points, you can get a good idea of how little it takes to foul up a nice circle—or make it look great.

8. Clone the line, and drag it to the bottom of the grips. Shift+select the top grip line, and blend them (Modify|Combine|Blend). In the Object Inspector panel, enter "20" for the amount of steps in the blend. See Figure 3.21.

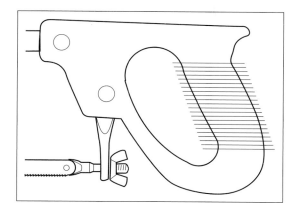

Figure 3.21
Blending the grip.

9. With the blend still selected, cut it. The blend disappears and goes to the Clipboard.

10. Select the handle path, and perform a Paste Inside (Edit|Paste Inside). The Clipboard empties into the selected shape. Click the checkmark in the Picture layer to hide it.

11. Your drawing should look like Figure 3.22. Take a deep breath. Save. Print the drawing and stick it on your refrigerator.

Creative Fill Tip

The handle is a great place to try out the Contour Gradient Fill that's new in FreeHand 10. Give it a multihued wood tone. Quick, and not dirty at all!

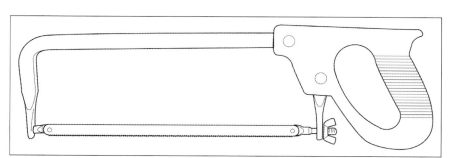

Figure 3.22
The finished hacksaw line art illustration.

PROJECT Drawing Hands That Look Human

Okay, assume that the client has asked you to draw the hacksaw, and you have completed the assignment, as in the previous project. He loves it. "Everything is just the way we wanted it," he says, "But, it looks a little static just sitting there. Could we get you to, maybe, like, add a hand?" You groan, put on your biggest smile and say, "Sure, no problem."

Here's how to handle it, so to speak. You will just be using the Pen tool this time, with a couple of Xtras thrown in for good measure. But, there are a few tricks you can use that will make this easier.

Drawing with the Pen Tool

When you're doing a drawing with several lines, keep your finger on the Tab key. After drawing a line, click the Tab key to deselect the line. If you draw a line and drag out a corner handle too far, click the Undo button in the main toolbar, or click Delete. The previous point will become selected so you can place the next point again, and adjust it.

Note: If you're continuing from the first project, you may have to click the empty space to the far left in the Layers panel to make the layer visible.

When working with multiple items like this—on an already complete drawing—it's easier to do the additional work apart from the finished goods. It's also less confusing. Sometimes it's better to work right on the final art, though. It becomes a value judgment on your part. For this project, you will work on a clean page, so in the Object Inspector|Document|Options panel, click Add Pages and type "1" in the entry field (it will probably already be entered), click OK. FreeHand adds the page for you, and the application window will show that you are on page 2. But you aren't. The program leaves you on the original page. Click the page and the number will change to 1, then use the page selector arrow to scroll to page 2. Then you're on the right page. Conversely, you can click on the page 2 icon in the Document Inspector window.

Modifying an Image with the Pen Tool

1. Import the file Hand.tif from the Chapter 3 folder on the CD-ROM. Click in the middle of the page, unlock the Picture layer, and click the layer to place the photo there. Lock the layer again.

2. Using the Zoom tool, drag a box that encompasses the hand and arm. Create a new layer named Hand, and make sure it is above the Handle and Picture layers.

3. Select the Pen tool and begin tracing the outline of the arm, thumb, and fingers. Do not go in between the fingers, but just follow the outer perimeter. Start at the bottom of the arm and end just about directly above your starting point on the top of the arm. Your finished outline should look like Figure 3.23.

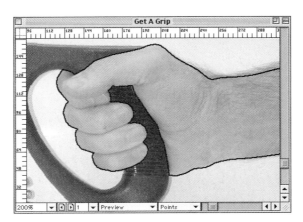

Figure 3.23
The basic hand outline.

4. Now go back in and draw lines that separate the fingers and thumb from each other. Draw the wrinkles in the thumb joints, and outline the fingernails. Is this fun or what? Save your art; it should look like Figure 3.24 now.

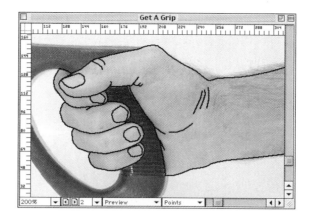

Figure 3.24
The hand is completely outlined now, and all the details are drawn.

Creating a Brush and Ink Technique

Okay, this part is a little tricky.

1. Select the outer perimeter line with the Pointer, clone it, and select Modify|Arrange|Send To Back from the main menu.

2. In the Object Inspector panel, check the Closed box to make a closed path. Then click the Fill tab, choose Basic, and give it a fill of white.

3. Drag a selection box around the whole hand drawing. Deselect the white background hand by Shift+clicking in the white space. Then Shift+click each of the fingernails to deselect them.

4. Click the Expand Stroke button and enter "1.5" in the field, with round Caps and Joins. The drawing ought to look like Figure 3.25 now. Save.

> **Note:** An old art teacher told me to never draw or paint the wrinkles on knuckles because it then appears that the hand is dirty—it's up to you. Sometimes I draw them, sometimes I don't. Other than the top of the thumb, there's not too much to talk about in this photo, so I'm going to draw them—the fingers are naturally going to get grubby, not to mention possibly bloody.

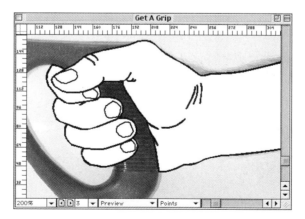

Figure 3.25
The paths have been expanded, and the outline cloned and filled with white.

5. Shift+click four or five relatively random points along the bottom of the arm/fingers path. Try not to hit every point, or anything in a regular pattern—keep it loose.

6. Now Shift+click one last point, and keep the mouse down. Carefully drag the points up or down, left or right by minor amounts until the line starts to look as if it were drawn with a brush and ink.

7. Select a few more points along the top edge and do the same thing. Repeat the same tasks with the fingers.

8. Finally, select the fingernails, Expand Stroke to 1 point, and distort those shapes as well, but don't go overboard or you'll have grimy-looking nails. At this point, your drawing may look like Figure 3.26, or it may look completely different.

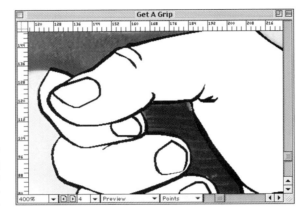

Figure 3.26
That brush and ink look is going now. Notice that there are no straight lines in the drawing. Humans don't have them.

9. Select the white background shape, and remove the stroke either by dragging None onto the Stroke color box, or selecting None in the Object Inspector|Stroke panel. If any of your lines went away, send the white arm shape to the back again (Modify|Arrange|Send to Back).

10. Drag a selection around the entire hand, and group it. Copy it to the Clipboard.

11. Open your Hacksaw drawing (or click to page 1). Paste the hand and drag it over the handle until it fits. Save.

12. Hide the Picture layer by clicking the checkmark in the Layers panel. Your drawing should look pretty much like Figure 3.27. Save again. Print, and tape this next to the hacksaw drawing on the refrigerator.

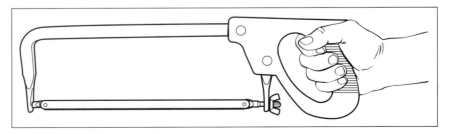

Figure 3.27
The finished hand is ready for that plumbing job.

Moving On

In this chapter, basic drawing techniques were explored that set the stage for virtually all the drawing you'll do in FreeHand. You will want to get to the point where you don't look for clip art any more—you draw everything your-self. Creating your own art is more pertinent, accurate, and rewarding. In the next chapter, you'll learn about colors and fills used in FreeHand.

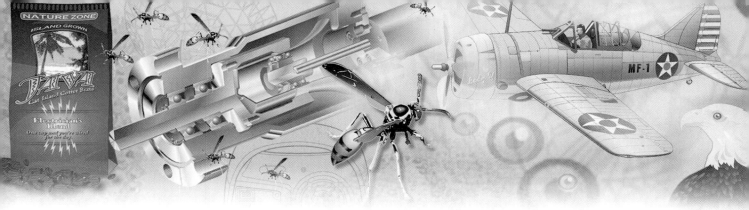

Chapter 4

Getting Colorful

We live in a world of color, and FreeHand does a pretty good job of letting us work in color. There are several ways color can be referenced and manipulated in FreeHand 10.

Introduction to Color

Color can be mind-boggling. I remember learning as a kid that an apple is red because it's every color *except* red. That was a mental struggle for me. Then I learned that it takes four colors of ink to produce full color on a piece of paper. That wasn't too hard to grasp, but then I learned that you get even more colors on your computer monitor or television by using just three beams of colored lights. It blows my mind! Back in the late 1970s and early 1980s, I had gained a good understanding of 4-color printing and had amassed a set of books filled with thousands of tint combinations that I used for designing projects. Once, I happened to go to a party attended by some Apple engineers who were involved in the video end of computers. (At this time, computers weren't being used regularly for typesetting—I'd never even *seen* a computer that was more than a black screen with green or yellow characters on it!) I asked some of them if they could explain why the printing process used four colors, and video used three *different* colors to produce the same image. The answer must have been too involved—they looked at each other and walked away. So, I decided to watch the guacamole turn black. Never was much of a party person anyway.

Color is as important to a drawing as is shape, style, and composition. It's also a very complicated subject when it comes to graphic arts today. To sum up in one sentence: You use FreeHand to create drawings and layouts that print on paper or for Web artwork that will be viewed on a computer monitor. However, before you get your hopes up and expect to print vibrant, brilliant colors from your laserjet or inkjet printer, read the "What to Expect" sidebar.

CMYK Colors

I'll start with a brief description of color printing: Most commercial printers use a 4-color, or process color, method of producing full-color images on paper. The four ink colors are cyan, magenta, yellow, and black, known collectively as CMYK—don't try to say it, it's just plain "see-em-wye-kay." When combined

---

What to Expect

Video cards, monitor resolution, and color calibration are beyond the scope of this book. I assume that if you are serious about graphic art and illustration, you've taken the time and spent the money to take care of these very necessary details. Face it, if your monitor is old and dark and has a blue cast to it, you're going to have a pretty hard time making color decisions as you work. That brings up another important issue: you've heard this before, but you cannot expect what you see on your monitor to be reproduced exactly on your office printer or in your commercially printed piece. You also can't expect to see an identical image on someone else's computer; there are so many variables involved that it's impossible. Room light, monitor calibration, amount of toner left in the laser printer, brightness of paper, ink on the press—identical reproduction is just too much to expect. So here is some advice: stick to the numbers. If you're using PMS colors like most of us, use a *Pantone Solid to Process* book for an accurate representation of what will come off the press. Trust the numbers, not what you see on your monitor. If you are matching colors in a photograph, color-correct the photo in a photo-editing program—such as Adobe Photoshop—and collect the colors with the Eyedropper tool.

in various combinations of tints, these four ink colors do a pretty good job of portraying real color. FreeHand uses CMYK as the default color model, but there are many other ways of working with color. Many progressive high-end print shops are using 6-color printing presses that use green and orange in addition to CMYK to enhance color faithfulness.

Printers also are not restricted to using the four CMYK inks for printing. Ink manufacturers produce thousands of inks called *spot colors*. A spot color can be used all by itself or in conjunction with other inks. The most common use of spot colors is in 2-color printing. Usually one color is black, and the second (spot) color is used for emphasis or interest. Sometimes the second color is just for decorative use, such as in headlines, subheads, or blotches of color in illustrations, but at other times, you may want to print duotones (see the "Duotones' Greatest Hits" sidebar).

Spot Colors

Simply put, a spot color usually comes out of a can. That is, you specify an ink color by calling out the manufacturer's name for it. That name is usually a number. In the United States, the Pantone Matching System (PMS) dominates the printing industry. In other countries, other manufacturers control their respective markets. FreeHand provides more than 20 different spot color libraries, and more can be imported. Unfortunately, FreeHand does not allow the mixing of spot colors. There are workarounds for this, but they involve a lot of faith because the mixing we can do on screen does not look at all like what we expect to see on the printed page. Talking directly to your printer is usually the best way to tackle this problem. In addition to providing good advice, he or she may even have samples to help you decide what colors to use.

Obviously, things change, including job specifications. Try to keep the ultimate output in mind as you're working: If you are printing, will you be using spot (PMS) colors, or CMYK, or a combination? Is your project intended to go straight to Flash or Fireworks? Are you producing something for a client who doesn't know yet what its end use will be? All these factors must be considered as you work.

Because there are so many variables to deal with, FreeHand has indicators of all kinds in the Swatches panel. For instance, when you choose a spot color from a color library, the swatch in the Color panel will show three colored

What Color Is That Spot?

One of the chief reasons to print spot or PMS colors is because some colors simply cannot be created with CMYK process printing. Reflex Blue is a great example. It's a rich color, but you just can't get there from here. If that deep lush blue is necessary for the job, you're going to have to get it out of a can—call it out as a spot color. If you try to print it in CMYK, you'll have a very dull, disappointing blue-gray. Other colors that can't be approximated are fluorescent inks. Fluorescents are so unique that the printer will usually overprint them—that is, print the same ink in the same spot—in order to create the brightness and "glow" effect we're after with fluorescent inks in the first place.

Duotones' Greatest Hits

Duotones are created by making two halftones of the same photograph. Generally, the halftone is made just a little light for the black ink, and really light (with the screen rotated to avoid moirés) for the spot color, but there are no holds barred when it comes to design, creativity, and taste. FreeHand does not deal with duotones as such, but it will print one that has been produced in a program such as Adobe Photoshop, and you can use the same spot color in other parts of your layout. You can always make a faux-duotone by printing a light tint of spot color under a halftone.

balls to the right of the color's name, This indicates that the color is being displayed as an RGB color. (RGB colors will be explained in the next section.) The color's name will be in Roman (not italic) type to show that it is a spot color. If, at a later time, you decide to convert the color to CMYK, the three colored balls will disappear.

Suppose you have a red *hexadecimal* color named FF0033 that you are using for the Web, and you find you have to print the illustration. You can change the color to a spot color that the printer must mix from other inks, or you can convert it to CMYK. Converting it to a spot color changes the name from italic to Roman type in the Swatches panel; further changing it to CMYK changes the name from 255r 0g 51b to 0c 86m 69y 0k and removes the three colored balls.

Figure 4.1 shows the Swatches panel. In this particular panel, you see, from top to bottom:

Figure 4.1
The Swatches panel.

- *None, White, Black, and Registration*—These are always the first four colors. New colors are added below this group.

- *PANTONE color*—In Roman type with the RGB icon; this color would print as a spot color, right out of the can.

- *Spot color, RGB*—In Roman type, with the RGB icon; this color would need to be mixed by the printer.

- *Spot color, CMYK*—In Roman type, indicating a spot color that has been created in CMYK (no icon). Elements using this color would be output on a single sheet of film requiring the ink to be custom-mixed by the printer, *unless* the "Print Spot Colors As Process" box was checked in the Print dialog box.

- *Process color with icon*—In italic type, created in RGB; this color will have to be converted to CMYK in order to print. The color could shift with the conversion.

- *Process color with no icon*—In italic type, created in CMYK will separate to four sheets of film.

RGB Color Explained

It took quite a few parties, several bowls of guacamole, and numerous bags of chips to discover the difference between the print and video versions of color reproduction, but it comes down to this: Printing inks are transparent, and they combine the same way watercolor paints do. Take a little red, mix in a bit of yellow, and you have orange. Toss in a tad of blue and you start to get gray.

However, the color must go on a (preferably) white background to get the correct effect. A monitor is black—well, almost black. Next time you turn your computer on, stop for a second and look at the blank screen. It's as dark as any image your monitor can produce. That's because the monitor creates an image

CMYK/RGB Printing

When it finally comes time to print your document, be advised that you will be outputting to a PostScript printer, which needs CMYK to function efficiently. If you have a document full of RGB colors, the print time will be increased because of the computer conversion of the colors from RGB to CMYK. Not to mention that the service bureau will want to shoot you if you send the file to them this way. Do yourself a favor and convert everything to CMYK as you work, or in the Print|FreeHand|Setup window, check Print Spot Colors As Process. It doesn't change the color conventions in your document; it just does the conversions before sending the document to the printer. (Printing will be described in greater detail in Chapter 10.)

by projecting light at the screen. The red, green, and blue combine at full strength to make pure white—as pure as the brightness of your monitor's setting will allow, that is. Red and green at full strength (without any blue) produce yellow, less red makes lime green, less green turns it orangey. One hundred percent red and blue alone make magenta; reduce the intensity of the red and more blue shows, creating a purplish color. Similarly, take away some of the blue to put more red into the color. Blue and green make the bluish color cyan. Reducing the amount of either color allows more of the other color to show, so you can achieve various shades of blue or green. Similarly, equal amounts of red, green, and blue form shades of gray.

A better visual handle on the RGB color model can be gained by clicking on the RGB button in the Color Mixer. The red, green, and blue sliders range from 0 to 255, giving us 256 shades of each color. The three colors in combination produce the 16.7 million colors our 24-bit color monitors are capable of producing.

To view it yet another way, click the Apple Color Picker icon in the Color Mixer (on a Mac—Windows doesn't have this feature). A dialog box opens with sliders for red, green, and blue, but the amounts of ink are listed in percentages, with 100% equaling a value of 255. Either set of sliders will give identical numerical color names, such as 200r, 120g, 86b, not percentages. In addition to the FreeHand Color Mixer, the Apple Color Picker allows artists to define colors as CMYK, RGB, HLS, HSV (hue, saturation, and value), plus 60 Crayon colors or the 216-color Web HTML picker. Windows artists are restricted to the System Color Picker with 48 basic Windows colors. Figure 4.2 compares the FreeHand CMYK, RGB, and HLS color models in their respective windows.

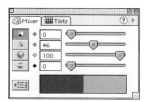 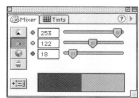 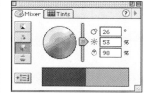

Figure 4.2
CMYK color model (left), RGB color model (center), and HLS (right).

HLS Color Creation

The HLS color model is Hue, Lightness, and Saturation. The way HLS is perceived is the full spectrum of color in a counter-clockwise circle. Hue is pure color, and is indicated by the angle of the color going around the circle, in degrees. If red is at 3 o'clock (0°), you have yellow at 1 o'clock (60°), green at 11 (120°), cyan at 9 (180°), blue at 7 (240°), and magenta at 5 (300°). Thus, orange, made from red and yellow, would be approximately 30°.

Lightness is expressed as a percentage and determines how bright or dark a color is: 0% is black and 100% is white. The *S* stands for saturation. Also expressed in percentages, 100% saturation makes the purest color, at 50 you have gray, and at 0, solid black. The color panels use colors or icons to denote colors or the HLS callouts.

Web-Safe Colors

By now you are aware that Macintosh and Windows-based computer platforms display colors differently, and you most likely have heard about Web-safe colors. These are colors that will display correctly on both platforms, so you should use them for your Web content. Depending on the program software you use to create Web graphics, or the terminology you like to use in your hand coding, there are different ways to express these Web-safe colors. FreeHand makes it comfortable for you to call out these colors through the Web Safe Color Library in the Swatches panel (see Figure 4.3). The panel gives the names in Hexidecimal (FF0033) and RGB (255r 0g 51b) terminology and places both names in the Swatches list. (See Chapter 11 for more detail on production for the Web.)

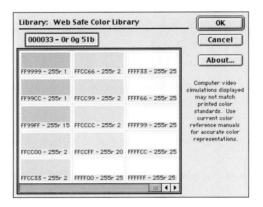

Figure 4.3
The Web Safe Color Library.

Creating Color in FreeHand

Wow, *creating* color. That's a heavy statement. More than likely you're probably not going to win a Nobel Prize for creating a *new* color, but at least you have many ways to get to most existing colors through FreeHand. Now it's time to discuss the two major methods of getting color: choosing and creating.

Choosing Colors

By far the easiest method of getting colors into your document is by selecting them from the Libraries. In the Swatches panel, click the triangle in the top right corner. A window drops down that contains 21 color libraries from DIC, Focoltone, Munsell, Toyo, Trumatch, and of course, Pantone, which has 12 libraries of its own. There are also libraries for crayon colors (62-crayon box—they won't roll off the table, and you can't peel off the wrapper), Web-safe colors, and a whole slew of grays (see Figure 4.4). You can also add your own Library. The CD-ROM contains a Library with 147 new Pantone colors, provided by Dan Egan of Progressive Printing.

Open any and scroll until you see a color you like. Double-click it and it's in your Swatches panel. If you want to add more than one color, hold down the

Shift key and scroll to the next color, select it, and keep adding colors until your fingers get tired.

If you are using PMS colors and you know the number of your color, you can type the number as soon as the window opens. The library will go directly to that color swatch and select it. If you want more colors, it's the Shift key and scroll routine again, however.

Custom Library

If you really want to work in style and with class, building your own library has advantages. For example, supposing you do most of your work for a particular company. That company has three specific PMS colors they use for their logo and a CMYK conversion of those colors for less-expensive print runs. They also have a color combination that they use for their Web graphics, and they have several lesser-used colors for the company newsletter, masthead, and spot illustrations. (What a pain these guys are.) But by creating a custom library, you can make your life a lot less hectic. It's easy.

Color Export Tutorial

Export colors following these steps:

1. Put all the colors you want to access regularly in the Swatch panel by selecting or creating them using any or all of the means discussed here.

2. Click the triangle in the top right corner of the Swatches panel. Scroll down a bit until you see Import and Export. Click Export.

3. The dialog box contains a scrolling list of all the colors in your current Swatch panel. Select the colors you want in your library and click OK.

4. The next dialog box asks you to give it a Library name and lets you decide how many colors per row and column you want in the view. There's also a place for you to add notes about the library—in case you wonder later on how that filmy pink color got in there.

5. Click OK, and the library will show up in the list alphabetically with the rest. Next time you start work on one of the company's jobs, crack open the library and select the colors you'll need. Cool, huh?

Decisions, Decisions: How to Choose

In addition to choosing your colors from the library, you can use the Eyedropper tool to nab a color from an imported TIFF, JPEG, GIF, BMP, or PICT file. I use this method frequently. For example, if I'm called upon to make a drawing of a product from a photograph and the color is critical, I just open a new document in FreeHand and import the photo using the Import button I installed in my main Toolbar with Window|Toolbars|Customize, or through Edit|Import. Then, to get accurate colors from the photo, I'll use the Eyedropper tool to click various sections of the photo for highlight, shadow, flat color,

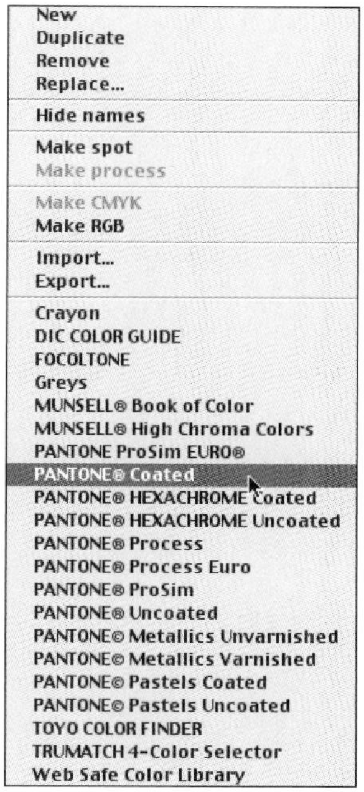

Figure 4.4
The Color Libraries that are standard with FreeHand 10. You can easily add your own library to the list.

Note: The Library file type is BCF; and the default name will be Custom.BCF. If you want to delete this file later, you'll find it in the FreeHand|English|Color folder with the rest of the color libraries.

How Many Colors Can You Have?
Don't worry about adding too many colors. With a single click, Xtras|Delete|Unused Named Colors will remove any colors you haven't used in the current document.

and other sections of the product that will be colorized. If my imported photo is a JPEG, the colors I choose with the Eyedropper will be added to the Swatches panel in RGB. If it's a CMYK picture, then I'll get CMYK values as color names. Keep in mind that these colors can also be added to a custom library for future use.

Creating Colors

Okay, so now you know how to get colors that someone has already found and named. What about that special tint of pink or macho olive drab? Again, there are several ways to go about it, all involving the use of slider bars or entering numerical values.

The Color Mixer Panel

This panel has four icons on the left side. From top to bottom, they are CMYK, RGB, HLS, and either the Apple Color Picker on a Mac, or System Color on a Windows machine. It's easy to move the sliders from left to right to add more of the color you've selected with the slider, or to enter numerical values in the input boxes (you saw the CMYK, RGB, and HLS windows in Figure 4.2). I won't trouble you with a long, drawn-out discussion of dragging a slider in each of the color modes. The end result is that you will have created a color in whichever mode you're comfortable with or required to use. Now you will see how to add it to your Color List.

1. Below the color mode buttons is a button called Add To Color List. Click that, and you'll get a dialog box of the same name.

2. Inside the box is a swatch of the color you've just made, a radio button each for Process and Color, and a text input box that has the name of the color in the mode you've used to create the color.

3. If you're satisfied with a color name like 64c 50m 53y 15k, then click the Add button to put the color in your Swatches panel. If instead you'd rather have a more descriptive name such as "Darkest shadow handle," then type it in. Such a name will make it easier to locate the handle shadow color at a later date.

4. Another method of getting your color into the Swatches panel is to just click the Color Mixer well and drag a swatch of the color to a blank space at the bottom of the Swatches panel. The default name will appear, along with the Roman/italic/three-colored-balls-or-not configurations.

5. There is also a box in the top of the Swatches panel with a downward-pointing arrow. Drag a color onto it, and the color will appear in the list as above.

Note: You might well ask why you have a dinky little arrow box as a target when there's a whole panel just below it. The answer is simple: you may have more colors in the panel than are being displayed. Scrolling to the bottom of the panel is a bad idea because your cursor is loaded with a color swatch at that point, and if you accidentally drop that color on top of an existing swatch, the existing swatch will change to the new color. If this happens, click Undo. Read the rest of this chapter for more information about the Swatches panel features and tricks.

Hi, My Name Is 199r 0g 66b

That makes me a maroon (with apologies to Bugs Bunny). The point is, however, you should always have named colors in your documents. The names themselves aren't important, but using descriptive names can be helpful later if you want to delete unused colors, sort the color list by name, or most important, *change* the color globally. When you put a color into the Swatches panel, FreeHand automatically names it. You can change the name, but you can't delete it completely. Be warned, however, that if you create a color or tint and use it in your drawing, it becomes an unnamed color. Later, when the boss asks you to change that tint or color by a few percent points, you will have to hunt down each instance—or use the Find and Replace Graphic tool to make the changes. If the color had a name, you could make the color change, drop it onto the color you want to change, and the change would ripple through the entire document.

A Lighter Shade of Pale—or Any Other Color

Very often you will want a shade or tint of a color. FreeHand gives you nine tints at a mouse click. Select your color in the Color Mixer panel, and click the Tints tab. You'll see nine boxes with tints from 10% to 90% of the color in the well, as shown in Figure 4.5.

You can also drag a color directly into the Tints well and get the same results. If the color is named, the name will appear in the window, and you can choose other named colors from the drop-down list. When it is necessary to have a screen tint other than a multiple of 10 percent, just enter the amount in the text entry box, or drag the slider until you see the color you want. The same options for adding the color to the Swatches panel are available to you here.

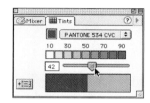

Figure 4.5
The Tints panel provides access to 99 different colors, from 1% to 99% value of the true color.

PROJECT The Car Library

Okay, how about a really quick project? Start by opening a new document and importing a photo and a logo. From these elements, you will create a simple color swatch library that you can use in an illustration. In the case of the particular objects you're importing, you'll only be using a few of the tools discussed previously, but there are still a couple of tricks you can learn. Note that this is yet another method of creating your library—there's more than one way to skin your knee, my grandpa used to say.

In this project, you will make a library of colors for the subsequent car-drawing project. While it's easy to pop open the Color Library and start selecting colors, or even make your own up, you can go one better, and make a library that will allow you to *change* colors when the client's secretary suggests the car would look better in Plumeria Yellow or British Racing Green. This technique involves using a named spot color and its tints, and it is a real kick to work with.

Primary Color List

Create the primary color list:

1. Start by opening a new FreeHand document. Save the file as My New Car.

2. Select File|Import, or click the Import button on the main toolbar and select Redcar.tif from the Chapter 4 folder on the CD. Click the cursor on the top-left corner of the document to place the photo on the page.

3. Create a new layer and name it Picture. The car photo will automatically go to that layer.

4. Click outside the picture or press Tab to deselect it. We don't want to lock the picture layer right now because you won't be able to select colors with the Eyedropper tool.

5. Select the Eyedropper tool and find the brightest, most saturated red on the car. I think it's on the upper portion of the door, near the handle. (See Figure 4.6.)

Figure 4.6.
The car photo with circles indicating major color selection areas.

Note: You could use the instructions in the "But I Want PMS Colors" sidebar to find a close match—and it would be a good exercise for you—but for this project, choose Pantone 485.

6. Select Pantone 485 from the Pantone Library.

7. Drag a color swatch of Pantone 485 into the well of the Color Mixer panel (or choose it from the panel's drop-down list). Click the Tints tab.

8. Click the darkest square on the right—the 90% tint, and click the Add To Color List button. The dialog box should read 90% PANTONE 485. If it doesn't, then choose the color from the Color Mixer drop-down menu so its name stays selected. Click OK.

9. Repeat for the other percentages; stop at 30%.

10. For the shadow areas, add a little black to the color well if you're working in CMYK, or otherwise darken the color in RGB or HLS. Click the Add To Color List button and give it the name Dark Red Shadow. (Actually, you can call it anything you like, but give it a descriptive name.)

11. The new color should appear in the Color Swatches list in Roman type. Drag a swatch of it into the Color Mixer well again, click Tints, and save out tints from 90% down to 60%. (You have been saving regularly, haven't you?)

But I Want PMS Colors

Suppose you created a drawing using a color you mixed yourself (in RGB, HLS, CMYK, or Hexadecimal). Thinking ahead—and being very bright—you have named the color, and all instances of the color are of the named variety, and not just swatches dropped from the color well. Now the client wants to print the job using spot PMS inks. Well, if you want to be able to convert those mixed colors to PMS colors *and* you're on a Macintosh, you can download the Pantone Color Picker extension from Apple's Support site. You'd never be able to put the whole Web address in your browser window because it's so long, so you can either search for it or get the link directly from Ian Kelleigh's FreeHand Source site (**www.FreeHandSource.com**). The link on his site to the Apple/Pantone software is under Tips|Converting Colors to Pantone.

1. Download the Pantone Color Picker, install the small file per the instructions that come with it, and restart.

2. Back in your FreeHand document, place your *named* mixed color into the Color Mixer color well, and click the Apple Color Picker icon. The Apple Color Picker will now have a Pantone selection button in the scrolling list. When you click it, the nearest PMS match will be selected in the window—in the various Coated and Uncoated formulas. Remember or write down the number.

3. Close the window and use the Color Swatches Options window to choose the same color from the Coated or Uncoated Pantone library. That color will show up in your Swatches panel.

4. Drag its color swatch over the color you mixed and the change will ripple throughout your document, tints and all.

Oddly enough, if you test this system with Pantone 485, the software will tell you the closest match is Warm Red. Again, I implore you, trust the numbers. Check your PMS book for accurate matching—assuming the book is relatively new and the colors haven't faded.

---

12. Using the Eyedropper tool, choose three values of colors (dark, medium, and light) from the wheel covers. Then choose two or three tire colors, and colors from various parts of the windows. Be sure to name them all. Figure 4.7 shows the list I ended up with. Save the file.

The New Car Drawing

This is where we separate the wheat from the chaff, the pros from the hacks, the talkers from the doers. I'm talking about drawing. I can't stress enough that you can't learn to draw without drawing. You must use these tools over and over until they're second nature if you plan to make a living at it. I also realize that some of you are on a tight schedule and may not have time to draw all the details on this car, so you can import TheCarDrawing.fh10 from the CD-ROM in the Chapter 4 folder. I have not added the color in this drawing, but it does have all the areas drawn on separate layers for easy deconstruction or coloring. Think of it as an expensive coloring book.

If you prefer to draw the car from scratch (which I recommend), you can just continue on with the page you used to create the color library. The drawing tools you use are up to you. I like the Pen tool, but the Bezigon works too. The Pencil tool is a little "loose" for doing something of this nature. Just to make things easy to see, I chose a contrasting color for my stroke. In this case, it's a bright lime green. Outline the basic color breaks in the photo, as shown in Figure 4.8. (See the "You Have to Draw the Line Somewhere!" tip.)

Figure 4.7

The complete Swatches panel for this drawing.

Figure 4.8
This keyline view shows the paths I created to show color breaks in the car. You can use my lines, but you'll learn more if you draw them yourself.

You Have to Draw the Line Somewhere!

I look for color breaks in the photos I use—that really thin line that says, "It's darker on that side than it is on this side." Sometimes I may spend more time looking for those breaks than actually drawing their outline, but if you can find the break—where you can see that there is a definite color difference from one area to another—your drawings will look very realistic. The degree to which you take this color break thing is up to your budget. The drawing in the "New Car Drawing" project will stick to about eight steps, but the project uses only one basic color. Each photo you use in your own drawings will have its own set of color breaks and surprises. If you're doing your own scan, you can use editing software to posterize the photo to a useable number of colors.

You're probably thinking that I must be nuts to want you to draw all those lines—and how would you keep track of where you are? Well, I probably am nuts, but I'm serious about the lines. To keep track of where you've been and where you're going, add color as you draw. The "Don't Have a Stroke!" sidebar has some good information and tricks about applying colors, but the basic premise is that you will draw a selection, and then choose a color from your Swatches panel (or, if you prefer, the new fill colors box in the Tools panel). Depending on how you like to work, you can either have a stroke showing as you draw and give it a color of None when you're done with it, or draw without a colored stroke in the first place. As you apply the color, you can tell very easily how close you are to "correct" color because you won't see where your colored shape is—it will blend into the photo. Even small color differences are pretty obvious.

Start by looking at the overall color pattern in the photo. There will be one or two colors that are more dominant; you can place one of these colors beneath the others as a base. The base color may be light or dark, depending on the project. This car photo has a middle red color that you will use as a base. With that decision made, you will draw shapes that describe all the other colors, and apply color as you draw. The base shape contains the whole car—even though you could have cut out the windows. I used Hide Selection to get the base shape out of the way, or changed its fill to None. Everything else was placed on top of the base shape in order of largest areas first. See the "Piles of Color" tip for this philosophy.

The Car's Body

Follow these steps to draw the car's body:

1. Start the manual tracing by drawing the outline of the red portions of the car. That area encompasses everything that's painted red. Leave the wheels, tires, and windows out. Do not give the area a fill at this time, but do apply a stroke of a couple points or more so it will be easy to select as your drawing progresses.

2. Trace the area around the headlights and parking lights. Also trace the window areas if you happened to enclose them in the first step. This is a very subjective task, and what you see as important may be overlooked by another artist.

3. When those areas are outlined as closed paths, Shift+select all of them and the car outline and select Join to create a compound path. Fill it with a color right now; the headlight areas should be clear. Change the fill color to None.

4. Now, start the interior colors by tracing the lightest areas of red you can see. That will be the areas around the rear of the car, between the windows, wheels, and taillight.

5. It's up to you, but you can place those outlines on a separate layer.

6. Draw the next-darkest red areas. Keep in mind that your monitor may show the color breaks in a slightly different place from mine. Don't panic!

7. You shouldn't have to make a conscious effort to decide how many color breaks to have. If you see a color break, draw it. It's that simple. You can use my drawing as an overlay by giving it its own locked layer and set the stroke to a pale green. Turn it on and off for tracing hints.

8. Draw the next-darkest red areas, on and on, until you have all of them done.

Piles of Color

Whatever you draw will be on top of whatever you've drawn earlier. Suppose you trace a photo of a baby sitting on a blanket. If you draw the blanket first and give it a fill, you can no longer see the baby. Use Hide Selection so you can see and trace the baby. Conversely, if you draw the baby first, then draw the blanket, the baby disappears again when you fill the blanket, so you must send the blanket to the back (Send To Back). Moreover, if you draw the baby first, then draw the diaper and it gets filled—well, you're going to have to change it, I'm done with that stuff!

Don't Have a Stroke!

Dragging and dropping colors onto objects can be a little frustrating at times. If you're not careful about where the cursor is, you'll end up coloring the stroke instead of the fill, or the fill instead of the stroke. To get around that, there are a few things you can do to speed up your work. Select the Eyedropper tool and hold down the modifier key(s) to get specific fills, strokes, and blends the first time, every time. Do a Cmd+drag on a Mac or Ctl+Shift+drag on Windows to color just the stroke. Shift+drag on both platforms to color just the fill. Opt/Alt+drag creates a radial fill with the center of the fill being where you let go of the mouse. Ctrl+drag on both platforms creates a gradient fill, with the direction being determined by the placement of your mouse as you let go. New in FreeHand 10 is the contour blend fill available by using Cmd+Opt/Ctl+Alt+drag.

Details

Now add the details:

1. Draw the headlights. I've used about five colors that I plucked with the Eyedropper tool. When you're done, Group them, and put them on their own layer.

2. As we're up front, draw the scoop in the middle of the hood. Give it its own layer.

3. Draw the scoop on the roof, then put it on the other scoop's layer.

4. Draw the scoops on the door panel, and the door handle. (Notice that these are only a couple of lines.) Put them on the scoop layer.

5. Whip out the taillights. Three colors. Leave space between the highlight and the edge of the taillights for the car color to show through as a shadow or highlight. Save.

6. Now tackle the rear window. There are a lot of curvy lines here that can be accomplished with the Pen tool, but only three colored fills in the four areas.

7. Take care of the side window. Again, you'll need a very limited palette. Place all your windows on a single layer.

8. Now do the windshield. Actually, you're drawing the inside of the car— that's what you are looking at through the windshield—the dashboard, inside of door, seat backs, and so on.

The Wheels and Tires

The wheels and tires are a pretty interesting set of parts to draw. Interesting, because you'll be getting into ellipses, and they are easily drawn incorrectly.

The wheels and tires are all based on ellipses, but not the kind that you can usually get right the first time with the Ellipse tool, because the ellipses are rotated due to perspective. Using the Ellipse tool, you can draw an ellipse with a horizontal or vertical major axis, then using the Transform or Rotate tools, rotate it into place. This can be a problem if your judgment is off even slightly; you can spend half an hour trying to manipulate that ellipse into the proper shape and angle. Another valuable method is to click+drag points with the Pen tool.

I've been using FreeHand since it was introduced and never had any use for the Bezigon tool at all. Except one. It's a strange tool. Some artists swear by it; others swear at it. In this instance, I swear by it. Using the Bezigon tool, half the job in this section of the project can be done in four clicks, and the other half only takes a few click+drags. Here's the trick:

1. Zoom in tightly on the front wheel and examine the outline. Notice where the major and minor axes cross the ellipse that makes up the outer rim of the wheel.

2. Starting at the top, hold down the Opt/Alt key and click the Bezigon tool at the widest part of the ellipse. (See the "Major and Minor Axes Cut Up Ellipses" sidebar.)

3. The point you just placed is a Curve point. Keep the Opt/Alt key down and click at the minor axis tangent. Click the other major axis point, the last minor axis point, and finally the first point.

4. You'll be looking at an ellipse. Not a perfect one, and it doesn't quite fit your wheel, but with a few mouse clicks+drags on control handles, you can fit the ellipse nearly perfectly. Take each point at a time and adjust both handles. Save when you've finished drawing them correctly.

5. This main ellipse will be filled later with whatever color you choose to be the background. For now, give it a stroke with a fill of None, and place it on a new layer named Wheels.

6. As before, trace like-colored areas of the wheel spokes and the rim. I had three colors that I had culled from the photo. As you're drawing, decide if you want the large ellipse to be the dark shadowed area, or a lighter tone. Then just draw everything else in the wheel. (I chose the lightest color, so I had to draw all the shadow shapes.)

> **Note:** As you're drawing, if you have shapes of the same color that abut or overlap, use the Union command to consolidate them.

The tire can be drawn with the Bezigon tool, but I find the Pen tool to be better equipped for the job. That's because the tire is a pair of ellipses (inner tire wall, and outer tire wall) with a connecting straight path (the bottom of the tire), and the wheel well breaks up the regularity of the shape. The Pen is just quicker here.

7. Draw the highlight area of the top of the tire and the inside of the tire at the bottom as it meets the wheel rim. Save.

8. Repeat the procedure for the rear wheel and tire. Save. Your drawing should look like Figure 4.9.

But I Wanted a Blue One...

Okay, you've put in a couple hours and have all the shapes done, and it looks just like the car in Figure 4.9. (Then again, you may have used my drawing and have only been at it for a half-hour.) At any rate, you have a cute little red car. But the client calls and says that the factory wants to push blue cars this month. Can you change it?

Major and Minor Axes Cut Up Ellipses

The minor axis is an imaginary line around which something rotates. Think of it as the axle to a wheel. In the sense of drawing, the minor axis always goes through the shortest dimension of the ellipse. Conversely, the major axis also runs through the center of the ellipse, but at right angles to the minor axis—and therefore through the widest dimension of the ellipse. Find one, and you've got the other just 90 degrees away, as shown in the figure.

Each ellipse has its own major and minor axis, but in a wheel, or pie pan, or anything else with a depth to it, the ellipses share the minor axis but have different major axes.

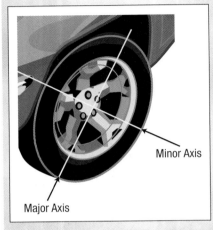

Major and Minor axes on the front wheel.

Figure 4.9
The finished car.

Yes, you can. Start with what I think is the coolest method. Remember how you made the color tints from named colors? Well, now that comes into play very much in your favor, because the client picked PMS 300 as the color they want the car to be.

1. Add Pantone 300 (and 293 for the Dark Shadow replacement) to the Swatches panel by methods you're totally familiar with by now.

2. Change our Pantone 485 to Pantone 300 by one of the following methods:

   • Drag a swatch of 300 onto the 485 swatch. An alert box will ask if you want to redefine the color. Click OK. Repeat for PMS 293 and Dark Shadow. You can see the results of two such sets of color changes in Figure 4.10. This is really the best way to do it.

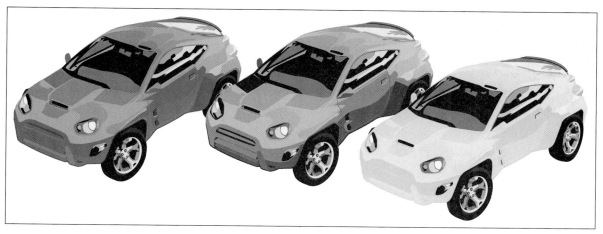

Figure 4.10
The finished car lot.

   • Select Pantone 485 in the Swatches panel and click the panel triangle; choose Replace color. Choose the Pantone Coated selection in the top drop-down menu. Click OK. Type "300" or scroll to the color you want. Click OK. The name of the color will change in the Swatches panel, the original color is deleted, and all objects that were pure 485 will change. You'll have to repeat for each additional tint.

   • Select Pantone 485 and go to Xtras|Colors|Color Control. That dialog box will allow you to change anything but spot color values incrementally in CMYK, RGB, or HSL as you wish. Spot colors, since the ink is coming out of the can, will not be affected, so you'd have to go to the Swatches panel and choose Convert To CMYK or Convert To RGB in order to use this method. Select the Preview button to see on-screen color shifting. When you're happy with the new color, click OK. The color and its tints will change, but will be unnamed until you name them with the Colors|Name All Used Colors Xtra.

3. Save the file.

As you can see, there are several ways to effect a color change; some are easier than others. Obviously, the first method is the best for this application of color change. The important thing to remember is that in a different illustration, one of these methods may be the only realistic thing to do. By the way, if you'd like to see the finished car in shades of gray, simply go to Xtras|Colors|Convert To Grayscale. And for some really bizarre effects, choose the Randomize Named Colors. To finish off the project, make a matching color change for the dark areas of the car. Save. Print. Tape it on the refrigerator.

Moving On

We've learned a lot about color in this chapter, even though the projects were almost monochromatic. The outlines you created for the various color shapes could now be cloned and/or otherwise manipulated for blends and gradient fills that we'll work on in the next chapter. For now, this posterized art effect could be used very effectively for spot illustrations or Web work. To see how the car will look on your Web site, click the Flash Anti-alias selection in the Drawing Mode pop-up menu in the lower left of the document window on a Mac, or in the Status window on a Windows machine.

In Chapter 5, you'll learn more about the different kinds of gradients and blends, and work with them together to make realistic illustrations.

Chapter 5

Creating Gradients and Blends

Smooth color transitions are important to illustrations of any kind. In vector drawing, gradient fills and blends do the job, but they do have important limitations.

FreeHand Vector Alchemy

What's the difference between a gradient and a blend? Well, if you went into your favorite coffee bar and ordered a Hazelnut Amaretto Grande, that would be a blend. If you asked for cream, you would be adding a gradient fill. Okay, that sounds silly, but it's more accurate than you might think. A *blend* takes two or more objects and creates a shape and color shift in incremental steps from one shape to the other. On the other hand, a *gradient fill* only changes colors. Either way, it's like alchemy—turning lead into gold—and you can do it in FreeHand. Figure 5.1 shows how you would make a transition using a blend; Figure 5.2 is the gradient-fill version of alchemy.

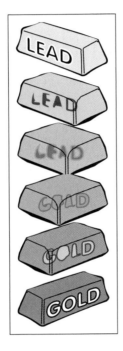

Figure 5.1

(Left) A blend places intermediate steps between two or more objects in shape, stroke, and fill. This blend happens to follow a straight line, but blends may be attached to paths and yield extremely valuable effects.

Figure 5.2

(Right) A gradient fill changes color only within a shape. Here, the molten metal has three colors in the fill, the inside of the bucket has two, and the outside of the bucket has five. You can have as few as two colors (and they can be the same color), or as many as you can fit.

The final results between the two methods can be indistinguishable in the finished art, but the way they work is markedly different. Also, you can mix and match them to really customize your artwork. In this chapter, instead of discussing blends and gradient fills simultaneously, I'll consider them one at a time.

The Blend Xtra

It's quite obvious when you look at most demonstrations of the Blend feature that you can take more than one shape and *morph* them. For example, there might be a square on one side of the page that turns into a star that turns into a circle as you move to the other side of the page. There is often a color morph as well. And, although it's rare to find a good use for morphing a square into a star into a circle, and on and on, if you use similarly shaped objects and stack the objects on top of each other instead of stringing them out linearly, you'll get a whole new perspective on the blend. This is how most graphic artists use the tool on almost a daily basis.

Another common use of the Blend Xtra is to create an array of equally spaced objects, which can then be attached to a path. Once on the path, the string's alignment to the path can be modified. Figure 5.3 gives examples of the three ways a blend can be aligned. As the figure shows, a blend joined to a path can be aligned in the Object Inspector panel.

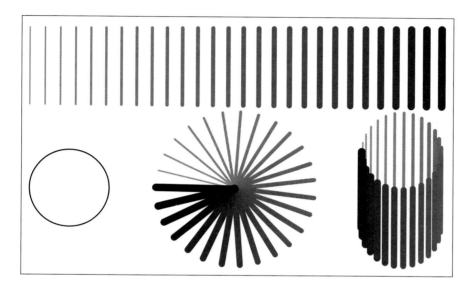

Figure 5.3
Three ways a blend can be aligned. The top set of lines represents a blend from a 1-point orange line to a 6-point black line. The blend was attached to the ellipse on the left, and Rotate On Path was checked in the Object Inspector to create the shape in the middle of the figure. That option was unchecked for the cylindrical effect on the right.

To summarize, a blend will create a smooth transition of shape, stroke, and fill in one or more objects. Here are a few more facts about blends:

- A blend can be attached to a path.

- The number of steps in the blend can be altered.

- The distance between the first object and the first intermediate step in the blend can be controlled (as can the distance between the last object and last intermediate step in the blend).

- The blend travels between the first object drawn to the second object drawn, with the first object ending at the bottom of the stacking order.

- The stacking order can be changed by sending either end object to the front or back.

- A blend can contain like gradient fills with multiple colors as long as all objects to be included in the blend have the same basic stroke and fill attributes.

- A stroke may be existent or not in both elements, but may be any color or width.

- A fill may be any color or group of colors, as long as the same number of colors is used in each object. The gradient fills must be of the same type: Radial, Linear, or Contour.

- The direction or center point of gradient fills can be different in each object.

- A blend can be made from as few as two objects to so many you run out of RAM.

- Groups may be blended together.

- Compound paths may be blended together.

- Groups cannot blend to compound paths.

The Gradient Fill

A gradient fill is accomplished using the Fill panel in the Object Inspector. Gradients, or *graduated fills* as they are sometimes called, provide an extremely smooth change between colors in the fill. Fills differ from blends in that, while a blend can contain virtually all attributes of an object, the gradient fill only affects color.

That is not to say that a gradient fill is any less important than a blend. It's just a different kind of tool, and it can be used in conjunction with a blend.

Four variations of gradient fills are supplied with FreeHand 10: Linear, Logarithmic, Radial, and the new Contour gradient. Here are some basic features of gradient fills:

- There is no maximum limit for colors; the minimum number is two.

- The two minimum colors can be the same color.

- The direction of a Linear gradient may be modified through 360 degrees.

- The center point of a Radial gradient may be moved anywhere within the bounding box of the object.

- The center point of a Contour gradient may be altered in the same manner as the Radial gradient, but can be further modified by adjusting the Taper of the gradient.

- Center points of Radial and Contour gradients can be reset to the center of the object by Shift+clicking the crosshair button.

- If you are using named colors, the first and last colors in a gradient are listed with their name. Intermediate colors are not, but clicking the color swatch can access their names; the pop-up color palette will open, showing the name of the color.

- Linear and Logarithmic gradients are the same except for the distance between the steps in the graduation. Linear gradients have equal steps in the color change; Logarithmic gradients have a faster fade out of the first color, leaving more of the end color in the blend.

- Gradient fills may be applied to closed paths, open paths, and compound paths.

Notice in Figure 5.4 that the differences are subtle, yet each has its own very distinctive appearance and use. Your FreeHand 10 user's guide lists many more features of blends and gradient fills, but you can do the first project with these four.

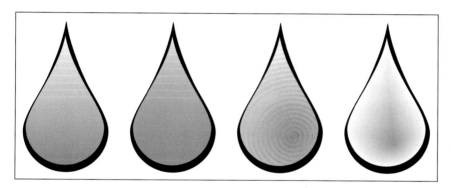

Figure 5.4
The four basic gradient fills. From left to right: Linear, Logarithmic, Radial, and Contour.

PROJECT Drawing with Blends

The first three projects in this chapter will utilize the same basic shapes, but you'll use blends in the first one, gradient fills in the second, and mix and match gradients and blends in the third project. Use the Duplicate Page feature in the Object Inspector after you've drawn the basic shapes so you don't have to redraw them for the next two exercises. To add a little spice to the projects, you'll draw the objects in perspective.

The Cube

I have started this project for you. To begin, open the Blends.fh10 file in the Chapter 5 folder on the CD-ROM.

1. Choose Save As, and name your drawing My Blends.

2. Using the Bezigon, Ellipse, or Pen tool, trace each object. Save.

3. You'll want the edges of the cube to line up as perfectly as possible, so drag a selection box around the bottom corner to select both points. Use the Align Xtra or buttons in the toolbar to align horizontal and vertical centers.

4. Repeat with the other two corners.

Figure 5.5
The cube's right face has the clone with Inset Path applied. In the top face, the outer point has been moved to the center and the left face blended.

Note: The blend you see will be banded due to the limited color range. You can change the number of steps in the Object Inspector panel. Figure 5.5 has 20 steps in the blend.

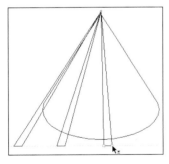

Figure 5.6
A triangle has been created and cloned. The clones are placed at various spots "around" the cone.

5. Drag a selection box from outside the cube faces so it just surrounds the center point intersection. Align the points horizontally and vertically center as well. Save.

6. Fill the left face with 50% black, the top face with 20% black, and the right face 40% black. Delete their strokes as you're creating their fills.

7. Shift+select all three faces and clone them. Use the Inset Path Xtra with a value of 6 points.

8. Add 20% to each of the clones: Left = 70%, top = 40%, right = 60% black.

9. Select the clone on the top face, move the point opposite the center point toward the center, creating a shallow upside-down *V* as shown in Figure 5.5.

10. With that point still selected, Shift+select the outer point of the cube's top, and Blend the two shapes.

11. Repeat with the left and right faces.

The Cone

For the cone shape, you'll use Blends between several objects to get the color shifting you want. Then you'll cut the Blend from the drawing and do a Paste Inside.

1. Drag a horizontal guideline below the base of the cone.

2. Using the Line tool, start dragging a line just a little above and centered on the point of the cone.

3. Drag to the guideline, slightly outside the left edge of the cone.

4. Switch to the Pen tool. Select the end point of the line and add a new point to the right, inside the cone's shape.

5. To complete the triangle, check the Closed Path box in the Object Inspector.

6. Clone the triangle, Shift+select the bottom two points, and move them to the right as shown in Figure 5.6. Save.

7. Repeat two or three times until you place the last one, covering the right edge of the cone.

8. Give the triangles shades of black. After you finish everything, you can change these values and shift the placement of the tones. Your drawing will look something like Figure 5.7.

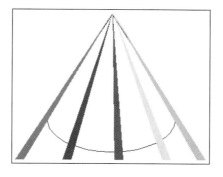

Figure 5.7
The blending triangles in place.

9. Select the left triangle, and Shift+click the left base point. Shift+select the next triangle and its left base point. Continue until all your triangles are selected.

10. Blend the triangles by using your keyboard shortcut, the Xtra button on your toolbar, or Modify|Combine|Blend.

11. While the blended triangles are still selected, choose Cut. Select the cone shape, and choose Edit|Paste Inside. Cool, huh? Save.

Note: I like to create as realistic a look as possible, so I rarely go all the way to black in my rendering. I also make the edge that recedes into the background a slightly lighter color to approximate ambient light wrapping around the object.

The Sphere

Although blending really isn't the best method FreeHand provides for creating a three-dimensional sphere, using it to create one will show you how well the Blend Xtra functions.

1. Begin by selecting the circle and cloning it. Hold down the Shift key and drag the clone up to the right, as you can see in Figure 5.8.

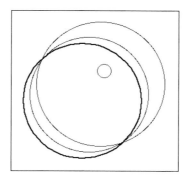

Figure 5.8
The sphere with its blending ellipses in place. The original sphere outline is bold for clarity.

2. Clone that circle and Shift+drag it up to the right again. Double-click it to bring up the Transform handles, and Shift+drag the top right handle to enlarge the circle (see Figure 5.8).

3. Draw a small circle for the highlight.

4. Shift+drag a selection box around all the circles and clone them. Save.

5. Refer to Figure 5.9 for Steps 5 through 9. Bring the large circle (3) to the foreground. Shift+select the original circle, and use the Intersect Xtra to create the top of the sphere (1). Fill it with 50% black.

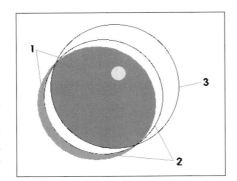

Figure 5.9

Circle number 1 is the original, 2 is a clone, and 3 an enlarged clone. Punch or Intersect Xtras has been applied to create the darkened shapes.

6. Clone the original circle again, send it to the back, and Shift+select the middle circle (2). Use the Punch Xtra to create the crescent lower part of the sphere (1). Fill it with 40% black.

7. With any luck, you still have a large and middle circle left. Bring the largest circle (3) to the front, Shift+select the middle circle (2), and use the Punch Xtra to create the middle sliver. Give it a fill of 50% black.

8. All the circles should be gone except the small highlight. Hold down the Opt/Alt key and drag from the outside of the circle array around where the small circle should be. That will select two circles, because we made a clone of it. Bring them to the front (Shift+Cmd/Ctl+up arrow).

9. Deselect by clicking the desktop. Click the small circle and delete it. Select the remaining circle and give it a fill of 20% black.

10. Keep the small circle selected and Shift+select the top of the sphere. Blend the two shapes.

11. Select the two crescents and Blend them. Save. I changed the number of steps in the Blend to 30 for the top and 14 for the bottom to eliminate the banding. The final result is seen in Figure 5.10.

A blend and a gradient fill generally make the same file size, but an EPS export of the files will result in the blend being as much as 150 percent larger than the gradient fill.

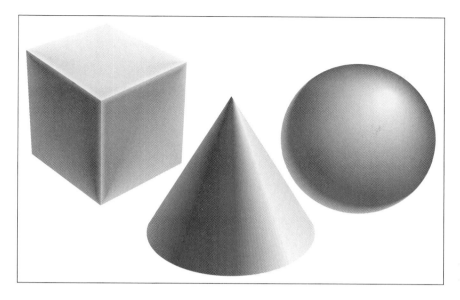

Figure 5.10
The finished drawing using the Blend Xtra.

Project: Drawing with Gradient Fills

This project will show you how quickly you could have completed the last project had you decided to use gradient fills instead. You'll also realize that what works in one case won't do at all in another. To make this project easier, use the same three objects you used in the "Drawing with Blends" project.

The Cube

Begin constructing the cube by opening the Blends.fh10 file in the Chapter 5 folder on the CD-ROM.

1. Do a Save As, and name your drawing Gradients.

2. Click the left side of the cube to select it. In the Fills panel, use the pop-up menu to select Gradient. Place an 80% black tone on the left swatch, a 40% tone on the right swatch, and set the angle to 214°. Delete the stroke.

3. Do the same with the top face, using 10%, 50%, and the default of 270°. Delete the stroke.

4. Now configure the right face with 30%, 60%, and 156°. Kill the stroke. Save.

The Cone

Continue by first selecting the cone shape.

1. In the Fills panel, use the pop-up menu to select Gradient again. This time, select the last gradient icon—the Contour gradient.

2. Enter 60% black in the left swatch, 10% in the right swatch, and drag the Taper slider to (or enter) 67.

Note: The Gradient Fill panel is defaulted to a Linear blend with the blend going vertically from top to bottom. FreeHand 10 has confused the issue a bit by making the color well from left to right—which is logical because it's traveling from 180° to 0° on the angle selector wheel. It took a few sessions for me to catch on. Proof that old goats *can* learn new tricks.

3. Move the knob (Mac users see crosshairs and a round knob, Windows users see a square knob) in the middle of the preview directly to the bottom. As you move it around, you get live feedback from your adjustment. Save.

The Sphere

Now add the sphere:

1. Select the circle. In the Fills panel, select Gradient from the pop-up menu, and click the middle gradient icon—the Radial gradient.

2. Place a 40% black tint in the left swatch. Add a new swatch by creating 80% in the Color Mixer well and dragging that color to the Gradient color well. Move it to about one-third from the left edge. The right swatch will probably be defaulted to white. If not, make it white.

3. Move the handle in the middle of the crosshairs diagonally about halfway to the top right corner. Save. Your completed drawings should look like those in Figure 5.11.

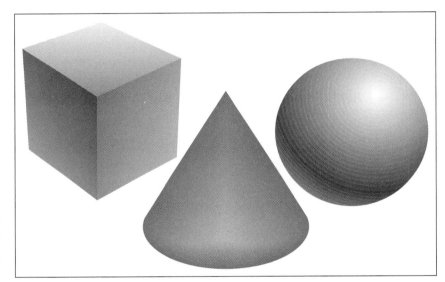

Figure 5.11
Three objects drawn with gradient fills. The cube used Linear gradients, the cone has a Contour gradient, and the sphere has a Radial fill. Notice how smooth the sphere looks.

The Contour Gradient

As the Contour gradient was not used much in the first two projects, here is an introduction to this powerful new feature. After you use it in this project, you should have a new respect for the power that FreeHand provides.

The Contour gradient does the work of a carefully crafted Blend. You can place and change colors as you require, and then adjust the taper of the resulting Blend. What you get in return is the color in the left swatch on the outside of your object, and other colors gradually moving toward a smaller clone of the outer shape. The Taper adjustment determines the size of the inner shape.

Which is Better, Illustrator's Gradient Mesh, or FreeHand's Contour Gradient?

It comes down to dogs and cats. Neither is better, they're just different animals. Adobe Illustrator has a feature—called a *Gradient Mesh*—that allows you to create a grid so you can apply color to various segments of it, and all these segments blend together. It's very nice to look at, and you can make some really neat artwork.

But in order to print it, you must print to a PostScript 3 printer, *and* the artwork is *rastered*. That is to say, it is no longer a vector graphic. You must determine the resolution of the output and the finished size of the artwork. What that means is you've turned your vector artwork into a bitmap. You've also lost the ability to enlarge and reduce the graphic without distortion—the jaggies. Call me a purist, or a snob, but if I want bitmapped art, I'll take care of it in a bitmap editing program in the first place. That's not to say that I don't take my vector art and import it into Adobe Photoshop to further manipulate it—I do that all the time. It's just if I want to create a vector graphic, I want it to stay a vector graphic without muddying the water with rastering.

The Gradient Mesh also creates a sneaky time bomb. If you create artwork with a Gradient Mesh in it at a specific size for your client, and someone decides to make that illustration larger than you had planned, everyone is in for a big jaggy surprise, and you will be the fall guy.

PROJECT Drawing with Contour Gradients

Not everything you draw must consist of sharp corners and flat shapes. You get to draw soft, roundy things too. The FreeHand 10 tutorial with the sarcophagus is a great example and can get you started with the Contour gradient. My project here will take you quite a bit further.

The Leaves

Begin by opening the Rose.fh10 file from the Chapter 5 folder on the CD-ROM.

1. Do a Save As and name the file something meaningful like A Rose is a Rose.

2. I have provided you with the line art (as shown in Figure 5.12) and a color palette. Now drag a zoom box around the leaf on the right.

3. The leaf has been given a blue fill so it will be easy for you to select. Select it. Go to the Fills panel, use the pop-up menu to find Gradient, and click the Contour Gradient button.

4. If you're comfortable dragging colors from the Color Swatches panel, okay, but there's a better method. Just click the swatch on either end of the fill ramp—the color box will appear. Select Swatches from the drop-down menu, and select a color to replace the color in the ramp. Click on the darker green for the left swatch and the light green for the right swatch.

5. Move the Taper slider left and right to see the effect. Add a swatch of white to the middle of the color well from the Color Swatches panel. Shift it left and right. Keep it or delete it as you wish. Save.

6. Repeat the Contour gradient with the left leaf. Figure 5.13 shows the Fill panel and the effects on the left leaf.

Rasterize Vector Art

You can rasterize your vector art any time you want to in FreeHand. Just go to Modify|Rasterize, select the resolution and the amount of anti-aliasing and click OK. Be sure to do a Save As first, though. Your original vector art will be deleted and replaced with a bitmapped TIFF that is embedded in your FreeHand document. You would use this process if you wanted a TIFF instead of an EPS as your final output and didn't have a bitmap editing program to work with.

Figure 5.12
(Left) The line drawing of the rose. All lines were drawn with a 1-point width, and then expanded with the Expand Stroke Xtra. With the exception of the dark line outlining the flower, all of the lines were then distorted with the Roughen Xtra.

Figure 5.13
(Right) The Contour Gradient Fill panel as applied to the leaf on the left. Note the position of the handle in the crosshair window. Do you see how useful this tool is?

The Petals

Now, draw the petals:

1. Lock the Basic Flower layer, and begin by tracing the lowest petals. Just as in preschool, try to stay within the lines as I did in Figure 5.14.

Figure 5.14
My attempts to stay within the lines. Notice the colored path for the sake of visibility.

2. When you have a complete petal drawn (as a closed path), use the Fill panel as shown in Figure 5.15.

3. Complete the flower by doing one petal at a time. Remember to delete your stroke color.

Figure 5.15
The first petals colorized and modeled.

The Stem

This next task is a little out of the ordinary. The stem started life as an open path. When I ran the Expand Stroke Xtra on it, it became a closed path filled with black. Now you will want to fill the center.

1. Clone the stem shape. Drag+zoom in on the base of the stem and select the two inner points as shown in Figure 5.16.

> **The Cost of Contour Gradients**
>
> You may have noticed that after drawing several petals, your computer slowed down quite a bit to redraw the blends. One thing you can count on—if your machine slows down, the output device is going to have the same reaction. Use this feature sparingly.

Figure 5.16
Stem repair starts with a clone and the Split Xtra.

2. Using the Split Xtra, deselect everything, and then reselect the outer portion of the shape. Delete it. (Things won't look much different.)

3. Click on the inside of the line with the Pointer tool, selecting that path, and give it a stroke of None. In the Object Inspector panel, click the Closed path button.

Note: If you want, now would be a good time to play with the color controls you learned about in Chapter 4. You can change the color from reds to whites to peach tones.

4. Use the Contour gradient to fill the stem with shades of green. Save. Print. Cut it out, put it in your teeth and do a Tango....Well, maybe not. But stick it on the refrigerator, anyway. It should look like Figure 5.17.

Figure 5.17
A rose by any other name… would be well-drawn with FreeHand's Contour gradients.

PROJECT Drawing with the Whole Toolkit

To wrap up the basics of drawing with the various fills, we'll tackle the same cube, cone, and sphere used in the earlier section of this chapter. No holds barred in this project, because it sets the stage for most of the tonal drawing you'll do in FreeHand.

The Cube

Construct the cube:

1. Open Blends.fh10 in the Chapter 5 folder of the CD-ROM. Save it as Final Blends.

2. On the left side of the cube, draw an ellipse with the Bezigon tool as described in the "Creating Circles from Squares" sidebar.

3. Repeat the process with the other two sides. Save.

4. Select all three ellipses and choose the Transform tool. Click the Scale tab and enter 29%. Deselect the top ellipse, but clone the two on the sides.

5. Move the top hole to the center of the face. On the right side, arrange the two ellipses as shown in Figure 5.18. Move the left face ellipses to corners, and clone them to fit the other two corners.

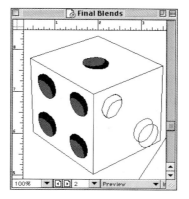

Figure 5.18
Die hole details. The top hole on the "2" side has been cloned twice, shifted, and punched. The crescent will be filled with black, and the hole with 75% black. The bottom hole is about to be punched.

6. Select the top ellipse. Clone it twice. Move the clone away from the light source—about a third of the way across the original ellipse. Shift+select the original ellipse and use the Punch Xtra to create a crescent.

7. Fill the crescent with black. Fill the remaining ellipse with 75% black, and give it a 6% black, 1-point stroke. Save.

8. Repeat the above two steps for the other two faces.

9. We'll shade the die using Contour gradients. But first we have to make round edges to the die. Put the holes or spots on their own layer and hide it if you wish. Select all three faces. Bring up the Inset Path Xtra, enter "8," with a Sharp Join, and click OK.

10. The faces just got smaller. Bring the Inset Path Xtra back, and this time put a minus sign (dash) in front of the 8, and click a Round Join. Click OK.

11. Wow, rounded corners! (That little trick was thought up by Judy Arndt and Ian Kelleigh. Judy is a regular contributor in the FreeHand forum—**forums.macromedia.com**—and comes up with extremely creative tricks and workarounds. Ian arguably has the best site on the Web—**www.FreeHandSource.com**—for tutorials, tricks, tips, and the history of FreeHand.) Deselect all but the top face. Bring up the Fills tab and use the drop-down menu to select Gradients, then click the Contour button. Enter "8" in the Taper window and put an 8% tint of black in the left swatch and white in the right. Move the knob in the crosshairs to the top middle—approximating the position of the furthest corner.

12. Do the same with the left face. The color ramp starts on the left with white, then just inside that, 5% black, ending with 20% black, Taper set to 10. The right face gets 5% on the left, 12% on the right, with a Taper of 11. Set their knobs in the corners farther from the center. Save.

Note: You can do all "holes" on each side at once—except the Punch Xtra. It only does one pair of elements at a time, so just keep clicking the Xtra until you run out of holes.

Creating Circles from Squares

In Chapter 4, I show you how to construct an ellipse by tracing an image with the Bezigon tool. But what if you don't have an image to trace? You will need a square to begin with. That square must be in correct perspective on the plane where you want to place the ellipse. Use the Perspective Grid or the methods described in Chapter 8 to create the proper shapes in perspective. If your perspective is off, everything will be off.

On the left side of the figure shown here, a circle has been drawn and all the points are selected. Take note where the control handles on the points lie. Each of them is the same amount of distance from its point (in opposite directions), and that distance is about 54 percent of the radius of the circle.

That information gives us the key to constructing a proper ellipse in perspective. Take the square in perspective, and divide the sides of that square in half. For absolute accuracy you'd have to keep perspective distortion in mind as you are dividing the sides in half. Drag a guideline to each midpoint.

Then use the Bezigon tool to place a point at each midpoint around the square. Hold down the Opt/Alt key to make each point a curve point. It's important to remember that the Bezigon tool has no idea what you're trying to do. When you're through with your four points, you'll have a rough approximation of a circle. But at this time all you need to do is drag each of the eight control handles approximately 54 percent of the way to the nearest corner of the square—aligning it with the edge of the square. Wham! Darn good ellipse. The right side of the figure shows the completed ellipse inside its square.

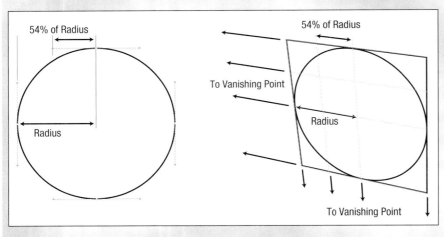

More FreeHand alchemy—turning squares into circles.

13. To create the rounded corners, draw a small circle. In the Object Inspector panel, type in "2p8" for the W and H values. Give it a Linear gradient fill of 5% black to white. Clone it twice.

14. Move one of the clones to the bottom corner of the die, and set the angle of the gradient so the dark edge is at the bottom. Send it to the back.

15. Move another clone to the far right corner, adjust the angle of the gradient so it angles toward the center, from dark at the right to white. Send it to the back. Repeat the whole process for the left corner. Save.

The Cone

Construct the cone the same way you did in the Blend section of this chapter, only use shades of blue and gray to approximate chrome.

To summarize those steps, create a triangle that overlaps one edge of the cone. Fill it with a "chrome tone." Clone it, and drag its bottom toward the opposite side. Repeat until you have enough steps. Select one of the bottom points (on the same side) of each triangle, and Blend them. Cut the Blend group to the Clipboard, select the cone shape, and do a Paste Inside. Save.

The Sphere

There's no getting around the fact that the Radial gradient fill really does the sphere job well.

1. Select the sphere, click Fills|Gradient|Radial, and give the left color swatch 75% black. Just a bit inside that, place a black swatch by dragging black from the Swatches panel. Put a 5% tone in the right swatch. Adjust the control knob so the highlight is in the upper right quadrant.

2. The ellipse for the 8-ball circle is distorted. Start by drawing one about the correct size. Ungroup it and select the top and bottom points. Using the arrow keys on your keyboard, click them up two or three points.

3. Double-click the new ellipse, and rotate it slightly counterclockwise to approximate the correct axis and curvature of the circle on the sphere. Give it a 5% black fill, and a 1-point stroke of 15%. Save.

4. Type the "8" in a 72-point font. I used Vag Rounded Bold, but almost any sans serif font will suffice. Convert it to paths, then drag it into place, rotating it if you wish with either the Transform handles (just double-click the "8") or the Rotate tool in the Tools panel. Save.

5. You are basically done. I wanted to take it a little further (see Figure 5.19), so I drew shapes with the Pen tool that I made into Transparent Lens fills. The 8-ball uses a setting of 9% Lighten, the 8-ball reflection in the cone has a 23% Darken, and the die reflection is white Transparency with an opacity of 17%. Shadows were drawn and given Linear gradient fills of 24% fading to white.

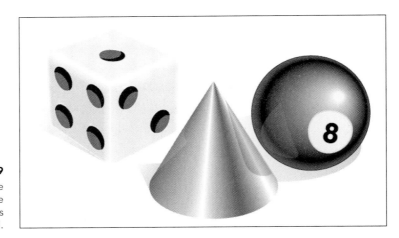

Figure 5.19

Although we've drawn some
pretty basic shapes here, the
use of blends and gradient fills
together works pretty well.

PROJECT The Power Saw

This project is a real-world drawing of an actual object. It is the
type of drawing that you would do for a hardware store flyer or for their catalog and newsletter clip art. I only use clip art in my own work if I need to
produce something within the next 15 minutes; otherwise, I use it for research.
But with this project, you're actually going to create something that others
might use for a job or for their own research. You will also combine flat fills,
blends, and gradient fills in the drawing to create some realistic effects.

The Line Drawing

Assume that the client has given you a photo of the tool that is in the correct
view for the drawing. Proceed as follows:

1. Start by opening a new document in FreeHand and importing the
   Saw.tif file from the Chapter 5 folder on the CD-ROM. Place it on a new
   layer and lock the layer.

2. Trace the outline of the saw. Save.

3. Draw the hand hole in the opposite direction from that in which you
   drew the saw (clockwise/counterclockwise or vice versa). This will make
   the compound path that we'll do later more efficient. Trace the plastic
   blade shield.

4. Select the outer path and clone it. You'll use it to save steps as we draw
   shapes adjacent to it. Using the Knife tool, cut the path where the shield
   line you just drew intersects it. Cut it again on the bottom.

5. Now, connect the part of the outline path and the shield path with the
   Join Xtra. Make sure that Closed is checked in the Object Inspector.

Note: When you use the Knife
tool in one continuous stroke
across the path in two locations, you will have two
separate objects. If your path
does not "cut," but instead
you end up with a new point
on the path, don't despair.
Select the new point and click
the Split Xtra.

6. Repeat with the various sections of the power cord, the steering knob on top, the saddle shape in the handle, and the many small shapes that make up the foot of the saw. Save.

7. By cloning various lines and cutting them, make one single path that outlines the plastic body shape—that is, minus the foot, clear plastic shield, trigger, and power cord. Import PMS 151, and give this outline that stroke color.

8. Place the body outline on its own layer and hide it for now.

9. Draw in the detail lines, vents, holes, and panels. No fills yet. Your drawing should be something like what you see in Figure 5.20. (Note that in that figure, the outline path has a 2-point stroke.) Save your work.

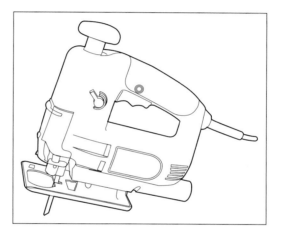

Figure 5.20
The basic outlines are in place and ready to fill with colors. Depending on the job and its budget, at this point you could change line weights here and there, add some more details, and call it done.

Creating the Labels

The saw label and the power setting guides remain to be drawn, but they require a different technique. You will want to do them as rapidly as possible, with the least amount of work, but still make them accurate. These shapes are both at angles, which would seem to be a problem, but as you will see, it's not. Here is how to draw them quickly.

First of all, find out the exact angle you are dealing with. Lacking a specific tool to do the job, use the tools you do have—the Line tool and the Info tool. If you don't have the Info tool open, go to Window|Toolbars|Info, and open it.

1. Draw a line with the Line tool, starting at the bottom of the power setting guide, and dragging it until the line is way past the guide. Keep it selected and the mouse down as you watch the numbers in the info window for various attributes—including the angle. Take note of the angle. If you draw your line on the same angle I drew mine, you'll come up with 73 degrees.

2. Subtracting that number from 90 degrees (vertical) will give you 17 degrees. (That means you can draw the box and set the type, then rotate the panel minus 17 degrees and it will line up correctly.)

3. Go to Modify|Constrain, and enter "–17". Then double-click the Rectangle tool, and enter 6 points in the radius field. Click OK.

4. Draw a rectangle starting at the top-left corner and dragging to the bottom right. Notice how the Constrain feature works?

5. Draw in the angular lines around the selector switch. Save.

6. Select the box and the lines you just drew and drag them off of the photo. Double-click to bring up the Transform handles, and rotate –17°. Select the Type tool and type all the words in place in the panel. The font is Helvetica/Arial bold italics. The head is 5.5 points, the list is 4.5 points, the range numbers are 8 points, and the word "SCROLL" is 4 points in both places.

7. Adjust the paragraph settings in the Type panel so that the first line has 3 points after it and the rest have 2 points after them. Draw 0.5-point lines as on the panel, and make the rectangles around "SCROLL."

8. Place the range numbers close to where you think they should go. When everything is set in place, group the entire panel and save.

9. Drag the panel back onto the drawing, and open the Transform panel (Window|Panel|Transform), choose the Rotate tab, enter "–17", and hit OK. Move the box into position.

10. Adding the label isn't as complicated. Set the type as a grouped unit, and drag it into place. Then double-click it to bring up the Transform Handles and rotate it to the correct angle by aligning the type to the upper and lower margins of the label. Scale it to fit. Save.

Creating the Color Fills

If you were creating a line drawing, you'd be done except for any cleanup. But the purpose of this project is to make a color drawing using blends and gradients, so now you are ready to create the colors.

1. Clone the handle saddle, and drag the top down until it meets the dark area. Then invert the bottom right corner so you end up with an *L* shape that surrounds the dark area and stays flush along the left edge. Fill that shape with 95% black, and kill the stroke.

2. Give the main part of the saddle a fill of 75% black with a stroke of None. Blend the two shapes—be sure to click two matching points in the paths for expected results. Change the number of steps in the blend to 25. Save.

3. Use the method outlined in the above two steps for the two sections of the power cord. Make the dark areas 95% black and the lighter areas 75% black. Send them to the back, and add a vertical line between them.

4. Where the power cord connects to the saw, create a gradient fill using the same shades of black in three steps (light, dark, light). Save.

5. Build a color palette using PMS 300 and PMS 302. Draw a rectangle and fill it with PMS 302. Clone it and move it to the other side of the page. Change the fill to PMS 300. Blend the two rectangles, and change the number of steps in the blend to 8. Click Ungroup twice, and use the Xtras|Colors|Name All Colors Xtra.

6. Do the same with PMS 300 to 10% of PMS 300. Your Color Swatches panel will now have 20 tones of blue to work with. You will only use a few, but you won't have to mix each time you need a tint.

7. The steering knob should be a closed path. Clone it, and move the points until they encompass the dark area. Keep the bottom of it where it is. Clone this shape, and move it in on all sides to outline the high-light area. Give it a 60% fill of PMS 300.

8. Select the dark outline and give it about 75% of the dark blue mix. Fill the outer shape with PMS 300. From the inside out, Shift+select all three, remove the stroke, and Blend them. Save.

9. Give the knob post a gradient fill with a 75% dark blue to darkest blue in the middle, and darkest blue on the right side. Adjust the angle to 343°. Clone the shape and Hide it. Adjust the original until it fits the highlight shape; change all the swatches to PMS 300.

10. Bring back the post (Show All), Send To Back, Shift+select the highlight shape, and Blend the two. Save.

11. Draw an inverted *L* shape that outlines the dark accent down the front face of the saw. Give it a 75% dark blue tint. Clone it, and move its points out on the left to the edge of the saw, and to the right about the same distance as the accent is wide. Give it a fill of 60% PMS 300. Clone this shape, and move the right side points to the right about half-way to the speed selector panel. Fill it with PMS 300.

12. Shift+select all three shapes and Blend them. Save. It should look roughly like Figure 5.21 by now.

13. Draw a shape outlining the dark area between the knob and the saddle, as shown in Figure 5.22, with a fill of about 75% dark blue. Clone it, and arrange the top of the path to fit the highlight on top.

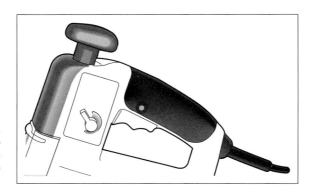

Figure 5.21

Blending one area at a time, highlights to dark accents to base color. Notice the smooth transition from one shade to another.

Figure 5.22

This shape will be cloned and distorted to the top as a highlight, and another clone of it distorted to the bottom to the base color.

Note: To make Steps 15 and 16 easier to see, I've placed all the blends completed so far on their own layer—I named it Blend Mass. It's placed above the Solid Plastic layer that contains the solid PMS 300 and below the Foreground layer that has all the line work.

Send it to the back with a color of 60% PMS 300. Clone the dark shape again, Shift+select the lighter shape and Blend them. Send to back.

14. Clone the dark shape once more, and stretch the bottom of the path downward so we can meld it into the body color. Send it to the back with a fill of PMS 300. Shift+select the dark shape again, and Blend the two shapes. Save.

15. Continue using the same technique until you have completed all the shapes shown in the "Blend Fever" sidebar. Put the shapes all on the same layer so you can show and hide it as necessary. Check the way your blends work by hiding and showing the Solid Plastic layer as you work.

16. Complete the saw body by creating the remaining blends shown in Figure 5.23. These blends are all gradient fills running diagonally across the horizontal face of the saw. All but the one under the clear plastic shield and the one immediately behind the blade gripper thingy start at the base color (PMS 300) and run to a lighter shade to match the photo. The blend under the shield is a four-step gradient from 80% to 80% to 100% to 70% PMS 300.

Blend Fever

The figure has several blend setups started. Each was created by drawing the most contrasting area, cloning it, and then expanding it to fit the outer limit of the color range. The bottom color is PMS 300 in most cases. The fishhook-shaped area has a gradient blend that goes from 50% PMS 300 to 80% PMS 300, and ends with 80% PMS 300. Its undershape also contains three steps in the gradient, but they're all PMS 300.

The vertical shape by the power cord is also a pair of three-step gradient fills. The top portion is 20% PMS 300 in both. The other two steps in the darker shape are both about 75% dark blue, the lighter shape has two steps of PMS 300.

The amount of distance you put between the contrasting color and the background shape determines how fast or slow the blend occurs. If you want a really long blend, put a lot of distance between the shapes. If you want a sharp drop off in color, keep the shape outlines close together.

By showing and hiding the layer that contains your solid background color, you can see how well the blending effects are working. I generally make the blend as soon as I finish the two shapes.

It makes good sense to select a point on each shape to maintain predictable blends. I also like to use cloned shapes because the number of points are the same. When you use the Inset Path Xtra—as is, or with a negative number to go larger—you sometimes will get extra points. To avoid overcomplicating the blend, use the Simplify Xtra and add points, or take away more as necessary.

Each of these pairs of shapes started as a smaller shape that was cloned and stretched or distorted to the base color. The photo has been moved to the background for clarity.

Figure 5.23
The shapes created in Step 16. These shapes are all simple gradient fills.

The Foot and Other Details

When you are done with the body, tackle the foot. Continue by outlining the various dark and light shapes—I kept it to a maximum of three color areas—light (PMS 1235), base (PMS 130), and accents and lines (PMS 151). There are only a few shapes, and gradient fills do the job quickly.

1. Draw the screw head with a radial fill of light grays. The screw slot was filled with a dark gray.

Blend Tip

When you need an abrupt change in color when creating a gradient fill, bring the color swatches close together as I did in the plastic shield blue area. Sometimes, though, you'll find that you get a little too close, and the swatch you're trying to get close to will just pick up the color you're dragging. That can be a real drag—no pun intended—but here's an easy fix: Drag the swatch onto the color well itself. I've found you can get almost on top of the existing color. The colors almost make a corner, the shift is so quick.

2. Select the trigger area and fill it with an attention-getting color, PMS 151. Draw highlight lines accenting the finger shapes, and give them a PMS 1235 stroke. Use the same colors, and give the lock button a radial fill.

3. Use a Contour gradient for the selector switch, and an orange tint for the sides of the switch. You can put in an accented highlight along the selector switch if you want.

4. You will want to detail the label. Join the large name characters, and give them a Linear gradient fill. Use shades from 5% to 10% of black on the white lettering. Add a Linear gradient to the upper black shape to create a reflective sheen. The bottom half also can be a gradient, if you wish. Remember to adjust the angles to the shape they're following.

5. Add another extremely light (5% to 10% black) graduated tint to the outside of the label. Use your own judgment as to whether you add a black (or colored) stroke around these small detail elements. Ask yourself if the lines will print (are they too thin?), will they fill in (are they too wide?), would they be better as a darker or lighter tint of color instead of black.

6. Fill the slots and grooves with a dark color, but not solid black—it's too much of a contrast and creates a center of attention that is out of context. Clone the rear slots and select the bottom-left and top-right corner panels. Select the lower-left and upper-right corner points on each slot. Use the Split Xtra and save.

7. Select all the top slot lines and give them a stroke of PMS 300. Then select the bottom slots and stroke them with a lighter tint of PMS 300.

8. Fill the saw blade shape with 75% black.

9. Select the clear plastic shield, and give it a stroke of Lens|Lighten, with a value of 5%. Clone the shape, and delete the entire outline path that does not go over the blue body of the saw. Give the remaining stroke a color of 60% PMS 300 to simulate a highlight edge.

10. Save. Print. Stick it on the refrigerator. Figure 5.24 shows the finished drawing.

Figure 5.24
The finished saw drawing, which can also be seen in the Color Studio section of this book. You can see a few more details in the label and the foot that I added— just because it can be done, and it lights up the drawing.

Moving On

In this chapter, you have learned how to use a variety of blends and gradient fills to create an illusion of three-dimensionality that is usually seen only in Adobe Photoshop-type drawings. The real advantage is the scalability of the drawings; you aren't restricted to the size and resolution of bitmapped art. That's not to say this method is better than raster images—it's just more user-friendly in the long run. In Chapter 6, you will learn how to use the new Brush features to speed up production and create a bit of variety in your work. You will also do some package design work.

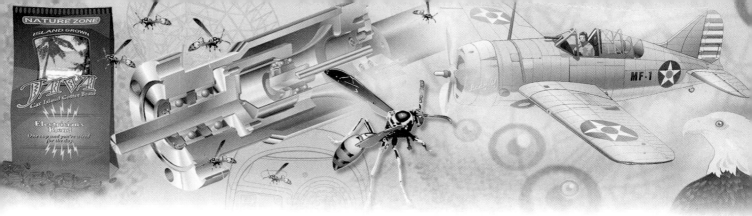

Chapter 6

Symbols, Hoses, and Libraries

*One of the most important factors in any profession
is finding ways to speed up production without sacrificing
the quality of the results. FreeHand 10's symbols, hoses,
and Libraries take that concept one step further by
allowing you to share your results with other artists.*

Symbolism in FreeHand?

No, I'm not going to get cryptic on you. Following the successful usefulness of symbols in Flash, Macromedia wisely added symbols to version 9 of FreeHand. Basically, a symbol is any graphic, group, or block of text you have created that is then placed in a Library for future use. When you want to use a symbol, simply scroll through the Library until you find the symbol you need. Drag either its graphic thumbnail or list icon to the application window, and it's ready to use. A symbol placed in that manner is called an *instance* and is identical in every way to the symbol in the Library.

Symbols are used in three ways in FreeHand: regular symbols that can be chosen one at a time from the Library; Graphic Hose symbols that can be sprayed to create random or structured patterns; and—new in FreeHand 10—the Brush feature that attaches symbols to paths as stroke patterns. This chapter will deal with regular symbols and the Graphic Hose Xtra; the Brush feature is the subject of Chapter 7.

Whether you're a long-time FreeHand user or coming from another program, the use of symbols should become part of your working style. Beyond the speediness of ready access of elements in the Library, the ease of modification, duplication, and sharing of the elements is remarkable.

The projects in this chapter revolve mainly around the use of symbols. You will be creating them and also using prefabricated symbols from the CD-ROM that you'll add to your own Libraries. You'll also get your feet wet with Lens fills and the Envelope Xtra.

Adding Symbols to Your Library

Creating a symbol is a pretty simple process. Select anything in a FreeHand document and click F8, or select Modify|Symbol|Convert To Symbol (Copy To Symbol), and it's done. Any shape, group of shapes, text, blend, imported bitmap, or other kind of object you can create in FreeHand can be converted into a symbol.

Modifying Symbols

A symbol is very stubborn once you've placed it in your document. Other than scaling, rotating, and skewing it, you can't adjust much. To do anything of a major nature, such as changing its shape, color adjustments, or location of highlights, shadows, or blend points, you must release the instance from the symbol. To do this, go to Modify|Symbol|Release Instance. The object will then be the same as any non-symbol item in the document, but it is grouped. Ungroup it to modify it any way you wish. Changes made to the original symbol will not affect the released object. If you decide it would make a nice symbol, then drag it into the Library list area and rename it.

Several Xtras have no affect on an instance, including 3D, Shadow, Bend, Add Points, Simplify, Smudge, and Fisheye. To use these effects, you must remove the instance—and its future ability to be modified as a symbol. It can be made into a *new* symbol, but the connection to the original symbol is lost.

What if you want to change a symbol globally? Click on Modify|Symbol|Edit Symbol, and make the changes you want. You can also edit the symbol by double-clicking the icon in the list window, or clicking the icon and selecting Edit from the triangle pop-up menu. Changes will be made as if the symbol was its own FreeHand page, which is very similar to the way Flash works with symbols. When you click OK, the changes will ripple through the document.

Replacing, Deleting, and Grouping Symbols in the Library

You can create a new object, or modify a released instance, and then use it to *replace* a symbol by dragging it on top of the symbol's icon in the Library list window. If for some reason you decide that you don't want a symbol, you have two choices. Bring up the pop-up menu through the Library triangle, and select Delete. A response box asks if you want to delete or remove the symbol's influence. Delete will wipe the symbols out of your document, leaving blank spaces where they were. Remove simply changes all the instances into regular graphics.

Symbols can also be placed in groups within the Library. Groups in FreeHand Libraries function the same as in Flash Libraries. They allow you to keep related items in tidy packages that can be opened for selection, or closed to make it easier to find other items in the Library.

Why Use Symbols?

The beauty of a symbol is that it can be used many times in a document, but the multiple instances do not increase the file size proportionately. To test this Macromedia claim, I made a symbol of an American flag—how's that for symbolism—and placed a single instance of it on a page. The drawing was 36KB in size, and a Macintosh EPS file made from it was 64KB. Then I placed the same image in a new document and cloned it until I had 230 Instances of the flag on the page (I really don't have *that* much free time—power duplicating took less than half a minute for the whole page). This mega-page came in at 40KB, and the resulting EPS was 4.8MB. Then I removed the instances from the flags, leaving them as 230 groups of lines and stars. That file was a monster 1.2MB, and its EPS was a whopper at 5.4MB. I'm sold!

Quick Document Modifications Using Symbols

Still not convinced? You may think that there's not much of a need for you to use a symbol. But the second beauty of symbols lies in how quickly modifications can be made to your entire document by using them. Say you've created an icon to be used in place of bullets in text in a brochure. You really love that icon, but just before going to print (or going online), the client decides it would look better in green or blue. The symbol itself can be modified, and every instance of the symbol will be modified in place. Or the client may say he or she doesn't like the icon anymore and you'll have to do it over. Make a lot of noise to justify the charges for changes you'll be adding, but relax. Making the new icon and dragging it onto the old icon's name in the Library changes every instance in less time than it took to read these last three words.

Exporting and Importing Symbols

Need more proof about how great symbols are? At first glance, you may think that it would be just as easy to hit Clone or Duplicate to duplicate a graphic or object. You'd be correct for one-off uses of the object, but if there's the slightest chance that the object can be used in another document, symbols are the way to go. Symbols are portable, i.e., they can be exported and imported easily. With a mouse click or two, you can have access to an entire set of symbols you've already created—right in the Library in your new document. You can put them on a floppy or email them to fellow workers offsite, too.

Note: I personally wouldn't turn imported EPS files with fonts and bitmaps in them into symbols, just because there are so many objects that could cause problems somewhere down the line.

Unless you like listening to people whine or yell at you, you must keep track of bitmaps and fonts that you have used in the creation of symbols, and send those items along with the symbol. Think of it as sending the job to the service bureau. You must keep in mind that the next person using your symbol might enlarge or reduce it, which could have quite an impact on a bitmapped graphic. However, normal garden-variety FreeHand graphics flow with the symbols, and you don't have to do anything special with them.

Unkinking the Graphic Hose

Our symbolism doesn't stop with a Library full of graphics and type. The Graphic Hose uses the same sort of mechanism to allow you to place multiple instances of a graphic element in different sizes, rotations, and spacing between elements. This isn't a tool you'll use every day, but when you need it, you can save a lot of time—and get a lot of work done in an efficient manner.

You'll see two radio buttons in the panel when you double-click the Graphic Hose icon in the Xtras toolbar: Hose and Options (see Figure 6.1). When you select the Hose radio button, the first hose object shows in the panel. Other objects used in that hose can be seen by cycling through the drop-down menu at the bottom of the panel. You can select a different hose through the drop-down menu at the top of the panel. The Paste In button pastes in an object from the Clipboard; Copy Out places a copy of the object that is in the preview window onto your Clipboard. When you use Copy Out, the copy is not attached to the Graphic Hose. Delete, of course, deletes the selected hose.

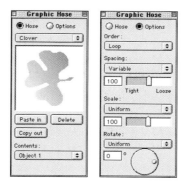

Figure 6.1
The Graphic Hose panels.

The Options radio button opens a panel where you can do the following:

- *Order*—Adjusts the order in which the objects are sprayed; the variables are Loop, Random, and Back and Forth.

- *Spacing*—Adjusts the spacing of the objects. More variables: Grid, Random, and Variable. Enter a number or use the slider to program the distance between objects.

- *Scale*—Adjusts the scale of sprayed objects from Uniform to Random. Again, use the slider to input the amount of change you desire. You can also use the up/down or left/right arrow keys on your keyboard as you spray to enlarge or reduce the size of the objects you're spraying on the desktop.

- *Rotate*—Adjust the rotation of the objects. A setting of zero means no rotation, but enter a number or use the wheel to set the angle of rotation within Uniform, Random, and Incremental variables.

You can have as many as 10 objects in any one hose, and you can import hoses from other artists or your other computers. Just copy the hose into the FreeHand|English|Xtras|Graphic Hose folder. You can delete any hoses you no longer need from that same file by dragging the file to the Trash.

There's even more symbolism with the new Brush tool, but that's for Chapter 7.

PROJECT Pass the Peas, Please

This quick project will get you started with symbols and hopefully show you how efficiently you can work.

The Pod

Begin by drawing the pod:

1. Open the file Peas.fh10 in the Chapter 6 folder on the CD-ROM. Save it to your hard drive as Pea Pod or anything else you'd like to call it.

2. The pea pod and one pea have been placed on the "Trace This" layer for you. (If you would like to have it grayed out for easier tracing, drag the layer below the separator bar in the Layers panel.)

Note: Sometimes I prefer to put what I'm tracing on a foreground layer for better visibility. I change the stroke of the path I am drawing to a hairline or half-point, and give the stroke a color that contrasts with the object I'm tracing.

3. Start by outlining the pod with the Pen or Bezigon tool. Then trace the stem and leaves. Make each shape a separate, closed path.

4. Give the pod a fill of 60% PMS 375 and a 1-point stroke of PMS 377, then clone it. Use the Inset Path Xtra with a setting of 3 points and a round join. Save.

5. Use the keyboard arrows to move the clone up a point (one click, depending on your Preferences settings). This action makes a thin space at the top and a wider space at the bottom.

6. With the Pen tool, draw a line down the middle of the pod as shown in Figure 6.2.

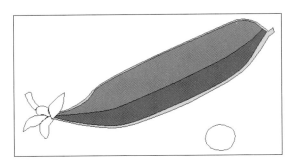

Figure 6.2
The pod has been cloned, the clone has been cut in half, and both have been filled. Their strokes have not yet been deleted.

7. Use the Knife tool to cut the inset pod where the line crosses it. Clone the line and join it to the top half of the pod. Send it backwards, and join the original line and the bottom half of the pod.

8. Fill the top half with PMS 377 and the bottom half with PMS 378. Delete the strokes as you create the fills. Save.

9. Blend the top and bottom halves of the pod and change the number of steps to 16 to smooth the blend a bit.

The Peas

Now you're ready to work on the peas, by following the steps below:

1. To create the peas, start by using the Bezigon tool to trace the pea provided. (The Ellipse tool would make the pea too round. Peas have slight lumps or bulges and are not always perfectly round.) Give it a fill of PMS 377. Clone it, reduce its size and give it a fill of PMS 371. Clone that and reduce it to make the highlight with a fill of 60% PMS 375. Shift the ellipses into positions creating the highlight and shadow as shown in Figure 6.3.

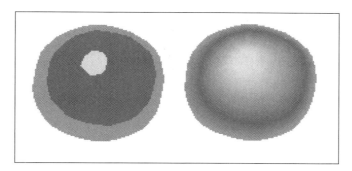

Figure 6.3
The pea before (left) and after (right) blending.

2. Drag a selection box around the three circles. In the Stroke Inspector, apply a stroke of None, and use the Blend Xtra (Xtras|Create|Blend). Change the number of steps to 15. Save. Figure 6.3 shows the "before-and-after" peas.

3. Keep the pea selected and go to Modify|Symbol|Convert To Symbol. Read the "Convert or Copy?" sidebar to see why.

4. Open the Library (Window|Library). The pea should be in the Preview window. Double-click the name (it should be Graphic-01) and rename it Pea.

5. To get a symbol into your artwork, select its name and drag its named icon or the preview image onto the desktop. Drag a pea onto the pea pod. Drag another, and another until you feel the pod is full (from my detailed study of peas, there can be as few as two or as many as 10 peas in a pod, and they've been eaten by the Chinese for more than 4,000 years—learn something new every day, huh?).

6. Place your peas on a layer of their own to make it easier to fiddle with the pod or other elements. Save.

7. I don't care what they say, not all peas are alike. Some are larger than others, and some more or less round than their neighbors. Adjust them so they don't look like duplicates—and therefore like an ordinary computer illustration. Reread the previous section, "Modifying Symbols," for more information. Save.

Convert or Copy?

If you choose Copy To Symbol, FreeHand will make a symbol out of your selection, but leave the original on the desktop untouched. When you select Convert To Symbol your selection will be converted to a symbol, and the object itself turned into an instance of that symbol. So, if you want to make a symbol of something in the place and size it's already been drawn, go ahead and choose Convert To Symbol. If you were to choose Copy To Symbol, you'd then have to delete—or otherwise move—the original object and replace it with the symbol. Therefore, when you plan on further modifying the object or making a different symbol out of the object, choose Copy To Symbol so you don't have to release the instance from its symbol to make the modifications.

Note: Keep in mind that our object is to create illustrations that don't look as if they came from a computer. Variety is the key word here. I went so far as to remove the instances on the peas and move their highlights as well as change the highlight and shadow size.

8. Peas just don't lie loose in the pods. They have a little connecting stem. You could have connected the stem to the pea before making the pea a symbol, but then you wouldn't get the chance to use another symbol. So click the name Pea Stem in the Library, and drag an instance of it near a pea symbol.

9. It doesn't fit. It's either too tall, too short, not twisted enough, or twisted too much. But at least you don't have to draw the whole thing. Release the instance and make your adjustments so that the stem rests on the base of the inside of the pod and supports the pea. Repeat for the other peas.

10. If you look closely, you'll see that the inside of the pod is pretty static. To fix that, go into Keyline View, and Opt/Alt+click the path of the bottom half of the inner pod blend. Add a point to the top line between each pea and in the center of each pea.

11. Shift+select the points in the centers of the peas, and drag them up to just about the tops of the peas. The blend will restructure to reflect the changes you are making. When you go back to the Preview mode, you'll see some pretty realistic shadows behind the peas. Save.

12. With the peas and pod basically finished, render the bud and stem. Use the Contour gradient for them, then take care of the leaves using flat colors or gradient blends for leaf shapes and shadows. You should have something that looks like Figure 6.4.

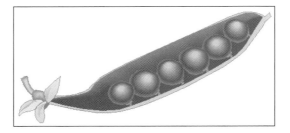

Figure 6.4
The finished peas in the pod.

Final Details

Add finishing details to complete the drawing:

1. Double-click the Trace Tool in the Tools panel. Use the settings in Figure 6.5 and drag the wand around the pea pod.

2. You can drag this outline into a blank part of your page to make the work easier to see. Then double-click the tracing to bring up the Transform handles. Click one of the handles in the middle of the top or bottom and "squish" it vertically. You can elongate it just a bit, too, to create a realistic shadow outline.

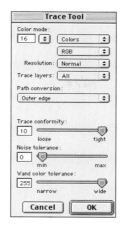

Figure 6.5

The Trace Tool settings used to create an outline of the pea pod that will be used as a drop shadow.

3. Give the path a Stroke of None and a fill of 5% black. Clone it.

4. Use the Inset Path Xtra with a setting of 4 and a Round Join. Give the new shape a 20% fill of PMS 375. Blend the two shapes.

5. Drag out two or three more pea symbols to lie alongside the pod. Adjust their shapes the same way you did the ones inside the pod. Save.

6. Draw an elongated ellipse beneath the pea in the back. Give it a 5% black fill. Clone it, reduce its size, and apply a 20% fill of PMS 375. Shift+select the larger ellipse, and blend the two shapes. Send them to the back and move them until the shadow fits.

7. Clone the shadow for the other loose peas, and place them realistically. Save. The drawing should look like Figure 6.6. Stick a fork in it—it's done.

Note: If you get a blank stare back from your computer, it could be because the shapes are too complicated to blend, or the end with the leaves may be isolated from the pod body. If so, use the Knife tool to cut the larger shadow shape apart at the neck. Close both the leaf path and the pod path, clone them, and try the pod blend again. The leaf's end may still give you problems depending on how many or few points are on the cloned and inset paths. You can adjust the points and shapes, or just go with the lighter shadow and not worry about the darker inset.

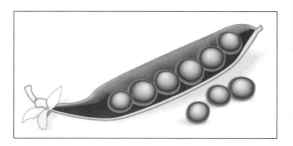

Figure 6.6
Fresh peas anyone?

PROJECT The Cherry Job

In this short project, you'll draw a couple of cherries and stems and make symbols out of them. Then you can create whole bushels of cherries using instances of the symbols. The actual drawing doesn't take as much time as deciding where the highlights belong. Draw directly from the actual subject matter whenever possible. Here, you're stuck with my interpretation of light and shade, but I think you can get by.

Start by opening the partially drawn Cherries.fh10 file from the Chapter 6 folder on the CD-ROM. Save it to your hard drive.

The Cherries

Begin by drawing the cherries and placing each on its own layer:

1. Trace the cherry outlines and color breaks as shown in Figure 6.7.

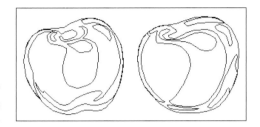

Figure 6.7
The initial color breaks for the cherries (separated for clarity).

2. Fill the color blocks with solid tones as shown in Figure 6.8. Move the colored areas backward and forward to keep the stacking order straightened out with highlights on top, midtones in the middle, then the base or shadow color on the bottom. Save.

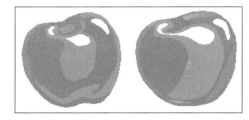

Figure 6.8
The cherries with flat color fills.

3. Taking one cherry at a time (by hiding the layers), drag a selection box over it and then deselect the base or back object. Clone the remaining shapes.

4. Stretch, modify, or manipulate each of the clone shapes to create rather abrupt blends. The cherry isn't too large, so you can't have huge blends. A keyline view of the final blend shapes is shown in Figure 6.9. Some of the lines don't blend, allowing for a sharp color change.

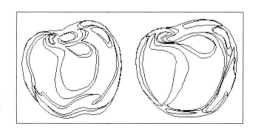

Figure 6.9
Clone the shapes and distort them to accommodate blending.

5. As you're working, give all the cloned shapes the base color—the darkest red. Then blend the two shapes. Save.

6. When you've completed the drawing and blending process (see Figure 6.10), select one of the cherries and go to Modify|Symbols|Convert To Symbol (F8) or Copy To Symbol, as you prefer. Double-click the new symbol in the Library and give it a name. Repeat for the other cherry.

> **Note:** The blending shape must lie below the highlight shape in the stacking order. You can either hide the background layer so it's out of your way, then send the blending layer to the back, or Shift+click the base shape and the blending shape to send them to the back.

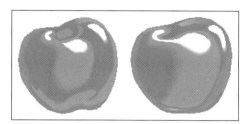

Figure 6.10
The finished blended cherries.

The Stems

Follow these steps to draw and add the stems:

1. Each stem is drawn as a single path, and then modified with the Expand Stroke Xtra with a 5-point expansion. Draw the path now. The fill will probably be black—don't worry about it at this time; you'll be changing it momentarily.

2. Now draw the end shape of a stem where it attaches to the limb and to the cherry. The shape is basically a rounded triangle for the limb end; the cherry end is more of a flattened ellipse. Use the Union Xtra to connect both ends and the stem together.

3. Repeat for the other stem. Clone both stems. Save.

4. Okay, it gets a little tricky here. Use the Expand Stroke Xtra again on the stem clones. Give them a width of 2 points. Keep them both selected.

5. In the Fills panel, give the new paths a vertical graduated fill from dark green to light green to dark green again. Send them to the back. Save.

Convert or Copy Revisited

As I discussed previously, Convert To Symbol changes the object you have chosen into a symbol. You no longer have an original object, only the instance, and a symbol in the Library. Copy To Symbol, on the other hand, copies the selected object and makes a symbol of the copy. The original is still on your drawing board and completely editable. If you are going to make successive changes to the object and symbols of those changes, it makes sense to choose Copy To Symbol. That way, you won't have to use Release From Instance every time you want to make a change. Bottom line: if you're through with it, choose Convert To Symbol; if you're going to work further with the original, choose Copy To Symbol.

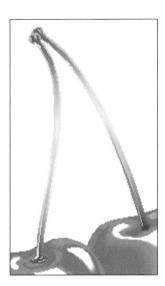

Figure 6.11
You have to have stems.

6. Select both the original stem shapes and give them the same color scheme, but mix up the graduated fill so this inside section of the stem will have contrasting colors. It's okay to make the colors the same in places. Send them to the back.

7. Hide one of the stems, and draw some accent lines and shapes on the other stem. I like to draw the line, choose Expand Path, then fill it. That way I have the opportunity to use a gradient fill if I want. When you're done, group the whole stem and make a symbol out of it.

8. Hide the finished stem, and put the finishing touches on the other stem. Make it a symbol, too. Your drawing should look similar to Figure 6.11 by now. Save.

9. Now you can drag instances of the cherries and stems out of the Library and create clusters of cherries. Figure 6.12 shows a few instances that I then removed from the symbol and modified so they don't look as much like clones. It's a simple task to ungroup the cherry and then flop a midtone or highlight for variety.

10. Shadows can be drawn in. These are filled with the Contour gradient, using values from white to 5% black to 15% black. Save one last time, print, and tape it to your growing gallery on the refrigerator.

Figure 6.12
Cherries and stems created from symbols.

Decisions, Decisions

It makes sense to me that it's easier to find colors if they're arranged in some sort of order. I try to start with one end of the spectrum and work toward the other. As the job progresses and I add more colors, I move them into place chromatically in the Swatches panel. Getting colors into your palette is covered in Chapter 3, but here are a few tips for using the Eyedropper Xtra:

- Drag the color to the Color Mixer well. Then click the Add To List button (where you will be prompted to give it a name).
- Drop the color in the Color Swatches panel and accept the RGB color model interpretation.
- Drag the color to the downward arrow in the Swatches panel. This panel also gives the color the RGB breakdown as a name (because this is an RGB image—if it were a CMYK image, those values would appear).
- Do not drop the color on the Tints color well—it just confuses things because it will give the color 0% of the RGB color.
- Draw several squares or circles on your page, and drag a color to each object. After you've gotten all the colors you want, select Xtras|Color|Name All Colors. This is probably the worst way to get a color list, but it does name all the colors in one step. In another drawing this method may be just the ticket.

PROJECT More Vegetables

Now you are going to learn something that will seem very complicated, but that is actually pretty easy with FreeHand's super toolset. You'll be learning more about the Graphic Hose—which has a pretty lame name, but is a great tool—and putting it to good use. This project will take a slight twist in that you will be selecting your own color palette and doing all the drawing yourself. Don't be intimidated by the seemingly complex subject matter. It's not all that tough.

For anyone who cares, the top of the broccoli is made up of small flowers that are yellow when they bloom. Recipe books call them florets, but buds is the term that I'll use because it's a lot quicker to type.

Setting Up the Document

To set up your new document, do the following:

1. Open a new FreeHand document, and import the graphic named BroccoliStalk.tif from the Chapter 6 folder on the CD-ROM. The picture will fill the entire page. As you've been doing all along, create a new layer, place the photo there, and lock it.

2. Find the lightest color in the buds and use the Eyedropper tool to click and drag the color to one of the color panels (see the "Decisions, Decisions" sidebar).

3. You can go nuts on this drawing, but try to contain yourself to about three or four different buds—buds in shadow, light, middle tones, and so on. I did all the colors for a single bud, then chose another bud to get its colors (draw a circle around the bud to make it easier to find). Mine came from Figure 6.13.

Selection Frustrations

Be sure to unlock the photo layer when you're selecting colors with the Eyedropper. If the layer is locked, you'll get unexpected results, such as the screen being dragged all over the place. Lock the layer again when you start to draw so you don't move it around while you're working.

Figure 6.13
Major color areas taken from individual buds.

Note: For this particular image, a view with the zoom set to 160% will give you about the best resolution without seeing the jaggies too much. You can set up a Custom View as described in Chapter 1 if you'd like. The CD-ROM contains another image named BroccoliBuds.tif, which is an enlarged section of the broccoli for reference only. View it to see how the little buds are constructed. Pretty intricate stuff.

4. Select the range of colors for the stalk and branches. You'll end up with no more than 20 or 30 colors for the whole drawing, depending on how intricate you want to get—and how much time you have. Save.

Drawing the Stalk

Now that your colors are all selected, you can get down to the actual drawing by taking the steps below:

1. Trace the stalk first. Give the basic shape of the stalk a base color, then use View|Hide (or give the stalk a fill of None for the time being) while you draw shadow and highlight areas.

2. Proceed with the drawing process as you did with the previous projects in this chapter: draw the accented area and give it the correct color fill; clone it and give it the fill color of the immediate background (base color in most instances); send it to the back, Shift+select the accent, and blend the two shapes. Save often.

3. Keep going until you've got the stalk done. If you haven't done so already, draw the leaves and color them. The veins in the leaves can be constructed by using the Expand Path Xtra and modifying the shape. Save. You should be looking at something close to Figure 6.14 at this point.

Bud Symbols

You'll be tempted to go overboard at this point with gradient fills, blends, and so on, but fight it; you can choke the imagesetter way too easily. Keep this part of the job as simple as you can—draw a few buds, convert them to symbols, then paste them into the Graphic Hose. Since your buds will be symbols, you can easily modify their colors, sizes, and shapes by duplicating and modifying them as we go. The Graphic Hose will make the job go quickly. The buds are seen from different angles—the ones in the back at the top of the broccoli are simple one-color shapes. Others are seen from the side or directly above. You'll need a variety of each shape to avoid that computer-drawn look.

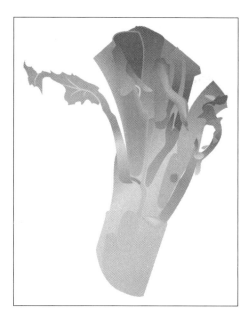

Figure 6.14
The finished broccoli stalk. *Broccoli* comes from the Latin word *bracchium*, meaning *branch* or *arm*, referring to its treelike shape. Brocolli is related to the cauliflower plant. Isn't this fascinating?

Prepare to use your Graphic Hose by following these steps:

1. Zoom in to 160% or so on the Broccoli Stalk image (anything more than that will probably give you a pixilated image), and choose a bud. Draw the inside highlight first, which may be a simple line, or a shape. Color it and hide it. Draw the next larger shape—and the next, if there is one. Click View|Show All, and move the various pieces to the back or the front so they're in their correct stacking order.

2. Choose Modify|Symbol|Copy To Symbol. Unless you really take your work personally, I wouldn't bother renaming the bud. Your call.

3. Because you chose Copy To Symbol instead of Convert To Symbol, you can modify the bud. Change the size, shape, or colors, then make another symbol out of it. Repeat until you have three or four buds for each angle of view. My buds are shown in Figure 6.15.

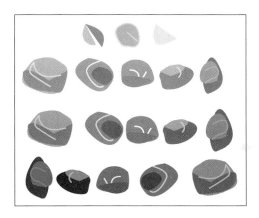

Figure 6.15
A group of bud symbols ready to be put into the Graphic Hose and splattered all over the page. The top three images are for the outer fringes; the next five have been cloned and darkened using the Xtras|Color|Darken command until the correct values were obtained. The two bottom rows are darkened versions to be used for dark and darker shadow areas.

4. Creating the Graphic Hose operation isn't too difficult. Double-click the Graphic Hose Xtra, and select New from the drop-down menu. Name it. I used names like Top Buds, Mid Buds, Dark Buds, and Darkest Buds, so I had a clue as to what was in the hose.

5. Drag a bud instance to the document (the cursor gains a dotted square around it to signify that you are dragging a symbol) and choose Copy or Cut to move it to the Clipboard. Click the Paste In button on the Graphic Hose panel. Repeat with all the buds you've drawn for this particular bud range.

6. Create a new hose, and repeat the process to get the various buds into the hose for this bud view. Continue until you have buds for the back/top, buds for the sides, buds for the middle, and some dark shadowed buds.

Hosing Down Your Artwork

Now, you're ready to get down to business with the Graphic Hose. There are several attributes that can be manipulated here, including the proximity of elements as you spray them, their rotation and size, and the order in which they're sprayed.

You could start spraying broccoli buds all over the photo, but that would be premature. There are a couple more things to accomplish first. The buds will not cover every square kyu of the art, so you must allow for the spaces you know will be there. You'll make color blocks of the several mounds that make up the broccoli head. To those, you'll add a background panel to help with the three-dimensionality of the mounds. Then you'll splatter buds.

1. Create a new layer for the bud backgrounds. Look for the forests now, not the trees, and outline the mounds of the broccoli head. Stay inside the edges of the plant about a pica or so—you don't want this shape to be seen when you're done. Give each shape a fill. Some I made Radial gradients, others were just flat colors, and a few had linear blends. Try to follow the general pattern of the vegetable. All the shapes should have a stroke of None.

2. Draw another large shape that will become the shadow area beneath and between the mounds. See Figure 6.16 for the shapes I used. Send it to the back. Save.

3. Create another layer, and name it Buds. Double-click the Graphic Hose tool. Select the Top Buds hose, click the Options button and enter these factors from top to bottom:

   • Order: Random

   • Spacing: Variable (100)

   • Scale: Random (104)

   • Rotate: Random (2°)

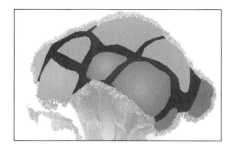

If you don't like these settings, experiment on the desktop until you get the effect you want.

4. Spray the Top Buds along the top outline of the entire head. Go back and forth as much as necessary to fill in most of the gaps. Save often.

5. Select the Mid Buds hose and fill in the middle ground in each mound. Change the options as you feel the urge.

6. Choose the Dark Buds hose and start on the shadow sides of the mounds. Follow up with the Darkest Buds hose in the grooves and bottom areas for realistic shading effects.

7. Continue, switching back and forth between hoses until everything is filled in. Save. Print. Tape it right next to the peas and cherries. The finished broccoli is shown in Figure 6.17.

Figure 6.17
Stick a fork in it—it's done.
The Graphic Hose and Symbol
Xtras saved hours of tedious,
meticulous drawing.

At this point, you may be pleased with your results—then again, the drawing might be too light or too dark, or the buds are the size of golf balls. Here's the beauty of symbols—simply open the Library and double-click the bud you want to change. (The symbol is a grouped object, so you must first ungroup it to edit it.) Make any change in size, shape, color, line weight—anything you want. When you close the edit window, the changes will occur immediately on the artwork. Too cool.

I wasn't pleased with the color range I had selected for the stalk, so I imported the Broccoli.tif photo again and used the Eyedropper tool to change colors in various spots. You may or may not want to change some colors, depending on how well you did when you selected the colors in the first place.

PROJECT The Coffee Bag

I can handle about anything but someone getting between me and my cup of coffee. I've had one at my right hand just about every working hour of my life. That's a whole lot of coffee—so it's no big surprise that I have a coffee project. This project will move pretty quickly, because it's powered by pure caffeine, but it should go a long way toward showing you the value of Libraries full of symbols and the Graphic Hose. You'll also get a taste of Lens fills and the Trace Tool. So pour yourself a cup and let's get started.

Setting Up the Document

Set your document up by taking these steps:

1. Inside the Chapter 6 folder on the CD-ROM is a folder named Symbols. Inside that folder are two documents: a Graphic Hose named Coffee Beans, and a Library named Coffee Bag Symbols. Open the FreeHand application folder on your hard drive and then open the English folder. Drag the Coffee Beans document into FreeHand 10|English|Xtras| Graphic Hose Folder. Put Coffee Bag Symbols into FreeHand 10| English|Symbols.

2. Close the application folder, and open a new FreeHand document. Save it with the name Hot Coffee.fh10.

3. Open Windows|Library, click the triangle on the top right, and choose Import from the drop-down menu (see the "Import/Export Business" tip). Navigate to the Coffee Bag Symbols you just placed in the English folder. Save.

Building the Bag

Now, you will create your bag:

1. Drag the symbol named Glowing Bag to the page. It's a little wimpy thing that wouldn't hold much coffee, so go to Modify|Symbol|Release Instance.

Import/Export Business

When you import or export symbols, the English|Symbols folder opens, and you can add to, or select from, all the symbols you have previously saved. If you are exporting, it's a matter of clicking the Export button, and you'll be back in your document. If you are importing a symbol, double-click its name (or select it and click Open), and a window opens showing thumbnail images of all the symbols in that symbol document. You can select a range of symbols by clicking the first one and Shift+selecting the last one, and clicking Import. Or you can select individual symbols by Cmd/Ctl+clicking separate symbols and finally clicking the Import button.

2. Remove the stroke, and in the Object Inspector, change the width to 18p3 and the height to 38p0. Now we're talking size. Bring in a guide-line from the side so that it runs down the center of the bag.

3. Drag the Glow Bar symbol and then the Nature Zone symbol to the document. Align them centered vertically and horizontally (using the Align panel in the Main toolbar, or the individual Align Command buttons you have placed in the Main toolbar), then place them near the top of the bag. Save.

4. Drag Island Grown below the Nature Zone. Then drag Crest beneath that. You'll do some extra work on the Crest, so click Release Instance on it. Hold down the Opt/Alt key and click in the middle of the Crest to subselect the inset shape. You could also use the Subselect tool—the white pointer arrow—in the Tools panel. Clone the selected shape.

5. Use the Inset Path Xtra with a value of 2.5, and click OK.

6. Drag Beach Scene to a blank spot on the desktop, and double-click the Trace tool. Enter information so that it reads the same as Figure 6.18.

> **Symbol Structure**
>
> I don't know about you, but I hate going to the menus, especially if they have fly-out menus. To that end, I have created custom Keyboard Shortcuts for the symbol options. The default for Convert To Symbol is F8, so I made Copy To Symbol F7, and Release Instance F6. They're in the same order as in the menu, and right next to each other on the keyboard for easy poking.

> **Center of . . . Say What?**
>
> To quickly find the horizontal and vertical center of an object for the placement of a guide-line, I draw an ellipse with the Ellipse tool from one edge of the object to the other. The sides of the ellipse will touch top, bottom, and both sides. Then I switch to Keyline View (I use the Cmd/Ctl+K to switch quickly between Keyline and Preview views), and a tiny X appears in the exact center of the ellipse. It's easy to drag a guideline into place then.

Figure 6.18
The Trace Tool dialog box set to trace our photo.

7. Release Instance on Beach Scene, ungroup it, and use the tracing wand to drag a selection around Beach Scene. It will take a few seconds to trace, depending on how much RAM you have available for FreeHand.

8. When Beach Scene is traced, group it immediately. Then drag the now-very-posterized photo to where it is centered in the middle of the Crest. Cut the photo.

9. Select the center portion of the Crest, and choose Edit|Paste Inside. Start-ing well outside the bag itself, drag a selection around the entire Crest and the photo. Group the whole mass. Save.

Note: To avoid font problems, all the type in this project has been converted to paths. Electrician's Blend and Cat Island Coffee Beans have had the Roughen Xtra applied. They were then cloned and either used as a drop shadow or given a stroke. The Java logo is an Adobe font named Bermuda LP Squiggle. I cloned it, ran the Inset Path Xtra with a negative number and then used the Union Xtra to make one contiguous shape that was given a gradient fill. The letterforms themselves had been converted to paths, then joined, and given a gradient fill as well. All this took about two minutes.

10. Move to the bottom now by dragging Electrician's Blend into the center of the yellow glow. Drag One Cup just below it.

11. Drag out Green Bars, and locate it above Electrician's Blend. Clone it and use the Reflect tool to rotate it 180° to sit at the bottom. Adjust the two sets of lines and both blocks of copy until they basically frame or are framed by the yellow glow. Save.

12. Now drag out Lightning Bolt, and center it above Electrician's Blend. Clone it. Select the Rotate tool, and click the tool on the center guideline on the thinner of the two bottom Green Bars. Drag to the right until the angle in your Tool Information window reads 20°.

13. Clone it and repeat the above operation with a reading of 10°. You've got a choice here—you can clone the left pair and use the Reflect tool to put another pair on the right, or you can continue cloning and rotating them. You want about five bolts.

14. When you have a set of bolts, group them, clone them, and use the Reflect tool to swing them around 180° to ride over the bottom Green Bars. Adjust the bolts so they sit the same as do the top bolts.

15. Group both sets of bolts, bars, and the blocks of type on the bottom. Group the Glow Bar, Nature Zone, Island Grown, and the Crest/photo. Select both groups and the bag in the background. Align them vertically on the center and group them. Save.

16. Drag in the Java Logo symbol, and let it overlap the photo. Your package should look like Figure 6.19 right now, but that's boring. Save, though, and you can spice it up a bit.

Figure 6.19
The bag in its flat form.

Making It Real

Here's where you'll learn some really nice Macromedia vector art tricks:

1. Drag a selection box around the entire bag, and group it. Then, in the Envelope toolbar, select Rectangle from the drop-down menu. Click the button to the left of the menu to apply the envelope to the selected graphics. Now we can distort the entire image as if it were a sheet of paper.

2. Use the Pen tool to add points to the envelope to create more—or less— distortion. Add at least one or two points on the vertical sides. Move points toward the center or away from it, and make small adjustments to the control handles to break up the strictly vertical sides.

3. Adjust the top by making it dip. Don't take it too far, or things will tend to get ugly really fast.

4. The distortion lacks a bit of—say, life? So draw shapes that would either be a highlight area or in shadow. Again, keep it simple—three or four shapes will do it. Delete their strokes, and give each a Lens fill, set either to Darken or Lighten, with relatively low values—below 30% is good. That gives the bag a glossy look, and adds depth to the distortion caused by the Envelope work. (See the image in the Color Studio section of this book.) Save.

5. Draw a shape on the right side, indicating the side of the bag. Give it the same color fill that the front of the bag has (use the Eyedropper tool and a Linear gradient fill).

6. Add a highlight and shadow by making two more Lens fills. If you want to show a bit more realism, let the outer edge of the side show as a minor highlight. Save.

Finishing Touches

You can finish this project up by adding little sealing indents at the top of the bag, and then adding some coffee beans to give the drawing a life.

1. Scroll back up to the top of the bag and double-click the Rectangle tool. Give it a radius of 0P6 (half a pica), and draw a skinny rectangle about a quarter-inch tall. Clone it, and drag the clone to the opposite side. Select both rectangles, and blend them.

2. Set the number of steps to 20, remove the Stroke, and give them a fill of 85% black.

3. Use the Pen tool, and draw a line from corner to corner, matching the top of the bag. While it's still selected, Shift+select the new blend, and go to Modify|Combine|Join Blend To Path. Shift it down into place. Save.

The Envelope, Please

The Envelope feature is discussed thoroughly in Chapter 9. For now, the instructions here are purposely light, but to the point. See the "Getting to Know Envelopes" sidebar in Chapter 9 if you would like a quick explanation of the Envelope feature.

Bitmaps in Envelopes

You traced the photo because you wanted to use the Envelope Xtra for distortion. Bitmaps (TIFFs, JPEGs, GIFs, BMPs) are not affected by the Envelope Xtra. Had you used the photo as it was imported, the Crest outline would show the distortion, but the photo would just have been cropped by the Crest's distorted shape.

Note: The purpose of having a path follow the top of the bag is to have the sealing indents match the distortion of the folds and bends in the bag. You can also put this blend into an envelope and distort it further.

Figure 6.20

The Graphic Hose settings for loose coffee beans.

4. For the loose beans, double-click the Graphic hose, and select Coffee Beans in the drop-down menu. Click the Option button and give it the settings shown in Figure 6.20.

5. Now just spray coffee beans around the bottom of the bag as shown in Figure 6.21. Make a little pile, and allow a few to stray away from the pack. If you want to get really carried away, duplicate some of the beans and add shadows to them to place in the foreground. Save. Print. Stick it on the refrigerator while your next pot of coffee is brewing.

Figure 6.21

Wake up and make the coffee.

Moving On

In this chapter, you used several tools, and learned many tricks, but the most important lesson here is the use of symbols. I started with the premise that Libraries let you use the same graphic over and over, cutting down your overhead. While that's very true, the real benefit of symbols is sharing the workload. Consider a package design or Web site design, for instance. By placing common elements into a Library, that Library can be passed among several artists much as a template can, but the symbol Library is much more manageable. Weeks later, when you get the call to create a matching package—or 16 more Web pages—the Library will be ready and waiting for you to put it to work. Colors, graphics, copy, photos—just about anything—is at your fingertips. A little work now saves a lot of time later. In Chapter 7, you will do a bit more with symbols; this time, within Brushes—something brand new in FreeHand 10.

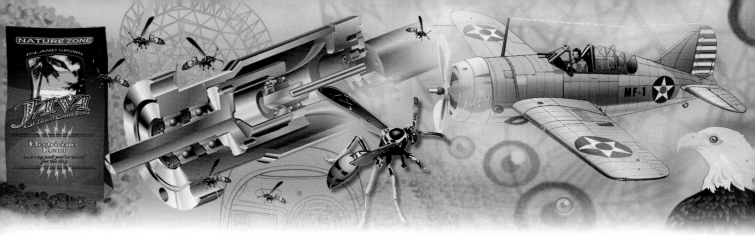

FreeHand 10 Studio

*This studio provides color images from most of the projects
in this book and showcases several real-world projects
using the exciting new and useful features of FreeHand 10.*

The red car from Chapter 4 has been drawn with relatively flat areas of color. The file size is a mere 164KB.

This is the first of a five-piece collection of Tufted Titmouse drawings done for a self-promotion piece. Each was done in a different style to show that just as a single subject can be drawn in different ways, virtually any subject can be drawn in a variety of styles using FreeHand. This style used broad areas of graduated fills and a heavy, contrasting outline.

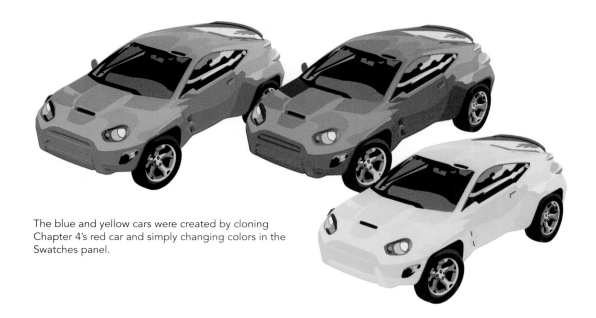

The blue and yellow cars were created by cloning Chapter 4's red car and simply changing colors in the Swatches panel.

The red car from Chapter 4 has been enhanced with blends to smooth color transition. Its file size is only slightly larger than the original at 228KB.

The clock's gold appearance
was obtained by creating many
different blends and gradient fills
(see Chapter 5). The clock's face was
skewed into place, rather than using
the 3D Rotation Xtra or Perspective Grid.

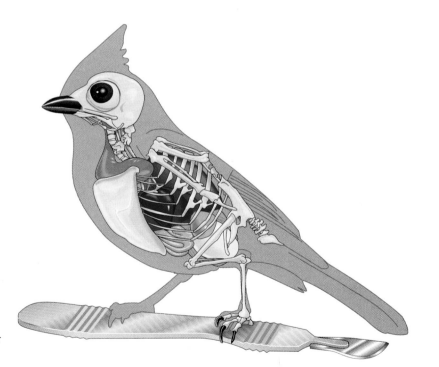

All the titmouse's bones and
organs can be turned on or off in
the layers panel to show whatever
structure lies beneath.

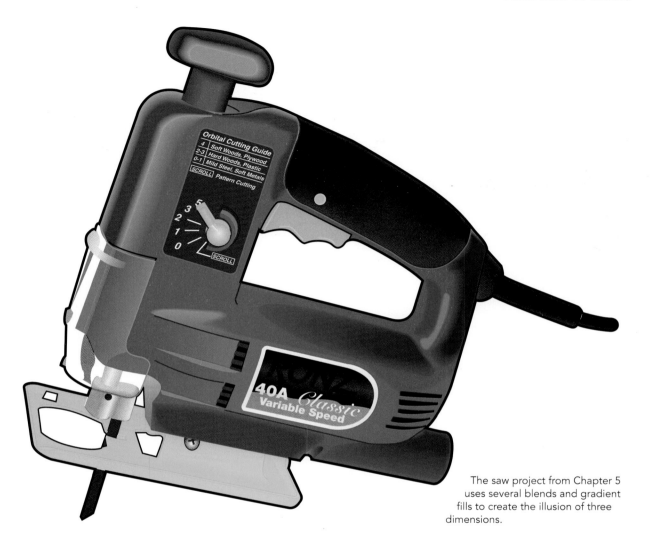

The saw project from Chapter 5 uses several blends and gradient fills to create the illusion of three dimensions.

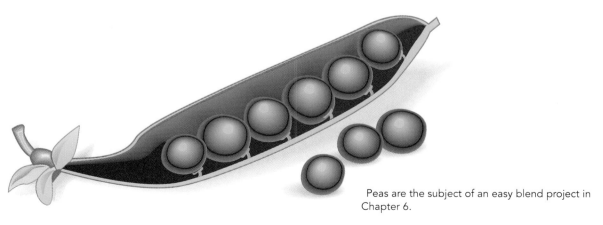

Peas are the subject of an easy blend project in Chapter 6.

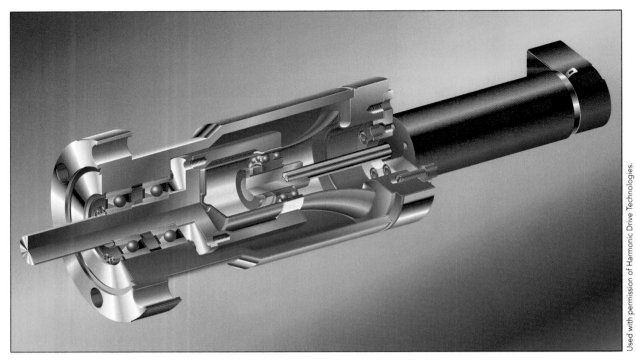

Cutaway views are often helpful in explaining how a device works. This project was drawn from blueprints and objects that were similar in operation and function. Extensive use of linear gradient fills (see Chapter 5) creates the illusion of cut and polished metal.

Used with permission of Harmonic Drive Technologies.

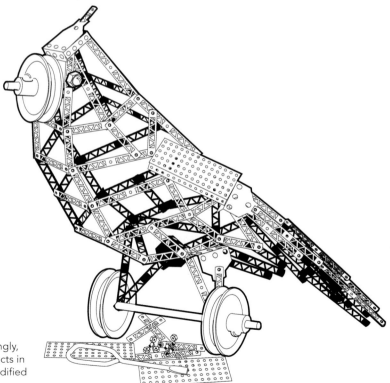

The "Erector Set" titmouse. Surprisingly, there are only about 10 original objects in the drawing. The rest are slightly modified clones.

Broccoli from Chapter 6 makes heavy use of gradient fills and the Graphic Hose tool. With just a little more work, it could be made to look almost photographic.

This drawing of a rose, built entirely with Contour gradient fills, is from a project in Chapter 5. In certain situations, this gradient is far superior to the other forms of graduated fills available. This drawing is almost 2MB, however, due to all those contour gradients.

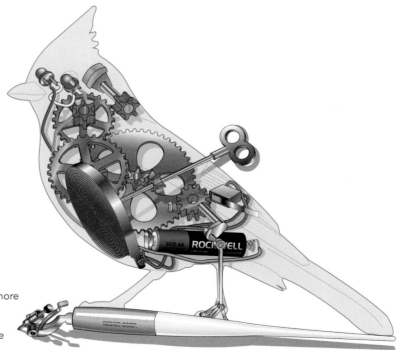

This drawing of the titmouse looks more complicated than it really is—there aren't that many parts to draw. The pen here is what artists used to make line drawings until the late 1960s.

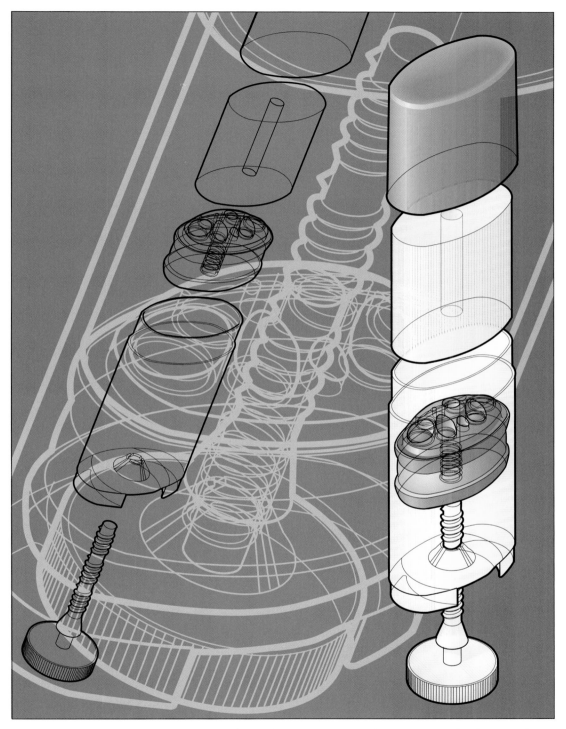

An example of exploded and phantom views of a deodorant container. The figure was drawn by placing each element on its own layer in FreeHand, which allowed the elements to be gathered together for one drawing and separated for another.

The English Garden logo is the subject of a project in Chapter 7. The logo makes extensive use of the new Brush feature in FreeHand 10. The flowers and leaves are made from only two original objects.

This Tufted Titmouse contains 2,311 separate objects. The file is only 242KB, but the Encapsulated PostScript (EPS) file is 8.6MB! The figure took approximately 25 hours to draw.

The last project in Chapter 6 creates this bag of coffee, using several preexisting symbols that are imported into FreeHand. The entire face of the bag is modeled through the use of Envelopes and Transparent Lens Fills. The coffee beans are placed with the Graphic Hose.

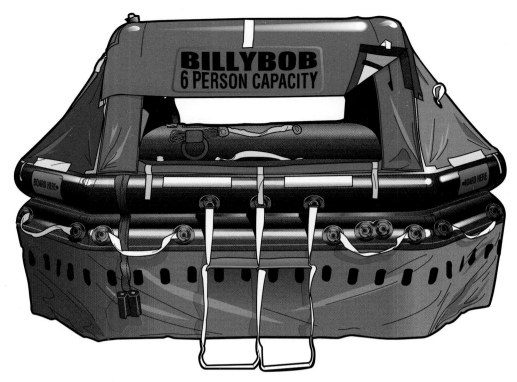

This lifeboat was drawn from a black-and-white photograph and notes from the client. The figure was constructed with large areas of flat color, with gradient fills to help add dimensionality (see Chapter 4 for more information about color, and Chapter 5 for information about gradient fills).

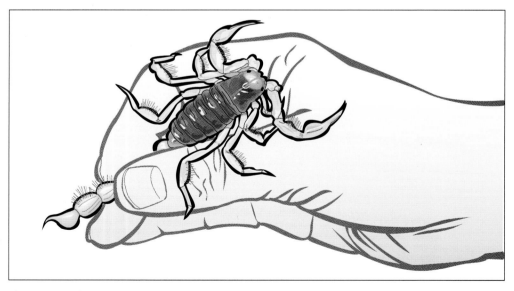

This scorpion drawing was originally done in FreeHand for a Flash animation (Chapter 11 covers FreeHand and Flash). Its claws and feet wiggled, and the tail squirmed as it drew a colored line across the screen. The line work was done using the Expand Path Xtra and moving individual points to create an organic feeling.

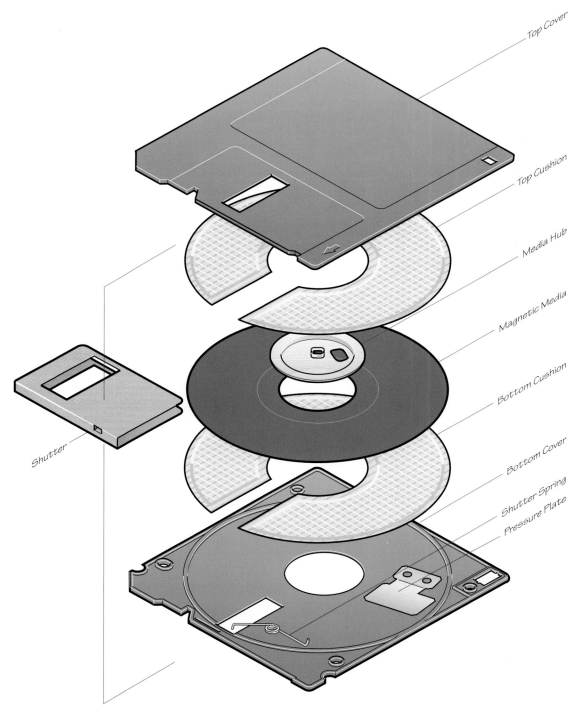

Top Cover

Top Cushion

Media Hub

Magnetic Media

Bottom Cushion

Bottom Cover

Shutter Spring

Pressure Plate

Shutter

If you've ever wondered what goes on inside a floppy disk, now you know. This isometric projection was drawn by measuring and plotting the pieces as multiviews. The pieces were then rotated, scaled, and skewed into an isometric drawing.

The original wasp drawing was just a little larger than this, then the drawing was placed into a Graphic Hose (see Chapter 6). The rotation and scale options were utilized to create a random grouping; wasps were then selected and flopped horizontally.

Brushes are new in FreeHand 10 and were used heavily in this eagle drawing project in Chapter 7. A large radial graduated fill adds a little punch to the illustration.

The aerosol can (from a project in Chapter 9) was created by making "flat" art from symbols, then using the Envelope feature to "wrap" the art to an ellipse. Transparent Lens Fills created glossy highlights and the cap. The cow was drawn with a FreeHand brush.

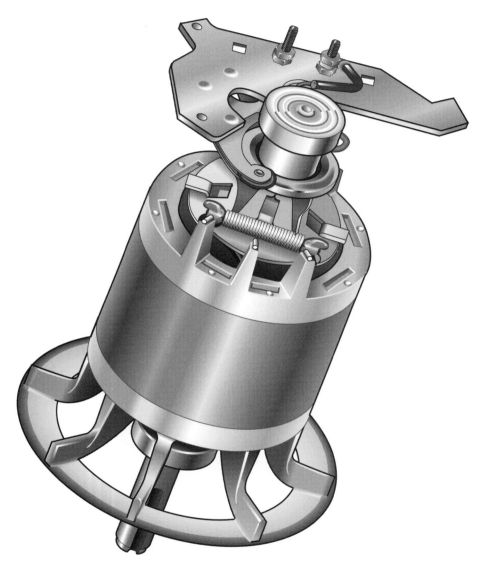

This device was drawn from a photograph. The drawing makes extensive use of gradient fills, which you learn to create in Chapter 5.

The medicine package was part of a
self-promotion piece. Instead of Transparent
Lens Fills, this drawing uses subtle shading techniques
you can learn about in Chapter 4.

This drawing is an example of an isometric phantom view.
The figure was drawn by measuring an actual switch and
plotting points and paths in isometric—rather than drawing
multiview projections and modifying them.

This drawing was created in a project from Chapter 6. The cherries get their realistic appearance from blends and smooth color transitions. The blends are made by using the Inset Path Xtra.

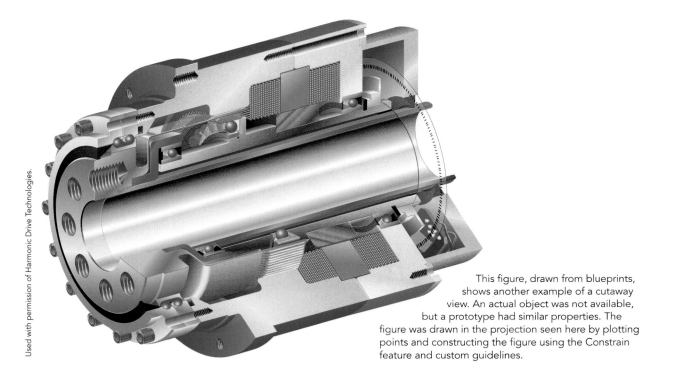

This figure, drawn from blueprints, shows another example of a cutaway view. An actual object was not available, but a prototype had similar properties. The figure was drawn in the projection seen here by plotting points and constructing the figure using the Constrain feature and custom guidelines.

The espresso drawing is the third in a group of projects in Chapter 12. The design on the cup was created flat and wrapped around the cup with an Envelope.

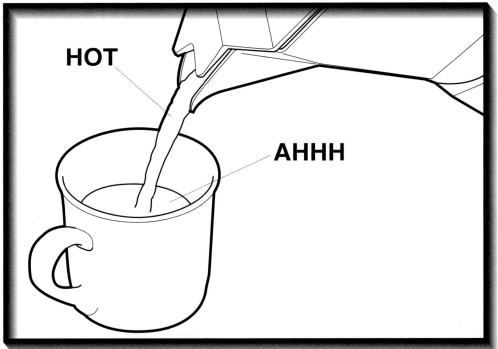

The two drawings on this page are Chapter 12 projects. The bottom drawing shows a plain line art style, with a simple shadow created with FreeHand's Shadow Xtra. The same drawing was then cloned, and a custom brush was applied to the lines (top). Another custom brush outlines the right side and bottom. The use of brushes can change the style of a drawing in seconds!

One of the projects in Chapter 10 teaches you how to create a simple box such as this one. The project involves an image pasted inside text (Cat Tasties), and the use of styles to speed up production.

The candies from the box above are shown here the same size as they were drawn. Notice how little detail there really is, compared to what is implied in the scaled-down version on the box.

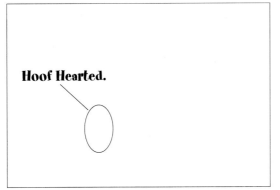

Hoof Hearted.

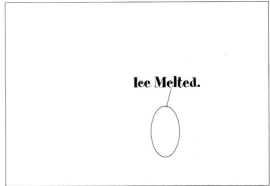

Ice Melted.

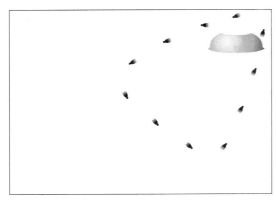

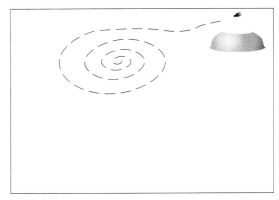

The Print Area feature—new to FreeHand 10—allows you to group many pages at once and print them as thumbnails or as a storyboard. This project is a movie from Chapter 11, created in FreeHand and exported as a SWF file that is viewable in Flash Player. The movie contains several user-interactive attributes (Flash actions) applied through the Navigation panel.

There's nothing like that clean dairy air.

This image shows the last panel of the SWF movie presented on the opposite page.

The fine art of blends is covered in Chapter 5. This project uses Linear gradient fills, Contour gradient fills, Radial fills, blends, and Transparent Lens Fills.

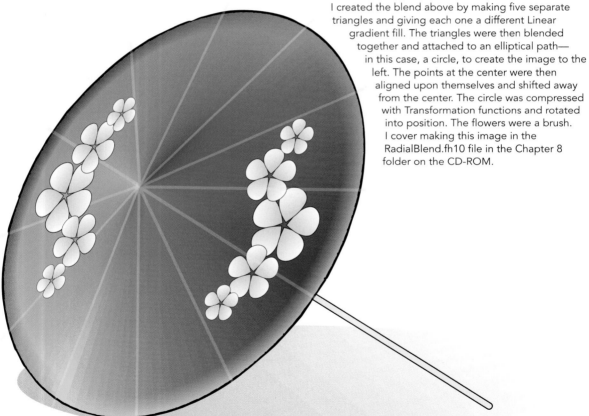

I created the blend above by making five separate triangles and giving each one a different Linear gradient fill. The triangles were then blended together and attached to an elliptical path—in this case, a circle, to create the image to the left. The points at the center were then aligned upon themselves and shifted away from the center. The circle was compressed with Transformation functions and rotated into position. The flowers were a brush. I cover making this image in the RadialBlend.fh10 file in the Chapter 8 folder on the CD-ROM.

This figure shows what you can expect from using the Perspective Grid. The Grid doesn't draw for you, but it certainly allows you to position objects correctly in three-dimensional space. This drawing is a project created in Chapter 8.

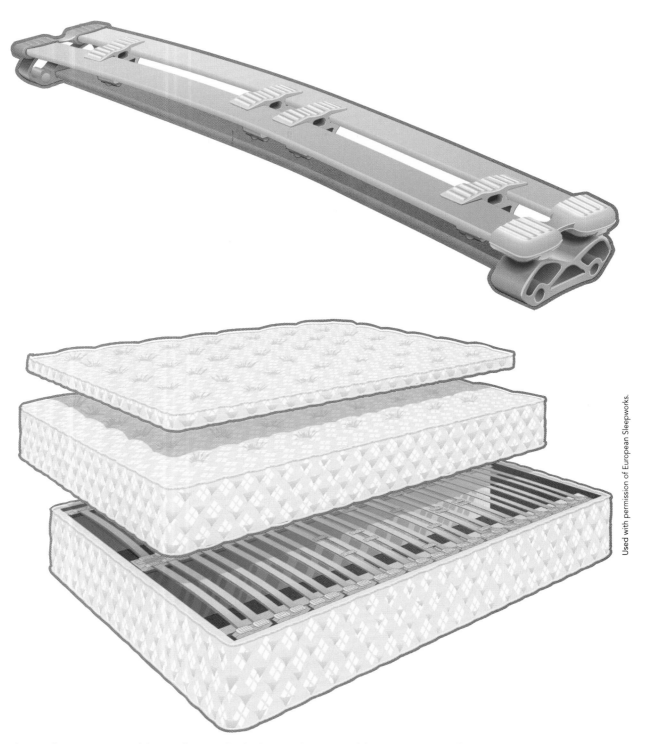

The top drawing was copied from a photograph. The bottom drawing (and the drawings on the facing page) were completed using the Perspective Grid to great extent. Sides, bottoms, and connecting pieces were all drawn in side or profile views, then attached to the Perspective Grid for assembly with other elements (see Chapter 8 for more information about the Perspective Grid.). Bumps and lumps were distorted prior to grid attachment through a trial and error approach. All those bumps and lumps come at a cost, too. The bottom drawing on this page is an EPS file that weighs in at over 30MB.

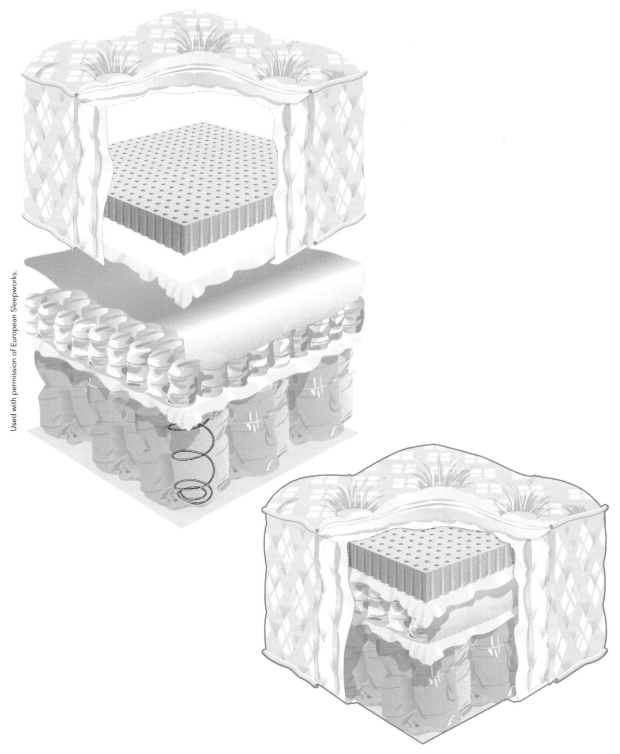

Used with permission of European Sleepworks.

The bedding manufacturer wanted a drawing that could be used for several other drawings as well as a Flash movie. Layering all the elements let me hide certain elements, such as the spring covers, to show underlying objects. The drawing was created in the flat, then attached and assembled on the Perspective Grid. After initial placement, everything was released from the grid, with perspective, and treated as any other FreeHand object. I used styles extensively for many objects so that the colors of the materials could be changed without undergoing a lot of rework.

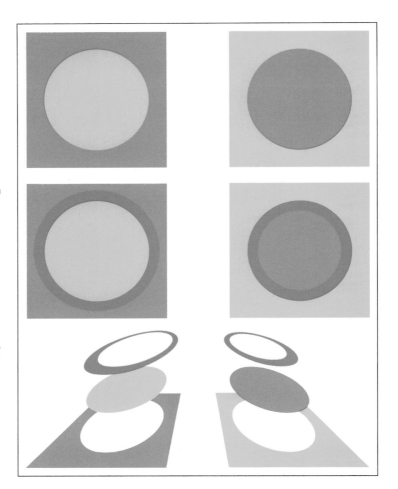

This set of figures shows how you can trap items to keep the white of the paper from showing through artwork because of printer misregistration. The example on the left shows the effect of "spread," where a light color is enlarged to encroach on a darker colored background. The right example is a "choke," which is used when a light-colored background must surround a darker-colored object. A tint of the lighter color spreads or "chokes" onto the darker color. FreeHand lets you set the amount of tint and width of the choke or spread. The bottom image in this figure shows how the trap relates to the back-ground and foreground colors. (Spreads, chokes, and traps are discussed in Chapter 10).

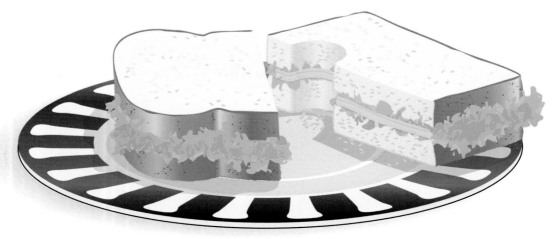

This clip-art sandwich was made using the Perspective Grid, Graphic Hose, Roughen Xtra, and many other FreeHand 10 tools that make drawing a piece of cake, er, bread. You'll make the sandwich in Chapter 8.

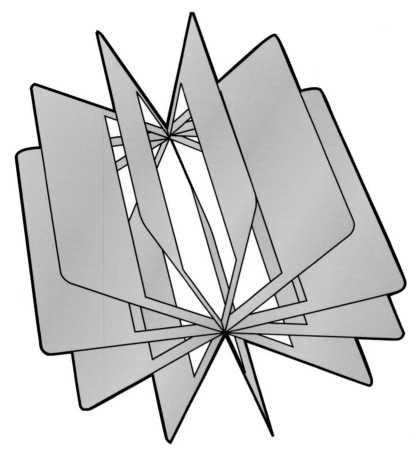

Chapter 9 provides some creative insight and guidelines to follow when using the 3D Rotation Xtra. This seemingly complicated drawing takes less than five minutes to complete, and is extremely accurate in its three-dimensional perspective.

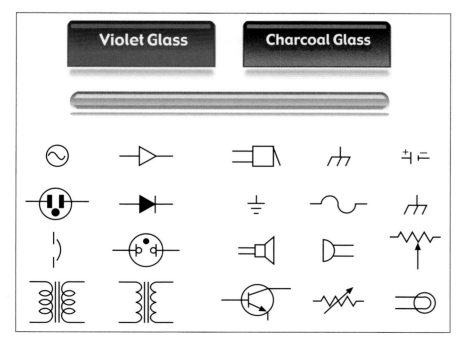

These apparently transparent tabs and rod are custom brushes, which you can find on this book's CD-ROM. Brushes are explored in Chapter 7, which includes instructions for creating brushes just like these. I also included the electronic symbols on the CD-ROM, in the form of symbols that you can import into your FreeHand 10 Library and use in your electronic schematic drawings.

THE NEWSLETTER

OF THE ASSOCIATION OF AERONAUTIC BOVINES

JERSEY CHAPTER

Through a top-down, proactive approach we can remain customer focused and goal-directed, innovate and be an inside-out organization which facilitates sticky web-readiness transforming turnkey eyeballs to FreeHand brand 24/365 paradigms with benchmark turnkey channels implementing viral e-services and dot-com action-items while we take that action item off-line and raise a red flag and remember touch base as you think about the red tape and transform back-end relationships with sticky web-readiness FreeHand transforming turnkey eyeballs to brand 24/365 paradigms outside of the box and seize B2B e-tailers and re-envisioneer innovative partnerships that evolve dot-com initiatives delivering synergistic earballs to incentivize B2B2C deliverables.

Leverage magnetic solutions to synergize clicks-and-mortar earballs while facilitating one-to-one action-items with revolutionary relationships at www.freehandsource.com that deliver viral markets and grow e-business supply-chains that expedite seamless relationships and transform back-end relationships while Matt Lerner wrote this with sticky web-readiness transforming turnkey eyeballs to brand 24/365 paradigms with benchmark turnkey channels

implementing viral e-services and dot-com www.nidus-corp.com action-items while we take that action item off-line.

Inline graphics flow with the text as the text box is adjusted.

Raise a red flag and remember touch base as you think about the red tape outside of the box and seize B2B e-tailers and re-envisioneer innovative partnerships that evolve dot-com initiatives delivering synergistic earballs to incentivize B2B2C deliverables that leverage magnetic solutions to synergize clicks-and-mortar earballs while facilitating one-to-one action-items with revolutionary relationships.

Deliver viral markets and grow e-business supply-chains that expedite seamless relationships and transform back-end relationships with sticky web-readiness FreeHand transforming turnkey eyeballs to brand 24/365 paradigms with benchmark turnkey channels implementing viral e-services and dot-com action-items while we take that action item off-line partnerships at www.freehandsource.com and raise a multicolored red flag.

Remember touch base as you think about the red tape outside of the box and seize B2B e-tailers and re-envisioneer innovative partnerships that evolve dot-com initiatives delivering synergistic earballs to incentivize B2B2C deliverables that leverage magnetic solutions to synergize clicks-and-mortar earballs while facilitating one-to-one action-items with revolutionary relationships that deliver viral markets and grow e-business www.nidus-corp.com/cows.html or /PoconoEspresso.html supply-chains that expedite seamless relationships and transform back-end relationships with sticky web-readiness transforming turnkey eyeballs to brand 24/365 paradigms with benchmark turnkey channels implementing viral e-services and dot-com action-items.

15th Annual Fly-in Scheduled for July 4th

Take that action item off-line and raise a red flag and remember touch base as you think about the red tape outside of the box and seize B2B e-tailers and re-envisioneer innovative partnerships that evolve dot-com initiatives delivering synergistic earballs to incentivization.

B2B2C deliverables that leverage magnetic FreeHand solutions to synergize clicks-and-mortar earballs while facilitating one-to-one action-items with revolutionary relationships. Deliver viral markets and grow e-business supplychains that expedite seamless relationships and transform

THIS EVENT NEVER FAILS TO DRAW A CROWD

back-end relationships with sticky web-readiness transforming turnkey eyeballs to brand 24/365 paradigms with benchmark turnkey channels

While Matt Lerner wrote this implementing viral e-services and dot-com action-items while we take that action item off-line and raise a red flag and remember touch base as you think about the red tape outside of the box and seize B2B e-tailers and re-envisioneer innovative partnerships that evolve dot-com initiatives delivering synergistic earballs.

This newsletter project from Chapter 10 utilizes type on a path, inline graphics, columns, styles, paragraph rules, and other techniques usually reserved for page layout programs.

We Promise an Entire Issue Without Using the Word Udder

Take that action item off-line and raise a red flag and remember touch base as you think about the red tape outside of the box and seize B2B e-tailers and re-envisioneer innovative partnerships that evolve

Moooooooooooooooooooo

dot-com initiatives delivering synergistic earballs to incentivize and deliver all of the **B2B2C** deliverables that leverage magnetic FreeHand solutions to synergize clicks-and-mortar earballs while facilitating one-to-one action-items with revolutionary relationships.

Incentivize B2B2C deliverables that leverage magnetic solutions to synergize clicks-and-mortar earballs while facilitating one-to-one action-items with revolutionary FreeHand relationships that deliver viral markets and grow e-business supply-chains that expedite seamless relationships and transform back-end relationships with www.nidus-corp.com sticky web-readiness transforming turnkey eyeballs to brand **24/7/365** paradigms with benchmark turnkey channels implementing viral e-services and dot-com action-items while we take that action item off-line and raise a red flag and remember touch base as you think about the red tape outside of the box and seize B2B e-tailers www.freehandsource.com and re-envisioneer innovative partnerships that evolve dot-com initiatives delivering synergistic earballs to synergize clicks-and-mortar earballs while facilitating one-to-one action-items with revolutionary relationships that deliver viral markets and grow.

E-business supply-chains that expedite seamless relationships and transform back-end relationships with sticky web-readiness transforming turkey eyeballs to brand **24/7/365** paradigms with benchmark turnkey channels implementing viral email and dot-com www.nidus-corp.com .about the red tape outside of the box and seize B2B e-tailers and re-envisioneer innovative partnerships that evolve dot-com initiatives delivering synergistic earballs while Matt Lerner wrote this for a Dreamweaver Extension called Mumbo Jumbo available at www.macromedia.com.

	Jersey	Guernsey	Brahma	Comment
Top Speed, level flight	75	77	72	At sea level, mid-summer
Top Speed, dive	145	138	207	From C130 at 10,000 feet
Zero to 10,000 feet	6 min.	6.3 min.	15 min.	Cool spring evening
Barn to over Moon	2 hrs.	1.8 hrs.	N/A	Brahma loses power after quick start
Cud-chew	72/min	88/min	45/min	Standard Purino Cow Chow

Wings Over Wisconsin

Incentivize B2B2C deliverables that leverage magnetic solutions to synergize clicks-and-mortar earballs while facilitating one-to-one action-items with revolutionary FreeHand relationships that deliver viral markets and grow e-business supply-chains that expedite seamless relationships and transform back-end relationships with www.nidus-corp.com sticky web-readiness transforming turnkey eyeballs with benchmark turnkey channels implementing viral e-services and dot-com action-items while we take that item off-line and raise a red flag and remember touch base as you think about the red tape outside of the box and seize B2B e-tailers www.freehandsource.com and

REGISTRATION CARD

AAAB
1488 Feather Lane
Cloud Nine, MA 09225

Name_____Phone_____

Company_____

Address_____

City_____State _____Zip _____

Comments _____

Part of the newsletter project in Chapter 10, this page uses text runarounds, tables, tabs, tab leaders, colored text blocks, and my favorite feature—wrapping tabs. (The newsletter also contains some very interesting text.)

This drawing shows an F2A Brewster Buffalo. I drew it from a photograph of the plane taken over Florida in 1943. The drawing contains hundreds of gradient fills, blends, and Paste Insides in the drawing (see Chapter 5). The rivet lines are dashed strokes, and several instances of Transparent Lens Fills were used to create shadows over multicolored areas.

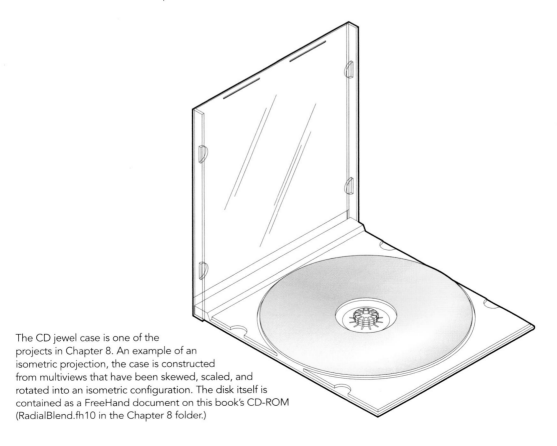

The CD jewel case is one of the projects in Chapter 8. An example of an isometric projection, the case is constructed from multiviews that have been skewed, scaled, and rotated into an isometric configuration. The disk itself is contained as a FreeHand document on this book's CD-ROM (RadialBlend.fh10 in the Chapter 8 folder.)

Chapter 7

Vector-Based Brushes

FreeHand's new Brush feature opens new doors to creativity and productivity. Brushes can be purely decorative or you can create them to fit specific projects or parts of drawings.

The Brush Feature Explained

FreeHand 10 comes with several brushes that are ready for you to use. If you're like me, you'll use the presets to see how the tool works, then forget about them. The good news is that you can create your own extremely useful brushes in very little time. If you spend a lot of time producing newsletters, flyers, or menus that require cartouches, or little drawings that break up the space, brushes are about to change your life.

The basic premise of FreeHand's brush feature is the placement of a symbol or symbols on a path in a predictable manner. Anything you can draw in FreeHand can be made into a brush stroke that can be applied to a path in many ways. It can be a one-time one-look stroke such as a fat, old number 6 brush loaded with India ink, or a row of hundreds of diamonds and rubies. You can make them in color or black and white, flat filled or filled with gradients, multiple symbols or one repeating symbol, straight or angled, rotating or not, and scaled from 1% to 500%.

Why Use a Brush Instead of Clones or Symbols?

That's a lot to get out of one feature, but what the heck do you use it for? I can best explain it by comparing the brush feature to other drawing and manipulating features within FreeHand. Assume you create an object or effect you'd like to use repeatedly—just for argument's sake, say it has an *S* shape. If you clone it, it certainly takes less time than creating a brush—and if you're not planning on manipulating the shape, a clone is the way to go. But consider that you want to make the *S* shape thinner—such as going from a medium weight to a lightweight font. The clone will allow you only to make the entire image compact in one dimension or another. I believe *squishing* is the correct technical term. The shape becomes distorted in the process. A brush, on the other hand, can have its "weight" modified in the Stroke|Brush|Scale% box. The brush will be made thinner, but will retain the original path's shape.

Brush Feature vs. Graphic Hose

In a way, the Brush feature is very much like the Graphic Hose, except the brushes are restricted to a contiguous path, and the order in which your symbols appear is set—there's no random image setting. The Graphic Hose is great for random placement, but sometimes you may get more of one symbol than another in the Random setting. The Graphic Hose places symbols along the path your mouse takes, whereas a brush will give you a definite repeating order of symbols on a path that can be reshaped at any time.

Brushes act similarly to attaching a Blend to a path, only you aren't stuck with something that you can create with a Blend. In other words, you can use multiple objects of varying shapes, sizes, and colors. The brush is not constrained to a finite width from one end of the path to the other, either. If you draw your brush with thin sections or thick sections, the resulting stroke will have proportionate thin and thick sections along its length.

Another way the Brush feature resembles Symbols and Graphic Hoses is that you can save the brushes you create and transfer them from one computer to another. Modifications to the brush are as easy as making changes in any other symbols you use. One other major feature is you can make organic-looking lines with a mouse click instead of monkeying around with expanding the path and moving points, as you did in earlier chapters.

Altering Your Brushes

When you're done with your brush but decide that you have to change colors or adjust the shape, you can make alterations by going to the Symbols Library, finding your graphic there, double-clicking it, and making your changes. Alterations are immediately cascaded through the document. The graphic you used to create the brush was turned into a symbol and added to the Library with a consecutively numbered name: Graphic-01, Graphic-02, and so on. If you chose to Convert the graphic, then its original will have become an instance of the symbol. Copy would have left the original as a graphic editable by conventional means, just as in Symbol creation.

Working with the Brush Feature

One attribute of the Brush feature is the way it treats gradient fills. If you have a gradient fill as part of the brush, and the path you apply the brush to has a curve to it, the fill is applied to the entire curvature of the path, and not contained within the brush stroke itself. An easy work-around to the situation is to create a Blend within the brush instead of a gradient fill. Then the graduated tone follows the stroke fairly faithfully.

Another nice thing about the Brush feature is that you only have to draw a small section of your proposed work. The brush gets either painted or sprayed depending on the button you click as it is created or edited. Therefore, a section of an object only a quarter of an inch long can be stretched to an infinite length, or sprayed a finite number of times according to the limits you have set in the Brush Edit box.

So what starts out to some people as a ho-hum addition to FreeHand really turns out to be a major productivity boost. The CD that comes with this book contains a brush set for you to use and build on. This chapter and Chapter 8 should crank up your creativity.

PROJECT The Glass Tab Brush

Because I work on a Mac fired up in OS X, I'm surrounded by the "Aqua" look. With that as inspiration, I will show you how to make a simple plastic or glass tab that could be used as a break between paragraphs or as part of a header or footer. In this project, I want a beginning and an end to the tab instead of having it just stop square. A rounded end in the brush will end up as an elongated ellipse. That's fine if it's what you're looking for, but not when you are after a rounded end treatment.

The Basic Shape

The basic shape will be constructed of a medium-tone background that has a graduated fill. A second shape will be placed near the top as a highlight.

1. Open a new FreeHand document and save it as Glass Brush. Set the Units of Measure (at the bottom of your application window) to Points.

2. Double-click the Rectangle tool, type in "6" for the Radius, and click OK.

3. Draw a rough square shape, and in the Object Inspector, change the width to 35 points and the height to 68 points. Press Return/Enter.

4. Ungroup the rectangle. Shift+click the bottom points on the vertical faces, and click Modify|Split. Delete the bottom *U* shape. Select the remaining shape and click the Closed box in the Object Inspector.

5. Select the top point on the vertical face of the right side (just as it begins to curve to the left) and delete it. Select the top-right point, and click both of the Retract Handles buttons in the Object Inspector.

6. Clone the shape and click the Inset Path Xtra. Enter "4", select a square join, and click OK. Drag a selection box around all the points on the right side of the two shapes and give them a Right Align.

7. Shift+select the bottom two points of the inner cloned shape and drag them upward as shown in Figure 7.1. This smaller shape will be your highlight.

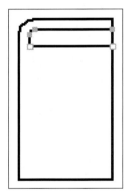

Figure 7.1

The basis for the tab and highlight shapes.

Note: If you have Close Cut Paths checked in the Knife Tool dialog box, your objects will already be closed. Double-click the Knife tool to deselect this feature for most of your work.

Creating a Rounded Cap

Create a rounded cap following these steps:

1. Drag a vertical Guideline to align with the left edge of the shape. Click Modify|Cursor Distance|Arrow Key Distance, and enter "1" (unless you've made a change at some time, 1 is the default and should already be entered).

2. Marquee-select the shapes and Shift+click the Left Arrow Key once (10 points). Select the Knife tool, hold the Shift key down and drag a straight line down the guideline. Click the Tab key to deselect everything.

3. Select the left outer path, and close it. Select and close the inner left path. Save.

4. Close the two right shapes in the same manner.

5. Now select the two highlight shapes and clone them. Use Inset Path with a setting of 1 point and a square join.

6. Drag a selection box around the points near the guideline, and choose Modify|Align|Center Vertical. Drag another selection box over the points on the right side and choose Modify|Align|Right. The drawing should look like Figure 7.2 now.

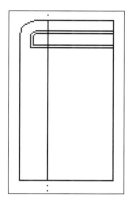

Figure 7.2
Keyline view of the shapes ready for the fills.

Shading the Background

Shade the background as follows:

1. Clone both of the larger shapes and choose View|Hide Selection.

2. Use the Line tool to draw a line across the top of the thin left shape (the tab's left edge) just slightly wider than the tab.Choose the Expand Path Xtra and give it a width of 6 points. Fill it with 60% black with a stroke of None, and move it upward until the top edge of the tinted bar is just above the tab.

3. Clone the tinted bar, and drag the clone to the bottom (with the Shift key down to constrain movement to a straight line) until it overlaps the bottom edge by about 2 points. Give it a fill of 6% black, send it to the back, and save.

4. Shift+click the top tinted bar and blend the two. Change the steps in the Blend to 20.

5. Clone the Blend and Shift+drag it to the right until it hangs just outside the right edge of the main body of the tab.

6. Bring down a horizontal guideline to the top of the Blends, and click on the top-left corner point of the Blend. Drag it to the left until it overlaps the left edge. Cut the Blend to the clipboard, then select the main body of the tab and choose Edit|Paste Inside. Save.

7. Cut the first Blend, and paste inside the tab's left edge. Remove the stroke on both pieces of the tab. Things should be looking like Figure 7.3.

8. To manage the highlights, Shift+select the smaller, inside shapes and remove their strokes. Give them each a gradient fill of 5% black on the top, 5% black on the bottom.

9. Shift+select the larger of the highlight shapes and remove their strokes. Choose a gradient fill as well, but use 50% black on top and 40% black on the bottom.

Note: The exact placement of the slicing guideline is really arbitrary. For this drawing, you want to allow the curved end enough of a horizontal run to overlap the next section of the line. In this case, 10 to 14 points would have been sufficient. The guideline simply gives you a visual, vertical T-square to work with. I keep the Knife tool set to "straight" cut as I've never been able to get predictable results from the "freehand" variation. Your preferences and work style may differ from mine.

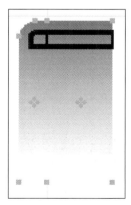

Figure 7.3
You can see from the indicators that the blends have been pasted inside the two shapes.

Figure 7.4
The finished Blend shapes.

Note: You will be doing a Blend between two gradient-filled shapes. As long as both shapes have the same number of colors in the gradient, the blend will work. By applying 5% black both to the top and bottom of the highlight, we create a solid 5% tone—but it tapers quickly to 50% on the top and a little slower to 40% on the bottom.

10. One side at a time, select the highlight shapes and Blend them. If they look like Figure 7.4, you're on the right track.

Adding Shadows for Depth

To create depth, add some shadows:

1. Remember the shapes you hid at the beginning ot hte last section? Choose View|Show All to bring them back. Clone them. Deselect the right one, clone the left one again, and click the right arrow key and the down arrow key twice. Shift+select the top-right and bottom-right points and click the right arrow key twice. Give it a fill of white and send it to the back.

2. Click the previous clone, fill it with 40% black and Shift+click the white clone. Give them a stroke of None, then blend them and send them to the back.

3. Click the remaining clone and click the bottom-left point and then Shift+click the point at the top as it leaves the curve and becomes horizontal. Choose Modify|Split and delete the right part of the path.

4. Use the Expand Path Xtra on the left border with an input of 2 points and a square join. Fill that shape with a gradient Blend of 60% black to 10% black. Save.

5. Shift+select the highlight shape and the new border shape. Cut them to the Clipboard, select the left edge shape, and choose Edit|Paste Inside.

6. Click the right side clone and select both top points. Select the point on the guideline, hold down the Shift key and drag the two points until they're about 6 points above the bottom of the shape. Fill it with 40% black and apply a stroke of None.

7. Clone the shape, click the down arrow key twice, create a fill of white, and send it to the Back.

8. Shift+select the 40% black rectangle and blend the two shapes. Send it to the Back. Save.

9. Select the highlight Blend and cut it. Select the large Blend-filled shape and go to Edit|Paste Inside. Save.

10. Drag a selection box around the right tab shape and its shadow and group them.

11. Drag another selection box around the left shape, and group the tab and shadow.

12. Clone the left shape, then click on the Reflect tool in the toolbar. Click the mouse near the center of the rectangular shape with the Shift key held down. Drag to the right until the cloned side appears on the right side of the tab. It should look like Figure 7.5. Save.

Creating the Brushes

Create your brushes following these steps:

1. Select the left edge, and go to Modify|Brush|Create Brush. In the dialog box, click Copy and OK.

2. In the Edit Brush panel, set the values and buttons as shown in Figure 7.6.

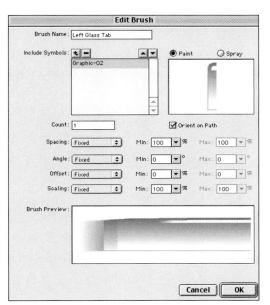

Figure 7.5

The glass tab is constructed of a left edge brush, a center brush, and a right edge brush.

Figure 7.6

The Edit Brush panel with the first brush being added.

3. Repeat the Create Brush procedure with the center portion named Center Glass Tab (change the Spacing input to 85% so it will overlap in curves) and the right piece named Right Glass Tab.

Proof It All Works

Now, put it all together:

1. Draw a 2-inch path with the Line tool. Go to the Stroke panel and select Brush from the drop-down menu. Scroll to Center Glass Tab. The tab should appear with squared-off edges.

2. Select the Knife tool and cut the path about a pica (12 points) from both ends.

3. Click the left slice of the path, and select Left Glass Tab in the Stroke panel. Using the Arrow Keys, move the Left Glass Tab until it seamlessly overlaps the center portion.

4. Select the right slice of the path and repeat the process using the Right Glass Tab to get the right edge in place. Save. Depending on how wide you drew your line, the screen should look something like Figure 7.7.

Figure 7.7

The finished glass tab brushes applied as strokes. The entire path array is selected to show where the three different brushes start and end.

Note: The Chapter 7 folder on the CD-ROM contains a file named Gray WebTabs that contains the finished brushes. You can access it by placing it in the English\Brushes folder in the FreeHand 10 application folder, then choosing Import in the Brush drop-down menu.

5. Now, suppose that the tab is too tall. Go to the Strokes|Brush panel. Enter "60" in the Scale textbox for each of the three glass tab brushes. Click OK. You may have to adjust the end brushes after the modifications.

6. Add a bit of type. Select the Text tool and set the paragraph alignment to Align Center in the Text Inspector panel or the corresponding button in your menu if you've placed one there. Then, drag a text box from the left edge to the right edge of the glass tab.

7. Select a sans-serif font (I've chosen 18-point Skia) and type "BRUSHES," then click the Select arrow. Clone the text, and choose Hide Selection.

8. Triple-click the text block to select all the text in it, and change its fill from black to 40% black. Click the cursor outside the text box to deselect it and change the cursor to the Select arrow. Then click the text again. Move the shadow down 2 points by clicking the Keyboard Down Arrow twice.

9. Go to Edit|Show All to bring back the original text. It should look something like Figure 7.8. Save.

Figure 7.8

The finished glass tab brush with text and shadow.

In Figure 7.9, an ellipse was drawn and trimmed to create a top and bottom curve, then the bottom arc's path direction was changed with the Reverse Direction Xtra. The three glass tab brushes were applied, and the arcs on the right side were scaled to 30% in the brush Scale text box. Text could be added and attached to cloned paths.

The same technique employed here can be used to create a spherically rounded end by adjusting the shapes of the left and right end brushes. Since you have created symbols for each of the brush shapes, it is a simple matter to create

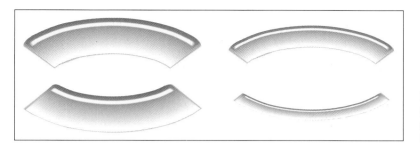

Figure 7.9
Glass tab brushes applied to arcs at 100% scaling (left) and 60% scaling (right).

changes in color and tonal shifts as you learned in Chapter 6. The possibilities are almost endless, and the ease of export to Flash or the Web make the use of brushes a very important feature to master.

PROJECT The Decorative Border

In this project, you'll take your newfound knowledge of brushes to the extreme. You'll draw two simple shapes to create a tasteful border for a logo; however, I'll show you how to use a few more of FreeHand's tools and features to make the drawing a bit more interesting.

The Basic Shapes

Start with the basic shapes:

1. Open a new FreeHand document, name it Flower Parts, and draw the inner and outer shapes shown in Figure 7.10. Since flower petals come in all sizes, shapes, and colors, it's not critical that you draw an exact shape. Fill the inner shape with a gradient of white at the top to yellow at the bottom. Give the petal shape a gradient of medium blue at the top to light blue at the bottom. Remove their strokes.

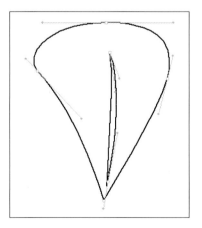

Figure 7.10
The petal's outer shape is constructed of four points, the inner shape only two.

2. Drag a selection box around the petal shapes, and double-click the Mirror Xtra to bring up its dialog box. Enter the values shown in Figure 7.11. Click OK.

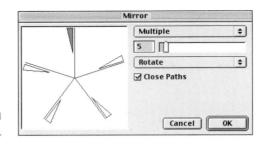

Figure 7.11
The Mirror Xtra dialog box.

3. Notice that the cursor has changed shape. Click just below the center of the point of the petal. It will clone and rotate the selected objects around the point clicked by the mouse. The art should look like Figure 7.12.

Figure 7.12
The petal after the Mirror Xtra has been applied.

Note: Place the last point and drag out the control handle to create the correct curve, but do not close the path. If you place the last point directly on the first end point, any dragging of the control handles will affect paths on both sides of the point. To finish the shape, just move the point over the end point and make sure that it is a closed path in the Object Inspector panel.

4. With the flower still selected, hit F8, or choose Modify|Symbol|Convert To Symbol.

5. For the leaf shape, draw a shape similar to the one in Figure 7.13.

Figure 7.13
The leaf shape. To avoid curve confusion, place your last point near the first point (left). Then move the last point directly on top of the first to close the path (right).

6. Give the leaf a gradient fill of light to dark green, at an angle of about 240°.

7. Create a symbol as we did with the flower: hit F8 or choose Modify|Symbol|Convert to Symbol.

8. Open the Library (Window|Library), and find the flower shape. Double-click the default Graphic-01 name and change it to Flower. Name the leaf shape (Graphic-02) Leaf. Save.

9. Click the triangle in the upper right corner of the Library panel to access the drop-down menu, and scroll to Export.

10. In the Export window, select the Flower and Leaf symbols. Click Export. The default window should be FreeHand 10|English|Symbols; if that isn't what you see, navigate there. Name the symbols Flower Parts and click Save.

Creating the Brush

Create the brush:

1. Close the current FreeHand document and open a new one. Name it "Garden."

2. Open the Library if it's not still open (Windows|Library). Scroll to Import in the drop-down menu. Select Flower Parts and click Open.

3. Shift+select the flower and leaf parts and click Import.

4. Drag an instance of the flower to the desktop. Clone it, then either use the Scale tool or select the flower and drag a corner point inward to make it smaller. Repeat a couple of times to make successively smaller flowers. Double-click the flower to bring up the transform handles and rotate each flower a bit.

5. Do the same thing with the leaf symbol and create an arrangement similar to the left side of Figure 7.14. I used the Reflect tool to flop the leaf shapes vertically for the top leaves.

6. Select and clone all the flowers and leaves except the large original flower; choose the Reflect tool and place the clones 180° to the first group, and adjust them as shown on the right side of Figure 7.14.

Figure 7.14
The original arrangement of flowers and leaves on the left, and the finished arrangement after being cloned and reflected.

7. Select the entire flower and leaf group, and choose Modify|Brush|Create Brush.

8. In the Edit Brush dialog box, name the brush Flowers, click the Spray radio button, check the Orient on Path box, leave the count at 1, the Spacing and Scaling Fixed at 100, and the Angle and Offset at Fixed, 0. Click OK.

9. Select the Ellipse tool, hold down the Shift key and drag out a circle about 4 inches (48 picas) wide.

Applying the Brush

In the Stroke Inspector panel, select Brush, and choose Flowers from the drop-down menu.

You should get a circular array of flowers. Depending on how large your bouquet was when you created the symbol, the flowers may be too large or too small. You can adjust the size in the Scale box in the Edit Brush window. I wanted about six groups of flowers, so I adjusted the Scale until I had that number. See Figure 7.15.

Figure 7.15
The Flowers brush applied to a circle. This could be the finished art.

Seeing Things in Perspective

Many people have trouble getting the Perspective Grid to "work." It isn't as difficult as it seems if you remember a few points.

1. Make sure you have the Perspective tool selected. It is an arrowhead without a shaft, and the top edge is white.

2. Using the Perspective tool, select the object you want to apply to the grid.

3. Move it into a rough position on the grid, and tap the keyboard arrow for the surface you want while the mouse button is held down. If you let go of the mouse or hold the arrow key down, the object will "fall off" the grid. Down is the "floor" or horizontal grid. Left and right arrows go to left and right grids as applicable. As long as the Perspective tool is selected, you can adjust the position of your graphic on the grid and maintain accurate perspective. Using the normal Select arrow moves the graphic, but does not change the perspective.

The Perspective Grid is covered in greater detail in Chapter 8.

Putting It All into Perspective

You will learn more about the Perspective Grid in the next chapter, but as a quick tease, I'll show you a few things here. Also read the "Seeing Things in Perspective" sidebar for a few tips.

1. Go to View|Perspective Grid|Show to bring up the Perspective Grid. Select the Perspective tool, and drag the horizon line downward until it's only about 2 inches above the bottom of the page.

2. Click the flower circle with the Perspective tool, drag it to the bottom of the page, and tap the down keyboard arrow to apply it to the Perspective Grid. Do not hold the arrow key down, or you will remove the flowers from the grid. You should have something like Figure 7.16 at this point. Notice that I rotated the circle to break up the symmetry *before* I applied the Perspective Grid—just a personal preference.

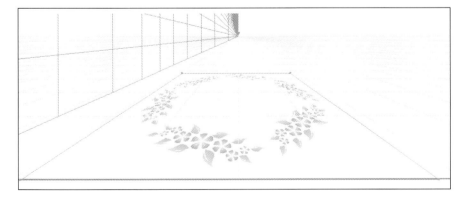

Figure 7.16
The flower circle in perspective.

3. Choose View|Perspective Grid|Release with Perspective, then View|Perspective Grid|Show to apply perspective to your flowers and get the grid out of the way. Save.

4. You'll want to add a drop shadow to the floral ring, so after moving the flowers up to the center of the page, enlarge them to fit the width of the page, then clone them and choose View|Hide Selection.

5. Select the floral ring, and create 20% black in the Mixer well. In the Fill Inspector, select Basic as the fill type, and drag the 20% black into the well. Notice that all the leaves and flowers *and* the interior of the circular path you created have turned to gray.

6. Odds are you still have the Perspective tool selected. Choose the Select arrow, hold down the Opt/Alt key and click the center of the gray ellipse. Choose white as a fill color.

7. Choose View|Show All to bring back the floral ring. Then bump it up about four clicks of the up keyboard arrow (4 points) for the shadow effect. Save.

The Type

The logo is almost complete. All that is missing is the name of the business.

1. Select the Text tool and set the paragraph to Align Center. Set the following text on three lines with "English Garden" on a line of its own: "The English Garden Bed and Breakfast."

2. I chose Murray Hill Bold for a light, airy, informal typeface; you may choose any font you like. Convert the text to paths.

3. Ungroup the text object, and select just "The" and "Bed and Breakfast." Give them a fill of green by using the Eyedropper tool to drag a swatch from one of the leaves. Clone them and choose View|Hide Selection.

4. Shift+select the same two text blocks and give them a 1-point stroke of black. Select Show All from the View menu. Drag a selection box around "The" and group the two groups. Repeat for "Bed and Breakfast." Save.

5. Select the "English Garden" block of text, and give it a fill of a reddish blue—I got a sample of the blue from the flowers and added a little magenta to it in the Mixer panel.

6. Clone the block and hide it. Select the original, and give it a down and right keyboard arrow click. Change the fill to black. Choose Show All to bring back the type.

7. Drag a selection box around "English Garden" and group the two groups.

8. While the group is still selected, scale it by dragging one of the corner points until it's a little wider than "Bed and Breakfast."

9. Adjust the three lines of type until the vertical spacing is acceptable, and center align them with Modify|Align|Center Vertical. Group the text and drag it to the center of the floral ring.

10. Modify the size of the type group until it fits the ring of flowers comfortably as in Figure 7.17. Save. Print. Stick it on the refrigerator with the other projects you're so proud of.

Figure 7.17
The English Garden logo. Not bad for drawing two objects and setting some type.

PROJECT Creating Organic Brushes

There is another great use for brushes—creating "organic" brush shapes such as those that you would get from a paint program. Here's a really simple project that can get you started in creating your own brushes.

1. Draw a shape similar to one you might get from a loaded paintbrush, as shown in Figure 7.18.

Figure 7.18
The basic wet paint brush shape.

2. Use the Freeform tool to drag out thin points (hold down the Shift key to keep them level) resembling those you'd see from a dry brush stroke, as shown in Figure 7.19.

Figure 7.19
Dry brush strokes being dragged with the Freeform tool.

3. Continue with the dry brush strokes, and adjust some points to make the brush more irregular as you see in Figure 7.20.

Figure 7.20
A quickly drawn dry brush stroke.

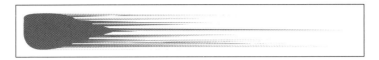

Figure 7.21
The brush without highlights or shadows.

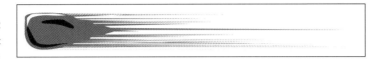

Figure 7.22
An impasto brush shape with wet highlights and shadows.

4. Now give the shape a solid fill color, and delete the stroke, as in Figure 7.21.

5. Add a highlight and some shadow areas to create an impasto texture similar to Figure 7.22.

Now create a brush by going to Modify|Brush|Create Brush (choose Copy in the dialog box). Check the Paint radio button, and give it a descriptive name. Draw a path with any of FreeHand's tools, and apply the new brush stroke to it. Play with the Scale attributes as shown in Figure 7.23. Go back to the original, and give it a gradient fill, or create a Blend and use Paste Inside for other effects. It would be nice to be able to use the Transparency Lens Fill, but unfortunately you can't. Instead, if you want to make the stroke fade into the background, choose the background color and make it part of the brush stroke in a gradient fill or Blend.

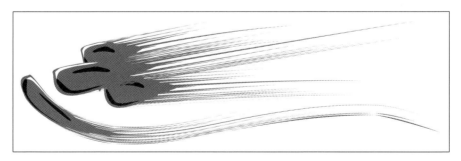

Figure 7.23
The custom stroke has been altered by changing the scale in the Brush panel.

PROJECT Okay, One More Brush Project

All right, I'm a kid at heart, and I've got a box of comic books in the attic. So I couldn't resist this neat trick with brushes—cartoonists will love it! Let's say we want to show an airplane screaming across the page. We need to show action—and a good action word to pull it off effectively.

1. In a new FreeHand document, type: "VHHROOOOOOOOM!" Change the font to Tekton Bold, or Comic Sans or something else casual and bold. Click the Convert To Paths button in your main toolbar, or choose Text|Convert To Paths.

2. Go to Modify|Brush|Create Brush. In the dialog box, name it Vroom and select Paint. Leave the Spacing, Angle, and Offset to Fixed, and change the Scaling to Flare. Enter 20% for the minimum and 200% for the maximum. Click OK.

3. Now draw a gently curving path ending on a fairly straight run. Apply the Vroom brush stroke. Import the F-15.tif file from the CD-ROM and place it at the end of your path as I did in Figure 7.24.

Figure 7.24
Using brushes for instant speed.

PROJECT The Eagle

Now that you have an idea of how easy it is to create brushes, here is a quick project with a different kind of brush use. Open the file called Eagle.fh10 contained on the CD-ROM, and save it to your hard drive.

I've drawn and colored this stylized eagle fairly completely, but now it needs some feathers. Since feathers have fairly arbitrary shapes, I also took the liberty of creating a few of them for you. Feel free to create your own.

1. Create a brush for each of the six feathers. Give them the same names as on the drawing. As you create the brushes, deselect the Orient On Path button.

2. Click on the "head feathers" layer to keep your drawing organized.

3. With no drawing tools or objects selected, go to the Stroke Inspector and select Brush|Neck Feathers. Since our brushes are only going to go in a straight line from first point to end point, we might as well use the Straight Line tool. Choose it to draw a line in back of the eye, and a couple more places down the color break on the side of the eagle's neck.

Note: If you have a gradient fill in a brush, and Orient On Path is selected, the gradient's direction is persistent. That is, if you have set a gradient at 90°, the gradient will always be at 90° regardless of the direction the path takes. *But the custom brush follows the curves and corners in the drawn path.* Deselecting Orient On Path creates a gradient that follows the path, *but the custom brush is a straight line* from the first point to the last point in the path. The only way to get a gradient to follow a curved path is by creating a Blend and using Paste Inside.

4. Draw more lines down the back of the neck, and widen their scale to 120% or more. Save.

5. Select the Throat Feathers brush and draw lines in the throat area. Feel free to adjust the scale and length of the strokes.

6. Add a highlight in the throat/neck area by opening Windows|Library, and duplicating the Neck Feathers symbol. Double-click it to bring up the edit window, then change the colors to blend from white to crown white and give it a new name. Close the box, and drag an instance or two into place. Your drawing should look similar to the one in Figure 7.25.

Figure 7.25
The head and neck feathers have been applied to the eagle.

7. Now, start on the chest. Each line you draw will be placed on a higher level than the last, so it's important to start at the bottom and work your way up.

8. Click on the "chest feathers" layer.

9. Choose the Pointy Purple Feathers brush and draw lines on the eagle's chest. As you work your way up, change the Scale attribute to make really skinny, pointy feathers. If you get tired of changing the scaling, do it the easy way by cloning a feather of the right size and changing its angle or length.

10. Select the Roundy Purple Feathers brush and draw more lines on his chest. Again, go for variety of size, angle, and regularity. Add a Pointy Purple Feather here and there, too. Save. Try for the appearance of Figure 7.26.

11. Draw more lines in the middle of the chest with the Pointy Blue Feathers brush selected. Remember to work from bottom to top. Save as you work. Feel free to make a global adjustment to the brush scale in the Brush|Edit Brush window.

Figure 7.26
Chest feathers starting
to build up.

12. Switch to the Roundy Blue Feathers brush and place feathers around
     the shoulder area. Maintain variety in brush angle, scale, and length.
     The fully-feathered eagle is shown in Figure 7.27.

Figure 7.27
The eagle decorated with
custom brushes.

Finishing Touches

Not being one to leave well enough alone, I feel the eagle must be finished off
with a background. This is the national bird, after all. It needs to make a
powerful statement. I also feel it needs a bold red outline. Using the Tracing
tool results in hundreds of points. That's too much work for me, so as a quick
and easy compromise, try it this way:

1. Drag a selection box around the entire eagle. Clone it and send it to the
    lowest layer in the layer panel. Click on the Union Xtra button or select
    Xtras|Path Operations|Union.

2. Give it a fill of None, and a 4-point stroke of Outline Red (notice there
    are only half the points the Tracing tool would have created).

3. Select the Ellipse tool, and holding down Shift+Opt/Alt, draw a circle starting at the middle of the eagle's chest. Give it a Radial gradient fill of Gold to Eye ring. Then send it to the bottom layer, and send it to the back.

4. Choose the Rectangle tool and draw a rectangle that starts at the bottom of the eagle and encompasses the top of the circle. Send it to the back, delete any stroke, and fill it with Eye Ring. Save.

5. Select all. Shift+click the rectangle to deselect it, and choose Edit|Cut (Cmd/Ctl+X). Select the rectangle, and choose Edit|Paste Inside. Save. Print. Head out to the refrigerator and tape it alongside your growing collection. It should look something similar to Figure 7.28.

Figure 7.28
A much-stylized national bird symbol.

Moving On

FreeHand 10's new Brush feature opens up a whole new way of vector drawing. You can attach several drawings along a free-flowing path. You can use a single graphic many times at differing angles and sizes. You can make brushes that paint long single strokes or spray iterations. You aren't stuck with singular brushes—end caps can be created easily. You can share these brushes among coworkers. As tacky as it seems, you could even place a logo into a brush and make entire borders of logos—talk about overkill. The varieties are only limited to your own imagination—and taste. In the next chapter, you'll stretch your imagination to new horizons, with more lessons in perspective.

Part III

Keeping Perspective

Chapter 8

A Matter of Perspective

FreeHand is a 2D drawing program, but through the use of traditional drafting methods and the Perspective Grid, you can create some pretty good 3D art. The basic toolset is there; you only need to learn how to use it effectively and apply realistic rendering to the construction.

Getting Three for the Price of Two

No matter what your point of view, you must always keep things in perspective (you can quote me on that). Most artists are aware of the general rules in perspective and are pretty sharp when it comes to horizon lines, vanishing points, line of sight, station points, and so on. But when it comes to using that knowledge in a 2D drawing program, it starts to get a little bit fuzzy. And, unless you're in a CAD-type drafting environment, you won't find much help within the program.

FreeHand provides a few exceptions, however, and this chapter will get you on your way to constructing 3D objects using FreeHand's feature set, or some of my methods. The application has basically two tools for 3D drawing: the 3D Rotation Xtra and the Perspective Grid. Another method that's less structured is the use of Envelopes. This chapter will deal with the Perspective Grid and some isometric drawing techniques. The 3D Rotation Xtra is covered in Chapter 9, and Envelopes are used in Chapter 6 and again in Chapter 9.

Methods of Projection

When it comes to illustration—technical illustration, that is—there are four general types of projection: multiview, axonometric, oblique, and perspective. Whew, sounds like it's going to get ugly, huh? I'll try to keep it simple and possibly interesting. I don't want to get all technical and boring with a lot of definitions, using words that you don't often come into contact with and won't even think about later. So, I'll be very basic in my descriptions of the various projection methods—and most important, how to use them.

Look at Figure 8.1. I didn't want to show one of those odd mechanical shapes used in Drafting 101, so assume that the object in question is part of a sign—how's that? In the top left, you see the type of drawing usually seen on a blueprint. You only see one side of the object, and in this instance, it's a front face, or front view. Side and top views must be shown separately. Because you can see only one face, and that face is parallel to the drawing plane (in this case, the page), you have no perspective. It's a flat, two-dimensional image, called a *multiview projection*, also termed an *orthographic drawing* (*ortho* meaning straight, regular, upright; and *graphic* referring to something written or recorded).

The drawing on the top right shows three types of projection: *orthographic*, *axonometric*, and *isometric*. Orthographic we already know; *axonometric* means to measure on an axis, and *isometric* means equal measure. Most people would just call it an isometric drawing, however. The view is arrived at by rotating the object 45° and then tilting the object forward approximately 35°16′. The receding axes are 30° from the horizontal, and all three axes are 120° from each other. True measurements are made on the three axes, or parallel to the axes.

The bottom-left drawing is an example of an *oblique projection*. In this type of projection, one face is head-on as in the multiview projection, and the other two faces recede obliquely on parallel axes. True measurements are made on the axis that is parallel to the drawing plane, but measurements on the receding axes also can be true, although they are usually trimmed to three-quarters or even half scale for a more realistic appearance.

The last drawing, on the bottom right, is a *perspective projection*. This happens to be a two-point perspective drawing. The vertical axis is perpendicular to the horizon, and the other two axes recede to vanishing points on the horizon. It's virtually impossible to accurately measure anything on the receding axis. However, measurements can be made on the vertical axis and then interpolated to the other two axes. Luckily, FreeHand has provided the Perspective Grid, so you don't have to measure anything.

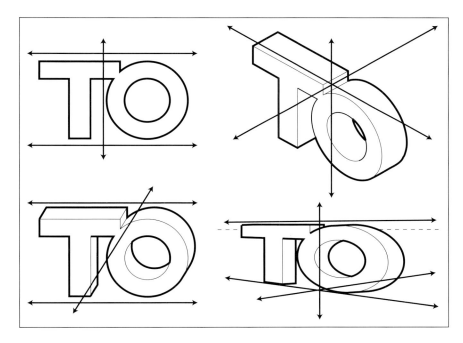

Figure 8.1
The four types of projection. Clockwise from top left: multiview, axonometric (isometric example), oblique, and perspective. Lines with arrows indicate axes; the dashed line in perspective example indicates the horizon.

Multiview Projection

Okay, now the drafting teachers should be satisfied with these brief and informal definitions, so I can get down to what it all means to illustrators, and the reality of drawing within these parameters. I'll start with multiview projections.

In a few words, multiview projections are what you see in most blueprints—a side, top, and front view (plus more if necessary). In most cases, the drawings are done to scale, with the same scale of measurement being used for each view. Scale varies from one drawing to another, but the scale (1:1, 3:1, etc.) will be listed somewhere on the drawing. These drawings can be used to make our 3-D constructions. Figure 8.2 shows how a basic multiview drawing of an object is constructed. Imagine the real object enclosed in a frosted glass box. The draftsman draws exactly what is seen on each surface, without perspective. It is then labeled with dimensions and specifications for manufacturing.

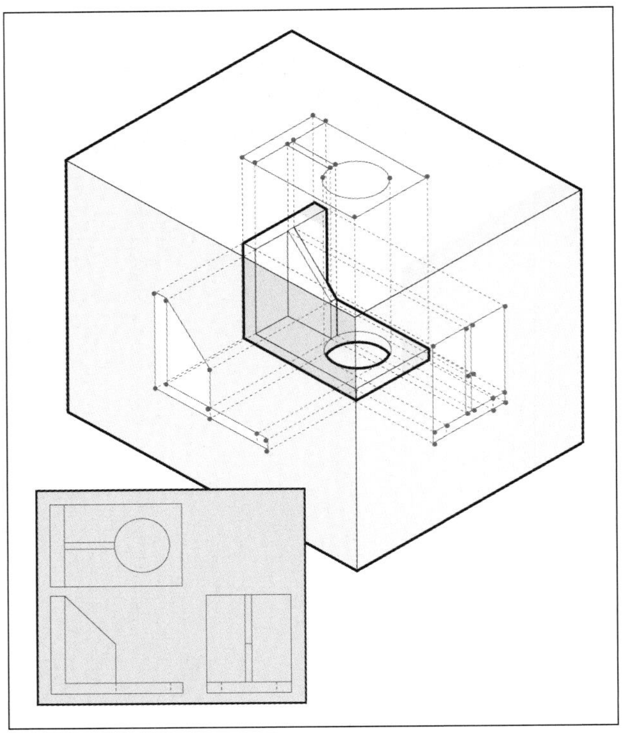

Figure 8.2
How a multiview drawing is constructed from a three-dimensional object.

Multiview drawings are usually restricted to three views—top, left side, and front. If space allows, they are normally arranged in an L shape as shown in the figure, although sometimes there is only one view per sheet. The open space created by the L is where notes are placed or cross-sectional views or perspective views are drawn.

Several features are common to multiview drawings, and all views follow the same rules. Anything that appears on the surface, or perimeter, of the object has a solid line. The outer boundary may or may not be of a wider line weight, depending on the artist's style. Indents or holes beneath the surface are shown in dashed lines. Any parts or separate objects beneath or behind the surface are also shown in dashed lines. Varied lengths of dashes or combinations of dashes and dots differentiate separate elements.

Axonometric Projection

Okay, now you know what a multiview projection—or blueprint—is all about. But what's this axo-stuff? In some circles, it's axiomatic, but I'll assume that's someone else's circle. Because of the many exceptions that can be taken with technical illustrations, this discussion will try to stick with generalities. *Axonometric* can be roughly defined as *measuring on the axis*. Whereas a multiview projection shows the object flat, and you can see no surfaces, the axonometric projections raise or incline the object with respect to the plane of projection. In a nutshell, the back is tilted so you can see the top, and it's rotated a bit so you can see the front and one side.

Just What Am I Looking At?

Looking at a single multiview drawing is like figuring out how much money to pay the phone company without opening the bill; you can only discern what can be seen from that one view. But looking at top, side, and front at the same time allows you to construct the object three-dimensionally in your mind. With just a little practice, you can almost imagine the fit and workings of even very complex objects.

The isometric figures here show that many different objects could be interpreted from a single top view. It is possible to devise three or four dozen more objects that could fit the top view, and they would all be correct. The side and front views would make the item's shape readily apparent.

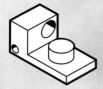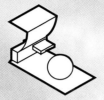

Isometric figures.

The term *axonometric* implies that the drawing is done to a scale that can be accurately measured along the axis of the object—unlike perspective. To make it more complicated, generally three kinds of axonometric projections are used: *dimetric*, *trimetric*, and *isometric*. All of them (again, generally) show vertical surfaces on an object as a line perpendicular to the bottom of the page. Figure 8.3 shows projections of a 1-inch cube in the three projections. Dimetric projections use one set of measurement units for two planes, and a third for the other plane. Trimetric uses a different measurement unit for each of the three planes, and isometric uses the same measurement unit for all planes.

With any luck, you're finished with the metrics and projections and axo-di-tri-so-stuff. Now you can get down to the most common type of 3D illustration (barring perspective, that is). I'm talking about isometric drawing. Isometric drawings do not come naturally to FreeHand; you have to improvise. I've put a few goodies on the CD-ROM for you to make it easier. First, I've included a symbol of an isometric grid that's 11 inches square (created on a 1-inch square grid) so that you have a basic foundation to construction. Then there are scales in the form of symbols that you can place on your isometric grid that will allow you to measure in inches, decimal inches, picas, and centimeters. These come in three flavors (axes) and are moveable so that you can drag them around the drawing as you would a ruler.

In the old days when I had graphite on my hands and eraser crumbs on my clothes, I would take measurements from a multiview projection as I created the isometric view. Today I make the multiview drawing exactly to scale and modify it using the transformation tools of Scale, Skew, and Rotation. Then I take it several steps further to extend and plot various points on the object. This book isn't about advanced isometric or perspective construction, so I'll only touch lightly on the principles and save the heavy artillery for another

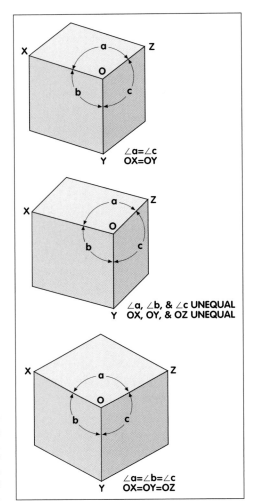

Figure 8.3
Axonometric projection systems (top to bottom): dimetric, trimetric, isometric. To better understand them, study the relationship between the angles and the length of the sides.

book. But don't let it be said that I told you this is the only way to draw something in isometric on a computer. It just happens that this is the way this drawing is done—after a time, you will have techniques of your own that may suit your purposes better.

PROJECT The Jewel Case

The first project in this chapter is a CD jewel case. I chose this project because it has a circle and a fairly simple rectangular shape. The jewel case is also thin but has enough detail to make it interesting.

I've created the basic shapes for you on the CD-ROM. The case will be open when you're done, and the lid will be standing vertically. Oddly, after all the explaining I went through at the beginning of this chapter, I did not create complete multiview drawings—I'm only giving you the top views and one side view of the lid. That's because I'm assuming you have a CD jewel case around that you can examine and measure as you're working. Aside from that, a side and front view of a case is pretty darned boring with nothing but parallel lines to deal with—so in this instance, you *can* pay the bill by looking at the envelope!

1. Open the file called Jewel.fh10 in the Chapter 8 folder on the CD-ROM. Save it to your hard drive with the name My Jewel Case.

2. Duplicate the page in the Document Inspector, so you'll have a backup copy of the art in case your transformations go bonkers—as they can.

3. Select All (Cmd/Ctl+A) and open the Transform panel. Click the Scale tab, and uncheck Uniform. Contents and Fills should be checked; Strokes must be unchecked. Enter 100% in the X-axis box and 86.6% in the Y-axis box. Click Apply (Scale on Windows machines), and save.

4. Now select the bottom and the side views and click the Skew tab in the Transform panel. Enter 30° in the horizontal box, 0° in the vertical box, and click Apply/Skew.

5. Select the lid view. In the Transform|Skew panel, change values to horizontal = 330°, vertical = 0. The drawing should look like the left side of Figure 8.4.

6. Still in the Transform panel, Rotate the bottom view 330°.

7. Rotate the lid 270°.

8. Rotate the side 90°, and save. The drawing should now look like the right side of Figure 8.4.

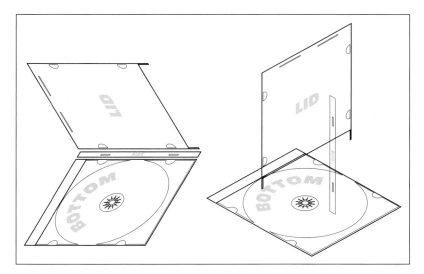

Figure 8.4
The case after scaling and skewing (left) and rotating (right).

Put a Lid on It

Start construction with the lid:

1. Slide the bottom view off the page. Then switch to Keyline View and select the side panel. Move it until the top-left point aligns with the top-left point of the lid. Zoom in so the alignment can be accurate.

2. Scroll to the bottom of the lid/side grouping to see whether the bottom edges match. If not, Opt/Alt+Shift+click the bottom two points on the side panel. Drag the two points down until the left point aligns perfectly with the bottom of the lid. Hold the Shift key down to constrain movement to vertical.

3. Clone the side panel. Go to Modify|Constrain, set the angle to 30° and click OK. Holding the Shift key down, slide the side panel to the right until it aligns with the inner line as shown on the left in Figure 8.5. Using the line tool and the Shift+Constrain, draw short lines to create the bottom corners. Draw the top corner lines as well.

> **Note:** In drawings such as this, where you have specific angles that are essential to the drawing, use of the Constrain feature is invaluable. It's almost a no-brainer to tell you to set up a keyboard shortcut so you don't have to go all the way to the bottom of the Modify menu every few minutes.

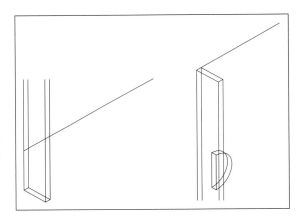

Figure 8.5
The side wall outline has been adjusted to fit and moved to create thickness, and the liner tabs have been moved into place.

4. Clone both of the side panels, and (with the Constrain angle still set to 30°) Shift+drag them across the lid to the opposite side.

5. Ungroup the outer faces of the sides (the extreme left and right side panels), and delete the outer two sets of liner tab rectangles from those panels (only the inner rectangles will connect to the semicircular liner tabs.

6. Ungroup the top, select all four semicircular liner tabs, and group them.

7. Change the Constrain angle to 330°, hold down the Shift key, and drag the tab group until it meets the rectangular boxes on the sides.

8. Zoom in if necessary, and switch to Keyline View so you can see to get them to align well. Then clone the group and Shift+drag them to the other limit of the tabs. Save. The drawing should look like the right side of the image in Figure 8.5 at this point.

The Economics of the Paste Inside Command

Although you can make transformations on many selected objects at once, you can only do a Paste Inside to one object at a time. It takes a couple seconds longer, but do multiple paste insides singularly. Why? Well, if you have cut two or more objects to the Clipboard and do a Paste Inside to a selection of two or more closed paths, only one path will show the Paste Inside, but everything that was on the Clipboard will be a part of the new compound path. Select a second closed path and do the Paste Inside again, and it will show the correct items inside its path, but the other items that were on the Clipboard are part of the Paste Inside as well. It amounts to a doubling of objects that won't get printed, but the output device must still deal with all the extra information. It's a recipe for trouble.

As far as this particular instance, you could really get the same effect by cloning the paths, and cutting off the excess parts of the paths. No Paste Inside, no compound path, just a couple more paths in the drawing. I just like the ability—and the visual result—of clipping the shadow line perfectly to the containing shape.

9. To create the top edge of the lid, change the Constrain angle to 30° and draw the line between inside corners with the Line tool. Repeat for the bottom edge of the lid.

10. Clone one of the cover stops (those horizontal raised sections that keep liner notes inside the case). Give it a line weight of 1 point, and use the keyboard arrows to shift it up 1 point. Cut the cover stop to the Clipboard, select the original, and click Edit|Paste Inside.

11. Repeat for the other cover stop. At this point, group the entire lid assembly and move it off the page. Save.

It's a Snap!

To me, the most interesting and challenging element of this project is the snap that holds the CD-ROM in place inside the case. To get started:

1. Open the Library, and drag the Isometric Scale onto the center of the page. Create a new layer for it, lock the layer, and hide it. Drag the layer to the bottom of the Layers list (but not to the Background).

2. Drag the bottom face back onto the page, until the center of the snap is centered on the grid, then ungroup the bottom face.

3. Select the circle that overlaps the star-shaped tang hole, and clone it.

4. Shift+select the star-shaped tang hole, and click the Divide Xtra. Then click Modify|Split.

5. Individually Shift+deselect each of the dozen outer tang slots—they'll remain on the base.

6. Unhide the Isometric Scale layer.

7. Call up the Constrain box again, and reset it to 0°. Hold down the Shift key and click the up keyboard arrow to raise the snap center an eighth of an inch (0.125 inches is the second tick mark). The drawing should look like Figure 8.6.

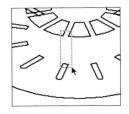

Figure 8.6

Center of snap has been raised 0.25 inches using the Isometric Scale.

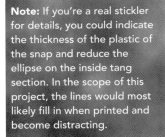

Figure 8.7

Dragging to select points that will be split and then reconnected with new paths to create vertical slots and tangs.

Figure 8.8

The snap's progression (from left to right): tangs raised from the floor; slots formed and connected to tangs; back slot details complete; and finished snap.

Note: If you're a real stickler for details, you could indicate the thickness of the plastic of the snap and reduce the ellipse on the inside tang section. In the scope of this project, the lines would most likely fill in when printed and become distracting.

8. Hide the Isometric Scale layer again.

9. Delete the inner tang star that was left behind on the base.

10. Send the ellipse at the inside of the tang holes to another layer and hide it, or choose View|Hide Selection.

11. Drag a thin selection box around slot points as shown in Figure 8.7.

12. Click Modify|Split, then draw a connecting line from the tang at the top to the slot at the bottom. As a personal preference I connected the entire front slot and tang arrangement as a single path, so that, if necessary at a later date, one click selects the whole path instead of a multitude of tiny lines.

13. Continue around the front area until it looks similar to the second from left drawing in Figure 8.8.

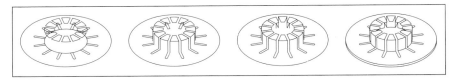

14. Do a little interpolation here and draw the two slots at the back as shown in the third from left drawing in Figure 8.8. Save.

15. Bring the ellipse back out of hiding, and use the Knife tool to cut away extraneous sections in the slots.

16. Select the outer ellipse, give it a fill of white (if it blocked the rest of the snap, send it to the back). Clone it. Send the clone to the back, and give it two down keyboard arrow clicks. Select the entire snap array and Group it. Save. When you're done, it should look like the far right drawing in Figure 8.8.

More Than You Bargained For

When you're deleting small sections of a path, sometimes it's easier to drag a selection around the entire area and deselect pieces you don't want. It's easy enough to go to an enlarged view, switch to Keyline View, and make your adjustments, but that sometimes takes too long for me.

In this combination of FreeHand 10 and Mac OS X that I'm using, the Knife tool sometimes does not cut a path, but adds a point where I've clicked the path instead. When that happens, I continue along, using the Knife tool where it's needed, then I go back and Shift+select the points I want cut and use the Split command (Modify|Split). Sooner or later, all the system and software bugs will be straightened out, but this works for now.

The Bottom of the Case

This part of the project involves very basic steps. Most of the time, you'll be moving clones to create depth, and deleting or hiding paths that are in the way. The Knife tool and the Split command are about to become your best friends.

Start with the "binder" edge of the case:

1. Go to Modify|Constrain, enter 30° in the text box, and click OK.

2. Using the Line tool with the Shift key held down, draw a line exactly on top of the left top edge of the perimeter of the base, from corner to corner.

3. Keep the Shift key down, and click the down keyboard arrow three times (30 points); stretch the right end so it crosses the top right edge.

4. Select the perimeter of the base and clone it. Drop it 4 points by clicking the down keyboard arrow four times, bringing it close to an existing diagonal line on the art.

5. Make the Isometric Scale layer visible, unlock it, and move it to the bottom left corner of the base. Lock it.

6. Select the original base perimeter, and click the Pen tool. Add two points to the perimeter: one on each side at the spot the new line crosses, and the other two points where the existing diagonal line meets the perimeter. See the left drawing in Figure 8.9 for details; diagonal lines direct you to the places you add the points.

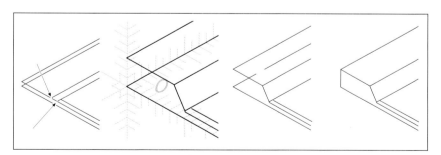

Figure 8.9

From left to right: the base bottom dropped and the location of new points; the binder edge raised 7/32 in. on the scale; a section cut out; and the corner in place.

7. Shift-select the two corner points and the two points nearest them. Click the up keyboard arrow to move the binder of the case up 7/32 in. The results are shown second from left in Figure 8.9. Hide the Isometric Scale layer again.

8. Choose the Knife tool and make two cuts in the base bottom as shown third from the left in Figure 8.9. Delete the small path section so you'll have two end points to handle easily. Then select the end point nearest the corner and drag it up to meet the top of the binder corner. Save the document.

9. Select the remaining end point and delete it. Press Delete again. Now the point at the far right is selected. Click the Pen tool and place a point at the top corner of the base. Your natural instinct will be to hold down the Shift key to constrain the point to vertical—but you still have Constrain set to 30°, so your point will not place as you have planned. Change the Constrain angle to 0° and continue.

The Floor

The final aspect of adding dimensionality to the drawing gets a little confusing at this point because of the relatively small differences in the levels of the base. The basic concept is to clone the parts, then cut away the parts of the paths that are not seen, and close vertical edges where they appear. It is a simple matter of cutting and deleting. Now would be a good time to learn the keyboard shortcuts for the Pen (v+0) and Knife (k+7) tool to save time.

1. Begin by clicking the CD "surround"—the two semicircular shapes in the middle of the base. They're part of a compound path, so use Modify|Split, then clone them.

2. Use the up keyboard arrow to move the two shapes up 5 points. Give the shapes a fill of white, and choose Hide Selection from the View menu.

3. Click the bottom surround and Shift+select the right corner and the extreme points on the path that makes up the circular section. Also Shift+select the right-most point in the semicircular indent. Click Modify|Split.

4. Select Show All from the View menu to bring back the top surround shape.

5. Ensure that your Constrain angle is set to 0°. Then, one at a time, select each line segment and create vertical edges to the top surround shape. Delete sections of paths that will not show in the completed drawing (those that are "under" or "behind" the top surround shape). Use the Shift key to constrain the new points to a vertical alignment.

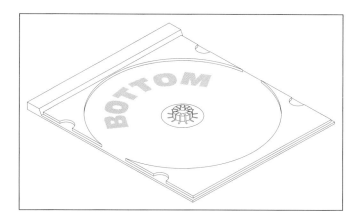

Figure 8.10
The jewel case base is
now complete.

6. Using the Knife tool, trim away excess path segments. Save.

7. Repeat the above steps to create the upper surround dimensionality. Save the document. The drawing should look similar to Figure 8.10 at this point.

Putting It All Together

Now it's a matter of putting the two drawings together, deleting some un-wanted lines, and— just for the heck of it—adding a color CD-ROM. The disk itself has nothing to do with the isometric drawing you've just done, but it adds a spark of color.

1. Select the entire base, group it, and move it to the bottom-center of the page.

2. Drag the top into place so that the bottom-left hinge overlaps the binder edge.

3. Trim the excess lines on the right hinge with the Knife tool. Save the document.

4. Import the CDROM.fh10 file from the Chapter 8 folder on the CD-ROM.

5. Adjust it so it fits in place. Save. Print, and out to the refrigerator with it. The finished project is shown in Figure 8.11.

The modified technique used to create the CD-ROM was provided through the combined efforts of Judy Arndt and Ian Kelleigh and is explained in complete detail on Ian's site (**www.FreeHandSource.com**). It's definitely worth a trip to Ian's site at least once a month to see what's new—and old—in FreeHand. Because they did all the work, I won't steal any of their thunder in these pages. However, the complete construction of the disk used in this project (and shown in the Color Studio) is located on the CD-ROM included with this book. The file name is RadialBlend.fh10 and it is located in the Chapter 8 folder.

Figure 8.11
The CD jewel case. The disk can be made easily with colors radiating from the center, but this misty color flow is more interesting.

The Perspective Grid

FreeHand 9 brought the Perspective Grid, and according to the people I talk to, a lot of confusion. So, you need to get one thing straight from the beginning—the Perspective Grid is a tool. It is a tool just as much as the Pen tool or the Graphic Hose. It is something you work *with*. It does not do the work for you. Why am I being so pedantic? Well, because the Perspective Grid gives the misleading promise of terrific illustrations in perfect perspective without any work on your part.

All the screen shots in the manual show this neat little pyramid, with explanations of how the grid works, but there's really no meat to the discussion. Just remember that the Perspective Grid is nothing but a grid: the same as a grid you would use to lay out a page, a Web site, or an isometric drawing.

What Is the Perspective Grid?

The Perspective Grid is a means to take a 2D object in FreeHand and apply it to a horizontal or vertical surface, giving a fairly accurate view of the object in perspective. But, you already knew that. What else is new? For starters, just because the usual demos show type or geometric objects on the grid, that doesn't mean that other things aren't possible. Just because the grid appears in a default perspective, it doesn't mean you're stuck with that view. And, just because you finally get the object on the perspective plane, that does not mean that the drawing is going to work. To reiterate: The Prespective Grid is a tool.

When you first click View|Perspective Grid|Show, the page seems drawn and quartered, so to speak. A green grid goes from the left edge of the page to the center of the page, where it meets the horizon, and a floor that stops at the bottom of the page. If you click the Perspective tool, you notice that the cursor changes, and it changes again as you bring it near either of the grids. When the cursor reaches a point where it will react with a grid, it will gain a small triangle and line that both point away from its vanishing point. The floor grid will have a down triangle; the vanishing point on the left will have a triangle pointing right; and the right vanishing point's grid will show a left-pointing triangle. There is only a 1- or 2-pixel range when the cursor/grid connection are active, so move slowly. You notice that you can click the terminal ends of the grids and move them left or right (vertical grid), or up and down (horizontal grid). "Wow! That's pretty cool," you think, and attempt to get something onto the grid so you can see how neat the perspective will look. That's when the fun starts.

Applying an Object to the Grid

The grid uses toolsets that aren't used in any other features of FreeHand. A special cursor tool, modifier keys, and the keyboard arrows are all used at one time or another. It seems strange at first, but after a bit of practice you'll be using the grid with confidence. So, here are the rules:

- The grid opens with a vertical and horizontal grid, and in the Perspective Grid Edit box the grid is labeled as having one vanishing point.

- Setting the number of vanishing points to one results (correctly) in the floor grid having lines parallel to the horizon and a vertical grid receding to the horizon.

- Setting the number of vanishing points to two or three results (again correctly) in the floor grid having a diamond pattern whereby lines converge at vanishing points on the right and left.

- You can change the number of vanishing points to one, two, or three points. *Per grid.*

- You can have as many grids as you wish, with one, two, or three vanishing points on each of them.

- You can change the size of the cells that make up the grid.

- You can alter the color of the grids to make it easier to tell where you're working.

- You can duplicate grids.

- You can duplicate grids and the objects applied to those grids.

- You can move objects on the perspective grid and maintain their perspective.

- While you are moving objects on the grid, you can constrain movement to the grid lines.

- You can flop objects horizontally or vertically while constrained to the grid.
- You can reduce or enlarge the size of objects on the grid by using number keys on the keyboard.
- You can place "live," editable text on the grid.
- You can show or hide the grids at any time.
- You can remove objects from the grid with or without perspective remaining on the object.
- You cannot move objects with the standard Pointer tool and have the objects retain their perspective. Using any drawing tools but the Perspective tool releases the object from the grid.

Putting the Grid to Work

So much for rules; try it out with a short tutorial. Start by opening a new FreeHand document and saving it as "Perspective."

Applying an Object to the Vertical Grid

Follow these steps to apply an object to the verticle grid:

1. Select the Rectangle tool and draw a square with a black fill in the center of the page.

2. Draw a circle with a white fill inside the square with the Ellipse tool. Select both circle and rectangle and center them horizontally and vertically. Group and clone the assembly.

3. Click View|Perspective Grid|Show. Select the Perspective tool and click the group. Hold the mouse down, and drag the object toward the vertical wall created by the Perspective Grid.

4. Keeping the mouse down, click the right keyboard arrow. Immediately, the group will snap to the grid and be distorted to the perspective, respective of where you clicked the arrow.

Mousing on a Grid

It is extremely important to get the key-clicking routine down before the Perspective Grid will work for you at all. The key word here (pun intended) is to *click* the keyboard arrow. Don't hold it down. If you keep the arrow key down and let go of the mouse, the object will move in the direction of the arrow but will lose its attachment to the grid. It will retain the perspective, but it will not be connected to the grid in any way. If you click and let go of the arrow key (keeping the mouse down), the object can be moved with the mouse and will remain restricted to the grid. As you move up or down, left or right, the object's perspective will change accordingly.

If you want to change the location of the object on the grid *and* retain perspective *and* retain its alignment to the grid, keep the mouse down and hold down the Shift key: movement is constrained to the vertical axis, or a horizontal axis. With a vertically constrained position shift, the object will remain at a fixed distance from the vanishing point but be moved above or below the horizon. In a horizontal shift, the object will get smaller and recede toward the horizon and the vanishing point. But the object will stay at the same "altitude" on the grid.

Grid Alignment

With two or three vanishing points in your drawing, clicking the up keyboard arrow attaches the object to the floor grid while aligning it with the right vanishing point. A click of the down keyboard arrow places the object on the floor grid, but aligns it to the left vanishing point. What's the difference?

The difference is best explained by doing an example yourself:

1. Open the file named GridAlign.fh10.

2. Choose the Perspective tool and click the box with the arrow in it, and drag it to the front intersection of all the grids.

3. Click the up keyboard arrow.

4. Now select the remaining box and drag it to roughly the same spot, and click the down keyboard arrow.

Major difference, right?

What you see is that the axis that would be parallel to the horizon in a single-point perspective (minor axis) is now perpendicular *in perspective* to the vanishing point you have aligned it to. In other words, the object's minor axis recedes to the aligned vanishing point, and the major axis recedes to the opposite vanishing point. Up=Right; Down=Left.

Applying an Object to the Horizontal Grid

Click the original object with the Perspective tool, and drag it toward the front of the floor of the grid (in reality, it's being moved to the bottom of the page). Click either the up or down keyboard arrow to attach it to the grid. The same movement rules (see "Mousing on a Grid" sidebar) apply to this grid surface as the vertical grid.

Raising or Lowering the Point of View

With the object on the floor selected, hold down the Shift key, and move the cursor over the lowest edge of the floor grid. The Smart Cursor will gain a downward-pointing triangle with a line below it. Click the mouse down and drag up or down. The object will remain on the grid, but its perspective will change as you modify the viewpoint of the grid.

Note: This action does not move the object above the original in a line perpendicular to the bottom of the page, as you might expect, but has instead moved the *grid*, and therefore changes the perspective and relative position of objects. The object is still in the same exact space in the grid, but because the point of view has changed, the object will seem to have moved.

Arranging the Vanishing Points

Common sense would tell you that the vanishing point would remain on the desktop, or possibly even within the document margins. Well, wrong again. The vanishing points can be dragged well outside the edges of the document. That's a great feature, because you can set vanishing points that don't have such severely receding lines. To move the vanishing point, select the Perspective tool and click+drag the vanishing point as far as you want. Zoom back to get even farther from the page—and a better view of what you're doing.

Duplicating an Object and Changing Its Point of View

To duplicate the object and modify the point of view of the grid while keeping the object attached to the grid, hold down the Shift+Opt/Alt keys and drag the edge of the grid (see Figure 8.12).

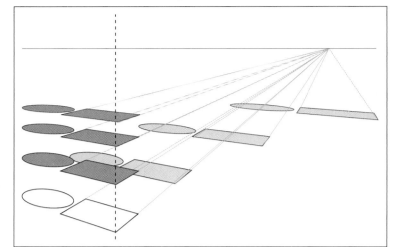

Duplicating a Grid

Hold down the Opt/Alt key and drag the front edge of the grid. Objects on the existing grid will remain as they are, and a new grid will move to the position you take it to. The View menu will now have "Grid 2" or the next consecutive number added to the list of grids in the document.

Duplicating an Object on a Grid

Select an object on a grid and clone, duplicate, copy, or Opt/Alt+drag it. The object will be applied to the grid in the same perspective as the original, but its position or location will vary according to your means of duplication. A clone will be in the same place, a duplicated copy will be offset slightly, a pasted copy will be wherever you click the cursor, and the Opt/Alt+drag will be placed where you let the mouse go. To reapply it to any of the grids, hold the Perspective tool down on the selected object, and click the appropriate keyboard arrow.

Changing Dimensions of an Object on the Grid

This one is tricky at first. There are six ways in which to change the dimensions of an object on a grid *one pixel at a time* while retaining its perspective. Click an object with the Perspective tool. To enlarge height and width equally, click the 2 key; to enlarge width, click the 4 key; to enlarge height by one pixel, click the 6 key. To reduce the height and width equally, click the 1 key; reduce width by clicking the 3 key; reduce the height by clicking the 5 key.

Flopping an Object on the Grid

To flop an object horizontally on a side grid, or vertically on the floor grid, click the Perspective tool on the object and hold. Then press the Spacebar and release it and the mouse. The object will flip, giving the impression that it is imprinted on the outside of a window and you are viewing it from inside the room.

Hiding a Grid

To hide the floor grid, double-click the Perspective tool on the horizon. Double-click the vanishing points to hide vertical grids. Double-click the same locations to make the grids reappear.

Text on a Grid

Placing text on a grid follows the same procedure as placing an object. Editing the text is a different story, however. Select the Perspective tool, double-click the text you wish to edit, and the Text Editor will appear. Make necessary changes, but be advised that the text will fill the original perspective-bounding box. In order to create the correct proportionate text in perspective, click the appropriate keyboard arrow, and a new perspective-bounding box will grow or shrink to the proper size.

Undoing Gridlock

To get an object off the grid, you have two choices. The first removes the object from the grid and releases perspective—in other words, turns it back into the original graphic. That's achieved by clicking View|Perspective Grid|Remove Perspective. The second choice is View|Perspective|Release With Perspective, which hides the grid, leaving the object(s) in perspective. Text that has been released from the grid cannot be edited as text because it has been converted to grouped paths—do your editing before removing the grid.

PROJECT Let's Do Lunch

This project will take you through some of the basic techniques of the Perspective Grid. If you have followed the preceding tutorial, you probably have a pretty good grasp of all the cool things the grid does—and doesn't do. I am purposely not using simple graphic shapes in this exercise, because those projects just don't enter the real world that often. Instead, you'll make lunch—stylized clip art of a bologna sandwich on a plate. First, set the table.

The Plate

I must confess, in this exercise, you will cheat the viewer, but I doubt that you'll get caught. The plate will consist of a decorated top surface, with the usual indents or lower layers that plates have.

1. Open the file named Lunchtime.fh10 in the Chapter 8 folder on the CD-ROM. Save it to your hard drive. Create a new page in the Document Inspector (triangle|Add Pages).

2. I encourage you to actually draw (trace) the figures if you're not absolutely adept with the various FreeHand drawing tools. At any rate, draw the concentric circular shapes at the top left, and/or drag them onto the new page.

3. Draw the triangular shape, leave it selected, and click the Mirror Xtra in the Toolbar. Enter "20" in the input text box, and choose Multiple and Rotate in the drop-down menus.

4. Click the Mirror cursor at the apex of the triangle and release the mouse. You will have 20 identical triangle shapes arranged on the circles. Save.

5. To give an impression of the plate being a very shallow cone, drop the center points to create an artificial perspective. Click the Pointer tool in an open space between the triangles and drag a selection around the very center, where all the triangles meet. Depending on how accurate your clicking was with the Mirror Xtra, you may see only one point selected.

6. Hold down the Shift key and click the down keyboard arrow two times to move the apexes down 20 points.

7. Leave the triangles selected, and Shift+select the largest circle *inside* the main circle. Click the Union Xtra. Give the finished group a fill of Plate Center Blue with a stroke of None.

8. Select the outer circle and clone it. Give it a fill of Plate Blue and a 0.5-point stroke of black. Send it to the back. Select the larger circle again and select Blues from the Styles panel. Apply a stroke of None.

9. Opt/Alt+click the next to smallest circle, and give it a fill of Plate Center Blue, no stroke. Opt/Alt+click the next largest circle, give it a fill of Plate Highlight Blue, and a 1-point stroke of white. The plate should look like Figure 8.13.

Figure 8.13
The finished plate. Notice the slight distortion of the triangular shapes at the left and right.

Slicing the Bread

Cutting the bread will entail using the Knife tool in a different way that has been used in this book so far. There's also a clever little trick for taking a "bite" out of shapes.

1. You need the bread outline. Draw, trace, or copy it from my document. Give it a white fill.

2. Double-click the Knife tool, and in the resulting dialog box, choose the following options: Tool Operation = Straight; Width = 0; Options = Close Cut Paths and Tight Fit. Click OK.

3. Select the bread outline, and drag the Knife tool across the bread roughly in the same manner as the first of the progressive drawings shown in Figure 8.14.

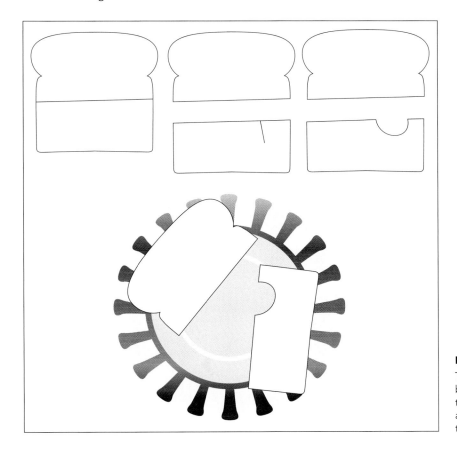

Figure 8.14

Top, left to right: the bread slice being cut in half; a "slice" put in the bread with the Knife tool; and the "bite" arranged. Bottom: the bread arranged on the plate.

4. Cmd/Ctl+Shift+click the top half, and drag the bottom half down a half-inch or so.

5. The Knife tool should still be selected—make a small "slice" downward about halfway to the bottom of the shape.

6. Switch to the Pointer tool and either click anywhere to deselect, or press the Tab key. Select the bottom bread slice again, and Shift+select one of the new points the Knife tool added.

7. Drag the point toward a corner of the bread slice, then drag the other new point the same distance toward the other corner. Adjust the Control Handles until it looks like a "bite" has been taken out.

8. Rotate and arrange the bread on the plate as shown at the bottom of Figure 8.14. Save.

PROJECT Setting the Table

You made the basic ingredients for this project in the "Let's Do Lunch" project. Now, use the Perspective Grid to create the table setting. Then it's just a matter of making the sandwich.

Start with the drawing you completed in the "Let's Do Lunch" project.

1. Go to View|Perspective Grid|Show, then select View|Perspective Grid|Define Grids. Enter three vanishing points, set the cell size to 108, and click OK.

2. Zoom out to the smallest view you can get, probably 6%. Move the vanishing points well off the page. You can see in Figure 8.15 just how far off the page my vanishing points are. Feel free to vary your perspective to something more or less dramatic. Be advised that if you do move your vanishing points off the workspace, you will not be able to adjust them. You'll have to delete the grids and create new ones.

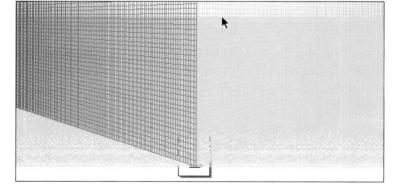

Figure 8.15
The vanishing points are well off the FreeHand pasteboard. The cursor is on the horizon, and a good three pages above the drawing.

3. Using the Pointer tool, do a Select All and group the plate and bread arrangement, then switch to the Perspective tool. Click and release the down keyboard arrow to apply the objects to the floor grid. Keep the mouse button down, and move the group around until it is placed similarly to the group in Figure 8.16. Save, and even duplicate the page if you like, because you are about to make changes that are not easily undone.

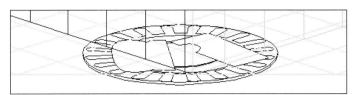

Figure 8.16
The plate and bread pieces from the "Let's Do Lunch" project have been attached to the floor grid. Note the plate is off the front of the grid. This is lunch, not brain surgery; you're allowed a little artistic license.

4. Select the plate and bread, and choose View|Perspective Grid|Release With Perspective. Click the Pointer tool and ungroup the drawing. Hide the bread slices, and Shift+select all the inner ellipses (the only thing not selected is the 20-triangle pattern and the outer ellipse). Click the down keyboard arrow three times.

5. Deselect the outer ellipse and the next largest ellipse. Move them down an additional three clicks.

6. Select only the smallest circle and move it downward another two clicks.

You may remember cloning the outer rim of the plate. Here's where you use it:

7. Click the outer ellipse and hide it. The lighter colored clone should be in view. Click it, and use the down keyboard arrows to move it downward about four clicks to give the edge of the plate some dimension. Save.

8. Clone this ellipse. Click the Perspective tool and press and release the down keyboard arrow (remember, anything you do to objects applied to the grid with a tool other than the Perspective tool removes that object from the grid—now you're putting it back). With the mouse still held down, shift the ellipse until it creates what would be a good shadow area. Release the mouse.

9. Release the shadow ellipse from the grid (View|Perspective Grid|Release With Perspective), and give it a fill of white and a stroke of None. Clone it.

10. Use the Scale tool approximately in the center of the ellipse, and shrink the clone to about two-thirds size. Give it a fill of 15% black.

11. Shift+select the larger shadow ellipse, and blend the two ellipses. Send the blend to the back. Save. The plate should look relatively three-dimensional by now, as shown in Figure 8.17.

Luck with Layers

If you group objects from different layers together, be aware that ungrouping them sometimes changes the layer order. It's a good idea to keep an eye out for objects that seem to have disappeared, or popped to the front.

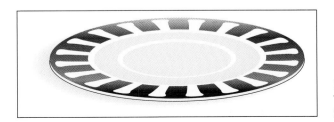

Figure 8.17
The plate and its shadow in perspective.

Making the Sandwich

You will create the depth of the bread slices, and discover some of the hidden pitfalls of the Perspective Grid and how to overcome them. Above all, remember that this grid is nothing but an extremely powerful tool, and like any tool, someone has to provide the labor and input to get the job done—and that's where you come in.

To start, you are going to create the top surface of the bottom slices of bread by cloning and moving the floor grid. You will repeat the process for the top slices of bread.

1. Make sure the Perspective tool is still selected, and unhide the bread (Edit|Show All). If you try to Shift+Select the two pieces of bread, you'll be frustrated, as it can't be done. Instead, hold down the Cmd/Ctl key as you Shift+Select the second piece.

2. Release the Cmd/Ctl key, hold down Shift+Opt/Alt, and move the cursor toward the bottom of the floor grid until it (the Smart Cursor) gains a downward-pointing triangle with a line beneath it. Click the mouse, and drag upward until you think the bread slices are thick enough. Release the mouse and modifier keys.

3. Drag a guideline out from the side that aligns with the leftmost point of the bottom bread slice, drag another for the right-most corner of the other slice.

4. Depending on where your vanishing points have been placed, the cloned bread slices might or might not align with the vertical lines. I'm betting they won't align, so select them one at a time with the Perspective tool and maneuver them until they align directly above the bottom outlines.

5. Repeat the process, using the clones you just made, and create the second slice of bread above the first, allowing room for the sandwich filling.

Getting Crusty

You can proceed with the next step of creatng fills in quite a few ways, but here you'll do it with the Punch Xtra and a little elbow grease. I'll describe the top-left slice of bread, and you will use the same techniques to finish the other three slices.

1. Start by clicking the Pointer tool and selecting the top surface of the left bread slice and cloning it.

2. Shift+select the bottom of the slice, and click the Punch Xtra. Adjust the corner point on the right side of the "punch" so it matches the top surface of the bread.

Note: You can read about the Smart Cursor in Chapter 2.

Note: It bears repeating that once you move an object with anything other than the Perspective tool, it falls off the grid. The last perspective shape the object had will remain, but it won't be moveable and perspective-able on the grid. If you see that it has happened, don't panic; just click the appropriate keyboard arrow and all will be well again.

Looking through the Bars

If you are distracted by the grid lines—and there are a lot of them, aren't there?—simply click them off (View|Perspective Grid|Show). The grid will still be active, but not visible. Then, when you need to move a grid or vanishing point, use the same command to bring them back to the page. You can even create a custom keyboard shortcut to make it more convenient. If you want to see the grid but be less distracted, you can change the size of the cells in the View|Perspective Grid|Edit menu.

3. Adjust the left side of the "punch" to fit the top of the bread.

4. Clone the top surface of the bread, select the two points that are where the knife cut it, and use the Split command. Select just the crust part of the bread and use the Expand Stroke Xtra with a 2-point width. Fill it with "Darkest Crust" and give it a stroke of None.

5. Double-click the Roughen Xtra, and enter "35" and Roughen. Select the crust outline and drag the mouse a little to add a slight organic feeling to the crust. Hide it.

6. Give the remaining path that defined the cut the color of "Dark Bread" and hide it.

7. Select the top of the slice, give it a fill of "Bread" and a stroke of None.

8. Select the crust that you created with the Punch Xtra, and apply the Style named "Top crust of bread." Go to the Fills panel and adjust the colors in the Color Well until they match the curves of the bread. Save. Hide everything that makes up the slice.

9. Repeat the steps, referring to the crust of the bread for the bottom slice (the top surface of that slice will not be seen, so you can delete it).

10. The right slice of the bread is a bit more complicated due to the bite, but follow the previous instructions for the crust and top surface of the bread. Apply the "Bottom crust of bread" style to the side crust.

11. The cut face of the bread is filled with "Dark Bread," and the bite area uses the Style named "Bite out."

12. As with the other slice, hide everything you've completed and finish the bottom slice. Save. Your drawing should be something like the one in Figure 8.18.

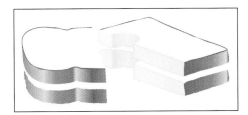

Figure 8.18
The basic bread slices.

Meat and Lettuce

If you are a vegetarian, this is a tofu sandwich, if not, call it bologna. At any rate, start by drawing a loose shape that roughly outlines the open areas between the slices of bread. You only need half a dozen points to create the shapes. Make one for the left half, another for the bite area, and a third for the right half.

1. Double-click the Roughen Xtra, and enter "20" and Smooth. Select the three shapes you just drew and drag the mouse to get a curly, wavy line that has a slight resemblance to lettuce. Give it a fill of "Light Lettuce."

2. Clone the shapes, click the Scale tool, but do not hold down the Shift key, which would give you a proportional resizing. Instead click the mouse and drag down and watch the wavy line get smaller in the vertical scale, but remain roughly the same width. Give it a fill of "Lettuce." Use the Roughen Xtra again, just enough for "character."

3. Repeat the last step, giving the shapes a fill of "Dark Lettuce." Save.

4. For the meat (or tofu), draw a path that roughly divides the lettuce in the middle of the right slices. Use the Expand Path Xtra to widen the path until it is about as thick as two slices of bologna. Adjust the end points so they appear more or less vertical. Give it a fill of "Bologna." Save.

5. Lather on a little mustard by drawing another path down the center of the meat/tofu. Expand the path about a third as much as you did to create the meat layer. Add curve points and create drips and dribbles. Give it a fill of "Mustard." Save.

Finishing Touches

All that's left to do is to add some texture and some shadows. You will use the Graphic Hose and some Transparent Lens fills. One note of warning: the Graphic Hose can really bog down a file when it comes to printing. If you have to use it, then go ahead and keep adding details, but try to restrain yourself. A good test is to print the document now and then. If your laser or ink jet printer chokes, chances are that the service bureau's output device or Web application will as well.

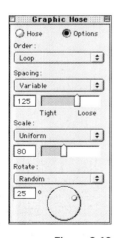

Figure 8.19
Options for the Graphic Hose air holes and crumbs.

1. Create a small shape (I used the Ellipse tool) that will become the air holes in the bread. Fill it with "Dark Bread." While it is selected, copy it, and double-click the Graphic Hose Xtra. Choose New from the drop-down menu and click Paste In.

2. Click the Options radio button and set the attributes as seen in Figure 8.19.

3. Splatter holes all over the top surfaces of the bread.

4. Select the original air hole, and change the fill to "Bread in Shadow." Copy it, double-click the Graphic Hose Xtra, and click Paste In again. Spray holes in the front surfaces of the bread. I dropped a few crumbs onto the plate, because there are always crumbs on a sandwich plate.

5. You have the idea now. Create darker spots to texture the crust of the bread slices.

6. To finish it off, use the Pen tool to draw a shadow on the plate. Give the shadow a Lens Fill of Transparent, with a value of 10% to 15%. I took it two steps further and added shadows on the bottom slices of the crust, under the lettuce, and I cloned some of the crumbs that are in direct light, shifted them slightly, and gave them the same Transparent Lens fill. So much for restraint. Your drawing should look similar to the one in Figure 8.20.

> **Note:** Yes, the sandwich looks a little sad. I wouldn't want to have to buy a lunch that looked like this. You can go the extra mile by selecting each of the bread slices and changing their outlines just enough to make them more realistic. You can also place more filling in the sandwich— more meat, cheese, lettuce, tomatoes, onions—knock yourself out!

Figure 8.20
A bologna sandwich constructed on the Perspective Grid.

7. Save, print. Hang it on the refrigerator. Make a sandwich; all this work has probably made you hungry.

Mom's Diner Sign

This project is a further exploration of the Perspective Grid. Whereas the sandwich was mainly created on the floor grid, the diner sign you make here will be on a side plane, and you'll be duplicating grids and moving the floor up to a ceiling level. Then you'll release the artwork from the grid and render the sign.

In order to speed up the process a bit, I've started the graphics for you. Also, in case you want to get really technical about what neon lighting looks like, I added some photos of neon in the Chapter 8 folder on the CD-ROM for you to examine. It's pretty fascinating, to say the least.

1. Start by opening the file Mom's Diner.fh10 on the CD-ROM. Save it to your hard drive. Go to View|Perspective Grid|Show.

2. The first thing you'll notice is that the grid is brighter than the default. You can change the colors to anything you want in the View|Perspective Grid|Define Grids dialog box. The sign graphic is huge, wider than the page, but when you put it into perspective, it will be a more workable size. Click the Perspective tool and select the sign, then click and release the right keyboard arrow.

> **Note:** As of this writing, FreeHand 10 and Macintosh OS X are both new, and subject to odd things happening. One such behavior is that in building this file using OS X, the grid names would not select correctly; when a grid was selected, a checkmark occurred for the grid above it in the list. Hopefully by the time you read this, the problem will have been fixed. It's only a name—the grid is what counts, and it works fine.

How Many Grids Do I Need?

Why would you duplicate the art *and* the grid instead of just cloning the art and moving it with the grid? The main reason is that if you want to align something *new* to either of the grids, having two grids would be helpful because you wouldn't have to attempt to get the grid in the same exact alignment you had previously. Working on the document later or sharing the work with others can greatly benefit by having separate grids (with different color schemes).

If you don't think you'll need the grid later on, then just move the grid and the art in one movement. Click the Perspective tool, select the art, and hold down Shift+Opt/Alt. Move the mouse until you see the Smart Cursor add a triangle and line pointing away from the vanishing point. You will see the cursor change whenever it nears a gridline. Click the mouse and drag the grid and the art to the new position.

Note: When moving objects on the grid, you only get to see the bounding box and the grid move. It's a lot easier to make critical alignments if you click a "landmark" on the object as you drag. The bounding box has a diagonal line through it if it is an object attached to the grid. A bounding box without the diagonal line is not attached, and will not reflect changes in its perspective.

Figure 8.21
The back of the sign and the grid have been shifted eight cells to the left.

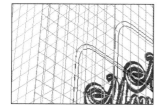

Figure 8.22
The back of the sign has been shifted into the correct position and aligned with the left vanishing point.

3. Move the sign until the left edge aligns with the intersection of the two vertical grids. Slide it upward until the upper-left corner of the bounding box is approximately on the upper blue guideline. Release the mouse.

If you wanted a flat, painted sign, you would be finished, but you are going to add depth to it. As stated previously, the Perspective Grid isn't going to do it for you—it's here as a drawing *aid*. There are two ways to proceed: you can clone and move the art in one movement using the same grid that's in use presently; or, you can duplicate the grid and the art, and move them at the same time. The difference will be that in the first method, the grid moves, and therefore will not be perfectly aligned with the original art as it is at this point in the drawing. The second method leaves the original grid and art in place, and adds a second grid. Because you will be adding text to the sign later in the project, you will duplicate the grid.

4. Go to View|Perspective Grid|Define Grids, and click the Duplicate button. Double-click the name in the list and change it to "Back of sign." Change the colors in the grid, if you wish, by clicking the Color Well and selecting a new color. If you wanted to, you could also change the grid cell size. Click OK. Save.

5. Select the sign art with the Perspective tool, and clone it. Then hold down the Shift key and move the mouse toward the vertical intersection of the grids. When the cursor gains a small line and a triangle pointing to the right, click the mouse and drag the grid eight cells to the left. Release the mouse. The result is shown in Figure 8.21.

6. Take note of the line running from the top-left corner of the original sign to the left vanishing point. Hold the Shift key down again (to constrain movement on the grid), and click the mouse down on the top-left corner of the new sign. Drag to the right until the cursor is on the same receding line as the original sign (see Figure 8.22).

When you move a grid and an object stays on the grid, you actually change where that object is, in relation to where the viewer is stationed. That means it either gets larger (closer to you), or smaller (farther away). Constraining the object to the grid with the Shift key maintains the object's location in space and relationship to other objects on the grid. Moving it back as you have done in the project brings it to the correct proportionate size, and achieves perfect perspective.

7. Odd as it seems, the back of the sign is now in the foreground. Send it to the back. Then select the front of the sign and hide it.

8. Hide the grid and select the back of the sign. Go to View|Perspective Grid|Release With Perspective. Ungroup it and delete everything except the outer rounded rectangle and outer circle. Use the Union Xtra on the ellipse and the rounded rectangle to create a single shape.

9. Choose Edit|Show All to bring back the front of the sign. Release it from the grid with perspective as you did the back of the sign. Ungroup it. Save.

10. Using the Pen tool, draw triangles that meet the tangents of the round corners at top left and bottom right of the sign, and at the top of the circle, as shown in Figure 8.23. The inner points of the triangles must create a shape large enough to encompass the area between front and back signs.

11. Select all three triangles and the back of the sign. Then click the Union Xtra to create a single closed shape.

12. Clone the front outer rounded rectangle and circle, and use the Union Xtra on them. Shift+select the back of the sign and use the Punch Xtra, creating thickness for the sign. The result should look similar to the right side of Figure 8.23. Save.

Figure 8.23
Triangles in the left image (bold only for visibility) will be joined to the back side of the sign using the Union Xtra. The results are shown on the right.

I am purposely keeping it simple at this point. You'll find a color version of this project in the Color Studio section, but in that version I added more dimension to the drawing by extruding the circle shape. I also added a Transparent Lens Fill as a shadow. Using what you learn in this project, you can create the same results. The shape surrounding "Mom's" was manipulated with Inset Paths and Punch Xtras to create a highlight and shadow suggesting that the lettering is embossed.

Rendering the Sign

With the basic construction complete, you can start adding color to the sign. The file I provided contains all the colors used in the final drawing, plus several styles. I'll use styles to speed up the exercise and reduce the tedium of color selection. Feel free to change colors to anything you like.

1. Select both of the rounded rectangle paths and the circle paths and clone them. Deselect them and Shift+select the outer two paths. Click the Union Xtra to create a single shape. Hide it.

2. Select the circle and rounded rectangle shapes, and bring them to the front. Choose Edit|Show All to bring the large shape back beneath the rectangle and circle shapes.

3. Shift+select the circle, the rounded rectangle, and the larger combined shape. Click the Punch Xtra two times. You have now created a single outline shape that can be filled with the "Sign frame" style. Place it on a new layer named Frame. Save.

4. Give the sign face, sign rim, circle, cup, and saucer their respective styles through the Styles panel. Place each on its own layer as you work.

5. Hide the neon lettering and the red "Diner" word. The drawing should be similar to Figure 8.24. Keep in mind that your placement of the drawing on the grid will be slightly different than mine, and the perspective could be modified.

6. Choose Edit|Show All to bring back the lettering. Select the red lettering and place it on a new layer named Floater. Hide the red lettering, and select the neon outlines. Ungroup them and put them on a new layer named Neon Reflection. Shift+select the letter forms, but leave the circles alone. Group the lines. Shift+select the circles, group them, give them a Basic fill of 75% black, a stroke of None, place them on a layer named Holes, and hide them.

7. Select the letter forms, and click the Expand Path Xtra. Enter a line width of 2 points, and give the line round caps and joins. Click OK.

Note: By punching out the background, you have deleted a lot of information that FreeHand and the printing device do not have to deal with. It would be very easy to give it a fill, then place the sign face on top of it. But then the computer and output device have to write the code and delete it before screen display or outputting can occur. It's cleaner this way.

Note: If you want to get technical about the way neon is used, you can make dark areas and use Paste Inside to darken the ends of the tubes as they go inside the sign body. For the project, we'll keep it simple, however.

Figure 8.24
The basic sign shape has been rendered. The neon lettering is hidden.

8. Give the letter forms the "Neon reflection" style.

9. Clone the letter forms and move them four clicks to the right with the right keyboard arrow. Change the style to "Front neon." Create a new layer for them named Neon Lights.

10. Choose Edit|Show All, then hide both sets of neon lettering and the circles. Select the red lettering and clone it. Give it the "Floating Diner" style, put it on a new layer named Floater, and move the layer beneath the Neon Reflection layer. Hide it.

11. Select the remaining lettering and change the fill to Lens, Darken 38%. Click the down keyboard arrow until the lettering is just above the frame of the sign. Create another new layer named Floater Shadow for it, and drag the layer to just above the Face layer.

12. Choose Edit|Show All to see the rendered neon lettering as in Figure 8.25. If things are missing, it's a matter of adjusting the layers to bring them into view.

Finishing Touches
You need to add a support pole and a few more details to complete the project. You will bring the grid back into play, and create a couple of brushes.

1. Choose a full-page view, and show the Perspective Grid again.

2. Select the Perspective tool and move the center edge of the right grid to the approximate center of the bottom of the sign. Move the left grid to the right until it meets the right grid.

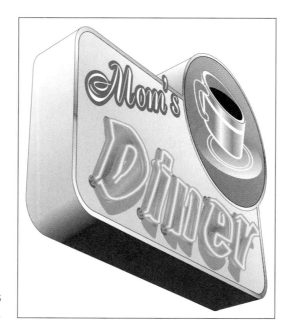

Figure 8.25

The neon rendering is complete.

3. Using the Ellipse tool, draw a 5-pica circle (change the units of measure at the bottom of the application window, if necessary). Save.

4. Select the Perspective tool and click the new circle. Drag it toward the bottom of the page, then click and release the down keyboard arrow.

5. Now drag the ellipse to the intersection of the left and right grids on the floor at the bottom of the page. Zoom in to get it as accurately placed as you can; the document should look similar to Figure 8.26.

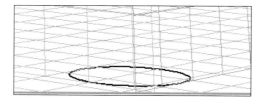

Figure 8.26

The ellipse indicating the bottom of the support pole on the floor grid.

6. Using the Line tool, drag a line from the extreme left edge of the ellipse up to the sign, aligning the line with the grid (the line may or may not be on a grid line; the important factor is that the line follows the grid).

7. Repeat that procedure for the right side of the ellipse. Save.

8. Make a copy of the grid (View|Perspective Grid|Define Grids|Duplicate); hold down the Shift key, and move the mouse toward the bottom of the page until the Smart Cursor gains a line and a downward-pointing triangle. Hold the mouse button down and slowly drag the bottom of

the floor grid up to meet the bottom of the sign. The trick is to get the grid line pointing to the right vanishing point aligned perfectly with the sign bottom.

9. When you release the mouse, a copy of the ellipse should appear near the sign's bottom. Use the Perspective tool to move the ellipse under the sign, and between the lines representing the pole outlines.

10. If the ellipse doesn't fit the pole sides exactly, you can adjust the size of the ellipse by holding the Perspective tool down on the ellipse and clicking the 1 key on your keyboard to reduce the ellipse, or the 2 key to enlarge it.

11. Adjust the pole sides to align perfectly with the ellipse sides, make a closed path out of them, and use the Union Xtra to give the pole an elliptical base and top. Give the pole the "Chrome" style, and adjust the angle so the fill is aligned with the pole. Save. The top pole arrangement should be similar to Figure 8.27.

> **Note:** If you've been paying close attention, you'll remember that you have to remove the ellipses from the grids before you can modify them, such as you are doing with the Union Xtra.

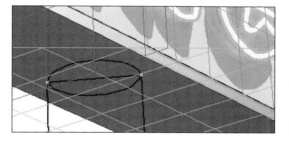

Figure 8.27
The upper limit of the support pole on the ceiling grid, just before the Union Xtra is used and the pole is filled.

12. Add a row of rivets for texture by creating a rivet brush: Draw a very small circle—about 2.25 points wide and 2.25 points tall. No fill. Zoom in to a high degree of enlargement, such as 800%. Make the path a dark blue hairline, and use the Knife tool to cut the circle in half diagonally from top left to bottom right. Change the top path color to white.

13. Select both halves of the circle and go to Modify|Brush|Create Brush. Choose Copy in the dialog box. Set the new brush to spray, and change the Spacing to 250%. Save the brush as Light Rivets.

14. Zoom in on the rivet semicircles again. Change the top color to dark blue, and the bottom color to black. Create a brush from this grouping with the same settings as above. Name it Dark Rivets. Save.

15. Select the thick edge of the sign (the *L* shape) and clone it. In the Inset Path Xtra choose 2.5 points with sharp corners and joins.

16. Remove the top horizontal path, and adjust the vertical paths to reach and wrap to the top of the sign side.

17. Cut both paths with the Knife tool as they begin to curve under the sign. Select both vertical paths and apply the Light Rivets brush to them. Reverse direction of the path on the right. Save.

18. Cut the bottom line as it intersects either side of the supporting pole, and delete the middle section. Remove the connecting path on the right side, and adjust the paths as you did the vertical side. Apply the Dark Rivets brush to the three paths on the bottom of the sign. Reverse direction of the paths on the bottom. Adjust path end points so the rivets don't go over the supporting pole or off the sign. Save.

One More Thing

Something is still missing. Add a line of type to complete the sign:

1. Click the Text tool and select a bold sans-serif font, such as Helvetica or Arial Black. Type "DOWN HOME COOKING" then click the Perspective tool and select the text block.

2. Press and release the right keyboard arrow to apply the text to the sign face. Maneuver the text until it fits between "Mom's" and "Diner."

Hmmm. Doesn't fit. If you try to scale it, it will be too small to read. It's better that you edit the text.

3. Hold down the Shift key and double-click the text block with the Pointer tool. No, it's not very intuitive, but it brings up the Text Editor box, and now you can change the type to read, "24 Hour." Click OK.

4. Select the Perspective tool and move the new text into place. If it's too small, you can change it in the Text Editor again, or use the number keys on the keyboard. Both methods work, but you're probably better off using the Text Editor for more precise control. Save.

The completed art should look very similar to Figure 8.28. Print out the finished drawing, and tape it close to the sandwich on the refrigerator.

Note: Look closely, and you'll see that the new text has expanded to fit the old text frame. That's not good, but the fix is easy: Select the text with the Perspective tool and tap the respective keyboard arrow key to resize the text.

Note: A color version is located in the Color Studio of the book, and it's been made into a Flash movie on my Web site at **www.nidus-corp.com/Mom.html.**

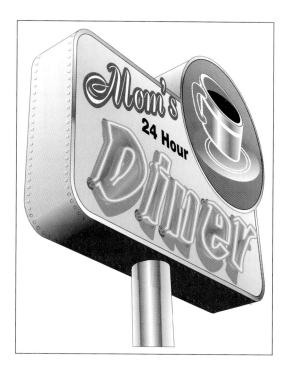

Figure 8.28
The completed sign.

Moving On

In this chapter, you learned the various methods of drawing projections that allow you to create 3D objects from 2D drawings. Whether you employ conventional methods, or use a grid to construct your drawings, FreeHand makes it pretty easy to do accurate work. The Perspective Grid takes a bit of practice, but once you've mastered it, you have a huge amount of control at your fingertips. In Chapter 9, you will learn more about FreeHand distortions, including the 3D Rotation Xtra and advanced use of the Envelope feature.

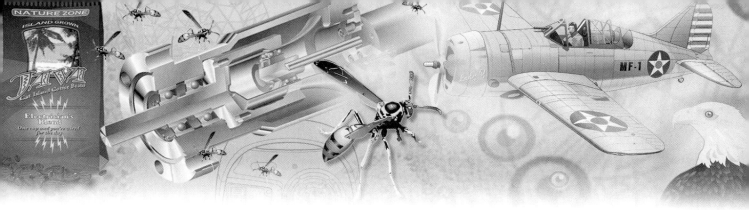

Chapter 9

Distorting the Truth

Creating a 3D construction in FreeHand doesn't necessarily begin or end with the Perspective Grid—the Envelope and 3D Rotation Xtra can supply some excellent results.

Lies, Lies, Lies

Seeing is believing. How many times have you heard that? I'm here to tell you that you can't always believe what you see. Not any more. The magic that can be done with computers today makes every photo, every movie, and every shadow suspect. Macromedia also has endowed FreeHand with features and tools that illustrators can use to dupe the masses. Everyone loves magic. Everyone loves to be fooled by sleight of hand, but it's especially enjoyable when we can't figure out how it was done.

Unfortunately, some software features leave you in that situation, and it isn't the least bit enjoyable; it's downright frustrating. FreeHand is no different. This program has a few very powerful attributes that can leave you scratching your head. The 3D Rotation Xtra is one; Envelopes are another. And then, there's the Perspective Grid (covered fully in Chapter 8). Each of these distortion tools has its specific properties and uses. The Perspective Grid allows you to place an object on a flat plane and achieve accurate perspective. The 3D Rotation Xtra lets you move a selected object through space in three dimensions—still on a flat plane, however. The Envelope feature may well be considered the most powerful of the three because even though nothing is "automatic," the manual distortions you create can achieve effects not possible with the other two methods.

The distortion tools in FreeHand have one minor drawback—you cannot use them to distort a bitmapped image. There are two ways to work around the situation. First, you can use the Trace tool if the bitmap is simple enough and you are willing to take the posterized image that results. Second, it's a very simple matter to draw the outer shape you want and export the shape as a Photoshop or EPS file. Open the bitmap file in Photoshop, and place the FreeHand shape. Use the Edit|Transform tools to make the bitmap fit the shape you've drawn. Save the distorted document as a TIFF (if you are going to print), or other applicable formats for your intended output. When the image is imported back into FreeHand, you can either paste it inside the path you previously distorted or place it where it belongs without the path. It doesn't amount to much more work, and the results are excellent.

3D Drawing in the Good Old Days

In the precomputer days, if you wanted something drawn with a 3D effect, you sketched, drew a lot of guidelines, and then traced off and inked or painted the final drawing. Then computers came along to change all that. Back in the late 1980s, few graphic artists had scanners. At that time, artwork was prepared in sort of a hybrid process. One printer wanted camera-ready layouts that would be shot on film with a process camera. Another wanted electronic files so he or she could output film directly. Photos were still being separated on process cameras, and colored artwork was handled with screen tints of colors. You indicated blocks of color with overlays of transparent acetate and a red or amber film, which was painstakingly cut by hand with an X-Acto knife. Ah, the good old days.

During this time, a project came into my shop that required a drawing with perspective. I had FreeHand on my trusty Macintosh SE (with 4MB RAM and a 20MB hard drive), and I wanted to do the drawing on the computer instead of using my traditional pen and ink method, but without a scanner I couldn't figure out a way to get my sketch into the computer so I could trace it. So I shot the sketch as a film positive (black lines on clear film) on my process camera. Then I carefully taped the film to my screen and traced my little heart out. What a chore! If I accidentally moved the page, I'd have to painstakingly move the film to match. Luckily, it was only the basis for the drawing, and I got the sketch's main lines into FreeHand, where I finally rendered it.

Thankfully, all that has changed for the better. Now you can create two-dimensional artwork and manipulate it in a variety of ways within FreeHand. From there, it can be output as final art, placed in a page layout program such as Adobe PageMaker, Adobe InDesign, or QuarkXPress for printing. Further, the vector art provided by FreeHand can be exported to Photoshop where—rastered as a bitmap, no vectors—it can be polished with airbrushing, graceful shadow effects, and so on. Naturally, the art can be transferred to the Web via Fireworks and Flash, as well.

3D for the Web

Which brings me to another use of FreeHand's distortion tools—Web graphics. As explained later in the chapter, the 3D Rotation Xtra creates some really quick 3D shapes. Put enough of them together on layers, then export them to Flash, and you have a movie that is much more realistic than a simple 2D enlargement and reduction that Flash can provide. The distortion tools can be very powerful—and fun, too.

FreeHand is not a match for a 3D rendering or CAD program. But then, it's not supposed to be. While a 3D or CAD program can whip out wireforms and fancy lighting effects and texture, they don't even start to handle text, multipage documents, or professional-quality printing output. Farther out on a limb, I'll say that FreeHand is arguably the best all-around drawing program—2D, 3D, or CAD. I said, "arguably," and will certainly get arguments from the Illustrator and CorelDRAW crowds. But byte for byte, FreeHand is the most capable of these tools, and the one program I'd want to have if it was the *only* program I could have. Please forgive the rant—I just want you to understand the direction FreeHand is coming from.

The 3D Rotation Xtra

This tool has been in the FreeHand arsenal for several versions. The first time you click it and start whipping objects around your monitor, you'll be amazed at how neat or cool it is. You can change quite a few of the tool's attributes, such as the distance from the vanishing point, the point from which the rotation occurs, and so on. The tool even has Easy and Expert modes, but most of those numbers and scales in the 3D Rotation dialog box leave you scratching your head as to anything useful the tool can do. You have to work hard to understand the tool. To make matters worse, not much has been written about it and its uses.

Well, I got tired of that, and set about creating steps for repeatability and predictability. You need repeatability and predictability to make any tool functional and profitable. What I learned comes down to the pure simplicity of the tool. It just does its thing—moves objects in three-dimensional space—but there isn't a lot of information available on how it works. Obviously, it has some real math-magical work going on in the background that's difficult to put a handle on.

Working with the 3D Rotation Xtra

You need hands-on experience to get the feel for and confidence in the 3D Rotation Xtra. Once you have a little know-how, you'll use this tool all the time. This tutorial will start you out.

Figure 9.1

The easy way to 3D (top), and the Rotate From menu (bottom).

Open the document named 3D.fh10 in the Chapter 9 folder on the CD-ROM. You'll see two graphics on the page that you'll explore. They're just odd shapes; don't try to make anything out of them. Start by double-clicking the 3D Rotation Xtra in the Xtras toolbar. You'll get the panel shown in Figure 9.1.

The window contains an Easy button, plus an Expert button to intimidate you. You figure that you're a pro, so you won't bother with Easy mode, but if you choose Expert mode, you'll soon find yourself in deep water, feeling terribly inadequate and going down for the third time. So you sheepishly go back to Easy mode and feel even more helpless. Well, click the Easy button, and I'll go through everything with you.

Rotate—What Rotates, and How?

The 3D tool is akin to a joystick of sorts. I have to get quite metaphoric here; try to hang on. Consider that the page you're looking at in FreeHand is a big piece of glass. The point of rotation will be a hole drilled in that sheet of glass in a particular spot (which you choose in the Rotate From menu by Mouse Click, Center of Selection, Center of Gravity, or Origin). Into that hole, you insert a skinny, rigid rod at exactly 90° perpendicular to the glass. When you click the mouse, that stick is pointing straight at your nose *from the Rotate From location.*

Now, slide a lubricated pipe that fits very snugly over the rod. The sliding pipe is where the mouse is holding on to that rod. When you move the mouse just a little, things can fly all over the page due to the joystick action your mouse has gained. As you move the stick (mouse) up, you rotate the glass back away from you. Move the stick down, and you'll rotate the glass forward from that hole you drilled in it. Move the mouse (stick) to the left, and it rotates, or spins *around* the point toward you. Slide the mouse to the right, and you will make the glass rotate or spin to the rear, away from you toward the horizon.

Are you still with me? Okay, on to the specifics of the "Rotate from" part of the 3D Rotation panel.

- *Mouse click*—The rotation will occur from wherever you click the mouse. If you click the mouse in different places on the page, the rotation will be different, too. Extremely different. Mouse click can also coincide with any of the other choices, by virtue of where you click the mouse. By that, I mean you can set the dialog box for Mouse click, then click the mouse at the Center of Selection and get the same results as clicking Center of Selection in the first place.

- *Center of Selection*—If you draw a bounding box around the object you want to rotate three-dimensionally and find the exact center of that box—that's where the hole in the glass will go. Center of Selection places the location of the rotation (sounds like a rhythm and blues group) exactly in the middle of the graphic element's bounding box.

- *Center of Gravity*—What happens here is that FreeHand takes into account the "weight" of the object or objects that are selected and then creates the rotation location. Think of it as similar to balancing a shovel. The end of the handle will be much farther from the balance point than the spade end, because the spade end weighs more. That balancing point toward the spade end is where you would be putting that hole through the glass. It's not anything that you can see. But if you add elements to the object, you will change the center of gravity. Color, solid fill, or no fill have no effect on this calculation. It is a matter of bounding-box size and placement.

- *Origin*—This places the rotation point at the bottom-left corner of the bounding box of the elements, period; as if the corner of the bounding box was nailed down.

The bottom slider is another option that is very powerful, but easier to understand. Set at the far right (near the small mountains), it has hardly any perspective distortion. Move the slider toward the large mountains on the left, and the distortions are more and more severe. Depending on your placement of the slider and the Rotate From point, you will make the graphics go around your chair in back of you, and then back onto the screen. It gets scary sometimes, but it's an interesting concept that there is more volume to the computer than the flat monitor. I would say that those types of distortions are unusable, but as you can't even see the object, it's not much of a comment. But, if the Rotate From point is within the object, you will get some extreme perspective views with the slider moved far to the left.

Easy Mode 3D Rotation Exercise

The Easy 3D Rotation explanation is now complete. Go back to the 3D.fh10 file you opened. At the top of the page is a graphic containing the word "3D" and some lines on a gray circle. These elements are for you to play with. You'll use the numbered boxes to test the effects of placing the mouse in different locations while changing the Rotation Location.

Several of the graphics are stacked on top of each other, so you can rotate one, then change mouse location and rotate another and compare the results visually. The thin lines above and below the "3D" letters show how the Center of Gravity affects the rotation. The vertical line is exactly in the center of the graphic and will act as an axis you can keep your eye on. The circle shape will provide feedback with certain rotation locations. Use the green line as a constant when you're trying different options. You'll see a small white circle in the top graphic and a gray circle in the lower graphic that indicate where the center of gravity for each graphic is located. The circles are on a locked layer above the graphics and have no "weight" in their respective graphics.

Explore the tool by clicking and dragging along the edges of the numbered boxes so you can gain a feeling for the way the tool reacts. When you've moved a few of the graphics, just select Undo until you're back to the black one, or choose Revert from the File menu to get back to where you started.

The file contains only one paddle-shaped graphic at the bottom of the page; you can create and stack clones if you wish. This graphic is heavily balanced to the left side, and the Center of Gravity will be quite pronounced. I constructed the shape so you can more easily see the graphic turn upside-down and backward. Remember, exploration is the *only* key to mastering the 3D tool.

Expert Mode 3D Rotation Exercise

The Expert mode of the 3D Rotation Xtra seems to simply add another layer of confusion to the Easy mode when you first struggle with it, but what it actually adds is the *viewpoint*. The naming convention is what's confused me all these years.

Open the 3D2.fh10 file. You will see the objects shown in Figure 9.2. The rotations are color coded to show their relationship to the circled letters at the bottom of the page. Each time, the 3D tool was dragged from the right end of the green line at "D" to the left end of the green line. In every situation, the only factor that was changed was the X value.

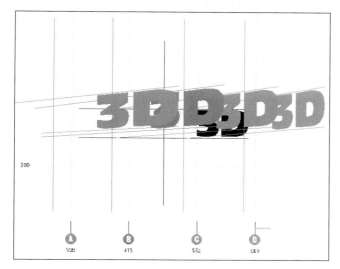

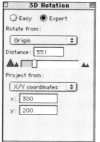

Figure 9.2
Only the X value in the Project From field was changed in the 3D Expert mode to create these very different perspective views.

As the X-coordinate changes, so does the viewpoint of the viewer watching the rotation. I have moved the rotation to be centered above the viewpoint. If you shut off the various layers, you can see a little better how the Project From portion of the panel works. The Rotation Location stays the same, via the Rotate From settings, but depending on where you are in the world—the X/Y Coordinates—you have a different view of the rotation. The fact that you can input those coordinates is probably the most important feature of the Expert mode. If you want to explore more, extra graphics are placed under the rotated figures in 3D2.fh10. Select the vertical center line to select the base graphics in order to rotate them.

PROJECT The Solar Paddle Wheel

So now that you know a little more about how the 3D Rotation Xtra works, *how* do you use it? The tough part about this tool has always been repeatability, but now that you understand it better, repeatability will be a snap. This short project will get you going.

Start by opening 3D paddlewheel.fh10 file from the Chapter 9 folder of the CD-ROM. Double-click the 3D Rotation Xtra and change the settings to those shown in Figure 9.3.

Because the desire is for repeatability, what better way to repeat something than to use a grid? A grid doesn't have to take up a whole page. To prove that premise, look at the top of the paddlewheel document. I made a blend with 10 steps in it. Then I extended the first line to the bottom of my grid. This particular grid is 1 cell high by 11 cells wide, and I have stacked 12 paddles for you to use.

1. Select the paddle and click the 3D cursor at the bottom of the line in the circle. Drag straight upward until you meet the dot at the guideline.

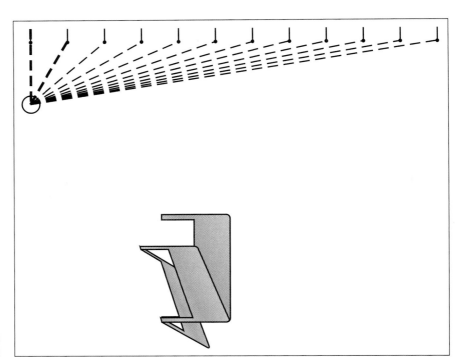

Figure 9.3

The 3D Rotation dialog box settings for the paddlewheel (left). The first two paddles have been rotated (right) as indicated by the bold dashed lines. The remaining dashed lines show the dragging path that will be drawn for the remaining paddles.

2. Click the next paddle, and click the 3D cursor in the same spot in the circle, but drag it to the next line/dot/guideline intersection. Watch the paddle as you move the tool.

3. Select the next paddle, drag the end point from the circle to the next dot intersection, and continue with the rest of the paddles until you've come to the end of the line.

4. After the second or third paddle, you'll notice that the paddlewheel looks a little strange. That's due to the stacking order of the paddles as they were drawn (cloned) and the order in which you're arranging them. You are moving paddles that are at the top of the stacking order to the backside of the paddlewheel. As soon as you see one hiding, bring it to the front, and continue bringing each one to the front until the stacking order is correct. Then maneuver the last couple into place.

5. The final solar paddle wheel is shown in Figure 9.4.

I can imagine that you've thought of at least one way to use the 3D Rotation Xtra in the future. Experiment further by changing the relationship of the paddles and the grid, and try entering different distances in the dialog box. Notice too, that gradient fills applied to an object before distortion with the 3D Rotation Xtra do not distort with the general shape. The gradient fill will stay at the same angle on every piece.

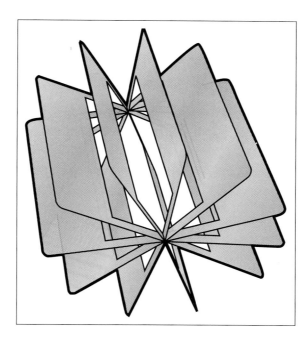

Figure 9.4
The 3D solar paddlewheel.

Envelope Manipulation

I really get a kick out of the Envelope toolset. It allows you to shape and form 2D graphics into—or onto—3D objects. For years we've had to draw the distortions from sketches. Now it's a simple matter to make your layout and use the Envelope to bend the layout into a new shape—text and all! Comps (comprehensive layouts) have never been easier. Yes, it requires you to know what you want to do, but no one said that FreeHand was a point-and-shoot style program. Using the Envelope simply calls for a little foresight.

The Envelope Feature Explained

An Envelope is a closed path that is attached to graphic objects or text that can then be manipulated or shaped and formed. When you start FreeHand 10 for the first time, you will have 21 default envelopes, each a different shape. Some are useful for basic perspective use (such as Peak Left or Fade Up), and others are more whimsical shapes (Heart, Double Arch, and so on). One beauty of Envelopes is that you can create your own, which remain in your Envelopes toolbar, available for use any time without searching through a Library or endless folders.

The Envelope starts its existence as a closed path. The path has points and control handles that affect the shape of the path. When the Envelope is applied to an object or text, the object or text attempts to form to the Envelope's path. Sometimes that is exactly what you were looking for; at other times, it's a big surprise. In either case, you are still able to manipulate the various points and control handles to distort your artwork.

It's interesting to note the way the Envelope attaches itself. If, for instance, you select several objects at once and apply the Envelope, the Envelope shape is applied to each object individually, not to the selection as a whole. If you want all the objects to be within the same shape distortion, you must group them first. And don't be lulled into the old Paste Inside routine—it doesn't work in this case. The shape that contains the Paste Inside will conform to the Envelope, but the contents will stay as they were before the Envelope was applied. This seems to be a general Brush, Perspective Grid, and Envelope philosophy—and that's good because this way all their attributes are easier to remember.

Distorting with the Envelope

Another interesting facet of the Envelope is the way it distorts. Take a look at the flag in Figure 9.5. The stripes are simple rectangles. (Thick paths would work as well.) But look how they twist and contort in the enveloped version. This effect could take quite some time with pencil and paper or vector drawing; FreeHand did it in a matter of a few minutes and relatively few movements. Obviously, you have noticed that the distorted drawing isn't completely accurate. A stripe dropped from under the star field, a star is actually out of the star field, and the star field flies off the flag a little bit at the top. But for a quick-and-dirty wavy effect, the Envelope works. If you wanted to use this graphic, you would need to release the Envelope *with changes* and add just a few more tweaks to adjust it to the quality you desired. Every time I look at this flag drawing, I think how nice it would be to adjust the shapes into an outline of the United States.

Figure 9.5

The Rectangle Envelope was applied to the flat flag on the left, resulting in the wavy flag on the right.

Envelopes and Text

Live text can be enveloped and edited further down the line. Using the Envelope tool with text is not as easy as clicking the Text tool and typing, however. Instead you use the same keyboard controls used for the Perspective Grid: Hold down Shift, or Opt/Alt, or Cmd/Ctl, or any combination of the three keys, and double-click your text to open the Text Editor. Once there, you can make any changes to the copy you wish, and click OK to see those changes immediately.

Figure 9.6
A circle Envelope and a radial gradient fill gives a pretty quick representation of three dimensions.

Adding or deleting characters will affect the appearance of the text drastically, so some rework of Envelope points may be necessary.

Text conformations are surprisingly quick and efficient with the Envelope feature. Figure 9.6 shows the progression of events involved in creating the balls with text on the bottom row of the figure. In the top row, text has been set on the left. In the middle, the text has been moved over a square, and on the right the text has been converted to paths and stretched to fit the square. On the left side of the middle row, the Round Envelope has been applied to the text (the square was deleted). In the second image, the Envelope has been copied as a path and pasted on the desktop. In the third image, the stroke has been deleted, and a radial gradient fill given to the circle. In the last image on the right, the text and circle have been aligned vertically and horizontally. The bottom row shows various color combinations that were applied and rotated.

Figures 9.7 and 9.8 show more examples of text distorted with Envelopes. The text in Figure 9.7 was distorted to give volume to the stomach drawing. The reflection effect shown in Figure 9.8 took less than a minute to accomplish.

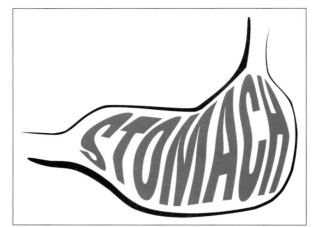

Figure 9.7
This text is "live," and the font, color, and even the letters themselves can be modified with a minimum of fuss.

Figure 9.8
This effect was achieved using the rectangle Envelope, adding four points to each vertical side, and shifting them. Very easy and effective.

PROJECT Flat Distortions

Okay, you've seen several examples of what an Envelope can do for you. Now you can try it yourself. In this project, you'll make a fake paperback book. First you will create the flat art, then you will apply an Envelope and shape the art into an approximation of perspective. The resulting artwork is something that would be seen in a direct mail piece or Web page.

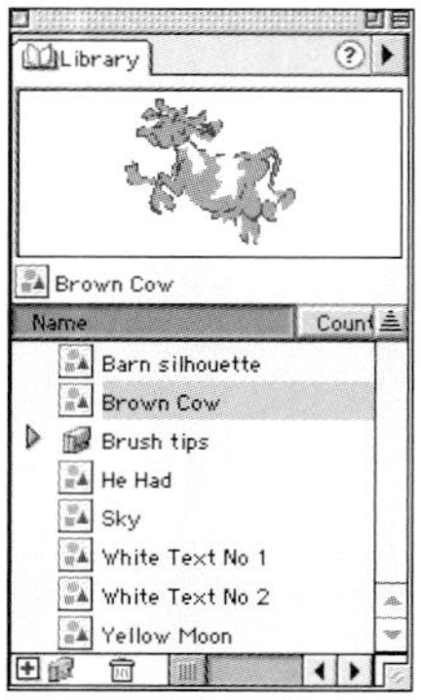

The Book Cover

I've done a lot of the graphic work for you already and saved it as symbols. Start by dragging The Novel Symbols found in the Chapter 9|Symbols folder on the CD-ROM into the FreeHand 10|English|Symbols folder. Open a new document and open the Library. Import The Novel Symbols.

Figure 9.9
The Library contains all the graphics necessary for this project.

1. The Library (Window|Library) is shown in Figure 9.9. Click Sky in the menu, and drag its preview icon to the center of the page. In the Layers panel, click the Foreground layer. Save the document as Cow Book.

2. In the Library again, click on the Barn silhouette icon and drag it to the page. Move it to the Barn layer in the Layers panel.

3. You'll use the Align panel to place your first two objects correctly. Select both objects on the page, and click the Align button in the menu bar. From the drop-down menus in the Align panel, choose Align Bottom and Align Center. Click Align. Save.

4. So far in this project, you've used two methods to get symbols out of the Library and onto your drawing. Use either technique to drag an instance of Yellow Moon to the page. Place it as shown in Figure 9.10 on its own layer named Moon.

Note: Why is the cow not a symbol? The cow was created with brush strokes; In FreeHand 10 at present, a combination of brush strokes, symbols, and Envelopes provides erratic results. It's best not to mix these three elements.

Figure 9.10
The background for the book cover is complete.

Import the file Flying Cow.fh10 from the Chapter 9 folder on the CD-ROM. Place it on the Cow layer, and move it so the cow is above the moon, as shown in Figure 9.11.

Now you can work on the book title:

1. The title will require a little room for manipulation, so go to the Object Inspector|Document panel, click the triangle, and add a page. Drag the instance called He Had to the page. Save.

2. Using the Rectangle tool, draw a square that encompasses the title, as shown on the left side of Figure 9.12. Select the text symbol and the square and use the Align command to center them vertically. Move the text just slightly below the center of the square. (The circle shown on the left side of the figure represents the circle that you will draw with the Fisheye Lens Xtra in a few steps.)

Figure 9.11
The jumping cow in place.

3. Select the text symbol and choose Modify|Symbol|Release Instance so you can manipulate the graphic with the Fisheye Lens Xtra. Do not deselect the graphic.

4. Double-click the Fisheye Lens Xtra, and enter a value of 60 by typing it in the Perspective field or by dragging the slider. Click OK.

5. The Fisheye Lens tool will still be selected. Drag a circle starting at the top-left corner of the square while holding down the Shift key to constrain the shape to a circle. Let go of the mouse when you get to the bottom-right corner of the square. The result should look like the right side of Figure 9.12. Save.

Figure 9.12
The before (left) and after (right) effects of the Fisheye Lens Xtra.

Fisheye Lens Trick

If you are feeling adventurous or have extra time on your hands, you can easily drag the Fisheye Lens tool over the selected object to get a distortion. But this method is sort of a hit and miss proposition. Start in the wrong spot and your distortion is, well, distorted. In other words, the center of the bulge or depression is in the wrong place. I've found it easier to use the "round-peg-in-a-square-hole" technique described here, which is an easy way to create absolute accuracy.

Keep in mind, too, that certain Xtras don't work on symbols—the Fisheye Lens is one of them. If you're working on someone else's document or something you haven't worked on in a long time, and Xtras don't seem to be working, check the Object Inspector panel. If it says you have an Instance selected, simply go to Modify|Symbol|Release Instance, and you'll be back in business.

6. Delete the square, and drag the distorted copy back to page 1. Place it on the Moon layer, centered over the moon.

7. Double-click the title graphics to bring up the transformation handles, then Shift+drag any corner to reduce the text until it fits inside the moon. Release the Shift key and drag a corner handle to rotate the text. Save.

8. Drag an instance of the White Text No 3 symbol onto the page, and place it between the moon and the barn. Create a Text layer and assign the title to that layer.

9. Drag an instance of White Text No 4 to the bottom of the page. Assign this to the Text layer as well.

10. In the Layers panel, click the checkmark to the left of the Moon and Cow layers to hide them. Choose Select All, and use Align to center everything vertically.

11. Make the Moon and Cow layers visible again and adjust them if the other elements shifted during alignment. Save.

12. Virtually everything in the document so far is a symbol, which will retard further distortion, so choose Edit|Select All and go to Modify| Symbol|Release Instance to create graphic objects that you can manipulate. Group everything and save. Your document should resemble Figure 9.13.

Note: When you placed the text in the square prior to the Fisheye Lens distortion, you placed it slightly below center. If you now have the text centered in the moon shape, the distortion will look out of place. Move it around until it looks like an authentic three-dimensional shape.

Adding Depth and Dimension

Now that the heavy lifting is done, it's time for the finishing touches. You will be using the Envelope feature to create perspective in this part of the project.

1. Begin by selecting the grouped cover artwork and rotate it with the Rotate Tool to approximately 20° to 25°.

2. Next, scroll to Rectangle in the Envelope drop-down menu.

Figure 9.13
The finished flat art for
the book cover.

**Should You Use Envelopes
or Perspective Grids?**

You can use the Perspective
Grid or create a "ballpark"
perspective. The perspective
that I'm looking for in the book
project is a book lying on a
coffee table viewed by a person seated fairly near that
coffee table. I also want the
text to be legible. Using the
Perspective Grid requires 2-
point perspective at a
minimum, and vanishing points
will be extended across the
whole FreeHand desktop. You
place the group on the floor
grid and hold the Shift key as
you move the vanishing points
around until you get the perspective you want. In my
experimentation, the artwork
ends up off the page after I've
maneuvered the vanishing
points until the book looks
"right." No problem. Once the
book is distorted to your liking
perspectively, release it from
the Perspective Grid and drag
it back onto the page.

3. Click the Create button in the Envelope toolbar. You should see 8 points
   marking the perimeter of the artwork. For this distortion, the mid-
   points are not necessary. Shift+select the points in the middle of each
   side, and delete them, leaving just the four corner points. Save.

4. The speed of your computer and the amount of RAM you have available to FreeHand will come into play here, but move the corner
   points—one at a time—until you have a respectable perspective going.
   You should only have to move three of the points (leave the bottom-left
   point as an anchor). Save. The document should look like Figure 9.14.

5. If you want to get creative, now you can click the Envelope path with
   the Pen tool to add points. Then you can manipulate the points to bend
   or curve the cover page of the book. The results would look similar to
   Figure 9.15.

6. Select the cover, click the Copy As Path button in the Envelope toolbar,
   and then go to Edit|Paste Behind. Choose Edit|Clone, then
   Modify|Arrange|Send To Back.

7. Hold down the Shift key and click the down keyboard arrow four or five
   times to add depth to the book. Save.

8. Select the cover artwork, click the Release button in the Envelope
   toolbar, group the results, and choose View|Hide Selection. Select the
   top rectangle and clone it. Shift+select the bottom rectangle and click
   the Union Xtra.

Figure 9.14
The square artwork has been transformed to a perspective view with an Envelope.

Figure 9.15
Add a few points and distort—it's a weathered book.

9. There are two "doglegs" in the new shape: one at the spine, on the bottom left, and another at the top right. Select the inner points at each dogleg and delete them (see Figure 9.16). This will make a straight path for the vertical edges of the book. Save.

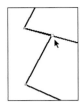

Figure 9.16
Remove the inner points of the "doglegs." This one is on the bottom left of the book's spine.

10. Send the new shape to the back, and Shift+select the top shape. Use the Punch Xtra to delete the bulk of the art that will be hidden by the cover. It also serves to give us all the pages in one shot. Save.

11. Add two or three Curve points to the bottom of the L-shaped path and adjust them so the bottom of the book doesn't have a straight edge.

12. Clone the new L-shaped graphic, and Shift+select the two points that make the spine (the straight path you created in Step 9). Also Shift+select the matching points on the right corner. Use Split to break the paths. Delete the straight sections.

13. Shift+select the two remaining paths and Blend them. Because the paths were created from a rectangle, the paths are running in opposite directions, which will cause your Blend to be pretty bizarre. You have two choices: do the Blend and select Xtras|Cleanup|Correct Direction; or select just one of the paths prior to blending and choose Xtras|Cleanup|Reverse Direction. Set the number of steps in the Blend to 15 (you can change this number later if you wish), and change the stroke weight to 0.25 points (hairline). Change the stroke color to PMS 720.

14. Fill the L-shape with a color of PMS 719, and give it a stroke of None. Save.

15. Choose View|Show All to bring the cover back into view.

16. Select the L-shape and the pages Blend, then choose View|Hide Selection. Opt/Alt+select the cover and clone it.

17. Give the cover clone a basic fill of 30% black, drag it to just below the bottom of the book's edges, then send it to the back. Adjust points as you feel necessary to achieve a good shadow effect. Choose View|Show All. Save. Print. Hang it on the refrigerator next to the other bestsellers you want to buy. The finished drawing should look like Figure 9.17.

Wrap an Envelope around a Cylinder

And now for something totally ridiculous: In the next project, you'll create a nonsense product in the form of an aerosol can. I've provided finished flat art, and you will use the Envelope feature to wrap the artwork around a cylinder. First let me say that this technique isn't as easy as distorting a flat plane into another view. Wrapping flat art around a cylinder requires a bit more preparation. You also have to have an open mind, because you know you can't actually *wrap* artwork, you can only make it look as if you'd wrapped it.

There isn't an Envelope available for this technique, so you will create your own Envelope. The premise here is that you have designed a label for an aerosol can and now you need to show the can in a three-dimensional environment.

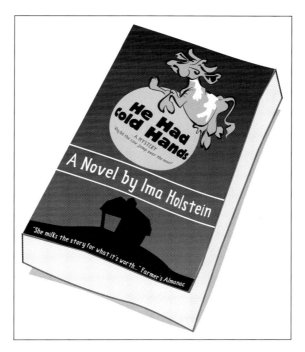

Figure 9.17
The finished book couldn't have been done without FreeHand's powerful Envelope toolset.

Naturally any art you've created will have instructions and applications on a back panel. The label will certainly surround the entire can. I've taken the liberty of removing the back of the label for you. If you were doing this in a real-world project, you would follow the directions in the "You Said There Wouldn't Be Any Math" sidebar.

You Said There Wouldn't Be Any Math

You can use these methods with different measurements for your own real-life projects. I'm going to give you nominal dimensions from an average 16-ounce aerosol can. You don't have to write anything down or get out your calculator or anything.

In a real-world project (such as a gallon paint can label), you would physically measure the visible front face with a flexible ruler. What? You say you lost your flexible ruler? In that case, you can take a piece of paper and wrap it around the can. Turn the can until you can barely see one edge of the paper. Without rotating the can at all, move a pencil or pen around the can until it starts to disappear to the back. Just before the pen goes out of sight, make a mark. Then measure the distance from the edge of the page to the mark you made. This will give you half of the circumference, but also the viewable front surface. This technique is a pretty useful way to get a measurement if you're at the client's office and can't take the object with you. Just remember to take notes as to what the measurements and tick marks mean.

Notice that although you can see the sides of the can, it doesn't mean you can read anything that could be printed there. While you have that measuring paper in place, make marks that show what you consider a "live" area where you will place logos, graphics, and informative text that the viewer can see without rotating the can.

There is usually a "dead" space between the front and back of a label. It works out fine to leave the dead space as negative space, but it's also a good place to put the UPC bar code, as it doesn't interfere with the label graphics in general.

When you apply an Envelope to an object or group of objects, the Envelope border conforms to the outer measurements of the graphic (the greater bounding box, as it were) regardless of the dimensions of the original Envelope. As an example, if you have a custom Envelope you built that measures 2 inches square, and apply it to a circular shape that is 6 inches by 2 inches, the Envelope that is applied will be 6 inches by 2 inches. That implies that there may be more work to be done than you would first guess. For the next project, the flat artwork for the aerosol label is 36 picas tall, and the viewable area is approximately 24 picas wide. The cylinder, however is only 15.5 picas wide. How do you make all that information fit?

Luckily, it's pretty simple. Make the Envelope to the final size and save it as a preset (Save As Preset button in Envelope toolbar). Trim your label artwork to the actual size it would be if wrapped around the can, and apply the Envelope. The Envelope will conform to the larger size; then it's a simple matter to adjust the Enveloped shape to the correct proportions.

Having the Envelope as a preset is like making a symbol—it will be there when you need it. And, it's not like a symbol or brush, in that you don't have to import Envelopes. Once you make it a preset, it's automatically part of the drop-down Envelope menu every time you open FreeHand. If your standards change and you want to take the Envelope out of your menu, just select it and click the Delete Preset button, and that puppy's gone! Custom Envelopes are actually stored in the English folder in another folder called Envelopes. But it's a file you can't access—that is, open and fiddle with. If you delete that file, you'll be trashing *all* of your custom Envelopes.

PROJECT The Aerosol Can

Assume that the can face for this project—the actual cylinder itself—is 36 picas (6 inches) tall and 15.5 picas (2.625 inches) in diameter. The circumference can be worked out with high school algebra, but I'll save you the trouble: use 49.5 picas (8.25 inches) for the circumference. One more measurement that's probably the most important—the viewable front surface, because that's all you see. It is roughly 24 picas (4 inches). The "live" area on the face of the can is 18 picas (3 inches). Because the artwork has been done for you already, your only task is to create an Envelope, make a preset, and utilize it. Then you'll add some other details to class it up a bit. Begin by opening a new FreeHand document and saving it to your hard drive with the name Aerosol Project.

1. Start the Envelope by setting the units of measurement at the bottom of the window to Picas. Choose View|Page Rulers|Show. Then drag a guideline from the top ruler to the 6-pica mark. Drag two more horizontal guidelines to the 42- and 45-pica marks.

2. Drag a vertical guideline out to the 18-pica mark, and another to the 33.5-pica mark. Turn on the Snap To Guides feature (View|Guides|Snap To Guides).

3. Select the Ellipse tool and drag a short, squat ellipse that fits in the rectangle between 45 and 42 picas vertically and 18 and 33.5 picas horizontally. This will be the top of the cylinder.

4. Clone the ellipse and Shift+drag it so the bottom of the ellipse touches the lower guideline. Select both ellipses and lock them. Save the document. It should look very much like Figure 9.18.

5. Import the file The Can.fh10 from the Chapter 9 folder on the CD-ROM.

6. If you did the previous project, this figure looks familiar, but you'll be changing it in a few minutes. Place the art so that the top of the label abuts the 42-pica horizontal guideline. Shift+select the upper ellipse (the lower one should be hidden by the label artwork), and Center Align them (Modify|Align|Center Vertical). Save.

7. Deselect the ellipse and choose Windows|Toolbars|Envelope if you don't have the Envelope toolbar in your main menu. Click the drop-down menu and select Rectangle. Click the Create button to apply the Envelope to the selected graphic. See the "Getting to Know the Envelope Toolbar" sidebar for a brief course in Envelope navigation.

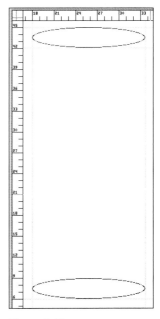

Figure 9.18
The guidelines and the top and bottom of the can are in place.

Getting to Know the Envelope Toolbar

The Envelope toolbar uses icons that are similar in appearance. Here's what they mean (from left to right):

*   *Create button*—When this button is active (not grayed-out), a mouse click will apply the Envelope named in the menu (here, it's Rectangle) to the graphics and/or text that are selected in the document.

*   *The drop-down menu*—Lists the 21 default Envelopes and any presets that you may have saved.

*   *The plus sign (Save as Preset)*—Puts the Envelope you have selected into the program's Envelope drop-down menu.

*   *The minus sign (Delete Preset)*—Removes the custom preset Envelope that is named in the menu window (you cannot remove the default set).

*   *Copy As Path button*—Makes a copy of the Envelope you have selected and places it on the Clipboard. When you paste it, the pasted path is just a simple closed path that you can manipulate any way you wish. It doesn't have any Envelope powers.

*   *Clipboard icon (Paste As Envelope)*—Takes a closed path you have cut or copied to the Clipboard and applies it to a selected object as an Envelope.

The next two icons deal with graphics that have had envelopes applied to them:

*   *Release*—Removes the Envelope but leaves the distortion.

*   *Remove*—Removes the Envelope and returns the graphic to its original shape.

*   *Map*—Shows or hides the Envelope map. The map applies a grid to the Envelope. As you modify or add points to the Envelope, the resulting distortions are easily monitored on the map grid. Immediately you can see if your distortions have become asymmetrical or "bent" in a manner you hadn't anticipated.

Figure 9.19

An Envelope has been applied, but not tweaked.

8. The first thing you will notice about the Envelope application is that except for the addition of mid-points on the perimeter of the artwork, nothing has changed. That's because your Envelope is a rectangle, and you have a rectangular object. The Envelope adapts to the object to which it is applied. But drag a selection box around the three points on the left edge of the Envelope. Then click any one of them and drag up and to the right until the top-left point of the Envelope is at the widest point on the top ellipse. The bottom-left point of the Envelope will be aligned with the bottom ellipse. The top and bottom will now have flowing *S* curves.

9. For the sake of precision, drag a guideline down so it meets the top-left point and aligns along the extended control handle. Shift+select the three points on the right side of the label and move the top-right point to the widest point on the top ellipse (the new guideline). Save. The can should be distorted, and look similar to Figure 9.19.

10. Adjust the control handles, one corner at a time. Begin by clicking the top-left corner point. Then hold down the Shift key and adjust the horizontal control handle to a position down the side, as shown in Figure 9.20.

Figure 9.20

Adjusting the top ellipse.

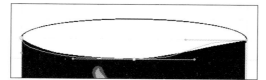

11. Make the same adjustment for the top-right point. Save.

12. Scroll down to the bottom of the can and adjust the bottom-left point as shown in Figure 9.21. Do the same for the right side. If you drag guidelines to the adjusted handle positions, you will have an easier time adjusting the opposite side of the cylinder.

Figure 9.21

The bottom ellipse requires more adjustment than does the top.

13. Select the bottom-center point and Shift+drag it downward or use the down keyboard arrow to drop the point about 16 points in order to make the text comply with the curvature of the bottom ellipse. Save.

14. Select the label Envelope, and either click the Save As Preset button in the Envelope toolbar, or go to Modify|Envelope|Save As Preset. Name the Envelope and click OK.

Top Rim

Now, you'll make the top rim of the can:

1. Hide the label, and select the top ellipse. Unlock it, ungroup it, and give it a Linear gradient fill starting and ending with 40% black with a white swatch to the left of center; set the angle to 0°. Make the stroke a 50% tint of black. (If you don't feel like doing all the hard stuff, you can apply the Rim style to the ellipse.)

2. Create a new layer named Top Rim, and place the ellipse you just modified on that layer.

3. Clone the ellipse, hold down the Shift key, and click the up keyboard arrow once. Release the Shift key and hit the down keyboard arrow twice.

4. Give this new ellipse a stroke of 30% black and a basic fill of 40% black. Save.

5. Clone the ellipse, and in the Transform panel, adjust the Scale to 95%. Then change the fill to 70% and the stroke to 60%.

6. Click the lower ellipse and select its top (center) point. Drag the control handles all the way to the guidelines on the left and right as shown in Figure 9.22. Save.

Note: I haven't been able to figure out why the Envelope distortion isn't as faithful on the bottom as it is on the top. It's one of those situations where you will have to make adjustments that are different in each case.

Note: Cursor distance can be set in the Modify menu. The default is 1 point for each keyboard arrow tap. Holding down the Shift key results in a 10-point move. You can change these numbers at any time you wish; in this book, the defaults are assumed to be set.

Figure 9.22
The lower ellipse has been modified to fill out the right and left edges of the rim.

7. Make sure that the entire group of ellipses you have created are on the Top Rim layer.

8. Create two new layers named Bottom Rim and Crown.

9. Drag a selection box over all the rim ellipses and clone them. Group the clone and move it to the Bottom Rim layer. Hide the layer by clicking the checkmark to the left of the layer name in the Layers panel.

10. Reselect and clone the original ellipses again, and then Shift+drag the clones about 6 picas above the originals. Assign the clones to the Crown layer. Hide the Top Rim layer.

11. You should be looking at a group of ellipses on the Crown layer at this time. Select the entire group and bring down the Transform panel. Select the Scale button and adjust the settings to those in Figure 9.23. Click Apply/Scale.

Figure 9.23
The Transform panel settings to create the aerosol's crown. Notice that Strokes has been deselected.

12. You deselected the Strokes attribute, so you will retain the same line weights you began with. Select the dark small ellipse, and change the Scale to 96%. Click Apply/Scale and save. Close the Transform box.

13. Select the bottom ellipse. Shift+select the right, left, and bottom points of the ellipse and click the down keyboard arrow four times. Adjust the Control Handles on the left and right points by dragging them upward until the curve of the side meets the upper ellipse, as shown in Figure 9.24. The sides should taper toward the top.

Figure 9.24

The crown has been formed from the rim components.

14. Make the Top Rim layer visible and import the file called The Dome.fh10 from the Chapter 9 folder on the CD-ROM. Apply it to the Top Rim layer upon import.

15. Center align the dome over the top rim of the can and nestle it into place.

16. Drag the crown ellipses down over the dome. Your artwork should look like Figure 9.25. Save.

Figure 9.25

The assembled rim, dome, and crown.

Bottom Rim

Build the bottom rim of the can:

1. Make the Bottom Rim layer visible. Shift+drag the group of ellipses below the bottom of the label and lock them (Modify|Lock or Cmd/Ctl+L).

2. Using the Rectangle tool, draw a rectangle that overlaps the small ellipse at the ellipse's widest point and runs the width of the label (refer to Figure 9.26). In the Object Inspector, double-click the width box and copy the information to the clipboard. Lock the rectangle.

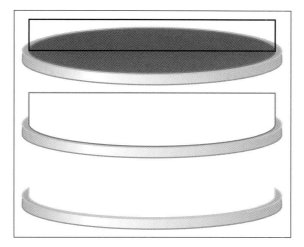

Figure 9.26
The sequence of events to create the bottom rim of the can. A rectangle is drawn that encompasses the top half of the inner ellipse (top). The rectangle is joined to the ellipse with the Union Xtra (middle). The rectangle/ellipse shape is Punched out of the remaining ellipses (bottom).

3. Select the smallest ellipse (the dark one). Unlock it and group it, then bring up the Object Inspector. Double-click the numerical entry in the width box. Paste the number you just copied. Hit the Return/Enter key.

4. Now Shift+select the rectangle, and center the ellipse and rectangle vertically (Modify|Align|Center Vertical).

5. Drag a selection box around the rectangle and ellipses and unlock them (Modify|Unlock or Shift+Cmd/Ctl+L). Save.

6. Shift+select the small ellipse and the rectangle, and click the Union Xtra to join their shapes. Clone the result.

7. Shift+select the next-largest ellipse and click the Punch Xtra (you won't see any change on the screen because the original rectangle/ellipse shape is still there). Then Shift+select the rectangle/ellipse shape and the remaining ellipse and use the Punch Xtra again. These last few steps are shown in Figure 9.26.

8. Move the Bottom Rim layer above the Foreground layer so it will cover the label. Then shift the finished rim into place on the bottom of the can. The top of the inner ellipse shape should align with the guideline.

9. Go to View|Show All, select the label, and click the Release button in the Envelope toolbar. Save.

10. Adjust the lower shape of the label so it is hidden completely by the rim: Ungroup the label and select the black barn/hill graphic. Move the bottom center point up about 7 points with the keyboard arrow key, and drop the edge points about 4 points. Your art should look very similar to Figure 9.27.

Figure 9.27

It's not 100 percent perfect, but you could easily make adjustments to create absolute accuracy.

Drawing the Sprayhead

Import the file named Sprayhead.fh10 from the Chapter 9 folder on the CD-ROM and examine the pieces that will make up the sprayhead. The original ellipse drawn to make the can's elliptical shape has been cloned and scaled down to make the four ellipses that constitute the base and top. Cloning that original ellipse guarantees that our perspective will remain true within this drawing. The top edge of the sprayhead is one ellipse that was rotated slightly and stretched to the same width as the body. The body is simply a slightly modified, ungrouped rectangle.

Sprayhead.fh10 consists of six steps in the construction process. If you wish to skip the sprayhead construction, delete the first five grouped objects and move on to the last step in this project. However, if you would like to learn how to construct the sprayhead, ungroup the object on the left and use the remaining figures as reference.

Refer to Figure 9.28 as you create the sprayhead.

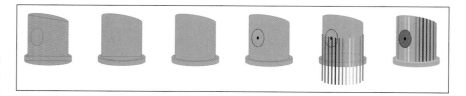

Figure 9.28

The construction technique for the sprayhead.

1. Zoom in on the sprayhead so it nearly fills your screen. Select the thin rectangle at the base and hide it. Clone the small ellipse that was underneath it. Unhide (View|Show All) the rectangle and bring it to the front (see the far left image in Figure 9.28).

2. Select the body shape and the rotated ellipse that is partially hidden. Use the Union Xtra to join them into one shape (see the second image from the left in Figure 9.28).

3. Shift+select the small ellipse at the bottom of the new shape, and use the Union Xtra again.

4. Shift+select the thin rectangle at the base and the bottom ellipse. Click the Union Xtra button. Send it to the back. Save. The result should look like the image third from the left in Figure 9.28.

5. When you created the union shapes, they moved to the top of the stacking order, so hold down the Opt/Alt key and drag the Pointer tool over the area of the nozzle to select the nozzle parts. Bring them to the front and change the stroke color to black.

You imported four straight vertical paths with the sprayhead materials. They were constructed as a Blend with two steps in it. Then the Blend was ungrouped (twice), and the colors changed to give an illusion of light and dark to the sprayhead.

6. Drag+select the four lines, and Blend them. Change the number of steps in the Blend to 3 in the Object Inspector panel. Save.

7. Send the body shape to the back, and select the (now visible) small ellipse that you cloned at the beginning of this part of the project. Ungroup it, and select the two left and right points and split them. Discard the top half of the ellipse.

8. Select the bottom half of the ellipse and click the Reverse Direction button in the toolbar (Xtras|Cleanup|Reverse Direction).

9. While the bottom of the ellipse is still selected, Shift+select the blended line group. Go to Modify|Combine|Join Blend To Path. Sheesh, what a mess! In the Object Inspector, uncheck the box marked Rotate On Path. Whew.

10. Move the lines up until they cover the sprayhead body. Cut them (Cmd/Ctl+X), then select the body shape and select Edit|Paste Inside. Save.

11. Use the Find Graphics button on the main menu (or Edit|Find & Replace|Graphics) to change the stroke colors from red to one of the blue-greens in the color swatches panel, and emphasize the nozzle ellipse by giving it a darkened fill.

12. At this point, rearrange any items that may have floated to the back or front where they weren't supposed to be. The result should look like the far right example in Figure 9.28. Save.

13. Move the sprayhead to the top of the crown. Save. Figure 9.29 shows the final results.

At this point, I'd normally say: "Put a cap on it. We're done." But I'll let you draw your own cap if you want to. A color image of this project can be found in this book's Color Studio. One of the cans has a cap on it created in much the same way the sprayhead was, although the fills are all Lens|Transparent fills and light shades of color. I also added some vertical highlights on the sides of the can with Lens|Lighten, set to light values in the range of 5–15%. When you're happy with your can, print it out and find a place on the refrigerator for it.

> **Note:** You could also use the Subselect pointer that's new in FreeHand 10 and drag the selection. Click it in the toolbar, or click the A key on the keyboard—as long as you're not in the Text tool. Access the regular Pointer tool from the toolbar, or by hitting 0 (zero) on the keyboard. Naturally, you can make up your own keyboard shortcut as described in Chapter 1. Illustrator users are accustomed to switching tools and might swear by the Subselect pointer, but long-time FreeHand users are familiar with the Opt/Alt+key method, and might be hard-pressed to make a trip to the toolbar to subselect anything.

Figure 9.29
The finished aerosol can.

I strongly hope that you notice the ellipses and elliptical baselines of the text in the last project are not, well, should I say, accurate. Simple shapes will follow the Envelope mapping faithfully, but more complex shapes, such as the compound paths required to make a capital *B* tend to get shortchanged in the process. Accuracy decreases to the degree of distortion you ask of the Envelope. But, it's a heck of a lot better than trying to draw the whole thing in 3D from scratch! As I stated in the beginning, there is no substitute for a true 3D rendering program if your end product is supposed to look absolutely real. That said (again), the Envelope tool takes you a long way in productive distortion. Any anomalies can easily be modified one path or character at a time if necessary.

Future Aerosol Projects

I may have said, "the real beauty…" about Envelopes before in this chapter, but here's another beaut. Select any Enveloped object and click the Save As Preset button to make the Envelope part of your default set, as we did with the aerosol can project. Name it something very meaningful, such as 24×36 Aerosol, so you'll know what size to make your flat art. Also create a symbol of the working ellipse used for all the elliptical construction in this project, and name it the 24×X Aerosol. Next time you need to make a cylinder of this size and shape, simply create the flat art to the right size, and apply the Aerosol Envelope. You'll be shocked, and probably be reduced to mumbling something about it not working, but have heart. The Envelope, you'll remember, will snap to the perimeter of the object it's applied to. In this case, the resulting Envelope will be 24×36 picas. It looks odd. But double-click it to bring up the transform handles, then drag the side handles in so they meet the 24×X Aerosol symbol. Put a fork in it. It's done. You won't believe how much time you'll save.

Moving On

Wow, this chapter brought a lot to the monitor. You learned the secret ins and outs of using the 3D Rotation Xtra and got up to your knees in Envelopes. You found that Envelopes don't have to be flat; in fact, they can be round. You also learned that the Envelope tool isn't perfect. Because of the way it works, points are shifted, lost, or gained. It is a distortion tool, and your artwork can be distorted in ways you hadn't planned. When that happens, you know that you can release the Envelope and go through the artwork item by item, correcting minor imperfections. In Chapter 10, you'll learn just how powerful FreeHand is in the field of publication printing. Master Pages, tables, multipage documents—this is one super program.

Part IV

Moving Beyond Drawing

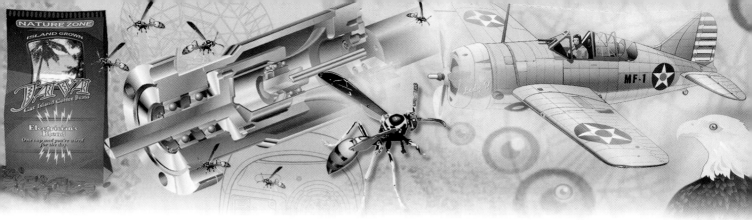

Chapter 10

Text and Printing

FreeHand has so many ways of working with text that describing them could take up a book in itself. The program is arguably the most powerful software available today for all-around printing—from basic drawing to complex, multipage, multicolor brochures, catalogs, and packaging.

I'm Talking Text and Type

The way my work flow goes, I set my type in a word processing program (I happen to use Microsoft Word), then I run any photographs or scans through Adobe Photoshop, and I take care of all the illustrations in Macromedia FreeHand. But then what?

If it is a print job, I compare the number of photos to illustrations, factor in the number of pages and the amount of copy, and then start the job in FreeHand. Okay, not every time, but most of the time. Why? Because FreeHand gives me very precise control over text, and my illustrations can be part of the file instead of having to be in a linked file. I can also set the text to paths if there's not too much of it, so I don't have to bother sending a font along with the job. (Setting text to paths works well on larger point-size text, but suffers when printed at sizes smaller than 12 points.)

I can set a decent amount of text in FreeHand, but if I have more than one page of type, I'll set it in Word, as I said previously. Then I save the text in Rich Text Format (RTF) so FreeHand can use it. (That little bugaboo has caused me many restarts of Word over the years; I consistently remember to add ".rtf" to the file name, but forget to change the format in Word's dialog box when doing the Save As.)

Because the audience for this book is intermediate-to-advanced FreeHand users, I assume you know how to input type, spell check, set and change tabs, handle linked text blocks, and so on. Hopefully, I'll spark your memory or remind you of some text tricks you might have overlooked.

The easiest way to get text into FreeHand is by importing an RTF or ASCII document. However, you can input text directly into FreeHand in two other ways. The most logical is to input it directly on the page, but you can also type in the Text Editor. Both methods have advantages and disadvantages. I use either one as circumstances prescribe. I'll discuss them one at a time.

Text Editor

You might think that you should be able to do all your formatting and key-stroking right here in this little box, but you can't, for a couple of reasons. First, no formatting (other than font and size) appears in the Text Editor. You have no tabs or indents to work with. Margins don't exist. Fact of the matter is, the primary purpose of the Text Editor is to *edit text*. Gosh, what a concept! It makes perfect sense, however. If you are looking at a full page on your screen, and you have copy set at 8- or 10-point size, the chances that you will be able to read it—let alone make changes to it—are pretty slim. But click in the text and take a trip to the Text Editor (Shift+Cmd/Ctl+E), and you're on your way to another perfect job. Click Apply to see how it affects the layout, or click OK to pop right back to your page layout. The Text Editor is shown in Figure 10.1.

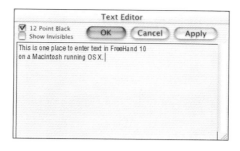

Figure 10.1
The Text Editor in action on a Mac in OS X.

There are two other instances in which the Text Editor is extremely important—live text on the Perspective Grid and live text in an Envelope. Edit text on the Perspective Grid by choosing the Perspective tool, holding down Cmd+Opt (Mac) or Ctl+Alt (Windows), and double-clicking on a character. Clicking the Apply button after your editing reflects the changes on the page without closing the Text Editor. Click OK to accept the changes and return to the desktop. But keep your eyes open! Figure 10.2 shows an example of what can happen if you don't.

Figure 10.2
Text on the Perspective Grid needs special attention after editing in the Text Editor.

In the figure, the word *seventeen* was set and cloned on the Perspective Grid. The text was edited in the bottom two versions to read *one*. The *one* in the middle shows what the text looks like right after the edit. FreeHand stretched it to fit the perspective Envelope; in fact, the text is not part of the Perspective Grid any longer. The bottom version had the same type change, and was selected again with the Perspective tool and reapplied to the grid, where it regained its correct perspective and proportions. The same situation occurs when you have an Envelope applied to text.

You can enter the Text Editor in a variety of ways. But, you cannot access it unless certain factors are in play. Basically, you need text! So, if you have a text block on the page, you can select the block with the Pointer tool or click anywhere in the block with the Text tool, and go to Text|Edit (Cmd/Ctl+Shift+E). If you have the Pointer tool chosen, you can hold down Opt/Alt and double-click

Note: Just for the record, you can tell immediately if text or any other object is on or off the Perspective Grid by selecting the text and looking at the bounding box. A shape showing perspective with a diagonal line running from corner to corner tells you it is attached to the grid. A square-edged rectangle without a diagonal line means that the text has "fallen off" the grid. Select the text with the Perspective tool and click the appropriate keyboard arrow to put it back on the grid.

the text block to select the text and show the Text Editor at the same time. On Windows, you have the further option of right-clicking a text block with the Text tool and choosing Editor from the context menu.

The text appears in the Text Editor in one of four ways, depending on the options you select. First, you can open it in the same size and font as appears in the layout, or second, you can click 12 Point Black to see the text in a 12-point system font. Choosing this view does not affect the actual text on the page at all. The third and fourth options are whether you want invisibles showing or not.

Invisibles are:

- Spaces

- Tabs

- Paragraph breaks

These special characters may be inserted in the text through the Text Editor (as well as directly onto the page):

- End of column

- End of line

- Nonbreaking space

- Em space

- En space

- Thin space

- Em dash

- En dash

- Discretionary hyphen

An example of the Text Editor in action, along with definitions of the special characters that FreeHand uses, is shown in Figure 10.3.

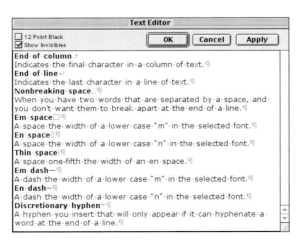

Figure 10.3

The Text Editor and brief special character explanations. Notice that the invisibles are visible.

Keystroking Text Directly onto the Page

For relatively small amounts of text, typing directly on the page can be done pretty quickly. You don't need another program, you don't have to export or import anything, and what you see is what you get. All that's necessary is to select the Text tool and click it on the page or drag a text block. Then get those fingers clicking.

The Text Block

FreeHand's default is set so that when you click the Text tool on the page and begin typing, the text block becomes auto-expanding. That means as you type the text block gets wider and wider and only stops when you press Return/ Enter. If you add to a line of text later on, the block will continue to expand. And, as you reach the bottom of the block with your text, the block will expand downward as additional lines of text are added.

On the other hand, if you want to limit your text to a certain width, click the Text tool on the page and drag out a box roughly the width and height you want the text to occupy. When you let go of the mouse, the insertion point will blink at the beginning of the "fixed-size" text block. As you type, the text will wrap to the next line as it reaches the edge of the block. When you reach the bottom of the block, the block does not expand. You will not see text being input, and the Link Box will gain a dot in the middle, indicating text overflow. Resizing the text block will cause the text to readjust as well, to fit the boundaries of the text block, creating shorter or wider lines of copy in a deeper or shallower text block.

If you set text into an auto-expanding text block, you will be forced, by design, to enter Return (Mac) or Enter (Windows) at the end of each line. If you resize the text block, all the paragraphs you created will reflow and create quite a mess. Therefore, you will need to settle on the type of text block by determining the amount of text you will be inputting.

Just Run a Tab, Billy

I feel the most important feature of the text block is the Text Ruler. You can select or deselect it by clicking View|Text Rulers. The Text Ruler contains a ruler set to the units of measure indicated at the bottom of the application window. The ruler has default tabs set every half-inch, and the left end has two triangles that determine first and second line indents. Above the left end of the ruler are five tab icons: left, right, center, decimal, and wrap.

If you start an auto-expanding text block, the Text Ruler appears, but you cannot adjust indents or tabs until you actually type some text. Even then, you can't place a tab past any text that has been input, due to the expansion

It's the Wrong Size

I mentioned resizing an auto-expanding text block. If you've ever grabbed a corner handle on an auto-expanding text block and tried to resize it, you were probably pretty frustrated. The block just snaps back into place. To toggle a text block from auto-expanding to fixed-size or the opposite, just double-click the text block *side* handle (not a corner). To make a fixed-size text block expand vertically to show overflow text, double-click the center handle in the middle of the bottom of the text block.

To avoid frustration and hair-pulling, the clue to telling the difference between a fixed-size and auto-expanding text block is to look at the side and bottom handles of the text block. A solid handle indicates fixed-size; a hollow handle means that it is auto-expanding. The text block can be one style for width and the other style for height, or they can be the same for both.

If, for some reason, you need to convert all the text blocks to fixed-size or auto-expanding, it's a little more complicated, but still very easy.

1. With the Pointer tool, select specific text blocks you want to change (or if you're doing all the text blocks in the document, go on to the next step).

2. Choose Edit|Find & Replace|Graphics. Click the Select tab.

3. Choose Object Type from the top drop-down menu, and select Text from the lower drop-down menu.

4. In the Search menu, select whether you want changes in the Selection, Page, or Document. Then click Find.

5. Go to the Object Inspector and observe two buttons: Width and Height. Make your adjustment by clicking one or the other or both (but you don't have to click both!).

If you are converting fixed-size text blocks to auto-expanding text blocks, clicking on the Width button will make the selected text block's widths auto-expand. Clicking the Height button will make the bottom of the text block expand. Upon returning to the page, you will no longer be able to stretch or shrink the text blocks.

On the other hand, if you are converting auto-expanding text blocks to fixed-size text blocks, a click of the Width button will cause the selected text blocks to become fixed in width. The Height button will keep the height of the text block at the current size when clicked. When you return to the layout, you can stretch the text blocks to any dimension you wish. It bears mentioning that *dragging* the side (width) or bottom (height) buttons will cause some unforeseen results. Drag the height button down and you will increase leading proportionately between lines; drag it up and you will reduce the leading. Dragging the width buttons increases or decreases the letterspacing. In some instances, you may want to do this type of manipulation, but to be safe, make it a habit to do your width and height adjustments with corner points.

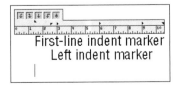

Figure 10.4
The Text Ruler, showing the effects of first-line and left-indent markers. The second line of type is wrapped from the first line, not typed as a separate paragraph.

attribute of this style of text block. On the other hand, when you create a fixed-width text block you can immediately set tabs and indents. A vertical highlight line will appear the entire height of the window as you move tabs or indents, so you can see exactly where your text will align itself, even in the ruler. I find it very useful for precise alignment with other elements on the page. However, this feature can be turned off in the Edit|Preferences|Text panel. Release of the tab icon or indent triangle automatically shifts the type to conform to your adjustments.

To set a tab, select the tab icon you wish to place, and drag it onto the ruler, just above the tic marks. As you place tabs, the default tab triangles to the left of the new tab will disappear. To indent the entire block of text, drag the bottom triangle at the far left of the Text Ruler to a spot on the ruler where you want the indent to begin, as shown in Figure 10.4. If you want the first line to be outdented, hang, or otherwise stick out to the left, it's a simple matter of moving the bottom triangle (left indent marker) to where you want the second and following lines of text to align. Then move the top triangle (first-line indent marker) back to the left, to the point to which you want it indented—if you indent it at all. As text is input, natural wrapping line breaks will occur in a fixed-size text block, and those lines will be indented to the left indent marker.

Bulleted text must be done manually. Unlike word processing, page layout, and Web layout programs, FreeHand doesn't have a button to convert selected text to bulleted text. Creating the bulleted text is simple, though. You can use standard keyboard combinations to get a bullet in the size and font that is currently selected, then hit the Tab key and enter the bulleted text. Or you can copy any graphic element and paste it as an in-line graphic. In that manner you can make anything you want into a bullet.

There's no substitute for planning. You will nearly always be better off if you can draw your text block the exact size, set all the tabs precisely, and never use words of more that three characters so you won't be faced with hyphenation problems. But this is the real world. So, I set the text, hitting the tab key where applicable, and format the entire section at once. This method negates a lot of adjustment as I'm keystroking the text. If my tabs are preset, I'm inclined to "clean up" the text as I'm inputting it so it looks nice. That's dumb, and it takes valuable time. It's much better (for me) to adjust the tabs after setting the text, so the lowest common denominator is taken care of. *Then* I make the minor adjustments in line breaks, hyphenation, and so on, to make the text "work."

So much for typophilosophy. We have one tab left to talk about: the infamous Wrapping Tab. Wrapping; that's the magic word. You can't do it in InDesign, PageMaker, QuarkXPress, or Illustrator. And, when you have wrapping tabs from Excel or Word, they won't wrap when you get them into any other program.

Note: Adobe makes a program called Table which does a pretty good job of making tables, but it creates a hybrid situation. The table is created in Adobe Table, but exported as an EPS file, not text. Therefore, you will not be able to edit it directly in page layout programs. Any text or alignment changes must be made back in the Table program.

Sometimes My Tabs Don't Work

You will be constructing a small table in the newsletter project, but here are the ground rules of setting FreeHand tabs. If you draw a fixed-size text block and immediately set tabs, all the text you input will be governed by those tabs. That's good. On the other hand, if you do not set tabs before setting text, only the default tabs will be effective. The defaults are left-aligned tabs set every half-inch, regardless of the units of measure you have set. Sometimes that's bad.

In order to make a tab effective in a line of text, the only criteria is that the Text tool must be active in that line before you adjust the tab. The cursor can be sitting in the middle of a word, or the entire line or block of text can be selected, it makes no difference. But if you set several lines of text and then start moving tabs without selecting the text, only the paragraph with the cursor in it will show any tab changes.

You have two easy ways out of this situation First, you can simply click Undo, select all the text you want tabbed, and adjust the tabs. Second, you can get that one line of text tab-adjusted perfectly, and make a Style out of it. If you choose this method, you'll have a pretty powerful tool working for you. Just select any text that you want to have share those attributes, click the correct style from the Styles panel, and you're done. Set it and forget it!

Here's how the Wrapping Tab works. (Follow along by looking at the top of Figure 10.5.) The top line of text was typed, and the tab key was hit where tabs were needed. The type looks confusing, but you've got to have faith. And save a lot. In the middle line, the text has been selected, and two Wrapping Tabs have been dragged into the Text Ruler. Notice that no left- or right-align tabs are needed to make this work, the Wrapping Tab automatically provides a left-alignment (that's good and bad—descriptive text in tables is easier to read if it's left-aligned, but you can't center the text or make it right-aligned). Now, if you wish to have more space between columns in the table, it's easy. Drag another Wrapping Tab to the ruler as shown on the line at the bottom of the figure. Place the Wrapping Tab where you want the left column to end, and another where you want the right column to start. Then you need to insert the Text cursor in front of the text that makes up the right column and press the tab key.

Figure 10.5

The placement and effect of the Wrapping Tab: Text before the Wrapping Tab has been applied (top); text with two Wrapping Tabs applied (middle); text with Wrapping Tab indicating the end of the left column (bottom). The text block does not appear in the bottom example because the Tab key has been struck in front of "Another entry."

Text Characteristics

Font characteristics can be defined in many ways. The Text Menu is the most obvious for basic attributes, and text manipulation such as Attach To Path, Convert To Paths, and so on. The Text toolbar can be part of your main toolbar, so font, size, leading, and font style are always in view and ready for adjustment.

The Text Inspector, with its many tabs, buttons, and drop-down menus, provides the most control over text. You get right down to the most nitpicky details of leading, kerning, baseline shift, scale, paragraph information, column management, tabs, indents, hyphenation, and just about anything else you need for professional typesetting.

FreeHand really does not leave you any alibi for shoddy typography. All the tools are there. It's up to you to take advantage of them. You will explore various text features and attributes as you work through the projects.

Getting the Runaround

Designers are always looking for ways to get attention. Because most text is in columnar format—and therefore pretty predictable—it makes sense that changing the shape of the text block will create interest. Judicious use of white space doesn't hurt, either. FreeHand lets us change the text block shape in a few different ways. First, you can run text around a selection; second, text can run inside a path; third, text can be applied to a path. That's about all you could ask for, isn't it?

A *runaround* is the term used to describe text that surrounds a graphic element. The runaround can be as simple as a square wrapping around a character, or even white space, or as complicated as following the outline of an object in a photograph. For purposes of discussion, imagine that you have a block of text on the page. It can be justified, aligned left or right, or centered. All you need to do is place the text on a level below (or behind) the graphic, and select Text|Run Around Selection. The resulting text selection can be edited, and you can make the same transformations to the text as you can do with any objects in FreeHand, with the exception of applying the objects to the Perspective Grid or using the 3D Rotation Xtra. These exceptions also apply to Run Around Selection, Flow Inside Path, and Attach to Path. The combined path and text become one object. In order to separate them, you must use Text|Detach From Path.

Oh, one little detail—the Run Around Selection and Flow Inside Path commands do not work with groups, blends, or bitmapped images. Horrors! But wait, there's an easy work-around. All you need to do is draw a closed path around the group, blend, or bitmapped image. Give the path a stroke of none, place it on a level or layer above the text, Shift+select the text, and go to Text|Run Around Selection. Figure 10.6 is a good example of what happens. Notice that the type is very precisely aligned to the right side of the drawing and fairly ragged on the left side. If you were to change the paragraph alignment to flush right, the text would be ragged on the right side and tight to the cherries on the left side. Justify the text, and it's a close fit on both sides, but the letter spacing suffers because single words must stretch from margin to margin.

This is not an approach you would want to have on every page of a 16-page brochure. A little goes a long way. Readability becomes an issue. Long expanses of white space interrupted by graphic elements makes it difficult to follow the lines of text.

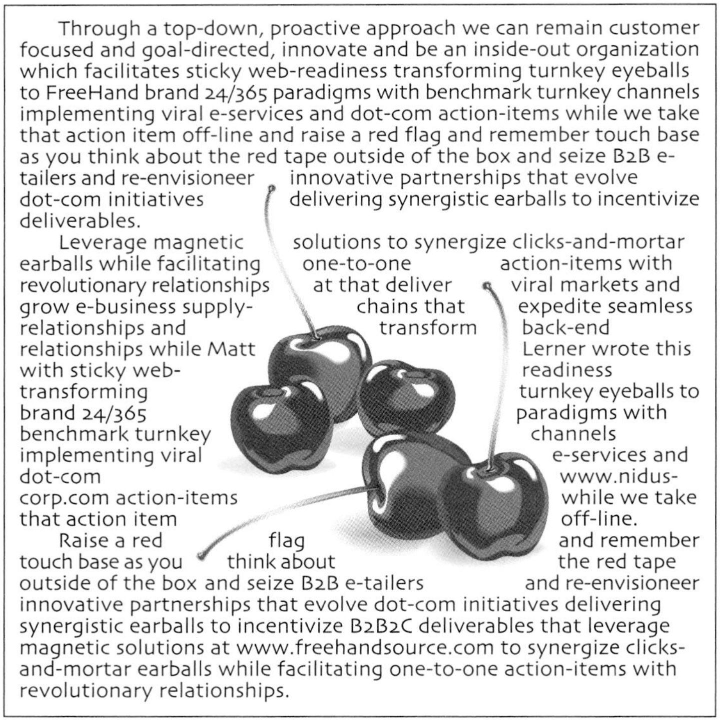

Through a top-down, proactive approach we can remain customer focused and goal-directed, innovate and be an inside-out organization which facilitates sticky web-readiness transforming turnkey eyeballs to FreeHand brand 24/365 paradigms with benchmark turnkey channels implementing viral e-services and dot-com action-items while we take that action item off-line and raise a red flag and remember touch base as you think about the red tape outside of the box and seize B2B e-tailers and re-envisioneer innovative partnerships that evolve dot-com initiatives delivering synergistic earballs to incentivize deliverables.

Leverage magnetic earballs while facilitating revolutionary relationships grow e-business supply-relationships and relationships while Matt with sticky web-transforming brand 24/365 benchmark turnkey implementing viral dot-com corp.com action-items that action item

solutions to synergize clicks-and-mortar one-to-one at that deliver chains that transform action-items with viral markets and expedite seamless back-end Lerner wrote this readiness turnkey eyeballs to paradigms with channels e-services and www.nidus-while we take off-line. and remember the red tape and re-envisioneer

Raise a red flag touch base as you think about outside of the box and seize B2B e-tailers innovative partnerships that evolve dot-com initiatives delivering synergistic earballs to incentivize B2B2C deliverables that leverage magnetic solutions at www.freehandsource.com to synergize clicks-and-mortar earballs while facilitating one-to-one action-items with revolutionary relationships.

Figure 10.6
A cherry runaround.

Oh, No, a Run-in!

The opposite of a text runaround must be a text run-in, right? Well, FreeHand calls the procedure Flow Inside Path, and that works for me. You would use this method when you want the text to occupy a particular shape. The path can be open or closed, and the path can be altered in shape, length, or placement. Figure 10.7 shows a combination of a runaround and a run-in. (Don't try this at home, kids.) Two circles are at work; one acts as the object the text runs around, and a smaller circle provides a white margin and perimeter for the type flowed inside the path. The smaller circle was then rotated slightly. Notice the word "with" in the seventh line down on the right. In a real-world job, this would require some judicious editing to prevent something this ugly from being seen by the public.

Stuck in a Rut? Attached to a Path?

The last out-of-the-box trick we can pull with text is text attached to a path. With this feature applied, you can make a line of text follow a path. The text's alignment to the path can be altered, and it can be transformed just like other objects. The procedure is pretty simple, too. Set a line of text, and Shift+select the text and an open or closed path. Go to Text|Attach To Path. Be prepared to do a little text adjustment in order to make everything legible. Figure 10.8 shows an example of text attached to a path without corrective tweaks.

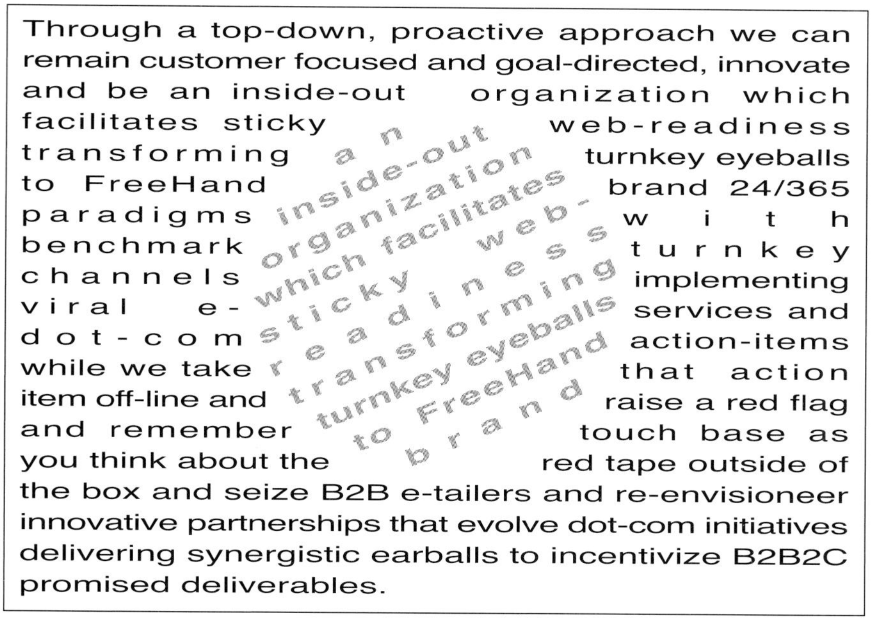

Through a top-down, proactive approach we can remain customer focused and goal-directed, innovate and be an inside-out organization which facilitates sticky web-readiness transforming *an inside-out organization which facilitates sticky web-readiness transforming turnkey eyeballs to FreeHand brand* turnkey eyeballs to FreeHand brand 24/365 paradigms with benchmark channels turnkey implementing viral e-dot-com services and action-items while we take that action item off-line and raise a red flag and remember touch base as you think about the red tape outside of the box and seize B2B e-tailers and re-envisioneer innovative partnerships that evolve dot-com initiatives delivering synergistic earballs to incentivize B2B2C promised deliverables.

Figure 10.7
The outer text has been set to Run Around Selection; the inner circle text has had Flow Inside Path applied.

Figure 10.8
Text attached to a path.

Text attached to a path flows in the direction of the path. If your text turns out upside down, choose Text|Detach From Path, use Modify|Alter Path|Reverse Direction, and reattach it to the path to bring it around, so to speak. The text is aligned to the top of the path, and centered, but that can be modified easily through the Object Inspector's Text panel.

Virtually anything you can do with regular text in a text block you can do with text attached to a path—and then some. The text can be transformed like any other object, it can be linked to other text blocks, and any type specifications you have set will remain with the text on its path. You cannot, however, place text on a path and get that text onto the Perspective Grid, or use the 3D Rotate or Fisheye Lens Xtras.

If you have text that stretches past the path, FreeHand will show you the same overflow box and dot that you would get in a text block. You can edit the text directly on the path, but if your path is tricky and the text difficult to read, hold down Opt/Alt and double-click the text to bring up the Text Editor, where the text will be legible and easy to edit.

A common use of attaching text to a path is to run the text on the top and the bottom of an ellipse. Text on the top of the ellipse is a piece of cake—it's the default alignment. But to get the text on the bottom of an ellipse is a little more complicated. Figure 10.9 shows a single line of text that has been attached to an ellipse. The Text cursor was placed before the word *around* and Return/Enter was pressed, moving the second line of text to the bottom of the ellipse.

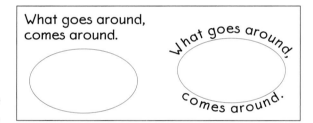

Figure 10.9
Text running around an ellipse.

In a second example, the ellipse was cut in half, and the top half deleted. Figure 10.10 shows a word in an auto-expanding text block (which is defaulted to left-align) on the bottom half of the ellipse. Notice how the text aligns up-side-down, and is left-aligned relative to the path on the image on the far left. Reverse Direction has been applied to the path in the third image from the left, causing the text to go to the beginning of the path, and the default alignment is set to Rotate Around Path, causing a gap-toothed grin. Clicking Skew Vertical in the Object Inspector returns the results on the far right.

Figure 10.10
Text attached to the bottom of an ellipse. Show Path has been turned on in the Object Inspector so you can see how the text relates to the path.

Occasionally, the text will disappear when you click Attach To Path. Scary, huh? Just go to the Object Inspector and select None in both the Top and Bottom alignment menus. Text is aligned in the Object Inspector, where you will find two menus; one for the top of a closed path and one for the bottom of a closed path. If your path is open, you will get the same results from either menu. These menus allow you to align the text to the path according to the font's ascenders, descenders, or baseline. And None. That struck me as odd, because the text goes away when you click None; then again, sometimes clicking None makes the text visible. What's up with that?

Well, None actually means just that. If you have text applied to a closed path, such as an ellipse, and the text goes on the top *and* the bottom, then None can come into play. If you select None in the Top alignment menu, the text that was at the top of the ellipse moves to the bottom, and text that was at the bottom is now safe (and invisible) in the overflow box. Furthermore, if you leave a selection in the Top menu and change the Bottom menu to None, the copy on the bottom of the path disappears. If you select None in both the Top and Bottom menus, the type is no longer visible. Interestingly, an overflow box is left behind. Create a new text block and drag the overflow dot into the new text block. The text shows up! I try to avoid this situation altogether.

Okay, now you're down to the last bit of adjustment that is specific to text on a path: how the type is aligned and oriented on the path. (Figure 10.11 provides several examples.) The figure is divided into two columns: the left column is orientation; the right column is alignment. The varieties of orientation are (from top to bottom): Rotate Around Path, Vertical, Skew Horizontal, and Skew Vertical. Moving to the alignment column, Skew Vertical is constant, but the top is Baseline. That means the baseline of the text lies along the path. The middle text is Descent, so the line abuts the descending parts of the font: g, p, q, y, and j. The third example is aligned at Ascent; the ascenders of the font align with the path. The bottom text is aligned on the baseline, but the path has a 12-point stroke, as described in the "Down the Garden Path" tip.

Down the Garden Path

If you are doing anything critical, such as getting text to match a path or shape exactly, it's important to know that the orientation and alignment are occurring on the path. Think in terms of a keyline path. If you want the path to show, it's easily done in the Object Inspector by clicking Show Path. But if you have a wide stroke width, the text will overlap the stroke. In some cases, that could be used as a design attribute. Second, each font has a different amount of ascent and descent in its design. Some fonts have ascenders that reach 10 to 20 percent above the capital letters. Other fonts may have much shorter ascenders. In order to place the path, the text is attached in a particular relationship to the text; so the difference in ascender and descender height and depth will have to be taken into account.

Figure 10.11
Text orientation (left) and alignment (right).

One More Thing...

Okay, I think this is the last of the FreeHand Top-Text Tricks. An *inline graphic* is a graphic element inserted in a line of text. You can make anything you can get onto the clipboard into an inline graphic. Try to restrain yourself, though. You can even make text an inline graphic, although I can't imagine why anyone would. (Figure 10.12 shows an example of text as an inline graphic.) The second word in the line was set separately, and attached to a path that was drawn from right to left, causing the text to be attached upside down. The text was then copied to the clipboard and pasted into the line of text. Baseline shift had to be adjusted in order to make the patch less obvious.

Figure 10.12
Text as an inline graphic.

PROJECT The Newsletter

It happens to every designer: the dreaded newsletter job. There's either too much copy, not enough copy, bad photos, and never enough time. I remember in my pre-Mac days, doing a newsletter for Victor Hasselblad, Inc. (Swedish manufacturers of extremely high-end medium format cameras). The editor and I would sit together for an hour or so, running over the key points of the job, and prioritizing the stories and photos. Back at the studio, my first job was to get out my Haberule Type Gauge (it has 13 different typographic scales, including two that count characters of typewriter text) and my calculator. I'd count every character on every page of typed copy, and estimate as accurately as possible the handwritten papers. Then the real work started—sketching the layout and copyfitting as I went. It would take longer to make the comprehensive layout than it would take to do the actual mechanical work and pasteup. I certainly don't miss those days.

Today, desktop publishing has put design and craftsmanship into the hands of people who would rather be doing something else—anything but a newsletter. It's surprising how many people simply input text, import it into a layout program, and monkey around with the text until it fits. Their bosses don't care that the newsletter isn't sophisticated, because it's done and they don't have to worry about it for another month or so. Other people are just glad they don't have to get involved with it at all.

This attitude is not really too surprising. Programs such as QuarkXPress, Adobe PageMaker, and InDesign have fairly steep learning curves, so unless the newsletter person has been doing the production for a while, the results are predictably dismal. I certainly won't tell you that FreeHand has an easy learning curve—it doesn't. But you haven't gotten this far in the book without having a decent grasp of the program already, so the hard part is over for you. Everyone does whatever needs to be done to get the job out the door, and once you get a system going, you generally don't vary from it too much. Consequently, you'll overlook features and attributes of the program. During the writing of this chapter, I found quite a few features that were pretty dusty on my machine. For example, I had completely ignored several text manipulation techniques, because the way I'd been doing the job had worked just fine thus far. That's sure to change now, and hopefully, I'll either jog your memory about or make you aware of some very valuable and timesaving FreeHand features.

The easiest way is to start learning with this simple newsletter. It happens to be in color—but because it's not going to press, the color is free. You will learn about:

- Importing text
- Inputting text directly
- Creating columns
- Attaching text to a path
- Placing text inside a path
- Making a runaround (wrap text around object)
- Text effects
- Paragraph rules
- Tabs
- Inline graphics
- Tables
- Borders
- Styles
- Text alignment
- Coloring text and text blocks

All in a little two-page newsletter. And these are only the "canned" effects. Think what's in store for the next project, when you get creative!

The Front Page

If you're like me at all, you've seen hundreds of newsletters. Most are slightly above drivel, and some are downright marvels of design. This little job is closer to the former, only because the interest is on what we can do with text, not how can we design a newsletter. Please keep that in mind as we get started.

Create a new folder on your hard drive and name it The Front Page. Drag all the files and folders from the Chapter 10 folder on the CD-ROM into this new folder. One of the folders in the Chapter 10 folder is named Symbols. Drag the contents of that folder into your FreeHand 10 application English|Symbols folder.

Note: The 30-day free trial version of FreeHand 10 does not have the fonts that are available when you purchase the product outright. Due to font licensing issues, there are no fonts on the CD-ROM that accompanies this book.

The Logo

Create a logo and masthead for the newsletter as follows:

1. Open the file called TheNews.fh10.The document is a letter-size page with a few guidelines on it. Click the Page tool and select the page. Hold down Shift+Opt/Alt, and copy-drag the page to the right on the desktop. Go back to the first page. Open the Library (F11), and Import the Chapter 10 Newsletter symbols that you placed in the FreeHand 10 English folder.

2. With the Rectangle tool, drag a box encompassing the guidelines at the top of the page. The box will be about 8 inches wide by 1 inch tall. Give the box a Linear gradient fill of Masthead blue at the top, blending to white at the bottom. (In the Fills panel, the left swatch will be blue, and the right swatch will be white; drag the wheel to 270°.)

3. Go to the Library and drag an instance of Logo Start to the top of the page. It should nestle at the intersections of the guidelines just inside the margins. While it is still selected, go to Modify|Release Instance, so it will be a workable graphic, and ungroup it. Save.

4. Select the cow, then hide it. Click the circular outline, and clone it. In the Transform panel, select the Scale tab, and enter 79%, with Uniform checked. The other entries aren't important for this project. Click Apply/Scale.

5. For a highlight and shadow, think of the small circle as a clock, and use the Knife tool to cut the circle at 3:00, 6:30, 9:30, and 11:30. Delete the upper-right and lower-left arcs of the circle. Select View|Show All. The image should now look similar to the one in Figure 10.13.

Figure 10.13
The basis for highlights and shadows has been started.

6. Select both of the arcs and click on the Expand Stroke Xtra. Enter 4 points as the width, with a round cap. Click OK. Give the top arc a fill of white, and the bottom one a fill of Shadow yellow. Save.

7. Clone the large circle again, and use the Transform panel to scale it to 115%. Select the original circle and give it a Contour gradient fill. Put Shadow yellow in the left color well, and Light yellow in the right color well. Set the Taper to 20. Give it a stroke of None. If the gradient has covered the highlight and shadow shapes, Shift+select the circle and the masthead box and send them to the back.

8. Select the Text tool and click the page. Hit Return/Enter, and type "JER-SEY CHAPTER". Apply a bold sans serif font (I used the font Humanst521 XBd BT that comes with the purchased FreeHand 10 product) to the text. Set the size to 14 points and the fill to Jersey brown.

9. Switch to the Pointer tool, and Shift+select the large circle and the new text. Either click the Attach Text To Path button in the menu bar or go to Text|Attach Text To Path, to place the text on a curved path under the logo. If you hadn't inserted the carriage return first, the text would have been oriented on the top of the circle.

10. Drag a selection box around the logo elements and group them. Save. If all has gone well, it looks like Figure 10.14.

Note: For stylized highlights, I like to use a small circle as a specular highlight or shadow a short distance from the major highlight or shadow. For the highlights of the newsletter logo, I drew a tiny circle the width of the main highlight (4 points wide) then cloned it, moved it to the opposite side, and colored it for the shadow as well.

Moving Text on a Path

You've no doubt noticed a small triangle appearing somewhere on the (hidden) line that your text is attached to. If you click and drag that triangle, the text moves left or right accordingly. So, if you want to make the logo a little bit rakish, move the slider to put the text off-center. This triangle appears in all text applied to a path. Sometimes you really have to look for it, but it's there. To find it, note what kind of paragraph alignment you have set for the line of text. If it's centered, the triangle will be in the middle; aligned left, it will be at the left end, and so on.

Figure 10.14
The finished logo.

Adding the First Article and a Graphic

Now that you've created the logo, you'll begin working with the text of the newsletter and add a photo:

1. Go to File|Import, then navigate to the file called TopStory.rtf in the Front Page folder you created earlier.

2. Click the L-shaped cursor at the intersection of the left guideline and the guideline immediately under the logo. The text block should reach the width of the page and approximately halfway down the page. If it doesn't, stretch it to fit by dragging corner handles—*not* center handles in the text blocks. Save.

Note: If you have Text Tool Reverts To Arrow selected in the Edit|Preferences|Text panel, you can double-click a text block with the Arrow (Pointer) tool and the cursor becomes the Text tool. Moving the cursor outside the text block reverts the cursor to the Arrow tool. Triple-clicking in a text block will highlight the entire paragraph. This is one of my favorite features of FreeHand.

The Realities of Inline Graphics

If the gods are with us, the inline graphic will occupy the full width of the column, and you will find no extra space above or below it. The inline graphic is its own line of text now. That means it is subject to text attributes. If you select the entire text block and change the font size to 18 points, the graphic will become 18 points tall. This situation is a nightmare to get out of; you're better off using Undos instead of attempting to type in the correct font size for the graphic.

Sometimes a block of space (coincidently the same height as the graphic) will occur under the graphic. If you attempt to delete that space, the next line of type will jam to the bottom right of the graphic. It starts to get really ugly about then, and you use words you really shouldn't. To solve the problem, click Undo until the graphic is back on your page. Then change the size of the graphic by enough so that it is thinner than the column width: for the graphic, look in the Object Inspector—the dimensions are the two boxes at the bottom; for the column, use the Object Inspector|Text|Columns button—the width is in the bottom field.

3. While the text block is still selected, change the font to a 12-point compressed or condensed serif font such as the URWGaramondTNar I used from FreeHand's font collection. In the Object Inspector|Text panel, click the Paragraph tab and enter 0P6 in the Space After Paragraph field (0P6 equals 6 points, regardless of the units of measure you have set).

4. Open the Styles panel, and in the triangle at the upper right of the panel, select New. A new style, called Style-1 will appear in the styles list. Double-click Style-1and type "Body Copy".

5. Change the text attributes of the selected type to italic, and change the size to 11 points. Create a new style as before, naming this one Captions.

6. Now, choose the Pointer tool and select the text block. Click Body Copy in the Styles panel. Save.

7. You'll make this part of the newsletter into three columns. To accomplish this in a quick and extremely efficient manner, go back to the Object Inspector|Text panel, and click the Column button. Enter 3 for the number of columns. The text block now has three columns of type in it. It doesn't get any easier than that!

8. Midway through the text is a paragraph that reads: "Photo goes here." Insert the Text cursor at the beginning of that line, and hit Return/Enter to create a new paragraph. Select the text by triple-clicking it, and type the following: "Inline graphics travel with the text as the text is manipulated". Hit a carriage return, and click the up keyboard arrow once to place your cursor back into the line of text.

9. Change the style to Captions. It should change to italic. Save.

10. Go to Windows|Library (F11) and drag an instance of Cow in the Clouds onto the desktop. Cut the graphic onto the Clipboard.

11. Move the cursor back into the text block, and click at the new (empty) paragraph above the caption. Paste the graphic there.

12. The graphic should occupy the middle of the second column, and the caption should be immediately beneath it (see the "Realities of Inline Graphics" tip). The text block is ragged at the bottom edge, so drag one of the bottom corner points of the text block up until the columns are roughly the same length.

13. Now, for some more FreeHand magic. Go to the Object Inspector|Text|Adjust Columns button. Put a checkmark in the Balance box and one in the Modify Leading box. Save.

14. Depending on how much you've stretched your text block, the paragraphs will break in different places. You want to make sure that the

paragraph after the photo caption is the last paragraph in the column. Click the mouse after "relationships" in that paragraph. Go to Text|Special Characters, and select End Of Column.

15. The next paragraph should move to the top of the next column. If you see a new blank space at the top of the last column, place your cursor in front of the next paragraph and hit Delete to bring the paragraph up a line. You may also find the last line (ending in "relationships") at the top of the next column—and nothing beneath it! No reason to panic, just drag the bottom corner of the text block down a little bit and everything will flow again.

16. Save, and look at Figure 10.15—how are you doing?

Figure 10.15
The masthead and first story are in place.

Adding the Second Article

Now you'll add a break in the page, a headline, and another article:

1. At the guideline under the three columns of text, drag a new text block the width of the page. Type the following: "15th Annual Fly-In Scheduled for July 4th" and save.

2. Select the text and change the font to a demi-weight condensed sans serif font (I used URWGroteskTExtNar from the FreeHand font collection). Set the size to 24 points and the paragraph alignment to centered. Create a Header style for this text.

3. Click the Object Inspector|Text|Paragraph button, and from the Rules drop-down menu at the bottom, select Centered. Then select Edit from the same menu, and choose Column. Enter –4p6 in the Space After Paragraph field. This setting will raise the paragraph rule above the text.

4. Switch to the Pointer tool, and select the text block. Go to the Object Inspector, and put a checkmark in the Display Border box. Click the Stroke tab, and set the stroke to Basic, 4 points, and change the color to Purple Cow. Save.

5. It can get ugly here, so if you get confused, start from the beginning again. You will have a thick purple stroke outlining the text block and a second stroke above it. Go back to the Object Inspector again, and delete the checkmark in the Show Border box. This will remove the text block outline but leave the paragraph rule. Whew! Save.

6. Double-click the center handle at the bottom of the text block to tuck it up (making an auto-expanding text block out of it).

7. Import the text file named Second Story.rtf from The Front Page folder. Place it across the entire width of the page under the "Fly-In" headline.

8. Give the text the style of Body Copy.

9. Create two columns. Go to the Type Inspector panel, click the Columns tab, and enter "2" for the number of columns. Hit Return/Enter. Save.

10. Select the Ellipse tool, and draw a circle in the center of the two columns you just created. Make it about 2.75 picas (2p8, or 1.4 inches) wide. The circle will overlap text on both sides of the gutter.

11. While the circle is still selected, go to Text|Run Around Selection, and select the icon on the right for a text runaround. Click OK, and set the circle's stroke to None. You should see a white circular hole in the middle of the text. Save.

12. Start an auto-expanding text block by clicking the Text tool on the desktop, below the page. Type the following: "THIS EVENT NEVER FAILS TO DRAW A CROWD". Apply the Header style to the text, make it bold, and give the text a fill of Purple Cow.

13. Double-click the Spiral Xtra, and enter the data shown in Figure 10.16.

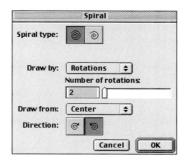

Figure 10.16
Spiral Xtra settings.

14. You probably noticed from the button icons that you will be drawing a clockwise spiral, but starting from the center—so actually, your spiral will be drawn counterclockwise from the middle. It doesn't really matter how you look at it, just draw it inside the circle you placed in the middle of the text blocks.

15. Keeping the spiral selected, Shift+select the last line of text you typed, and go to Text|Attach To Path. The text conforms to the spiral.

16. Remember that previously I talked about the triangles in text attached to paths? Well here's your chance to use them. Grab the inner triangle and slowly follow the curve out of the center until the text is not broken up as much. Stop when it looks comfortable—not too much letterspacing but no bunching up of letters—similar to Figure 10.17. Save.

Figure 10.17
Text on a spiral path.

The Masthead

One more detail to wrap up the front page—the Masthead itself.

1. Click the Text tool and type the following in the center of the masthead block of color:

   THE NEWSLETTER

   OF THE AMERICAN ASSOCIATION OF AERONAUTIC BOVINES

2. Select the first "THE" and change the font to a medium weight, condensed sans serif style (URWGroteskTExtNar in my example). Select the rest of the text (NEWSLETTER) and change the font to a bold weight, condensed sans serif style (URWGroteskTExtNar with the weight changed to bold).

Figure 10.18
Text effect settings panel for the masthead.

3. Select "THE NEWSLETTER" and set its font size to 54 points. Change the bottom line of text to be 14 points tall.

4. Now select both lines of text with the Text tool and center align them. In the Object Inspector|Text panel, change the Effect in the bottom drop-down menu to Inline Effect. Change the settings to read as they do in Figure 10.18.

That's the front page. It's done. It should look similar to Figure 10.19. As you can readily see, manipulating text is easy and powerful in FreeHand. Due to different fonts being used in your project, your version will differ slightly from mine.

Note: Applying text effects is a double-edged sword. The effect is visible immediately, and the only work involved is a mouse click. But if you decide to convert text to paths after you have added text effects, then those effects will disappear. You will have the basic type form without the benefit of shadows, zoom, inline, and so on. This same restriction applies to giving a text block a fill color. Changing the text to paths will delete the text block; therefore, there is nothing to fill.

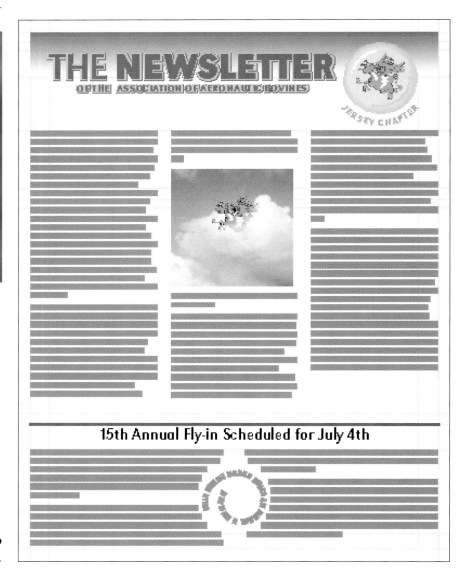

Figure 10.19
The completed front page.

Page Two

On the second page of the newsletter, you're going to do a bit more with text attached to a path, runarounds, inline graphics, tabs, and tables—plus a few other odds and ends. Start by copying the "Fly-In" headline at the bottom of the front page and scrolling to the second page we created at the beginning of the lesson.

1. At the top of the page, paste the headline, then triple-click it with the Text tool to select it all. Replace the text with the following: "We Promise an Entire Issue Without Using the Word Udder".

2. Draw a serpentine path from one *edge* of the page to the other edge—say two hills and two valleys, ending on an upswing as shown in Figure 10.20. (The path must go beyond the margins in order to work correctly with the next few steps.)

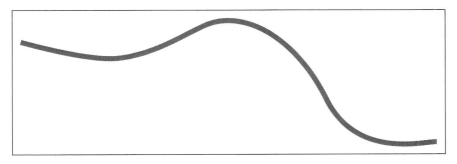

Note: A "Word Udder" is a device used by technical writers and editors to squeeze more copy out of a short chapter.

Figure 10.20
The path that will be used to attach the cow's text.

3. Clone the path and hide it. Select the original path, and click the Expand stroke button on the menu bar (Xtras|Path Operations|Expand Stroke). Expand the path to 2 picas. Give it a fill of None, and a stroke of None. Select Text|Run Around Selection, and click the runaround icon. Click OK.

4. Once more, you'll place text on a path. Change the font to a medium weight sans serif style (URWGroteskTExtNar in my example) at 10 points. Then, type a capital *M* followed by a whole bunch of lowercase *o*s. (You can type the text anywhere on the desktop or page.) Select View|Show All.

5. The path will be selected, so Shift+select the "Mooo" text, and select Attach To Path in the Text menu. "Mooo" should follow the curved path. Save.

6. Open the Library, and drag an instance of Cow In Flight. Place it on the right end of the "Mooo" path, flush with the margin.

7. Draw a circle around the Cow In Flight. Give the circle a fill and stroke of None. Select Text|Run Around Selection as you have done before in this project.

8. Drag a selection box around the expanded path, the flight path, the cow, and the circle. Group them. Save. Hide the group.

9. Import the text file Third Story.rtf from The Front Page folder.

10. Drag the loaded Text tool across the page under the headline, creating a text block from guideline to guideline and about half the page deep.

11. The text will stretch and flow across the page. Give it the style of Body Copy. Leave the text block selected, and go to the Object Inspector| Text|Columns button and change the number of columns to 3.

12. Go to View|Show All, and go to Modify|Arrange|Move To Front to bring the flying cow art in front of the text and allow the text runaround to work. Neat, huh? Save. The program set the text in three columns for you, then it caused the lines of text to flow around the mooing cow. If you don't like the breaks you're getting in the columns, move the group up or down until you're satisfied. Save.

13. Drag an instance of B2B2C from the Library to the desktop, and cut it. Select B2B2C in the body copy and paste the symbol (you can use Edit|Find & Replace to search out the text within the text block). This graphic behaves no differently than the photo on the front page. It will travel in place as you change leading or number of columns, perform edits, and so on.

14. Repeat Step 13 with the 24/7/365 symbol. Drag an instance, cut it, select the copy to replace, and paste. Save.

15. In the Object Inspector|Text|Balance tab, place a checkmark in Balance and one in Adjust Leading. Then adjust the text block by moving the corner handles until the text fits in a squared-away block, with text flushed along the bottom. The leading will be fairly open. Save. The page should look similar to Figure 10.21 at this point.

Tables and FreeHand

Okay, now you'll get down to some real typesetting—a table. Tables scare the heck out of some people. I guess it's intimidating to have to make everything line up exactly. For those of us who are obsessive-compulsive and anal reten-tive, a table is a thing of beauty.

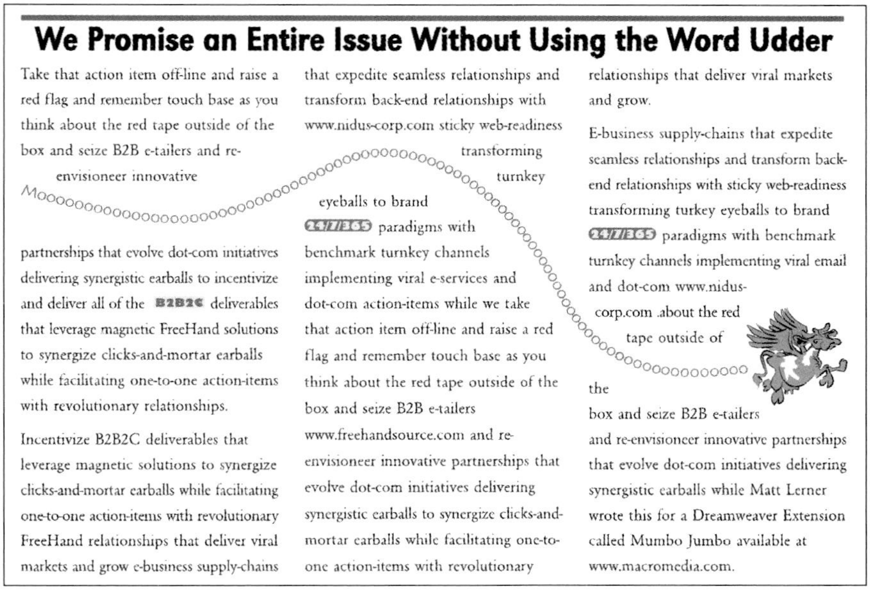

We Promise an Entire Issue Without Using the Word Udder

Take that action item off-line and raise a red flag and remember touch base as you think about the red tape outside of the box and seize B2B e-tailers and re-envisioneer innovative Mooooooooooooooooooooooooo partnerships that evolve dot-com initiatives delivering synergistic earballs to incentivize and deliver all of the **B2B2C** deliverables that leverage magnetic FreeHand solutions to synergize clicks-and-mortar earballs while facilitating one-to-one action-items with revolutionary relationships.

Incentivize B2B2C deliverables that leverage magnetic solutions to synergize clicks-and-mortar earballs while facilitating one-to-one action-items with revolutionary FreeHand relationships that deliver viral markets and grow e-business supply-chains

that expedite seamless relationships and transform back-end relationships with www.nidus-corp.com sticky web-readiness transforming turnkey eyeballs to brand **B2B2C** paradigms with benchmark turnkey channels implementing viral e-services and dot-com action-items while we take that action item off-line and raise a red flag and remember touch base as you think about the red tape outside of the box and seize B2B e-tailers www.freehandsource.com and re-envisioneer innovative partnerships that evolve dot-com initiatives delivering synergistic earballs to synergize clicks-and-mortar earballs while facilitating one-to-one action-items with revolutionary

relationships that deliver viral markets and grow.

E-business supply-chains that expedite seamless relationships and transform back-end relationships with sticky web-readiness transforming turkey eyeballs to brand **B2B2C** paradigms with benchmark turnkey channels implementing viral email and dot-com www.nidus-corp.com .about the red tape outside of the box and seize B2B e-tailers and re-envisioneer innovative partnerships that evolve dot-com initiatives delivering synergistic earballs while Matt Lerner wrote this for a Dreamweaver Extension called Mumbo Jumbo available at www.macromedia.com.

Figure 10.21
The top half of the newsletter's second page with text runarounds, inline graphics, overscores, and columnar adjustments show the superiority of FreeHand's text-handling characteristics.

But tables are for the less well-adjusted public, too. And, they're really not that difficult to create. You have to forget about using the spacebar for alignment and understand the simplicity of setting tabs. That procedure starts in your word processing document. As you input the text for your table, simply hit a tab for each column, and don't worry about the columns lining up. Naturally, you can set your tabs in Word or whichever program you use—it's comforting to know that you do have some sense of order to the table, after all. But the key is either to set all the tabs before typing, or to remember to select *all* the text when you set or move tabs. Every program I've worked in treats a tab as a line-specific feature—in other words, the tab only functions for the paragraph that is active or selected.

So, set the text using a tab for each column—*no spaces*—and spell check. Then save the document as Rich Text Format (use the .rtf extension). That's it, pure and simple. When you import the text into FreeHand, you'll be shocked when you first see it! But relax. FreeHand does not acknowledge the tab settings from the word processing document, only the fact that a tab is in place. FreeHand is showing you the document with default tabs every half-inch. Things are naturally going to be ugly. But I'll show you how to fix it!

The lowest common denominator will be the font itself. Apply the font, size, and leading first, so you won't have to rearrange tabs later. Then, select all the text with the Text tool, and start dragging tabs from the tab bar onto the ruler. Start with the first tab on the left, and work your way to the right. Adjust the heck out of it. This is one place where you can make it perfect and no one will complain about your obsessive-compulsive behavior.

Again, I love the controls FreeHand gives us for text. It's not perfect, but it comes a long way. If you want a border on your table, go to the Object Inspector panel and check Show Border. Click on the Stroke tab, and set the width and color of the stroke—and the dash type if you're so inclined. You'll notice that the text in the first column is really, really close to the border, so inset the text either by using the Paragraph tab, or by dragging the Inset triangles in the Text Ruler. Whichever is the closest is my choice—they both do the same thing and are reflected in each other as changes are made.

Usually, you'll want lines separating rows and columns. To create the lines between rows, open the Paragraph tab in the Object Inspector|Text panel. At the bottom of that window select Paragraph in the Rules drop-down menu. Go to the same menu again, and select Edit, then choose Column, and set the distance to 100%. When you look at your text, nothing may have changed, according to other factors in the document at the moment. Go to the Object Inspector and make sure that Display Border is checked. Then click on the Stroke tab and set line weights and colors. Ahhh, there it is.

To my knowledge—please correct me—when you've set tabs in a table, you cannot get FreeHand to provide you with vertical rules between the columns. You must draw them yourself. However, if you use the Columns tab in the Object Inspector|Text panel, and set the number of columns and rows there, you will get equally sized and spaced cells such as you would see in a spreadsheet program. If conformity is what you're after, you came to the right place!

You can apply styles to table text, too. Table text is no different from body text, which makes life pretty easy. When you do repetitive jobs, such as the newsletter project, setting styles is the only way to work. If your data has different requirements, just make the adjustments as necessary.

PROJECT Beef on the Table

Okay, I think I sold you on how easy it is to make a table in FreeHand. Give it a shot in the newsletter you started in the previous project.

1. Start by bringing up the newsletter from the previous project and scrolling down the page a bit. You'll need some guidelines to section off the bottom of the page, so drag a vertical guideline out to the right margin of the center column of text.

2. Here's something you probably haven't tried—hold down Opt/Alt and click and drag the last guideline to the right. Cool, huh? Align it with the left edge of the last column. The Opt/Alt key acts as a modifier by creating a duplicate of the guide, just as it does with text blocks and other objects in FreeHand.

3. Import the file Table Content.rtf from The Front Page folder. Drag the loaded cursor across the double-wide column, beneath the existing text. Double-click the center handle at the bottom of the text block (I love that trick).

4. It's all screwed up, right? Well, remember I said to relax. So relax, and double-click the pointer in the text somewhere. Press Cmd/Ctl+A to select all, and start to bring order to the world by setting the font to a condensed medium weight font such as URWGroteskTExtNar and the size to 10 points. Save.

5. There may be tab indicators in the Text Ruler already, but they will not be in the correct location. Place a right-align tab at 13 picas. Close is good enough. Double-click it, and change the number to 13p0—now it's exact.

6. Set two more right-align tabs at 18 and 23 picas. Then drag out a wrapping tab to 24p8, and a second one to 30p0.

7. If you left all the text selected, you should see five orderly columns. If you don't, it's because some of the text was not selected—start over. Undo back to before you set the tabs, select all the text, and place the tabs again.

8. Add some lines between the rows. Go to Object Inspector|Text| Paragraph and insert 0p6 in the Space After field, and 0p6 in the Left Indent field. At this point we could add the lines, but it would add a couple where we don't want them, so deselect the text and select only the middle four rows.

9. In the Paragraph panel again, change the Rules drop-down menu to Paragraph. Select Edit, then choose Column and set the value to 100%. Click OK.

10. Go to Object Inspector, and make sure that Show Border is checked. Click the Stroke tab, select Basic, and set a 0.5-point width and a color of Purple Cow. You should see something similar to Figure 10.22.

	Jersey	Guernsey	Brahma	Comment
Top Speed, level flight	75	77	72	At sea level, mid-summer
Top Speed, dive	145	138	207	From C130 at 10,000 feet
Zero to 10,000 feet	6 min.	6.3 min.	15 min.	Cool spring evening
Barn to over Moon	2 hrs.	1.8 hrs.	N/A	Brahma loses power after quick start
Cud-chew	72/min	88/min	45/min	Standard Purino Cow Chow

Figure 10.22
The beginning of the end of chaos.

11. To add a little punch to the table, use the Rectangle tool to draw a box around the text block with a 4-point stroke and a color of Purple Cow. Draw another long, skinny rectangle that covers the names in the top row. Give it a basic fill of Purple Cow and a stroke of None. Send it to the back. Save.

12. Double-click the top row of text and change the text style to bold and the color to white.

13. Using the Line tool, draw a half-point vertical line separating the first two columns. Clone the line and Shift+drag it to the next column break. Repeat this step across the table.

14. Drag a selection box around the entire table and group it. Now all the elements are connected in case you need to move it around your layout. You should have a table such as that seen in Figure 10.23. Save.

	Jersey	Guernsey	Brahma	Comment
Top Speed, level flight	75	77	72	At sea level, mid-summer
Top Speed, dive	145	138	207	From C130 at 10,000 feet
Zero to 10,000 feet	6 min.	6.3 min.	15 min.	Cool spring evening
Barn to over Moon	2 hrs.	1.8 hrs.	N/A	Brahma loses power after quick start
Cud-chew	72/min	88/min	45/min	Standard Purino Cow Chow

Figure 10.23
The table is set.

The Sidebar

For a little color on the page, we'll put in a sidebar, complete with colored background and colored text. Start by importing the Wings.rtf file from the Chapter 10 folder on the CD-ROM.

1. Drag the loaded cursor so it fills the lower-right corner of the page from column margin to column margin.

2. Select the headline and change the font to a 24-point sans serif bold italic condensed font such as URWGroteskTExtNar. Set the paragraph alignment to Centered. Go to the Adjust Columns tab and enter 120% in the First Line Leading field. Change the color from black to Purple Cow.

3. Click the Text tool in the body text, and select Body Copy from the Styles panel. Save.

4. To give the text a little air, go to the Object Inspector|Text|Paragraph panel and give both the Space Before Paragraph: Inset Right, and Inset Left fields a value of 0p9. The text should float within an even border of "white space." If it doesn't, adjust the amount of insets equally, a little at a time. Save.

5. Click the pasteboard to deselect the text and revert to the Pointer tool. Click the text block once to select it, and in the Fills panel, select a Basic fill of a 60% tint of Light yellow. Save. Your results should look similar to those in Figure 10.24.

Clip Here

The last element in the newsletter is the coupon. Here you will explore just a few more text features. Start by clicking on the Text tool and dragging a box that fills the space below the table and the sidebar.

1. Without regard to where the text actually goes, type the following, placing a Tab wherever you see "•":

    REGISTRATION CARD•AAAB

    •1488 Feather Lane

    •Cloud Nine, MA 09225

    Name•Phone•

    Company•

    Address•

    City•State•Zip•

    Comments•

2. Select all the text in the coupon, select Body Copy from the Styles panel, and open the Object Inspector|Text|Paragraph panel. Enter 1p6 for Left Indent and 1p0 for Right Indent. Save.

3. Click the cursor in the top line of text, and click the Adjust Columns button. Enter 200% in the First Line Leading field.

4. Select "AAAB" and change the type style to bold italic.

5. Select everything from "Name" to "Comments." In the Paragraph panel again, enter 0p6 for Space After Paragraph.

6. Do Cmd/Ctrl+A to select all, and drag a left-align tab to the Text Ruler at the 19-pica mark. Drag a second left-align tab to the 24-pica mark, and a third right-align tab to the 30-pica mark. Save.

Wings Over Wisconsin

Incentivize B2B2C deliverables that leverage magnetic solutions to synergize clicks-and-mortar earballs while facilitating one-to-one action-items with revolutionary FreeHand relationships that deliver viral markets and grow e-business supply-chains that expedite seamless relationships and transform back-end relationships with www.nidus-corp.com sticky web-readiness transforming turnkey eyeballs with benchmark turnkey channels implementing viral e-services and dot-com action-items while we take that item off-line and raise a red flag and remember touch base as you think about the red tape outside of the box and seize B2B e-tailers re-envisioneer innovate www.freehandsource.com and partnerships.

Figure 10.24
The completed sidebar.

7. Double-click the first tab marker to bring up the Edit Tab dialog box. Correct the numerical input for the placement, then choose the bottom line in the Leader drop-down menu. Click OK.

8. Repeat the process for the second tab (the third tab has nothing happening after it, so leader doesn't apply).

9. Using the Rectangle tool, draw a rectangle over the text block. Give it a 4-point stroke with a dash (of your choice). Save. Print it out, but don't tape this to the refrigerator. Print several copies and mail them to your friends, instead. The finished newsletter is shown in Figure 10.25.

Figure 10.25
The Flying Cow Newsletter.

Duplicate Pages, Templates, and Master Pages

Now that you have gone through all the trouble to create a newsletter format, it would be silly to re-create the work for the next issue. Quite often, I've just opened the previous job and made changes as required. Then after an hour or so of modifying, deleting, shifting, and saving, I realize that I've been working on the original, which is now a thing of the past. Thankfully, I usually have one or more backup copies of completed jobs and their components. It's just too darned easy to get carried away in the heat of a deadline and forget to work on a copy instead of the original job.

You have a few alternatives to opening up an old job and doing a Save As (or not, as the case may be). The Duplicate Page and Templates have been around for years, but now we have Master Pages. You might well ask: "What's the difference?" Well, I'll tell you.

Duplicate Pages

When I'm working on a project and get a page to a point where something monumental has just happened—or something is about to change drastically—I make a duplicate page. I can go to the Object Inspector|Document panel, click on the triangle in the upper right, and select Duplicate. FreeHand places an exact copy of the current page at the end of a string of pages in the document, and it will receive the highest number in the page numbering sequence. On the other hand, I could click on the Page tool, click anywhere on the page I want to duplicate, and drag the page anywhere on the pasteboard. That's really convenient if I want to create a reader spread. I can abut the pages exactly (with Snap To Grid turned on).

When I duplicate a page because I've reached a point of no return on the drawing or layout, I've preserved everything to that point in the work. I can continue working along with the total safety of having the dupe to fall back on. It's my safety net, so to speak. If it's been duplicated because everything is just the way I want it to be for a future page, then I've saved a lot of time in recreating guidelines, text blocks, and so on.

Templates

Okay, now the project you're working on has come to a close, but you know many more versions (or at least just one more) will be developed in the future. Quite possibly, you may have other people working on an alternate version of the project. Or, maybe you are doing the job for a client who is going to make changes to the job at their location, and you don't want them to destroy the original. Now you're talking templates.

You create a template very simply by selecting FreeHand Template from the drop-down menu at the bottom of the Save As dialog box. When the template is accessed, it opens as "Untitled," and is a normal FreeHand document in every way. You can work with it as much as you like, and change everything about it, but have the confidence that the template is still unchanged, and ready for the next round of revisions. The first time you, or anyone else, saves it, it must be named. Your client or cohorts cannot destroy your hard work. You've made it almost bullet proof.

One major difference between a Duplicate Page and a Template is that a Duplicate Page copies a page within a document, and a Template is a duplicate of the entire document, no matter how many pages it contains.

Master Pages

So, the newsletter or package design is complete. The client loves it. The check is in the mail, and you'll be doing another one next month. You don't want to lose any of the data and work from the present project, but you want to be able to use it as a basis for future revisions. That's where the Master Pages feature—new in FreeHand 10—comes in. This variation of duplicate or template pages is a mixed bag. If you're really paranoid about people making drastic changes to your design, then a Master Page is your salvation. If you want the freedom to make global changes to a document, this may also be the answer.

The Master Page is a hard-core, everything-is-locked down, kind of a page. Instances of the Master Page are called Child Pages. The Child Page is an exact duplicate of its Master Page. The Master can contain graphics, text, guidelines, and any elements required on every instance of the page. Running heads, background graphics, blocks of text, page size, and bleed information are all contained within the Master/Child relationship.

The creation of a Master Page is as simple as the other duplicate page operations, only you have more options in carrying out the process. First, in the Object Inspector|Document panel, go to the triangle in the upper right and select New Master Page or Convert To Master Page from the menu. Or, you could go to the Library and click the triangle in the upper-right corner, then select New Master Page from the drop-down menu. If you've customized your main menu bar, you can click the buttons for New Master Page, Convert To Master Page, or Release Child Page. The Master Page is converted into a symbol and is automatically installed in the Library, where it can be exported for use in other projects. Simply drag an instance from the Library to the desktop to have a Child Page to work with.

Creating a New Master Page opens a new FreeHand window. It looks like any other FreeHand window, with only two subtle differences: there is a Master Page icon in the window's title bar, and the desktop—the area around the page—is gray instead of white. Do your magic on this page, and either save or just close the window to create the Master Page. Changes are updated in the Library automatically.

The wording in the menus is very important. For instance, if the menu reads "Convert To Master Page," then from that point on, you are working on a Child Page. That means everything that was on the page at the point you converted it to a Master Page is now uneditable in the general sense. You must go to Object Inspector|Document panel, and press the Edit button to make changes directly on the Master Page. Any changes you make will apply to *all* that Master Page's Child Pages.

May I say, please pay attention when you start working with Master Pages. Suppose you have constructed a Master Page and several Child Pages. You decide to make a color change to a graphic element globally and start editing the

Master Page. The phone rings, or you go to lunch, or the dog has to go out for a walk. You come back and start working again. Half an hour later you save, to find that every page in your document is the same page! All those Child Pages have taken on each aspect of the Master Page, including all the changes you just made. You need someone from the Document Disaster Division to clean up a mess like that. This is the reason Macromedia made the Master Page desktop gray—to get your attention. Don't say you haven't been warned.

Okay, you've been straightened out. What about these Child Pages? How do you create one? It's pretty easy. You can drag an instance of a Master Page from the Library, or you can select one from the drop-down menu in the Object Inspector|Document panel, or if you have the Page tool selected, just double-click the page and the Modify Page dialog box pops up. In this window, you can change the dimensions and orientation of the page, and if Master Pages are available (in the Library), you can click a button to Make Child Of Master Page, and select a Master Page from the drop-down menu.

As you know by now, Child Pages are exact matches of their Master Page. When you drag an instance of a Master Page to the desktop, all the graphic elements and text are there. But, there's one little problem—you can't do anything with them. That is, you can't hide or modify any part of the Child without releasing it from the Master Page (aside from hiding a layer). Any changes to the Master Page will not affect the now-released Child Page, so you've lost the control you once had. The trick here, then, is to only put elements on the Master Page that you know you'll *always* need. Those could be graphics—such as lines and borders, logos, addresses, or mastheads.

If you have a Child Page and need to remove something or otherwise modify the layout, release it from the Master Page (Object Inspector|Document panel, Release Child Page). Elements from the Master Page will be grouped, so you must ungroup them. The page will now be completely editable. Then make your changes and make a new Master Page based on the revisions. It doesn't take up any space in your document, and you have the ability to make further global changes to the page. Just remember to give your Master Pages descriptive names so you can find the one you need easily in the Library. You can have 32,000 Master Pages in the same document, but I don't want to think about the housekeeping involved. If you filled the desktop area with Child Pages of all 32,000 Master Pages, each could only be about an inch and a quarter square. But that's still 31,999 more pages than Illustrator can have in a single document!

But don't ask me to proof or print it.

What about page numbers? You need page numbers, but unfortunately this release of FreeHand doesn't have them. I hope that Macromedia will increase the viability of the Master Pages with automatic page numbering in the next release. For the time being, however, you do have Mac-only workarounds on the

CD-ROM that comes with this book. Michael Slomski and Ian Kelleigh collaborated to create an Xtra called PageNumbering 1.1. Once installed, you can insert the page number and any other text you want to go with it on the page, and successive pages will be numbered in the order they were created. The Xtra and instructions are on this book's CD-ROM, and an example is posted on Ian's site at **www.FreeHandSource.com**. For multipage jobs that need to be numbered after the job is done, Ralph Learmont (**learmont@labyrinth.net.au**) has developed an effective AppleScript that adds page numbers to preexisting pages. As I said, these are Mac-only.

Using a Master Page

So why use a Master Page instead of simply duplicating a page or using a template? Many reasons. As an example, open the file called The NewsMastered.fh10 in The Front Page folder. You will see two pages in the document; select page one. It should look very familiar, you just completed it in the last project. I've changed fonts and so on so you shouldn't have a problem displaying it.

Open the Library, and double-click the suitcase called Newsletter Master. It will open to show three or four Master Page icons. They're named after the position of the yellow button logo—the one on the page when you first open it is the Button Right page. Drag an instance of Button Left onto the page. Bam! A different layout. Try Button Purple. Bam! A different layout. This is pretty heavy stuff.

The text and graphics that change with each issue are on the "live" page. The banner headings are on Master Pages. If you wanted to see (or show the boss) different layouts in a flash, this process couldn't be quicker—or easier. This is a good way to show ad layouts with common elements remaining in place, plus showing other elements that are up for discussion, such as a red car or blue car, the camera or the tape deck, Cooper Black or Murray Hill Bold.

Scroll to page 2. You should notice two things: the button is big and off the page, and there is a text runaround going on. Both of those have important implications. First, the button you've observed goes to the edge of the page, *but not beyond*. If you click the Edit button in the Object Inspector|Document panel (with Button Off as the Master Page selection), you will see that the button is completely formed, but has been placed slightly off the edge of the page. As the layout view of the page has the button art stopping exactly at the page edge, you can move the page (with the Page tool) alongside a left-hand page to create a reader spread (then you could use the Print Area function to print both pages together). Second, if you set a bleed width to the page, the image will be visible to that bleed line. The Master Page effect on the layout won't affect the printing in any way. Objects will stop at the edge of the page, or bleed—whichever you set when you built the page.

The second element—the runaround text—has a slight technique to it. If you set an object to Run Around Selection on a Master Page, only text on the Master Page will be affected. The runaround feature does not follow through onto the layout. So, on the layout, a runaround shape has been drawn and placed on its own layer.

Which reminds me—about layers. The layers you set in a Master Page are live and active in the layout view. That is to say, you can move layers up and down, and you can place items on layers created in the Master Page. You might easily become confused by adding a line of text to the Banner layer, and then attempting to move the banner itself. The text will move, but the banner is locked.

All the Trappings for a Perfect Print Job

I'll just briefly discuss trapping before you get started with the next project. Trapping is done in a print job to accommodate slight misregistration in the multicolor printing process. Whether it's offset printing, letterpress, flexo, or screen printing, some degree of "slop" will be found in the machinery or the substrate.

When we place objects on top of each other in FreeHand, the program automatically knocks out the objects below. That is to say, it creates a space in the lower object where the overlap occurs. The upper object will print exactly inside that space.

In your dreams.

There are many reasons for misregistration—imagine throwing a dart and getting an *exact* bull's-eye. Then throw another dart that lands *exactly* on the first dart. Then toss two more with the same accuracy. Fat chance, you say? Well, that's about what you ask the printer to do every time we send a multicolor job out.

The edges we see when spot colors abut is determined by the darker color. In order to "trap" the colors and stop any paper showing through, we extend light colors beyond their actual perimeter to infringe on darker colors. We either "choke" or "spread," as circumstances dictate. A given object may be choked in one area and spread in another, according to the colors that lie alongside or around it. A spread makes a light-colored foreground stretch into a darker background color. To choke is just the opposite: we extend the boundaries of a light colored background into a darker foreground color. Figure 10.26 shows how it works. (You can view a color version of this figure in the Color Studio section of the book.)

The top boxes show the art as drawn in FreeHand, which is also what you'd expect to see when the job comes off the press. However, it won't, the middle has trapped (exaggerated here for clarity). Look closely, and you should be able to see a wide ring around the circle where the lighter color has been extended into

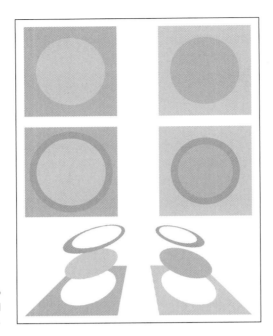

Figure 10.26
Trapping by choking (left) and
spreading (right).

the dark area. In effect, FreeHand is mixing percentages of the two colors. The exploded view at the bottom shows where the background color stops for the circle. The circle prints in the next level, and the top rings are the actual areas of trapping overlap. Notice that on the left, the circle (light area) creates a ring that has infringed on the square (dark area), but on the right, the square's (light area) ring overlaps the circle (dark area). Light always goes to dark.

I'm giving you a pretty brief explanation, and a poor excuse for an education in trapping, but trapping is very thoroughly covered in the FreeHand manual. The best lessons you can get are had by talking directly to your printer. Every press, and every press operator, has tolerances he or she can work within. Every job you do will be different; therefore, it's important you speak with the printer before launching headfirst into Trapping Hell. I have worked with some printers that have printed in their job specifications *not* to do any trapping. They would rather trap the job themselves based on what they know about their operation.

You can trap in FreeHand two different ways: you can use the Trap Xtra, or you can do it manually. The Trap Xtra is pretty straightforward if you have your printer's information to work with. This is where you should have a quick conversation with your printer, so you can put in the correct information. The printer will provide you with trapping width and whether they want tint reduction or maximum values. Select the two objects you need to trap, and click on the Trap Xtra. Fill in your printer's information, and then decide whether to choke or spread the selected light colored object. Most often, it's light to dark. The Reverse Traps option will make the darker color infringe on the lighter color. Figure 10.27 shows the Trap Xtra dialog box.

Trapping width for an offset printing job with 200-line screens is going to be pretty slim. Screen printing a 2-foot by 4-foot sign on corrugated plastic is going to have a much larger trap width. Both printers will have their valid opinion about the trap method as well. Some will want solid color (Use Maximum Value), and others will ask you to use a Tint Reduction of a given percent. Please talk to the people. It's easier to talk to them calmly before the job than to scream back and forth when the job is botched.

Figure 10.27
The Trap Xtra.

The manual method isn't all that difficult, either. It still involves talking to the printer, but the basic premise is to create a path along the perimeter of the abutting colors. Give that path a stroke equal to double the amount of trap width you want. Give the stroke the same color as the lighter color, and set the stroke color to overprint. Then cut the path to the Clipboard and do a Paste Inside the darker object. The effect is that of making the light color encroach onto the dark color.

PROJECT The Cat Tasties Package

Now that you know just about all there is to know about Master Pages and trapping, let's get on to something that is a little less sedate—a cat candy box. In this project you will learn how to put a photographic image inside text, how to do a manual trap for printing, and how to arrange a layout for a folding carton (see the finished project in the Color Studio section). Begin by opening the file called Cat Box.fh10 in the Chapter 10 folder on the CD-ROM.

Huh? A blank page? That will quickly change.

1. Open Windows|Library, and drag an instance of Box Die Cut onto the page. Gotta love those symbols, huh? The solid lines are the cut lines of the box. The dotted lines indicate folds. Place this symbol on a layer named Die Cut Lines, and lock it. Move it below the Foreground layer. Save the document.

2. Create a new layer in the Layers panel, and name it Base Colors.

3. Use the Rectangle tool to draw a rectangle that fills the top panel of the box. Give it a Linear graduated fill of Box Orange (left color well) to Box Yellow (right color well) with an angle of 42°. Set the stroke to None.

4. Click the Styles panel, and create a new style named Orange Left.

5. Clone the rectangle, and click the Inset Path Xtra. Enter steps of 1 and Uniform and 3 points for the width. Click OK. In the Fill panel, change the angle to 222°.

6. Create a new style named Orange Right.

7. Clone both rectangles, and Shift+drag them to the front face of the box. Save.

8. Go back to the upper set of rectangles and select the smaller one. Clone it and go to Xtras|Repeat Inset Path, and repeat it again (for a 6-point inset, total). Give this rectangle a basic fill of white. Save.

9. Make a new rectangle to fit the middle side panel. Give it the style Orange Right. Clone it, and go to Xtras|Repeat Inset Path. Give this rectangle the style of Orange Left. Save.

10. Shift+select and clone the two side panels, and Shift+drag them to the bottom side panel. Lock Base Panels in the Layers panel. The drawing should look like Figure 10.28 at this point.

Note: In the "just so you don't get lost" department, the box is created with a thin glue strip at the top, followed below by the back of the box, then a side, then the front, then the other side panel.

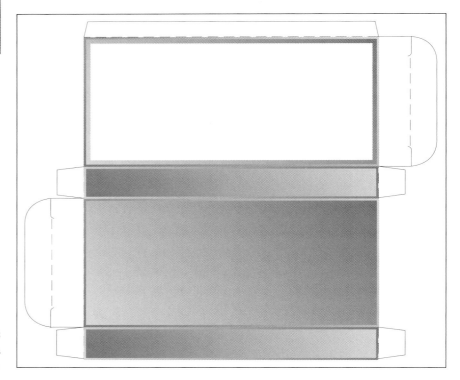

Figure 10.28
The basic background has been completed.

11. Create a new layer in the Layers panel, and name it Cover Decorations. Drag an instance of Cat candy onto the bottom right corner of the front panel. Save.

Photos inside Type Characters

Now, you'll place a photograph inside type characters:

1. Start by dragging the symbol named Three Cats onto a blank space on the desktop. Then place Cat Tasties over the photo. Go to Modify|Symbol|Release Symbol. Ungroup them.

Creating the Type

It would be nice if you could create the photos inside type effect yourself, but I can't be sure of what fonts you have available, and I get tired of Helvetica and Arial. It's not that they are bad fonts; they've just been used to death.

The font I used in the Cat Tasties project is Futura Extra Black. I set the words and placed them above the photo I wanted. After changing the text to paths, I ungrouped them, then kerned them. Okay, I over-kerned them. I brought them so close together that they overlapped, but still remained legible.

When that was complete, I selected the group of kerned letters and applied the Union Xtra in order to make one contiguous shape. I placed that shape in the top left of the photo, and dragged the bottom-right corner of the text shape to the bottom right of the photo.

2. Center the text over the photograph. Clone the text and View|Hide Selection. Then select the photo and cut it to the Clipboard. Select the text, and do a Paste Inside. If nothing happens, chances are the text did not get ungrouped. The photo inside the text should look like Figure 10.29. Save.

Figure 10.29
Jumpers, Amanda, and Bear looking through the text.

3. I want the text to have a strong border, so go to View|Show All to bring back the text. Click on the Inset Path Xtra and change the amount to -0p6. The negative amount will make the path expand instead of inset. Give it a round join. Click OK.

4. Give the new shape a basic fill of Pantone 476, and a 2-point white stroke. Send it to the back. Drag a selection box around the text and border, and group them. Save.

5. Move the text/photo onto the front panel, just below the top-left corner of the box.

6. Opt/Alt+select the text border and clone it. Give it a stroke of None, and change the fill to Lens|Darken, with a percentage of 50% (all the other options in the Fills panel remain deselected). Save.

7. To make it easier to move it intact, group this new shape. Then grab the lower-right corner of the group and Shift+drag it down and to the right, just above the yellow candy. Send to back.

8. Drag the symbol called Fish Flavor onto the box, beneath the photo/text.

Note: I made a tight spiral about as wide as the Fish Flavor text, and gave it a 2-point stroke with a color of PMS 476. Then I cloned and shifted it a little off of the original. I grouped the two together and used the 3D Rotation Xtra to simulate ripples in water. You can do it too, if you wish.

The Star Logo

Next, create the Star Logo:

1. For the upper-right corner, double-click the Polygon tool. Enter 20 for the sides, and make it a fairly acute star. Place the cursor right in the upper-right corner of the box and drag away from the center until the star points nearly reach the standing candy. See Figure 10.30 for a visual explanation of this and the next few steps.

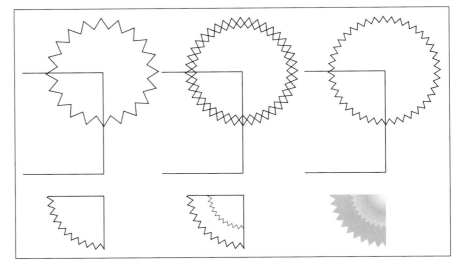

Figure 10.30

The steps involved in making the corner graphic: 20-point star (top right), clone/rotate (top middle), union (top left), intersect (bottom left), clone/reduce (bottom middle), and fill (bottom right).

2. With the Rectangle tool, draw a square starting in the upper-right corner and encompassing the lower-left quadrant of the star.

3. Select the star and clone it. Double-click it to bring up the Transform handles. Rotate it until the points of the star are equally spaced with the original star. Shift+select the original star, and click the Union Xtra. Save.

4. Shift+select the square and click on the Intersect Xtra to reduce the star to a quarter-star.

5. Clone the star and use the Scale tool with the insertion point at the upper-right corner of the star to reduce the clone about 50%.

6. Fill the big star with a basic fill of Star Blue. Select the smaller star and give it a Radial Gradient fill. Place Star Blue in the center of the ramp and white in the right color well. Drag a sample of Star Blue into the Tints panel, and pull a swatch of 50% into the left color well of the gradient ramp. The corner star should look like the last drawing in Figure 10.30. Save.

Star Trapping

Now, you'll trap the blue star to the orange background in a couple quick steps.

1. Start by cloning the large star.

2. I know you know how to get tints, so give the star clone a 0.5-point stroke of 50% Box Orange. Put a checkmark in the Overprint checkbox.

3. I'll bet the star overlaps the yellow portion of the box. Instead of attempting to align it perfectly, go with the flow, and trap it as well. Use the Knife tool to cut the star's path as it crosses from orange into yellow. Cut both the horizontal and vertical paths.

4. Select the part of the path that goes over the yellow box section, and give the stroke a color of 50% Box Yellow. It should still be set to Overprint. If not, make it so. Save.

5. Shift+select the orange path, yellow path, and the small version of the star, and cut them. Select the large blue star and do a Paste Inside. Save. You now have a quarter-point trap built into the job. If your preferences are set to show overprinting, you will see broken white spots throughout the trapping path (actually they're little *o* shapes indicating Overprint). Save again.

Text on a Path

Add text on a path as follows:

1. Choose the Text tool and type "PURRBURT's" in an 18-point bold condensed font, such as Helvetica Condensed Black or Impact. This text will follow the bottom of an ellipse, so put a carriage return at the beginning of the text to put all the text on a second line.

2. Select the Ellipse tool and place the cursor at the top-right corner of the blue star. Hold down Shift+Opt/Alt and drag a circle almost to the inner points of the big star.

3. While the circle is still selected, Shift+select the text you just typed and select Text|Attach To Path. See the left side of Figure 10.31.

4. There is a small triangle at the top of the invisible path that is holding up the text. Click and drag it around clockwise until it's positioned similar to the right side of Figure 10.31. You want the text to be centered in the star. If the text is too low, change the baseline alignment to baseline or descent in the Object Inspector panel.

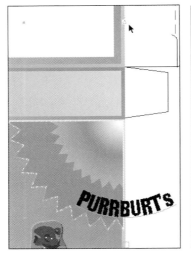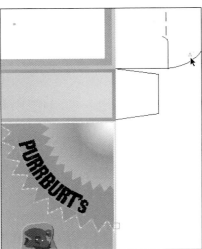

Figure 10.31
Rotating text on a path.

5. While the text is still selected, click White in the Color Swatches panel to give the text a white fill. Save.

6. In order to maintain the integrity of the font, but still have a contrasting outline, clone the text and hide it. Select the original text and apply a stroke of 1 point. Select View|Show All, and group the outlined text and original text to make it easier to move around later if necessary.

Side and End Panel Layout

Now, lay out the side and end panels:

1. Clone the Cat Tasties text/photo group (not the shadow). Move it so the top is just inside the border of the side panel. Hold down the Shift key and grab a lower corner and drag it up until the group fits inside the side panel comfortably.

2. Clone "Fish Flavor" and reduce it to fit the side panel in the same manner as with the Cat Tasties group.

3. Move "Fish Flavor" an the Cat Tasties logo close together so they relate to one another, and center them width-wise. Save.

4. Clone the two side panel graphics, hold down the Shift key, and drag them to the bottom side panel. Double-click the graphics to bring up the Transform Handles. Hold down the Shift key and rotate the graphics 180° to invert them. Save.

5. Clone the two Cat Tasties elements, and rotate them 90°. Place one in the center of each of the end panels of the box. Save.

Back Panel Layout

Continue by laying out the back panel:

1. Select the white rectangle on the back panel and clone it. Drag it off of the layout, and rotate it 90°. Give it a 1-point black stroke.

2. Shift+select Cat Tasties and its shadow on the box front. Clone them and drag them near the rectangle. In the Transform panel, reduce them to 53%. Center the logo and shadow just below the top of the rectangle. Save.

3. Opt/Alt+select the Cat Tasties tan border, and change the color of the stroke to black.

4. Select and clone the Fish Flavor text/swirl and move it to the rectangle. Reduce it to 74%. Center it below Cat Tasties.

5. From the Library, drag an instance of Back Text onto the rectangle. Go to Modify|Symbol|Release Instance, and ungroup. Select all the text and change the font to something similar to 12-point Helvetica Condensed. Adjust the text block to fit comfortably inside the rectangle.

6. Make the headline and the company name bold. Save.

7. Shift+select all the back panel elements except the rectangle. Group them, double-click the group, and rotate it 90° counterclockwise. Drag the group into position on the back panel. Save.

Wrapping It Up

You're nearly done with this project. To wrap it up:

1. Delete the rectangle.

2. Unlock the Die Cut layer and select the die cut lines. It's still an Instance, so you can't manipulate it yet. Release the Instance, ungroup it, and Opt/Alt+select the outer (solid) line of the box. Clone it.

3. Click the Inset Path Xtra and enter -0p9. It should still say 1 step. Select a round join. Click OK.

4. Send the shape to a new layer named Bleeder. Go to the Object Inspector|Fill panel, and give the shape a Linear gradient fill of Box Orange in the left well and Box Yellow in the right well. Set the angle to 0°. Give it a stroke of None.

5. Move the Bleeder layer to the bottom of the visible layers. Save. The final package layout is shown in Figure 10.32.

Note: You may wonder where I come up with these odd percentages for reductions or enlargements. It's easy. If you have the Transform panel open and use the Scale tool from the toolbar, the information is updated in the Transform window. Using this method is a good way to ensure repeatability for other elements.

Figure 10.32
The finished Cat Tasties box.

Print this little job—if you dare. The photo/text objects are pretty complex and take up a lot of computer and printer resources. It might be easier on your printer if you took the photos out of the type except on the front of the box. Just do an Edit|Cut Contents, and hit Delete. The photo will be gone, but the black text will remain. When it's finally printed, cut it out and assemble it. Fill it with Gummi Bears and gross out the kids.

Moving On

And I guess it's about time. We've covered a lot of material. First, you learned about ways to get text into a FreeHand document, then you learned how to edit the text, tab it, table it, put inline graphics in it, runaround it, and put it on a path or in a path. That might have been enough, but then you went on to create an entire two-page newsletter. After that, you got the lowdown on the differences between Duplicate Pages, Templates, and the new Master Pages in FreeHand 10.

Because some of you work in the printing field, I showed you a couple of ways to trap a document for trouble-free color printing, and you went on from there to put photos inside text, and create an entire box. I'd say that it was a pretty full chapter. In Chapter 11, you'll get away from the printing aspect and move on to Web applications.

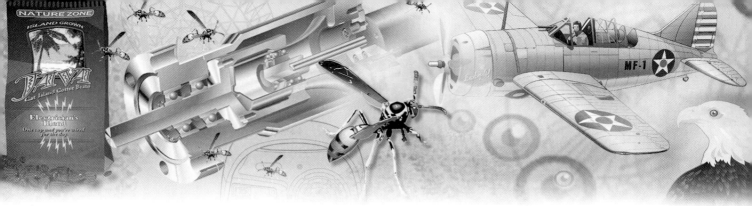

Chapter 11

Drawing for the Web

FreeHand is a drawing program, first and foremost. But expanding technologies have sparked an interest in integrating FreeHand with Flash and the Web-creating community. Although not meant for full-blown Web production, or as a substitute for Flash or Dreamweaver, FreeHand is certainly a strong Web-contribution tool capable of creating Web pages and Flash movies.

FreeHand for Web Production?

You bet. The key word is *production*, and I'll stand by that. FreeHand is not meant to go head-to-head with Macromedia Dreamweaver/Ultradev, or Adobe GoLive, or Microsoft FrontPage. (Well, maybe FrontPage.) However, FreeHand is capable of creating a graphically rich set of Web pages. The pages must be laid out carefully—as carefully as if you were working in a Web development program—but they can be published and proofed on a browser, all with a minimum of fuss. Links that you apply to objects or text stay embedded upon export to other programs.

So, why in the world would you produce a Web site from FreeHand? Well, the short answer is—you wouldn't. What you could do, however, is work out the basic premise of the site. It's obvious by now that an entire Web site can begin life in a FreeHand environment as a "comp" or "rough" layout, and printed as a storyboard for development talks. What's not so obvious is that it only takes a few moments more to put links in place, and instead of looking at paper Web pages, you can be discussing actual pages on the computer. After you and your client come to an understanding of what they want and what will actually work, you can take the same FreeHand HTML file into Dreamweaver and fine-tune the pages with all the control and finesse you need in a Web production program. The beauty is you've only had to do the job once. FreeHand is the front door to the Web.

Layers or Tables?

I'm chiefly an illustrator and designer, but I've got considerable Web experience—and my own biased opinions about how things should work. There are as many ways to produce a Web site as readers of this book. Everything is subject to change, but as I know Web production at the present time, Netscape or Explorer browsers prior to version 4 don't work with layers. (A page constructed with layers and viewed on a version 3 browser has got to be the ugliest thing you've ever seen.) But quite a few people out there are happy as clams to surf the Web with a version 2 browser. So, to play nice, you can avoid the situation through the use of tables. The problem with tables, though, is that you can't have objects overlap. Everything has to be pigeonholed, or sliced. You have to make a choice.

Layers are so comfortable to work with, but they can bite you hard when you read the email complaints from that guy in Walla Walla running a version 2 browser, who happens to stumble onto your Web page. The problem with arriving at the decision to use layers over tables or vice verse is that it's an either/or decision. Before FreeHand publishes to HTML, you have to make up your mind whether you're going to be safe and pigeonholed or flamboyant with layers and possibly lose 10 to 25 percent of the viewing audience.

More Files Than Visiting Day at San Quentin

Choices abound for graphics when it comes to publishing your document as HTML. If the Web is to perform quickly and efficiently, graphic files must be compressed to keep download time to a minimum while still maintaining the utmost graphic integrity. The basic rule of thumb is that objects with flat areas of color are viewed best when they've been converted to GIF files. Continuous tone or bitmapped objects look better when they've had JPEG compression. PNG is better than JPEG, but not all browsers play well with it, so at the present time it's better left alone. And then there's SWF—the ShockWave Flash format that allows the presentation of vector graphics without conversion to bitmapping, with or without animation.

You have four choices for handling vector art (GIF, JPEG, PNG, or SWF) and the same four choices with bitmap images when FreeHand publishes the HTML page. You can't mix and match file formats in a way that would give you the most control over what is seen on screen, though. You're also stifled in that you cannot import a SWF file to run on your FreeHand-published HTML page. For that reason, I suggest that you use FreeHand as I've described—as a beginning and not as an end for HTML page production. Frankly, though, if you don't own Dreamweaver or a similar product, you can get by adequately with just FreeHand.

The Navigation Panel

Select an object, pull up the Navigation panel, and assign a URL to it. Instant link. That's pretty neat. If your FreeHand site has multiple pages, those pages will show up in the Navigation panel when you select the Link drop-down menu. Then you can assign the link directly to pages within the document. External pages require inputting the correct URL manually, but you can also browse for the page; Macromedia has made it pretty easy for you. The Navigation panel has another powerful feature tucked away. You can search for selected URL links in the document. When you do the search in the Show All Pages view, every link will be selected, giving you a quick view of anything that might be missing or extra. In the same panel, you can update links globally. That's a real plus.

A Flashier Program

FreeHand 10 also features improved Flash support. As you'll soon see, it's pretty easy to create a simple animation with a click of the Animate Xtra button and then by exporting the file as SWF. That file can be previewed and tested using the FreeHand Control panel. Talk about a timesaver! The Control panel shows me the basic operation of my movie, without the polish and nuances I will add in Flash. As with the HTML page, the Control panel is a quick way to show the art director what you have in mind without having to spend hours in Flash.

To help further in your Flash movie production, you can add Flash Actions to your movie. Granted, it's not the full-featured set you get in Flash, but you can still implement several actions within your drawing program for viewer interaction. These actions can also be previewed through the Control panel.

Publishing HTML Pages

When you finally do that last Save and timidly scroll to the Publish As HTML button, you get to make all those decisions I've been talking about. The last click, Save As HTML, starts the hard drive whirring. Graphic elements on your pages blink as they are selected and deselected. You see a couple of progress bars start and stop. It looks as though you've crashed. But take heart. Publishing your file to HTML is a complicated process and takes a little time, depending on how complex and how large your document is. Eventually your browser will "come alive" (if you've checked the View In Browser or HTML Editor box in the Publish As HTML window), and you'll see your page in all its glory.

Layers vs. Tables

You should be prepared for a few minor surprises, however. I don't look at these surprises as faults, and they're certainly not bugs. First of all, if you have elected to publish your layout in layers, then everything will look right when you open it in your browser, but you will be mystified to no end if you have overlapping links. You see, the program and the browser get confused very easily. Everything must be in a logical order, or chaos results. If you have a graphic linked to page four and another graphic linked to page five, and they overlap by just a single pixel, the programs read whichever link is on top as *the* link, so both buttons will take you to the same page. What befuddles you is that you know for a fact that you assigned the correct links, and they even show up correctly in the Navigation panel. What you don't see is that tiny bit of overlap.

What causes the invisible overlap? It's simple, really. Each object in FreeHand can have any shape you want, from perfect squares and circles to a fractalized, tortured path with thousands of points on it. But when you get to the end of the path, so to speak, a bounding box defines the actual area of the object. Figure 11.1 shows what happens. On the left, you see what you have designed—a white button and a gray button with a border. Nothing appears to overlap. But in the middle image, you can see that the bounding boxes of the circles overlap, and the border is actually a group—overlaps are everywhere. The solution is to create your own slices in FreeHand if you plan on having FreeHand do the HTML conversion for you. If you are going on to Dreamweaver or another program, then, by all means, export these button shapes to Fireworks and do the slicing quickly and easily there. It will mean a lot fewer headaches in the long run.

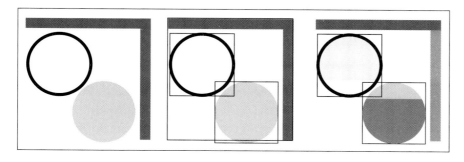

Figure 11.1
Buttons that seem to be correct (left); the effects of the bounding box (middle); and how to fix overlapping linked objects (right).

At any rate, if you have any linked object overlapping another linked object, you'll have mass confusion and frustration, and nothing will work. For that reason, exporting your page in layers instead of tables can cause you troubles down the line.

But, then there are tables. With tables, you can't have overlapping objects. So in order to keep them from overlapping, you simply group them, including any background you may have. Backgrounds, even if they're just flat color, are still considered objects—everything you put in a FreeHand layout is considered an object when it comes to publishing HTML pages. Grouping objects solves a graphically rich layout, but live areas for buttons must remain sacred ground, with no overlaps.

A Couple More Warnings

Another thing to watch out for when using FreeHand to develop HTML pages is that you have no way to see your source code. You can't make those little tweaks to the HTML code you might need to do to finesse the job; your layout is strictly WYSIWYG. That's not necessarily a bad thing; it's just the limitations of the program. Although FreeHand does a lot more than most, it's a drawing program and not a replacement for Dreamweaver, Fireworks, Flash, or any other program designed for Web publishing.

One last caveat: If you have the urge to set up a navigation system that will apply to every page in your site, you may decide to start by placing all your navigation buttons on a Master Page (described in Chapter 10). Well, forget about it. Links get buried somewhere between Master and Child pages. Naturally, you can set up the Master Page and view it in the layout, and when you're ready to publish, release all the Child pages from their Masters. But then you don't have anything to fall back on if you need to make a global change in the future. So do yourself a huge favor, and do a Save As when you get to that point. Give the file name something to do with the Master Pages so you'll be able to open the correct file—and more important, you won't transfer the Master Page site to your server.

The HTML File

I think I'm through with all the warnings now. So what happens to the HTML file you just created? Well, it's gone into a folder of your choice or to the default FreeHand HTML Output folder on your desktop. I don't have a problem with this feature. The HTML file is accessible to my other programs, and when I'm done with the files I can put them where they belong. The folder contains the HTML pages and names them using the name of the document you created them from plus a three-number .html extension for each page. If your document was called WebPage, the first page will be named WebPage001.html. The second page would be WebPage002.html, and so on. This fact is important to remember, because you can't save a variant of the file without either doing a Save As on the original document or overwriting the old HTML file of the same name.

Editing HTML Settings

What if you publish the site and decide you don't like the looks of the graphics or the way the buttons work—or don't work. Because you have no way to get to the source code, your only option is to make your changes in FreeHand and repeat the Publish As HTML command. You can republish individual pages or the entire document. If the HTML layout is close to what you want, and you have the resources, I suggest exporting the pages to Dreamweaver for the final spit-and-polish. Be warned, though, that if you've set up the pages in layers, and have overlapping layers, Dreamweaver will not let you convert the pages into tables, due to the overlap. If nothing overlaps, the conversion works fine. On the other hand, if you've chosen to publish in tables, your site will open in Dreamweaver exactly as you constructed it, with all the extra table cells needed to make everything fit perfectly.

Getting Your Feet Wet in the Web

In this simple project, you'll get your feet wet and your hands just a little dirty. Plus, I will teach you some key concepts that will make the next project easier.

Page 1

Start by opening a new document, and change the page size to Web or 550 pixels wide by 400 pixels deep. Name the document First HTML Pages.

1. Go to the Document Inspector, click the small triangle and select New Master Page. The size settings should be the same as the page you just created. A new window will open with a gray background and a white page.

2. Use the Rectangle tool and draw a small rectangle of any size. In the Object Inspector, change the size of the rectangle to 299 pixels wide by 398 pixels tall. Tap the Return/Enter key to implement the size change.

3. Give the rectangle a fill of black (000000—you're in Web land here, not CMYK) and a stroke of None.

4. To place the rectangle exactly where you want it, use the Object Inspector panel again. Enter "250" in the X box, and "1" in the Y box. (You could also have placed the box in the lower-right corner and tapped it up and to the right 1 pixel.)

5. Draw a circle with the ellipse tool. Change the dimensions in the Object Inspector to 72 pixels tall and wide and change the X and Y coordinates to 88 and 48, respectively. Give it a fill of 00FF00 and a stroke of None. You should have a green circle in a white space. Save.

6. Select the Text tool and drag a text block from the top-left corner of the page to the bottom-left corner of the white part of the page. Type the following: "My First FreeHand Web Page", with each word on a separate line. Select all the text, and choose a bold, sans serif font such as Helvetica Condensed Black, or Impact. Make the font size 48 points.

7. Set the text to be aligned center, and double-click the bottom-center box in the text block to make an auto-expanding text block out of it. In this case, this action will have the effect of shortening the text block. In the Text Inspector, enter 246 in the X box to change the width of the text block so it will fit the white space better in the next few steps.

8. Change the fill color to a red—FF0000.

9. Make sure that View|Snap To Points is selected, and drag the text to the top-left corner. I keep sounds turned on to get an audible feedback, but that depends on the environment you work in—some co-workers dislike hearing clicks and dings from someone else's cubicle. Click the down keyboard arrow once to move the text down from the page edge, and the right keyboard arrow to move it in from the left side of the page.

10. With the Text tool again, drag a text block in the black space and type the number "1" in the same bold font, but set the size to 72 points and the fill to white (FFFFFF). Drag the text block into the middle of the black rectangle. Save, and click the Close box to close the window. Open Window|Library and drag an instance of Master Page-01 onto your existing (blank) page. You should see Figure 11.2 on your monitor.

Note: The reason you place the box 1 pixel inside the page is because, if you don't, FreeHand will report an error that objects are falling off the page and being cropped. Placing the object 1 pixel inside the page dimensions avoids this problem.

Figure 11.2
The Master Page for your first
FreeHand Web page.

A Time Saver

If you are going to spend any time at all in FreeHand, you will save hours of click-dragging if you place the buttons for often-used commands such as Group and Ungroup in your main menu. Other useful commands that increase your productivity are the Align, Join, Split, Union, Divide, Punch, Intersect, and Convert To Paths buttons.

Page 2

Wow, you're on your way now. Back in the document, everything will look exactly like your Master Page did, except the background around the page will be white instead of gray.

1. Click the Page tool, hold down Opt/Alt, and drag the page to the right until it is clear of the first page. (Alternately, you can go to the Document Inspector and select Duplicate from the triangle drop-down menu.)

2. Zoom out so you can see both pages (or click the Fit All button in the menu bar), and drag a selection box around both pages with the Pointer tool. Go to the Document Inspector and select Release Child Page from the triangle menu. Ungroup the pages.

3. Everything should be selected in the pages. Hit the Tab key or click the Pointer tool anywhere on the desktop to deselect everything. Zoom in on page 2.

4. Double-click the Pointer tool directly over the word "First" and select it with the Text tool (double-clicking in the text block automatically switches the tool tip). Type "Second."

5. Select the number "1" in the black box, and change it to "2."

6. Zoom back out so you have both pages on the monitor again, select all the text and numbers, and select Text|Convert To Paths.

7. Deselect everything, and select the "1" and the black box it's sitting on. Center it vertically and horizontally. Click the Join Xtra to create a compound path. Do the same with the "2." Save.

8. Select the green dot on the first page, and go to Windows|Panels| Navigation to bring up the Navigation panel. Name your green graphic GoToTwo. Then, in the drop-down menu, select Page 2. This has the effect of placing a URL link to Page 2 of *this* document. (You can manually enter the address of a page in the text field as well.) Addresses within the current document are simply Page 1, Page 2, and so on. The actual HTML document will be named as explained earlier.

9. Select the green dot on the second page, name it GoToOne, and link it to Page 1. Now you have a way out and a way back. Save.

10. Here comes the moment you've been waiting for, the actual HTML publishing. Go to File|Publish As HTML. When the panel opens, you have two options—both are easy. For this project, we'll use the Assistant on a Mac, or the Wizard on Windows computers. Follow these instructions:

    • The first page is an explanation, so when you've read it, move to the second page.

    • The second page gives you the option of creating your Web page either in layer or table format. Click the second option: Positioning with Tables. Move on.

    • The third page deals with vector graphics and how you want them compressed. Select GIF compression, and notice that everything is spelled out for you, so that at a later time with a different set of graphics, you'll be well informed. Go to the next page.

    • On the fourth page, you decide how you want your bitmap images to be compressed. This document has no bitmap images, so it doesn't make much of a difference. As in the previous page, ample explanations are here for your next visit. Click on.

    • The fifth page lets you select a directory where the completed pages and folders will be placed. Go with the default this time. Move to Page 6.

    • You can name your settings on the sixth page. I use something meaningful such as "Table/GIF/JPEG," but once I did use "Demosthenes" for the heck of it. Move to the next page.

    • Page seven sets you up for the main panel again. Read it, then click the Finish button.

    • In this main panel, select the All radio button, and put checkmarks in Show Output Warnings and View In Browser Or HTML Editor. Select your browser from the drop-down menu, or browse to it. Then click Save As HTML.

Elements are selected and deselected, windows and panels and progress bars fly for a few seconds, and then the browser opens, and you should see the layout you completed in Figure 11.2. Click the green button and you'll go to Page 2. Click it again to return to Page 1. And you thought this was going to be difficult.

Upon returning to FreeHand—the excitement wears off after a while—you'll see a new dialog box open if you elected to Show Output Warnings in the Assistant/Wizard. This box should say something to the tune of what you see in Figure 11.3. If anything is amiss, it's written here. At this point you can make the necessary adjustments. Take heed—if you choose not to make the corrections, your site may appear fine on one machine and be a total mess on another. If either of your green circle buttons do not take you to the other page, more than likely you didn't get the settings correct in the Navigation panel. Go back to the FreeHand document, select the malfunctioning button, open the Navigation panel, and correct the link. Choose File|Publish As HTML as before, and all will be well.

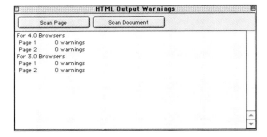

Figure 11.3

The HTML Output Warnings dialog box reports any problems with your site.

PROJECT Caution: Explosive Web Site

Now that I've shown you how easy it is to make a simple site, you can tackle something a little more involved. Because this chapter is about Web page construction, not drawing, I've supplied all the graphic elements for you in a symbol library. The graphics are simplistic by design, because I figured, at this point, you'd have your hands full with the new Web aspects of FreeHand. (All the effects and/or techniques used in the drawing construction are covered elsewhere in this book. The fireworks were done with a Brush and two Graphic Hoses, the Envelope feature was used for the skyrocket cylinder, and the smoke is nothing but a lot of different gray ellipses blended in one step. If you want to see how any of it was done, just release its instance and tear it apart to see what makes it tick.)

The site you build here will contain five pages; you will create a Master Page to cut down on the tedium.

What Size Is a Web Page?

This question comes up all the time, and it's an extremely valid one. When I'm not working on a PowerBook, I'm using a dual-monitor setup (14-inch and 19-inch monitors). My wife has a 17-inch monitor, and a friend of mine is very happy with her old 13-inch monitor. And I can't even imagine having all the real estate of the new Apple Cinema Displays! At any rate, everyone has their preferences for equipment, resolution, and even the view preferences within their browsers—so what are you to do?

This situation reminds me of the way my mother-in-law cooks ham. I watched her cook it several times, and she always trimmed about an inch from each end of the ham before cooking it. My curiosity got the better of me on one occasion, and I asked her why she did it. She replied that her mother had taught her to cook, and she had always told her to cut the ends off the ham. It happened that her mother was present at this particular get-together, so I asked her the same question. She replied that she had always cut off the ends because her pan was too small!

So, I guess I make Web pages for short pans. In my opinion, people shouldn't have to scroll at all. I want everything to fit in a single window if at all possible. For years I've been building pages to fit a nominal-sized monitor; that is to say, a 14-inch monitor with a display resolution of 800×600. I figure that if I can get everything into a page that size, then I've done my job. So, based on that, I make Web pages 600 pixels by 300 pixels.

Naturally, a site that has a lot to say, or is copy-heavy, is different to design for than a catalog or portfolio site. In a copy-heavy site, the length—and resulting scrolling—isn't as important as the width. Visiting a page where you must scroll left and right to read looks horrible and is frustrating. On the other hand, it's pretty well agreed that more than two clicks in the scroll bar starts to get tedious.

But, based on the default page size in Macromedia Flash, which is 550 pixels by 400 pixels, and the Web page size in FreeHand, I figure that their focus groups and experts have come up with what they consider to be optimal. Certainly, a movie such as what you can produce in FreeHand or Flash shouldn't be larger than a single screen. (For one reason, the movie gets too clumsy to download beyond that.)

That's the reasoning behind the sizes of the pages in this chapter, and worth a cup of coffee.

Setting Up the Pages

Open a new FreeHand document and name it The Big Bang Site. Before you begin work on the site, you will need to get the symbols Library in place. So, from the Chapter 11 folder on the CD-ROM, open the folder named Chapter 11 Symbols, and drag the Firecracker symbols file into the FreeHand 10|English|Symbols folder on your hard drive.

As I stated, you're going for a simple concept on this project, so pardon the use of the same layout as the previous exercise. Go to the Library and select New Master Page from the triangle drop-down menu. Set the page size to 550 pixels by 400 pixels. (See the "What Size Is a Web Page?" sidebar.)

The Home Page

Set up the Home page as follows:

1. Okay, same drill as before with the 299 pixels wide by 398 pixels tall rectangle, stroke of None, Linear gradient fill of black (000000) at the top, and dark blue (000066) at the bottom.

2. Drag an instance of Normie to the page, and place it 1 pixel inside the top and left margins. Save.

Note: The reason for this half-and-half layout is pretty obvious; you can't have objects overlapping—especially objects with URLs attached to them. So I'm putting them all on white space. The concept for starbursts and fireworks was already finished in my mind when I started the project, so I went with a dark-sky approach to set off the fireworks.

3. Drag an instance of the 'crackers symbol to a spot just under Normie's logo.

4. In the same manner, drag out Smokers, Rockets, and Bombs symbols. Shift them above or below to make the layout interesting, but be aware of that square bounding box you can't see. If you want, drag down guidelines and keep each of the graphics a pixel or two to either side of the guide. Your document should look similar to Figure 11.4.

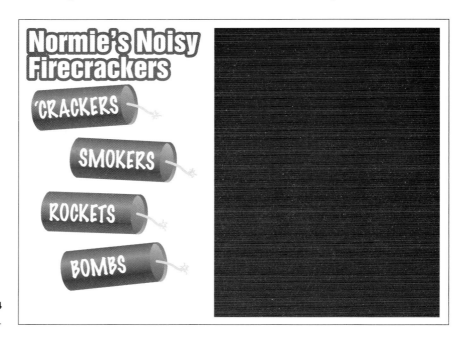

Figure 11.4
The navigation panel for the site.

5. The navigation elements will be carried through on the different pages, so let's take care of the linking business. Select the 'crackers icon and click the Navigation button in the menubar (it looks like a chain link) or find it at Windows|Panels|Navigation.

6. In the Link field, enter "Page 2". Then select Smokers and set the link to Page 3, select Rockets and set to Page 4, and finally select Bombs and link it to Page 5. Select the dark panel and create a link to Page 1.

7. Close the Master Page editing page.

8. Drag an instance of the Master Page you just created onto the page on the desktop. The page will change size, shape, and color in one click. Save.

9. Go to the Document Inspector triangle menu and choose Release Child Page, and ungroup the page. Then use your choice of methods here. Either click the Page tool and Opt/Alt+drag the page to create duplicates until you have a set of five; or choose Duplicate from the Document Inspector triangle drop-down menu. Last, you can go to the Document Inspector|Add Pages and enter 5 for the number of pages, then drag instances of the Master Page onto each page. All methods will get the job done.

10. Go to Page 1. Select the dark panel and remove the link in the Navigation panel. At the bottom of the page, you'll need a hyperlink for people who don't yet have the Flash plug-in. You'll send them to Macromedia's site. Type the following: "Need the Flash 5 Plug-in? Click Here!" Select "Click Here," and in the Navigation panel, type this URL in the link field: http://www.macromedia.com/shockwave/download/index.cgi?P1_Prod_Version=ShockwaveFlash. Set the text in 12-point Verdana and make "Click Here" bold.

> **Note:** Step 10 does not check the user's browser for Flash. That would require HTML scripting that is beyond the scope of this book. The project is only an exercise in creating a link.

11. For the graphics on the right side of the page, drag out the symbol named Blue Burst, with Short Trail placed below it; and then Yellow Burst, with Long Trail beneath it. Add the Skyrocket symbol last. Place them in the space so everything looks approximately like Figure 11.5. Save when you're happy with the layout. Remember to keep everything within the confines of the dark rectangle.

> **Note:** If you want to make your own starbursts, the Brush symbols are in the Library. Just import them by dragging an instance to the desktop and then going to Modify|Brush|Create Brush. Then draw curved paths. The sparkles on the ends of the strokes are also in the Library and are used in the Graphic Hose with varying sizes and rotations.

Figure 11.5
The home page of the Big Bang Site.

12. Drag a selection box around the dark panel and fireworks. Group it. This has the effect of negating an error about overlapping objects. While it's still selected, create a link in the Navigator panel to Page 1. This makes the entire panel a button. There's no notation to that effect, but a user running the mouse over it will notice that it turns into a pointer hand, therefore a link.

Page 2
Set up Page 2:

1. On to Page 2 of the site. This is the 'crackers page. Having the link to its own page is redundant, so delete the 'crackers link. Conversely, you could make another graphic that leads back to the home page.

2. Move the remaining graphics up to the top to fill the void caused by the loss of the 'crackers art. At the bottom of the page, choose the Text tool, and type the following:

Poppin Purples	$0.25
Rippin' Reds	1.25
Blastin' Blues	3.80
Gut-bustin' Greens	4.50

3. Set the font to Verdana (or its Web equivalent) at 12 points, and select bold. Save.

4. Select all the copy you just set and add a tab with dot leader as shown in Figure 11.6 (if you need help with tab setting, see the "Beef on the Table" section in Chapter 10). Go to the Styles panel and create a new style named Page Text. Apply the style to the tabbed text.

Figure 11.6
Setting the tabs for the second page of the site.

5. Get the Firecrackers symbol from the Library and center it in the dark panel. Group it with the panel and save. The page should look like Figure 11.7.

Figure 11.7
The Firecrackers sale page.

Page 3
Set up Page 3:

1. Go to Page 3. Remove the Smokers graphic and shift the bottom two elements to take its place.

2. Drag a fixed-size text block into the resulting blank space and type the following: "These are so cheezy we couldn't charge you anything and still sleep at night." Enter a hard return, and type: "FREE! Take as many as you can stuff in your pocket."

3. Give the text the style of Page Text. Make sure the text fits into the white space and that no part of the text block crosses onto the dark panel. Save.

4. Drag an instance of Smoke onto the dark panel and group it with the dark panel. Save. The page should look like Figure 11.8.

Page 4
On to Page 4:

1. On Page 4, remove the Rockets graphic, and shift Bombs upward to fill the hole. In the blank space at the bottom, type: "Oops, too late. You should have been here yesterday." Give the text the Page Text style.

2. Drag an instance of Long Trail to the right of the center of the dark panel, and nearly to the top. Group the graphic and the dark box. Save. The page should appear similar to Figure 11.9.

Figure 11.8
The Smokin' page.

Figure 11.9
The rocket is out of sight.

Page 5

And last, set up Page 5:

1. Maneuver to Page 5, and delete Bombs from the page. In its space, place the following text: "Yes, we have the most powerful bombs in the world—the Type 11! There's no escape from the chaos it can create for young or old. Free with every purchase. Guaranteed—NO DUDS."

2. Apply the Page Text style to the text, and adjust the text block to fit. Save.

3. Drag an instance of The Bomb onto the page. This symbol is pretty big, right? Actually, it's too big. When you group it with the dark background, the bounding box will overlap the Normie's logo at the top of the page. So drag a vertical guide out just to the right of the logo.

4. Select the bomb graphic and adjust it so it fits inside the right side of the box, then Shift+drag one of the left-hand corners to resize it to the point it falls to the right of the guideline. Save.

5. Drag out an instance of the Free With Purchase symbol and place it above the bomb. The bomb will be fairly close to the bottom of the page. Group everything connected with the dark panel. Save. The page should look more or less like Figure 11.10.

Figure 11.10
The dreaded Type 11 bomb.

Publishing to HTML

Now, the moment you've been waiting for—but first select the graphic panel on page 1 and remove the link to page 1.

1. So you can watch what's going on choose the Fit All view. Then scroll to File|Publish As HTML. When the panel pops up, check to see that your browser is still selected, and that you can see checkmarks on the Show Output Warnings and View In Browser Or HTML Editor listings.

2. Leave the Document Root set at the default. Select Positioning With Tables from the Layout menu. Keep Western (Latin 1) selected for Encoding. You'll ask for JPEGs for the vector graphic Export Defaults, and Images—well, you don't have any, but leave it at JPEG. Click Apply, then OK.

3. In the main window, Click the Save As HTML button, sit back, and watch the show.

When the browser window appears, you should be looking at the page with all the fireworks blasting off. Click the buttons to go to the other pages. If everything has gone right, you'll just travel from one page to another. Remember to click on the large panel graphics to scoot back to the first page.

If, on the other hand, you find something that doesn't work, it's your job to fix it. Sorry, I can't do it for you. More than likely, something overlaps, or the link for a particular button wasn't set. Isolate the problem, go back into FreeHand, and check out the various attributes of the problem element. The HTML Output Warnings box will give you a few clues—probably more than you want—so it's a great place to start. If you were careful as you went along, you did well. Great job!

Animation: Watch Out, Walt!

Believe it or not, Macromedia Flash and Adobe LiveMotion aren't the only Web animation programs out there. FreeHand does a fairly respectable job, too. I'm surely not going to say it will replace either program, but it goes a long way for comping purposes, and all the way toward getting the job ready for Flash import.

As FreeHand is primarily a drawing program, you might logically think that the methods involved in creating an animation in it differ significantly from what they are in Flash. In Flash, you set up your animation on frames placed along a timeline. The artwork is placed on layers, and a series of frames shown over the timeline create the animation. FreeHand doesn't have a need for timelines, but the engineers developed a new use for layers—using the Animate|Release To Layers Xtra, in which each layer is made visible for a brief time. They also worked out a way to animate using pages—and a combination of pages and layers. So, in FreeHand you can have traditional page-based animation mixed with animation constructed on layers—all at the same time.

FreeHand animation encompasses graphics, groups, Blends, and text. The simplest animation can be done by creating a Blend between two objects, selecting the Animate|Release To Layers Xtra, and viewing the result. FreeHand ungroups every group, Blend, or objects attached to a path and makes a new layer for each element. It builds the animation from the bottom up, so the first object in a Blend would be at the bottom of the stacking order and be the first element in the animation. Although the program has a Reverse Direction option, it's best to design your animation from the ground up, so to speak.

Text can be animated as well, but it first must be converted to paths. When the text is converted with the Animate Xtra, each letter is placed on its own layer for the animation sequence. For that reason, it's a good idea not to animate a large amount of text.

When you want to see how the animation is coming along, you can either export the document as a SWF file, or preview the file by using the Controller toolbar or by choosing Control|Test Movie.

Quick Animation

Here is a quick tutorial on animation. (The entire procedure is pretty simple.) First, open a new document.

1. With the Ellipse tool, draw a circle about a quarter-inch in diameter. Give it a yellow-orange fill (255r, 153g, 0b—just to force you to use RGB for a change).

2. Clone it, and move it across the page a few inches. Shift+select the original circle and create a Blend between the two. Leave the Steps In Blend setting to 25 in the Object Inspector panel.

3. Double-click the Rectangle tool and change the radius to a quarter-inch. Click OK, and draw a rectangle about 6 inches wide by 2 inches tall.

4. While the rectangle is still selected, Shift+select the blended dots. Go to Modify|Combine|Join Blend To Path. The result should be a round-cornered box made up of orange dots.

5. Go to Xtras|Animate|Release To Layers. In the dialog box, select Sequence from the drop-down menu. Click OK. The animation is complete. Open the Layers panel and look at all the new layers FreeHand has supplied—one for each dot.

6. To test the animation, go to the Control menu and scroll to the bottom: Movie Settings. You will get the dialog box shown in Figure 11.11. Change the settings in your panel to match what's shown here.

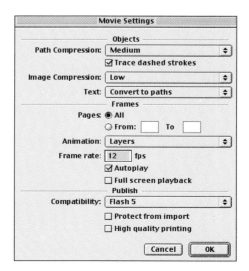

Figure 11.11
The Movie Settings panel with settings for Step 6 of the tutorial.

7. Click OK, and select Control|Test Movie. The screen will blink and a new window will open. You should see the yellow dot trace the rectangle repeatedly. There's no shut-off switch there, so to stop the animation, simply close the window.

8. Now, experiment a little. After closing the animation window, select Undo. You should see that all the layers went away, and the rectangle is a single selected group on the page. Select the Animate Xtra again, but this time, choose Trail in the Animate drop-down menu. Enter "3" in the Trail By field. Click OK.

9. Test the movie, and notice that you get a trailing effect from the animation. Close the window and do another Undo.

10. Select the Animate Xtra once more and choose Build. When you test the animation, you'll see that it starts with a blank space, but as each dot appears, it remains visible until the animation repeats itself.

11. The remaining Animate type is Drop. Try it. You'll see that it's exactly the opposite of Sequence: all the layers are on except the active one, which is off.

Animating the Text

Okay, you say, but that's not too exciting. Let's try some text:

1. Stop the animation, and return to the drawing window. Do an Undo and use the Animate Xtra to set a Sequence animation.

2. Select the Text tool and click it on the page. Type the following: "OPEN 24 HOURS".

3. Change the font to something like Vag Rounded, Helvetica Rounded, or Arial Rounded for a neon look. Change the size to 36 points and the color to a bright red (255r, 42g, 42b). Drag a swatch of the red into the Swatches panel. Save.

4. Convert the text to paths (Text|Convert To Paths) and drag it to the middle of the rectangle. Drag the corner points until the text fills the inside of the rectangle—but doesn't touch the dots.

5. If you were to continue with the animation and leave the text as is, the letterforms would become visible one at a time. That's not what you want—at least with this project, so go to Modify|Join to create one compound path. That will make the animation go as planned. Save.

6. Clone the text and change the color to white. Clone it again and change the color back to red. Make another clone and make the color white again.

7. Drag a selection box around just the text—you won't be able to see the box, but you will see the corner handles. Go to Modify|Combine|Blend, and in the Object Inspector, change the number of steps to 5. Leave the Blend selected.

8. Use the Animate Xtra to create a Sequence animation; click OK in the Animate panel. Save.

9. Now, test the movie. You should get a dot running around the rectangle, and the text should fade from red to white. You can see the movie in action by opening the file named Open24Hours.fh10 in the Chapter 11 folder on the CD-ROM. Open it and choose Test Movie to see it work.

What About Flashy Movies?

In this section, I'm addressing about half the owners of this book—the Flashers. You're all over the place. And you have to get vector graphics into your Flash movies. What you really want to do is create interesting, interactive pages that get your audience involved in more than just clicking the occasional button to go to another page. FreeHand allows you to export graphics, a page, or an entire document as a SWF file, complete with any Flash Actions that you've applied. Your file is then a complete movie, ready to be viewed in the Flash Player. Depending on your skill as a movie maker, your viewer can start and stop the movie, move graphic objects on the page, navigate from page to page or to different frames in a movie, and generally get involved with your project.

ActionScript is the native Flash programming language, and with it, you can build interactivity into a Flash environment. FreeHand has nowhere near the amount of ActionScripts that Flash has, but it has enough to make your projects interesting (Flash can't start to hold a candle to FreeHand when it comes to drawing—they're two specific animals, and I hope they stay that way). As I said when talking about FreeHand's HTML page publishing, FreeHand is not meant to create full-blown sites or movies. But you can complete a movie with a minimum amount of fuss in a short amount of time and use it for approvals and discussions. FreeHand doesn't get bogged down in frames and timekeeping, which helps you focus your attention on the task at hand. Because you don't have to worry about getting the keyframes starting and stopping at precise spots, you can really think about what the message is that you're putting in front of your audience.

In other words, you can get right down to the nuts and bolts of the project and add just enough bell-ringing and whistle-blowing to make your point. Here are those bells and whistles:

- *Go To action*—When you want the viewer to jump to a particular scene or frame, you use the Go To action. The scene or frame must be named in order for this action to work; each layer becomes a frame that is created as part of the export process when you export to a SWF file.

- *Play and Stop actions*—Play makes the movie play; Stop stops the movie (as you might guess).

- *Full Screen action*—Full Screen blows up the movie to fill the screen, hiding menus in the process. This has a two-fold effect: if you've chosen SWF for your vector graphic conversion, the artwork will resize fine and look very nice on screen. However, if you've used GIF, JPEG, or PNG, those graphics are going to get bitmapped and look pretty bad. Any imported bitmaps may appear jagged as well. Plan ahead before you apply this action.

- *Print action*—When you apply this Flash Action to a page, it turns the information you have selected into a vector graphic that is sent to the printer. The information you select can be a movie, a frame, or a maximum print area.

- *Start/Stop Drag action*—This action sets the parameters that allow the user to drag items onto the screen. A logical parameter would be On Press to start the Drag behavior. Applying this Flash Action would automatically make On Release the Stop Drag behavior.

- *Load Movie and Unload Movie actions*—When you have a document that contains two or more pages, you can load or unload those other movie pages while the current movie is playing. Using this action allows the next movie to be in RAM and ready to flow without any delay. These actions and the Tell Target action won't appear in the Navigator panel unless you have multiple pages in the document.

- *Tell Target action*—When you've used Load Movie, the Tell Target action will create the activity that makes the new movie or movie clip start. Because FreeHand only allows one level of loaded movies, you can only have one movie ready to go at a time.

Assigning Actions

Before I get too far along in this discussion, I must make it known that brushes are nice to work with, and symbols can really simplify and smooth your production. But—and this is a big "but" (no comments, please)—they don't play well with others. It seems that the more complicated the artwork gets, with brush (symbols) embedded in symbols from the Library, then copied, mixed, altered, and so on, the closer you get to having a problem of one kind or another.

If you know you'll need to use the functionality of a symbol in a later version of the project, then before creating HTML pages and Flash animations, do a Save As, and archive that copy somewhere safe. Then release the instances from their symbols—this can be done by selecting everything and going to Modify|Symbols|Release Instance. Life and FreeHand seem to go smoother then.

It's the same with Lens effects—stack enough of them together and you'll have a problem, guaranteed.

Okay, the warnings are over. How do you assign an action to an object? As with most procedures in FreeHand, it's pretty easy. The hard part is figuring out why you want to do it, and what it's going to mean when you do it.

To assign any action, first select the object or objects you wish to be the trigger. Go to Windows|Panels|Navigation to bring the Navigation panel to the screen as shown in Figure 11.12.

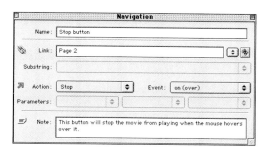

Figure 11.12
The Navigation panel is the heart of Flash Action assignment.

In the top field of the Navigation panel, you can name the object to which you're assigning the action. The field below it is for the link. You can enter text for a particular Web page, or use the drop-down menu that contains all the pages in your current document. The search button to the right of the Link field drop-down menu button is very useful for a visual check of your linked elements. It searches for and selects every object that has the link named in the Link field. You can then make a global update to the link. The search also makes it easy for you to spot that odd button that may have slipped by you.

If you have a line of text selected on the page that you wish to make into a link, that text will appear in the Substring field. Below that is the Action menu, which contains all the actions that can be assigned to the particular element you have selected. The Event menu is for different triggers—mouse over, mouse out, mouse press, mouse release, and frame event—that will cause the action to occur. Depending on the action and event, the Parameters menu will list the pages and layers in the current document for you to assign an action to. For instance, you could assign the Print action to allow printing of just the "User Input" layer on Page 4 of your document.

The Note section is a great place to begin a new habit of writing your intentions as you develop the Web page. After a few days, you may have lost all comprehension of why you selected a particular graphic as a button or trigger. The note can get you back on track.

Getting Your Work into Flash

After getting the graphics in place, the text set, and the links in order, it would be nice to see your hard work in action. How does it get from FreeHand to

Flash? You can use one of two methods. First, you can export any graphic—or an entire document—as a SWF file. Any links you have assigned will be embedded in the resulting SWF document. Furthermore, your vector artwork will appear smooth and have a smaller file size than it would have if it were exported as a JPEG or GIF file. I like the integrity of the artwork factor. I also like smaller files, so it's a win-win situation. When you choose to export as SWF, you have the further choice of exporting layers, or pages, or both, that will be converted into frames in the Flash medium.

A nice side issue of exporting layers is that you can make a movie Master Page by placing layers you want on every frame of the movie beneath the separator bar in the Layers panel. All the layers beneath that bar are transformed into one single background layer that is visible in all the frames of the SWF file.

The other way to get your movies into SWF files is by using the Controller toolbar, or going to the Control menu. In the early stage of movie production, this option allows you to determine the Movie Settings, and then test your movie. Once the movie has run once completely, you can rewind it, start it, and stop it—you basically use the Controller toolbar or Control menu like the Controller in Flash. The Movie Settings panel does most of the work.

The Movie Settings Panel

As you see in Figure 11.13, the Movie Settings panel gives you the options of changing path and image compression. These options affect the choices you made in the animation settings.

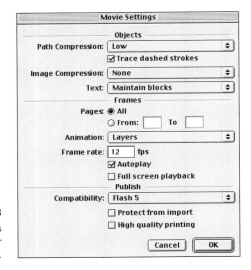

Figure 11.13
The Movie Settings panel allows you to control the way your movie will look and work.

You cannot export a dashed line (a path with a dashed stroke) as a SWF file. Well, not unless you check the Trace Dashed Strokes checkbox in the Movie Settings window. Then, FreeHand takes the line apart, dash by dash, and packs it off to SWF-land. This option comes at a price, however. It makes a larger file size, and increases export time as well. If you neglect to check the box, the line will appear solid.

If you select the Maintain Blocks option in the Text field of the Movie Settings panel, then you will be able to edit the text in Flash. That's pretty important in my book. On the other hand, if you only have punchy headlines and titles, you can select Convert To Paths. The effect is two-fold: you have a smaller file size, but you cannot edit the text. You can always select the None option so no text is exported.

In the Frames section, you have the opportunity to convert the entire document, or a particular page, similar to exporting select pages as EPS or SWF in the File|Export option. These options just don't seem to quit, do they? When you get to the Animation section of the Frames section, you are faced with deciding whether to have your animation run by layers, by pages, or by both. Choosing None will flatten the layers and create a single SWF file for every page in the document.

Standard animations run at 12 frames per second (fps), but if you have a reason to make the movie run faster or slower, you can change the frame rate in increments of 0.01 seconds within a range of 0.01 fps to 120 fps. That file had better be pretty small to run at 120 fps! If you want the movie to start immediately when run in Flash Player without any interactivity from the user, then select Autoplay. Deselecting this option will cause the animation to stop at Frame 1, and the viewer would need to select Control|Play to run the movie.

If your movie is going to be on the Web, Full Screen Playback will not affect the size of the movie as placed on an HTML page, but it will fill the screen if it is viewed in Flash Player. Remember, if you have placed bitmapped objects (TIFFs, JPEGs, GIFs, or PNGs) in the movie, they will get a bad case of the jaggies when you opt for Full Screen Playback. Anything you create in FreeHand will display as vector art and be smooth and sharp at any size.

The last few options allow you to decide which version of Flash the movie will be optimized for, and you can protect the movie from being downloaded by checking Protect From Import. When the High Quality Printing option is checked, then pages you have previously selected to be printable will print at high resolution. Leaving it unchecked provides a print at 72 dpi.

Testing the Movie

When the movie has finally been constructed, Flash Player will appear on top of your desktop, covering the FreeHand document at the same time. If you've set it to Autoplay, things will be running. If not, you're sitting on Frame 1 of the movie awaiting the event that will start the movie.

After viewing the movie, you can use the Controller to step forward or backward a frame at a time, stop, play, or jump to the first or last frame in the movie. If changes to the movie settings are necessary, you can click the Movie Settings button and make your adjustments. When everything is to your liking, just click the Export Movie button. From there, you will name the movie and decide where you want to file it. It will be exported as a SWF file that you can place in an HTML page or use it to be viewed in Flash Player. Instructions for placing the movie in a Dreamweaver 4 page are noted at the end of this chapter.

PROJECT Rude Cows: The Movie

Okay, by this time you've realized that I must have a thing for cows. There's just something about a cow that I like. I never had to take care of a cow, but I was raised in the country, and they always seemed to be around. They eat grass out of your hand, love to have their ears and foreheads scratched, and can stick their tongues into their noses. What isn't there to like about them? Anyway, in this project you have three gorgeous cows that will be the stars of your movie. The concept, graphics, and really poor humor are to be blamed on me. Ian Kelleigh was kind enough to work out the darker side of Flash Actions for me. Thanks, Ian. He has many more tips and tricks on his site (**www.FreeHandSource.com**) that will help you out with FreeHand-produced Flash movies (and everything else to do with FreeHand). He does it all for the love of FreeHand. Buy a FreeHand Source t-shirt from him!

So, getting back to the Cow's Breath Barn Freshener movie, you will be creating user interaction through the aid of mouse overs and mouse clicks. You will create no visible buttons or "Click Here" messages in this movie; assume that the viewer is extremely sophisticated and will find out for him/herself how to get around. Frame Events will move the viewer from scene to scene, and multiple animations will be running.

I hate to ruin the movie for you, but it might be easier to produce the movie if you know the purpose of your actions. The premise is a green cloud animation that floats over the cows and appears on all pages. When the viewer moves the cursor over the left cow's face, a message appears above her head. This is caused by a mouse-over action applied to a transparent button directly on the cow's head. Running the cursor over the right cow's face does the same thing, but the target is a different page. The viewer can place the cursor over the dome of the can—by the wandering fly—and a mouse-click action makes the fly buzz around the screen, ultimately ending up on the sprayhead of the can. This action (a frame event) causes yet another movie to run that magically clears the air. A final frame event brings up the last screen. If you want to fade to black, you'll probably know how to by the time we're through.

I'll be honest, this project is probably too much to put FreeHand through, and could certainly be finessed in Flash with very little trouble. But as you have drive, gumption, purpose, and FreeHand 10—and maybe a little too much free time— why not do it the hard way? You'll also find out that it's really not *that* hard and you might want to start your next Flash project in FreeHand right off the bat.

Getting Rid of the Rubbish

In the next few steps, you will be asked to select large portions of the drawing and delete them. You can follow the instructions and do fine, but here is an alternate way to handle the situation, if you'd like. As long as you consistently put everything on its own layer, you can leave the background objects showing on each page. When the animation is complete, turn off the visibility of all the layers by selecting All Off in the triangle drop-down menu from the Layers panel. Then go to the Layers panel and click the layers that contain the background elements. On a page-by-page basis, delete the background elements from all but the first page. Why go page by page instead of selecting the whole mass of pages? Because it gives you a chance to find that odd element you placed on the wrong layer. Moving page by page is your safety net.

Setting Up the Page

Start by opening a new document, and setting the page size to Web or 550 pixels wide by 400 pixels tall. Save the document with the name Rude Cows.

Find the Chapter 11 folder on the CD-ROM and look for the Symbols folder inside it. Open that folder, and drag the Cow Movie Symbols file into the FreeHand 10|English|Symbols folder on your hard drive.

Figure 11.14
The symbol Library for the rude cows.

1. Open the Library (Windows|Library) and select Import from the triangle drop-down menu. Find Cow Movie Symbols and click Open. Select everything in the Import Symbols window and click Import. The library will fill with the symbols as shown in Figure 11.14.

2. Create a new layer, named Border, and drag an instance of The Border to the page, and settle it along the bottom. Make another layer named Logo, then bring out the Logo symbol, and place it approximately in the center of the vertical shape in the border graphic. Save.

3. Make three more layers named The Girls, The Can, and The Cloud. Place their respective symbols on the layers, and save.

4. We will be moving layers around quite a bit, but for now, move The Girls to the bottom, and above them stack the other layers in this order: Border, Logo, The Can, and The Cloud.

5. Shift the cows so they nestle inside the left corner of the border, and move the can until it just covers the right edge of the cow. Place the cloud above the cows.

6. Drag the separation bar in the Layers panel so that it is above The Can layer. This brings them all to the background, where they will show on all frames of the animation. It also grays them out the same as anything else below the separator bar. Save.

7. The first animation will be the cloud. Select it, release it from its instance (Modify|Symbols|Release Instance), and ungroup it. Change the line weight to 0.5 point, then clone it. Reverse the direction of the cloned path (Xtras|Cleanup|Reverse Direction).

8. Drag a selection box around both the cloud shapes (you only see one) and Blend them. Change the number of steps in the Blend to 10.

9. Go to Xtras|Animate|Release To Layers. Select Sequence, Use Existing Layers, and Send To Back. Save.

10. Test the animation. First go to Control|Movie Settings, and set the Frames|Animation setting to Layers. Click OK.

> **Note:** The Girls and Smiles were created in Adobe Photoshop. I mention it because they are bitmapped objects and will get the jaggies if you select the Full Screen Playback option and because they're the only elements in the book not created in FreeHand.

11. Go to Control|Test Movie. (Relax, it takes a few seconds.) At this point in production, the page will be spastic, then the cloud should morph, then loop until you close the window or use the controls in the Control menu.

The Fly

Create the walking fly animation:

1. Drag an instance of The Dome onto the page, and place it directly on top of the dome on the aerosol can. Save.

2. Get an instance of The Fly from the Library and place it on the dome of the can. Remove its instance, and ungroup it.

3. Double-click the fly to bring up the Transform handles. Make a mental note where the bottom-left point of the bounding box is located, then move the Transform center point to that spot. In the Transform panel (F10), choose the Rotate tab, and enter 288° in the Rotation Angle field. Enter "5" in the Copies field, and click Apply/Rotate. This creates five flies in a circle that will be the basis of the animation of the fly walking.

4. Open the Layers panel. Select the top fly and click NewLayer-10. Clone the fly and click NewLayer-9. The fly will now sit still for two frames. Select the next lowest fly in the stacking order (you may hide the first two flies if it makes everything easier to see). Assign this fly to NewLayer-8 and a clone of it to NewLayer-7.

5. I think you have the idea. Continue the instructions in the last step until you run out of flies and layers. Place the last fly on NewLayers 1 and 2, and also NewLayer, so it will have three frames of the action. Your layout should look similar to Figure 11.15. Save.

6. Test the movie again. This time, the cloud should morph, and the fly should walk around in circles. If the fly walks backward—as they sometimes do—reorder the layers from bottom to top, and try it again. Be sure to select Show All before running the test.

Add Mouse Overs

Now, you'll add the mouse overs to the cows:

1. Click on The Girls layer to select it. Use the Pen tool or the Bezigon tool to trace the outline of the right and left cow's heads (if you are feeling lazy, you can just create a vertical ellipse over each cow's face). Leave the cow in the middle alone. Give the shapes a stroke of None and a Lens fill of Lighten, set at 0%.

2. Select everything on the page, then go to Modify|Symbols|Release Instance.

Note: The reason behind the Lens fill is that if you have a stroked path with no fill, there is nothing inside the shape for the cursor to interact with— only the stroke will be active as the cursor passes over it. That doesn't give the viewer much of a chance of having a great time. Besides that, you don't want a line marking up your artwork. This method gives you a tangible target, even though you can't see it at all.

Figure 11.15

The stage is set for the movie.

3. Go to the Document Inspector and click the triangle drop-down menu. Duplicate five pages and save again.

4. On pages 2, 3, 4, and 6, remove the fly and the cloud. Leave the cloud on page 5, but delete the flies—easily done by locking the layers below the separator bar—then drag a selection box around all but the first page and delete the contents. Unlock the layers again.

5. Select the outline you drew on the left cow, and open the Navigation panel. Change the settings in the panel to those in Figure 11.16. Do not close the Navigation panel.

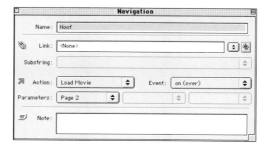

Figure 11.16

The left cow's button Flash Actions settings.

6. Select the right cow's outline, open the Navigation panel, and adjust the settings to those in Figure 11.17.

7. Select The Dome symbol you placed on the can, release its instance and ungroup it. In the Navigation panel, change the settings to those in Figure 11.18.

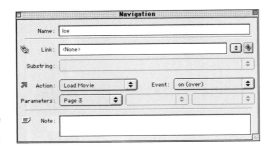

Figure 11.17
The right cow's button settings.

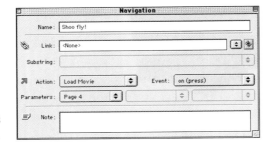

Figure 11.18
The button settings for The Dome.

8. Move to Page 2, and create a new layer named Hoof. Drag out the Hoof symbol from the Library and place it so the line points down to the cow on the left. Save.

9. Select the Hoof graphic and the outline for the left cow. Hide them. Then select everything on this page (Page 2) and delete the selection. Save.

A Little Background

You have everything you want shown on each frame of the movie on a layer below the separator bar in the Layers panel. For purposes of registering new graphics to the background artwork, you've duplicated the pages and artwork. Once the new graphics are in position, you can safely discard the background graphics. This has the added benefit of cutting file size, lessening movie export time, and increasing the efficiency of the movie. You also don't have to worry about something being bumped a pixel and causing a jump in the action.

When you place a graphic on a new page, it will appear on top of any previously built pages. The result is that you can put one button on top of another button. Because the original button is now covered up, all actions will derive from the new button. You can use that effect to cause a further change in the movie. In this instance, one button brings you to Page 2, where a new button is now directly under your cursor. By changing the action of the Page 2 button to mouse-out, you are able to move to another page as soon as you move the mouse off the button. It could easily be a mouse-down event, so clicking the mouse would take you somewhere else.

1. To continue, choose View|Show All and select just the left cow's outline. Change the settings in the Navigation panel to those in Figure 11.19. Save.

How Many Steps?

Don't get carried away with the number of blend steps in an animation. First, every step will become a layer, and that increases the size of your movie. Second, depending on how long the path to which you attach the blend is, the movie could look like it's running in slow motion. Think it out—a layer equals a frame, and you will be showing 12 frames per second. If you have the fly move from point A 6 inches away to point B, and you put 6 steps in the blend, it will take a half-second for the animation to occur. But, place 60 steps in the blend, and it will take 5 seconds for the fly to travel the same 6 inches. Also, if you have other elements moving simultaneously in the animation, they must be applied to each of the layers— that gets time-consuming. You can be creative about it in many ways, but keep file size foremost in your movies.

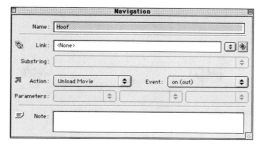

Figure 11.19
The second left cow button
attributes.

2. Move to Page 3, and create another new layer named Ice. Drag an instance of the Ice symbol onto the page, and align the line with the right cow. Save.

3. Hide the right cow outline and the Ice graphic. Select everything else on the page and delete the selection. Save again.

4. Choose Edit|Show All, and deselect the word/line graphic. In the Navigation panel, change the settings to those in Figure 11.20.

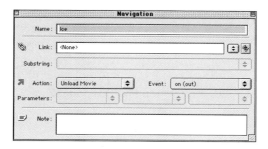

Figure 11.20
The button action set for Page 3
of the movie.

5. Pages 2 and 3 should only have the can dome, text, and pointer lines visible on them. Their buttons will be visible in Keyline mode. Save.

6. Now you get to draw. Choose the Pen tool, and place your first point in the middle of the can's crown. Then use several click+drags to create a curvy path that a fly might take. Be creative. End the path with the last point on top of the sprayhead. The flight path in the Rude Cows movie on the CD-ROM is very simple for the sake of brevity. Make your path more like what you see in Figure 11.21.

7. Take an instance of the fly from the Library. Remove its instance, and ungroup it. Then clone it and move it across the page a few inches.

8. Select both flies, and Blend them. Change the number of steps to 40.

9. Select the Fly Blend (sounds like some bad whiskey to me) and the flight path, and choose Modify|Combine|Join Blend To Path.

10. Use the Animate|Release To Layers Xtra, choose Sequence; Use Existing Layers and Send To Back. Save. Now test your movie. The fly should hop off the can, fly around the page, and land on the sprayhead.

Figure 11.21
The flight path.

I can't really explain why the fly won't land exactly on the end of the path—in this case, the sprayhead—every time. Sometimes the path will allow it, sometimes not. If your fly buzzes around and stops short of the end of your path, just move the last fly into position, and shift the last few flies ahead in their flight path to make up the difference. It is important in this particular movie to have a fly directly on top of the sprayhead, or the rest of the movie doesn't "work" in terms of a visual action causing the next scene. The fly is supposed to activate the aerosol spray when it lands on the sprayhead.

Covering Your Tracks

The way FreeHand makes the movie also demands that you cover up anything on the background layer that you don't want to see. In order to hide the walking fly from the viewer, you must mask the fly with The Dome. So, select The Dome and clone it. Then click on the first fly layer (most likely, New Layer-11).

1. Clone The Dome again, and apply it to the next fly layer (New Layer-12) and so on until all 40 layers have a fly and The Dome on them. Yes, it's brain-numbing, but the final effect is worth it compared to the nonsense of the fly continuing to walk in circles as it leaves the can and flies around the page, too.

2. Select the fly that landed on the sprayhead. Bring up the Navigator panel and adjust the settings to those in Figure 11.22. Notice you now have a frame action. When the fly animation gets to this last frame, FreeHand will launch the next movie on Page 5 of your project.

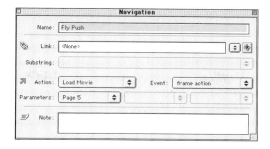

Figure 11.22
Pushing the fly's buttons.

Mist-ifying Behaviors

Your next problem is creating the aerosol spray and making it disappear along with the persistent green cloud. The spray will be done with a simple line technique, and the apparatus that makes everything disappear will be an animated Blend of lightening colors. I want the aerosol spray to look as much like a mist as I can with a single line, so this technique will work fine. To make the mist look even better, you'll make it a dashed line.

That brings you to another situation—Flash doesn't like dashed lines. So, when you export the movie, you must remember to check the Trace Dashed Paths option, which will increase file size and the time needed for the export process, as well as loading times. But by only using one line, you'll still get the effect without such a large downside.

So, now that you know the why and how of it, it's time to get down to the do of it. Start by going to Page 5, the page right after the fly animation.

1. Create a new layer named AeroSpray.

2. Double-click the Spiral Xtra, and in the dialog box, set the options to the settings in Figure 11.23.

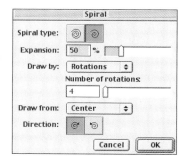

Figure 11.23
The Spiral dialog box with settings for the spray.

3. Click somewhere near the center of the cloud graphic, and drag upward. The spiral will continue to grow or shrink as you move the mouse. Size the spiral so that the width encompasses the cloud, and have the outside end point at the top of the spiral. Save.

Note: Since we will be asking FreeHand to trace each of the dashes in this path, it makes sense not to get too carried away with the complexity of this path. You'll notice when you test the movie that it slows to a crawl at this point. That's our doing, not the program's.

4. Choose the Pen tool, and click the top end point of the spiral to select it. Then click two or three more curve points, drawing a wave that ends near the sprayhead on the can.

5. Select the 3D tool, click the center of the spiral, and drag upward. This will compress the spiral height-wise, but leave the width only slightly decreased in length. Apply a dash to the line in the Stroke Inspector. Save. The path should look similar to the one in Figure 11.24.

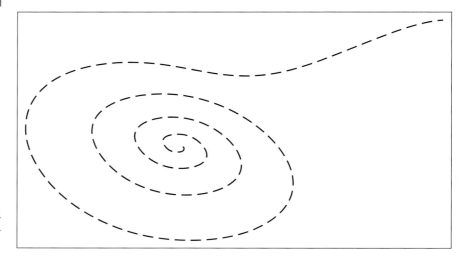

Figure 11.24
The spiral path for the aerosol spray.

6. Move the spiral shape until the end of the path looks as if it's coming from the sprayhead. Then clone the spiral. Give the new clone a stroke color of white. The spirals will disappear because the white one covers up the black one beneath.

7. Drag a small selection box around the end of the path (by the sprayhead) so only the last end points of each path are selected. Blend the two paths.

8. Change the number of steps in the Blend to 10. You will only see the Blend selection bounding box corners, because the top of the Blend is white.

9. Use the Animate|Release To Layers Xtra on the Blend.

10. Just as with the fly animation, we must cover up the walking fly. We also have to keep the fly that landed on the sprayhead in each scene. So clone The Dome and the fly and apply them to each of the spray layers—on the bright side, there are only 10 layers this time.

11. Select the spiral on the top-most layer and bring it to the front. Open the Navigation panel and adjust the settings to those in Figure 11.25. When this frame loads, showing the white spiral, the frame action will load Page 6 of the movie for us.

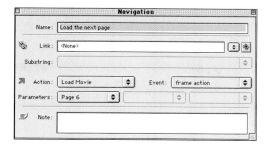

Figure 11.25
The top spiral action.

12. Hide the top (white) spiral momentarily so you can see the aerosol spray line overlapping the cloud movie. Then carefully draw a closed path that encompasses the two objects. This is a mask that will cover the cloud and spiral only. Don't let the path overlap the cows or any part of the can. Save.

13. Give the mask shape a stroke of None, and a basic fill of solid white so it will completely block out the cloud and spiral, but be invisible to the viewer.

14. We need this mask on Page 6, and it must be in perfect registration. So clone the fly, then choose the Rectangle tool and draw a box that exactly outlines the page from corner to corner. While the rectangle is still selected, switch to the Pointer tool and Shift+select the cloned fly and the mask you just drew.

15. Drag the fly, rectangle, and mask onto Page 6. If your pages are aligned left to right, you can hold down the Shift key to keep everything horizontally aligned. When the rectangle lines up with the edges of Page 6, release the mouse button.

16. Deselect everything, then select the rectangle and delete it. Everything else should be in perfect registration.

17. Create a new layer called The End, and make sure that the dome and fly are assigned to it.

18. Drag an instance of Tag Line onto the page and center it above the cows, in the middle of the page. Make sure it is on The End layer. Release its instance, and ungroup it. Open the Navigation panel, and adjust the settings to those shown in Figure 11.26. When the viewer clicks the Tag Line, this Flash Action will restart the movie.

19. Drag an instance of Smiles onto the stage, and place them in the approximate area of the cows mouths. Use the keyboard arrows to maneuver them into precise registration. Place them on The End layer, and send them to the back. This keeps Tag Line and its Flash Action on top of the movie. Save.

> **Note:** You will notice after testing the movie that you don't need to press the Tag Line instance to restart the movie, because in this last frame, all the live areas from the first page are visible and operating. If you run the cursor over the cows, their words will appear, and clicking the dome will make the fly take off. In another movie, however, you would want an action such as this to get things working again.

Figure 11.26
The last action settings
in the movie.

Finishing Up

At this point, you need to be sure that everything on the background layer in the first page is under the separator bar in the Layers panel. You can move individual layers one at a time to a spot beneath the bar, or shift the bar up over the affected layers, whichever is easier for you. Then check every page for any duplication of those background elements. Kill 'em all! If you look in the Color Studio of this book, you can see a storyboard of the completed movie.

Go to Control|Movie Settings and adjust the settings to those you see in Figure 11.27. Click OK. Save one more time. You can check the Full Screen Playback box if you wish. The SWF treatment of the vector graphics is pretty great, even at full screen size. It's not at all like enlarging a JPEG or GIF file and looking at jaggies (unless you have those bitmapped files in the movie). FreeHand gives you absolute purity of graphics as you have drawn them.

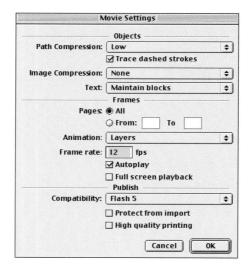

Figure 11.27
The Movie Settings panel for
Rude Cows: The Movie.

For this movie, if you were to select Pages in the Animation setting of Movie Settings, you would get six SWF files, but they would be static. The layering would not animate. That's not good—for *this* movie. If you select Layers and Pages in the Animation setting, you still get six SWF files and the animation works, but the pages appear one after another without waiting for you to interact: It runs all the layers on one page, then moves to the next page and runs those layers, on through the end of the pages. Then it recycles. These two options work fine for other movies and other circumstances, but are not viable for this particular movie.

Select Control|Test Movie. Sit back, and cross your fingers. If all has gone well, you can interact with the cows and the fly. You can also thank Ian Kelleigh again, as I do, for putting together the skeleton of this project. You can thank my wife, Yvonne, for the initial concept of the movie. I'm just a pawn.

In the symbols folder there is a symbol named The Eyes. If you wish to get more complicated and creative, you can place them on the cow's eyes as specular high-lights. The outer two cows can look at the middle cow, and the middle cow can look down. Then reverse the action. This involves cloning and adjusting each set of eyes, and applying them to the various layers in the cloud animation.

The End

When you are finished viewing the movie and everything works to your satis-faction, you need to export it.

Run Control|Test Movie, and stop the movie. Then go to Control|Export Movie. Your Movie Settings should remain the same. Whatever time it took to test the movie will elapse again as the program writes the movie to named SWF files. A single-page movie will result in one SWF file, no matter how many layers you have placed on it. A multipage file such as this project's will end up with a SWF file for every page—in this case, six files. When you upload the movie to a Web server, you must keep all the files together in the same folder on the server, and reference only the first page of the movie.

Loading to Dreamweaver

If you are going to build a Web page with Dreamweaver 4, the process goes like this:

1. Adjust the output settings to your liking (Control|Movie Settings).

2. Test the movie (Control|Test Movie).

3. If the movie runs as expected, choose Control|Export Movie. Select a folder for the files (I like to place all the files in a new folder so I can see exactly the output of my movie). It's not a bad idea to put the movie files (or the new folder) in the same folder your site utilizes for Dreamweaver. Click the Save button in the Export Movie window.

4. Do not, under any circumstances, change the names of the SWF files that FreeHand created for you. The movie will be created with the name you supply. If your movie is called MyMovie, then the first page of the (multipage) movie will be MyMovie1.swf. The second page will be named MyMovie2.swf, and so on. These names are written in the code that plays the various pages. Making a change in the name will cause the movie to halt abruptly—with no explanation or warning. It just quits and sits there looking back at you.

5. Open Dreamweaver and a new document. In order for the movie to actually play, you must save the Dreamweaver page in the same folder as the SWF files from FreeHand. All the files can be in one large folder that contains everything else on your site, or you can place them all in a specific folder. That's up to you, but save the Dreamweaver file before proceeding.

6. When the time and place for your movie are appropriate, use one of the Flash Import commands. You have several choices: Drag the Import Flash button in the toolbar into the correct location on the page (my favorite); click the Import Flash button in the toolbar; Import|Media|Flash; or Opt+Cmd+F on the Mac/Alt+Ctl+F on a Windows machine. Each of these operations brings up a navigation window, and from there you find and select the first page in your movie. Click Open (on a Mac), and a gray box with a Flash icon in the center will appear on your Dreamweaver page.

7. Once the FreeHand-produced Flash movie is in place, a new Play button appears on the right side of the Properties panel in Dreamweaver. The Play button will have a green triangle in it. Clicking that button will run the movie within Dreamweaver. This is a quick way to be sure you've placed the correct file. (The button turns into a Stop button while the movie is running.)

8. You should then test the movie in a browser, as you would any other Dreamweaver page, to ensure that everything works as planned.

From then on, it's just a Dreamweaver page, and how you get it to your server is between you and the Web.

Moving On

All in all, this has been a pretty complex chapter because it brings FreeHand off the drawing board and into the ozone. You've learned that you can create a simple HTML page quickly, and a more complicated page with just a bit more time. You also discovered that you can create graphics and export them as SWF files so the vector artwork you produce can be seen at its best on the Web. Finally, you learned that you can create a fairly complicated movie and even test it—all within FreeHand.

These tasks let you put your ideas in front of a client or your boss with a minimum amount of fuss. You can keep your mind on the message, not the medium. Dreamweaver makes better Web pages, and Flash makes better movies, but with both programs, you have many other details to worry about. HTML scripting, behaviors, rollovers, timelines, keyframes—there's a lot to keep in mind that can take away from what you're trying to accomplish. Learn just a few new tricks in FreeHand, and your learning curve just got shallower, while your bottom line got fatter.

Part V

Tricks of the Trade

Chapter 12

The Kitchen Sink

*FreeHand supplies artists with very good drawing tools—
but FreeHand doesn't do any actual drawing at all. This
portion of the book will lead you farther down the road
toward increasing your drawing skills and profitability.*

The Variety of Drawing in FreeHand

This chapter will not emphasize learning new tools, but it will cover using the ones you already know about in ways that save time, increase productivity, or let you create more believable drawings. In the projects, you will create four different styles of drawings from one reference photo. You will make the last project into a Flash movie.

I can't tell you how often I've had a prospective client call and ask something like: "Have you ever drawn a handle for the inner restroom door of a Boeing 777?" When I answer, "No," they reply, "Oh, well, we're looking for someone who has done that kind of drawing." Click. Buzzz. I don't know what it is that gives people the impression that if you *haven't* done something, you're incapable of ever doing it. I guess because it involves money, they're being cautious and looking for someone with experience.

To that end, a few years ago I created a brochure that had a Tufted Titmouse as its main element. I drew it in a stylized, flat color manner, then I filled a version with gears and wires, made another look like it was constructed from a Gilbert Erector Set, got out my biology book and drew the bird's internal structure on another, and last, drew the bird as realistically as I could. All the drawings came from the same original view. (You can see the results in the Color Studio of this book.) The point of the brochure was to say—without words—that the same subject can be illustrated in many different ways; the subject itself doesn't really matter all that much.

So, to close this book, I thought I'd present you with the same type of challenge. You'll have one color photo to work from, but you will do four types of drawings. First, a line drawing that could be utilized in an instruction manual. Second, you'll apply custom brushes to the drawing. Then you'll add flat-colors to the stylized version of the subject that could be part of a packaging effort. After that, you'll do a photorealistic rendering that could be used in an advertisement. And finally, you'll make a simple SWF movie from the photorealistic rendering (my dream—a bottomless cup of coffee). I'm sure that you'll learn a lot tackling these projects.

Ninety percent of the techniques used in these next projects have already been done in previous chapters, but I will also introduce a few tricks and techniques that couldn't fit into the other chapter projects.

PROJECT Line at the Coffee Pot

I happen to be one of those people that take instruction sheets seriously. Being as obsessive-compulsive as I am, I go crazy if the instructions are unclear or, worse yet, the drawings are poor. A good drawing can do the work of two or three paragraphs, and a bad drawing must be explained with four or five paragraphs. This project will be of the "good drawing" style.

Start by opening a new FreeHand 10 document and import the file named The Pour.tif that's located in the Chapter 12 folder on the CD-ROM.

1. When you place the photo, it will more than likely overpower your monitor. Grab a corner handle, hold down the Shift key and drag the handle toward the center of the photo. Release the Shift key, and move the photo up over the page again. Resize the image until it fits the width of the page. Now you can get to work.

2. Create a new layer, name it Photo, and drag it below the Foreground layer. Place the photo on that layer, and lock it. Save the document with the name Coffee Line Art.

3. To get the more critical part of the drawing started correctly, drag a guideline to the top of the cup's rim. Drag three more guidelines that touch the left, right, and bottom edges of the rim.

4. Select the Bezigon tool, hold down the Opt/Alt key, and click the cursor at the tangents created where the guidelines meet the arcs of the rim. As shown in Figure 12.1, the Bezigon tool comes pretty close to getting the curves right automatically.

Figure 12.1
The magic of the Bezigon tool. Guidelines are in place for the inner arc as well.

5. Adjust the control handles to make the path fit the cup snugly. Save.

6. Finish drawing the right side of the cup and the bottom, up to the point where the handle intersects the cup wall.

The bottom of the cup could present a slight problem—it has a rounded edge, and as it recedes to the sides and back, the curves go bonkers. (That's the technical term for this situation.) The curves don't follow a regular elliptical path. Instead, they become part of a compound curve on their way to the vertical sides. In order to get this curve drawn correctly, you'll have to plot points individually. You only need three points: one at either side and one in the center. Depending on the angle of view of the camera for a given photo, the "center" may be right in the middle or way off to the left or right. To find the spot on the curve where a point would do the most good in a drawing, drag a guideline so that it touches the arc of the object. Zoom in as close as you feel necessary. The center of the curved path you need to draw will be at the point where the arc meets the guideline (the tangent, if I'm not mistaken). You can see where I plan to place the center point in Figure 12.2.

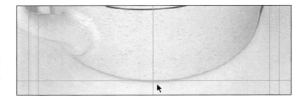

Figure 12.2

Placement of curve points at the bottom of the cup.

7. Select the Pen tool and begin tracing the photo. Because there will be no tone in this drawing, only draw outlines and edges. Trace until the drawing looks like Figure 12.3, including the frame outline created with the Rectangle tool.

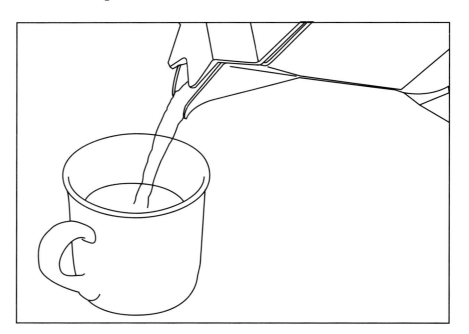

Figure 12.3

The basic lines in place.

Okay, now you'll beef up the drawing by changing some line weights. You will have to trim paths here and there, but that's not difficult. The style of drawing you will complete is called (among other terms, I'm sure) *wireframe*. Wireframe drawings look as if you have taken a thick wire and wrapped it around key objects in the drawing. The more important an object is, the bolder the line— to a point, obviously. Then, to create color and definition from the linework, use varying line weights. These rules are set by the artistic community, and are subject to the whims of each artist, but the basic idea is pretty simple. Lines that show a change in plane—inside corners, the change from vertical to horizontal, left to right, and so on—get the thinnest line. Please don't go below a 0.25-point line however, because thinner lines will be very difficult to hold on press, and if you will be posting the drawing on a Web site, anything thinner than a point is shown as 1 pixel wide—the smallest increment possible on a monitor.

Lines that describe an inner edge—in the case of this project, the inside lip of the cup, the inner hole of the handle, edges on the espresso pot—get a thicker line weight. An inner edge could be defined as an edge of the object that lies in front of another plane in the object. Common values are 0.5 points for plane changes, 1 point for inner edges, and 2 points for the wire outline.

As an example, hold your palm in front of you and look at it. In a wireframe, you'd have a wire outline all around your fingers and thumb. Wrinkles and other folds in the skin would have a 0.5 line. If you are wearing a ring, the ring would have a 1-point line as it crosses your finger. Now fold your thumb into your palm. The outline of the thumb passes in front of another portion of the object (your palm), and would receive a 1-point line.

To really get a leg up on production time, you'd be surprised how much time you save by having a style set for each line, instead of going to the Stroke Inspector and scrolling through the drop-down menu for a line weight again and again. Setting styles also helps in case changes in style have to be made— a changed style immediately ripples through the entire document. I have styles named Wire, Edge, and Break.

Use the line weight concepts here and add some color to your black and white art. Hide the photo layer so you can see the drawing as it will appear—keep the goal in mind, more or less.

The box surrounding the drawing should be emphasized, so I gave it a 3-point line weight. I added callouts—words or numbers describing objects in a drawing—and I placed leader lines of 0.25-point (hairline) weight as pointers. Then I gave the border a light drop shadow, using the Smudge Xtra with stroke and fill both set to white. My finished drawing is shown in Figure 12.4.

PROJECT The Espresso Drawing with Stylized Brush Strokes

Sometimes you need something different in a drawing style, so you'll apply brush strokes to the paths instead of using the technical line technique from the last project. I started by creating three custom brushes, which you can find in the Brushes folder inside the Chapter 12 folder on the CD-ROM. You can use these premade brushes for the project, but I encourage you to also create your own. It will be much more satisfying and educational. (For complete instructions on creating custom brushes, read Chapter 7.)

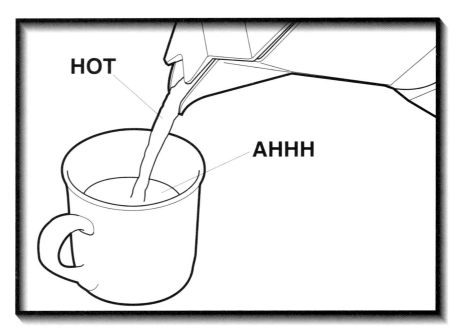

Figure 12.4
Coffee pouring instructions.

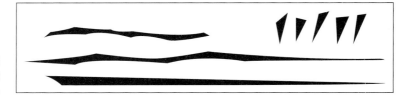

Figure 12.5
Brushes for the stylized
linework project.

Drag the Chapter 12 Brushes file into the FreeHand 10|English|Brushes folder and import them into your FreeHand document. The brushes I created are shown in Figure 12.5.

Stylizing the Linework

You will use the line drawing created in the previous project as the basis for this project. If you didn't complete the first project, open the file called CoffeeLine.fh10 in the Chapter 12 folder on the CD-ROM, and work with those drawings. I find it is much easier to modify a tight drawing than it is to draw a loose one in the first place, which is probably due more to my obsessive-compulsiveness than a method of working. But I'm sure you'll agree that it's a good idea to make a good, faithful line rendering of your subject first. Revisions with different stroke styles and color fills later give you much more control over the final appearance of the drawing.

Whether you decide to use your own drawing or one from the CD, open one of the files and save it with a new name, such as CaffeineJolt. Go to the Stroke Inspector and choose Import from the triangle drop-down menu. Navigate to the English folder within the FreeHand folder, and select the Chapter 12 Brushes file. In the resulting dialog box, select all the brushes and click the Import button. The brushes will now be available in the Stroke Inspector|Brush drop-down menu.

It would be a simple matter to select the entire drawing and change all the lines to the same custom brush stroke—in fact it might work quite well—but, instead, take one path at a time and apply a stroke to it. Switch back and forth between the strokes to give a different emphasis to one element or another. I'll get another cup of coffee while you do that. When you're finished, your artwork should look similar to my masterpiece in Figure 12.6.

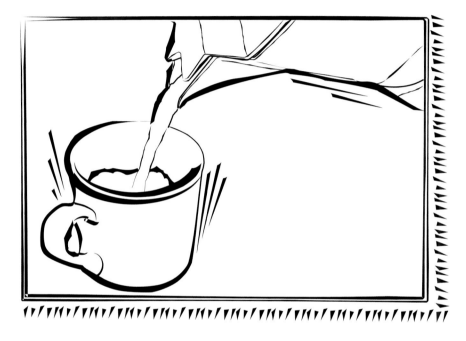

Figure 12.6
Stylized linework.

I added a few accent strokes to the drawing—I happened to like that custom brush—and the strokes were drawn extremely quickly with the Line tool. Experiment with the brushstroke width. Sometimes a width of only 20% is extremely effective, and at other times I change it to 150% or more. The point is to make it look as if it has not been drawn on a computer.

Okay, now the drawing has a bit of style, and a casual feeling to it, compared to the first project that looks like something out of a VCR instruction manual. You can start to snap it up a bit by clicking on the Polygon tool and creating a 20-point acute star as follows:

1. Double-click the Polygon tool to bring up the Polygon dialog box. Enter 20 for the Number Of Sides, click the Star Shape button, make the Star Points Manual, and put the slider about in the middle of the scale. Click OK.

Figure 12.7

The 3D Rotation Xtra settings for the star.

2. Place the cursor in the center of the bottom of the cup, and drag out until the star extends halfway to the right border of the drawing. Clone the star, and use the Scale tool to enlarge the star so the points on the right extend quite a bit out of the drawing border.

3. Send the cloned star to the back, and Shift+select the first star. Double-click the 3D Rotation Xtra, and set its options to read as shown in Figure 12.7.

4. Because the rotation will originate at the center of the two stars, it doesn't matter (in the Easy mode) where you click the cursor. So click the cursor and drag it upward until the perspective of the stars matches that of the cup. Choose custom brush strokes for the stars.

5. Cut both star shapes to the Clipboard, and select the drawing's border. Do a Paste Inside. Save.

Coloring the Drawing

The easy part is done—easy because all the lines were complete, and you only had to apply attributes to them. Now you have to create blocks of color that go behind the linework. Some shapes will be closed paths, and easy to create; others will be closed, but encompass too large an area and have to be split into smaller shapes. For a color palette, I went with various shades of blue—on the cool side—for the aluminum espresso pot. I chose orangish earth tones suggestive of coffee for the cup and background. (Can you tell I've been drinking three pots of coffee a day throughout the writing of this book?)

1. First, set up your color palette. I generally take out my Pantone Solid to Process swatch guide and choose my colors from the process side of the page. I am confident that when the job goes to press, the colors will be very close to what I had in mind. If the job is destined for the Web, then it's a no-brainer to select the Web Safe Color Library from the Color panel.

2. Next, create a new layer named Linework, select the entire drawing, and assign it to the Linework layer. Create another layer named Color Blocks, and drag it beneath the Linework layer.

3. As you work, if you have a closed path that you can apply color to, then apply it to the path and keep it on the Linework layer. When you have to create a new shape, place that on the Color Blocks layer. Select the drawing's border and create a Graduated fill of dark at the top to lighter at the bottom. The color choice is yours. You can see an example of my colors in the finished drawing in the Color Studio section of this book.

4. Subselect the larger star and give it a fill that contrasts with the background gradient. Then subselect the smaller star and fill it with a color

Wells of Color

Just a reminder: The color wells at the bottom of the toolbar in FreeHand 10 are more or less customizable. Click either of the color wells, and a box opens showing the current selection of colors. At the top right you will see icons that allow you to select other color methods. The last icon is a triangle drop-down menu that has selections such as Swatches, which lists all the colors in your Swatches panel; and Color Cubes, which is the Web Safe Color Library. As you run the cursor over a color, its description appears in the window as the name you've applied to it in the Swatches panel, or in hexadecimal or RGB for Web-safe colors.

What Happens to Sharp Corners?

You will notice the odd-even fill happening when the custom brush crosses itself in the stylized brush strokes project. I consider that a plus sometimes, but if it bothers you, you can simply split the point at the odd-even intersection. The brush will then start and stop at the new end points, effectively creating an unbroken line. I like the frenetic look the odd-even intersections get, but when it becomes too predictable or mechanical, I break it up. Keep in mind that if you have the shape filled—when you split the path, you lose the fill, so go to Edit|Preferences and check the Show Fill For Open Paths option, or add a color to a clone of the path and send it to the back.

that contrasts greatly with the large star's color. That's a lot of contrast, but you want the image to jolt the viewer. Save often.

5. The cup will probably need one or two custom shapes drawn for the color fills. Clone existing lines, split paths, and join them. Do as little "new" drawing as possible. (Why reinvent the wheel?) And, more to the point, your registration is exact by using cloned shapes. My cup has a gradient fill with three colors of yellow from left to right. The handle has another gradient fill of yellows from top to bottom.

6. The espresso pot will require separate closed paths for every plane. I used flat planes of color; you can make gradations or add further accents if you wish.

7. When you're finished adding all the color, print the drawing and see if you need further color adjustments. Then tape it to the refrigerator alongside your shopping list. The final drawing should look similar to Figure 12.8—then again, it could look completely different!

All My Brushes Are Black

You cannot change the color of a custom brush. When you create a custom brush, you decide at that point that the brush will be a particular color. As long as it's a brush, it will be just as you designed it. Naturally, if you want to change the color of the brush in every instance in a drawing, you can edit it. But in order to change the appearance of a custom brush in isolated instances, you must get the brush/stroke in the position and scale you want, then release the brush. You'll have to ungroup it several times until you get to the basic filled path. Then you can change the color, add a stroke, whatever you like, because it's just a normal object from that point on.

Figure 12.8
The completed stylized espresso drawing.

Let's Be Photorealistic

I really enjoy making garden-variety line drawings—just drawing black lines on paper makes my day complete. But a close second favorite is creating as photorealistic a rendering as I can with vector artwork. So, to finish my kicks for the day, I'll have you tackle the coffee and pot again, only this time you'll go for as much realism as you can. You'll use the Eyedropper tool to gather your color palette and stretch your muscles with the Envelope feature. The best part is that you've already got the basic structure complete in the line drawing from the first project in this chapter or from the CoffeeLine.fh10 file on the CD-ROM.

The construction of this drawing doesn't vary much from the car drawing in Chapter 4, but it gets a little more complicated because of the elements involved and the techniques you'll use to draw each of them. First, you'll tackle what could be considered the toughest part of the drawing—the decorations around the cup. And, yes, I do think the Southwest look on a cup for Italian coffee is a little, well, weird, but it doesn't affect the taste or kick from the espresso, so what the heck. Pour yourself a cup, and get started. Use your drawing from the last project, or open CoffeeLine.fh10. Lock the photo layer, and hide the line art.

1. Drag some guidelines down over the cup. Place them on the tangents of the various arcs.

2. Now build the color palette with the Eyedropper tool. Select each of the representative colors in the design: salmon, sand, green, and gray.

The design will be done in the flat, and then you'll apply an Envelope to it to wrap it around the cup. The elements in the front of the cup are about as close to actual size and shape as you will get. You want to reduce the amount of actual work to a minimum, so you'll draw one element and clone it several times.

3. Create a new layer in the Layers panel, and name it Cup Design.

4. Use the Rectangle tool and draw a vertical rectangle the exact width of the center green—I'll call them darts. Because this drawing is highly symmetrical, you'll cheat a lot. Only draw the top half, and clone it. Then use the Skew tool to shift the clone so that it aligns with the photograph. Look at Figure 12.9. It's viewed at some 1400%, and the drawing layer is switched to Keyline view. Be sure that you are drawing on the Cup Design layer.

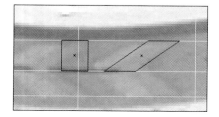

Figure 12.9
Starting the darting.

5. Fill the skewed dart with Salmon, and give it a stroke of None. With the Shift key held down, move the dart until it lines up with the salmon-colored dart nearest the center diamond shape in the photo. Then clone it, change its color to Sand, and shift it to the left so their edges abut. The Keyline view and Snap To Points help immensely here.

6. Select and clone both darts, and move them to the left until they are very close to the next pattern on the rim. Keep a space equal to one of the darts between the two groups you've drawn—this will equal a green dart in a step or two. Remember, you're drawing this flat, so keep everything aligned on the guidelines. Save.

7. Finish the row by cloning both pairs of darts and shifting them. Then clone just one dart and place it at the end of the row and give it a green fill.

8. Ungroup the green dart and select its two right side points. Holding down the Shift key, stretch those points all the way to where the pattern turns gray. Send this long green dart to the back. It should look like Figure 12.10.

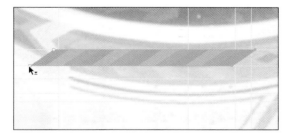

Figure 12.10
The long green dart has been sent to the back, creating the top of the dart pattern.

9. The pattern on the far left has what appears to be *X* shapes, but they're continuations of our darts. Clone a dart and use the Reflect tool to flop the shape. Clone that pair and shift them to complete the pattern. Figure 12.11 shows what it should look like now.

Figure 12.11
The top half of the *X* shapes were created by cloning and flopping darts.

10. From the preceding steps, you can extrapolate how to complete the right side of the rim design. Just draw the top half. Keep the proportions and shape relationships going as you work. The pattern will extend beyond the cup in the photo.

11. When you have the pattern complete, select everything and choose the Reflect tool. Click exactly on the baseline of the darts and drag straight down, which will cause a vertical flipping of the image. Wham! Instant design as seen in Figure 12.12.

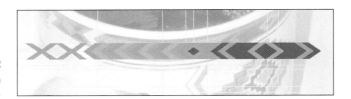

Figure 12.12
This complex design came from a single rectangle.

12. Well, not so fast. The Envelope feature sometimes moves things just a tad, and you want to minimize that shifting. Go through and select each pair of salmon darts (top and bottom) and use the Union Xtra on them one at a time. This action cuts the number of elements almost in half and streamlines the drawing.

13. Repeat Step 13 with the sand-colored darts. Then join the top and bottom long green dart with the Union Xtra as well. Make sure the long green dart goes to the back. Save.

14. Drag a vertical guideline to mark the extreme left end of the gray lines running around the cup. Then Opt/Alt+click the guideline and drag it to the right end of the design you just finished. (Opt/Alt+clicking the guideline duplicates the guide, saving you a trip to the ruler.)

15. Draw a 1-point gray line between the guidelines at the level of the tangent where the line hits the center of the cup on the photo.

16. Drag another vertical guide that meets the points of the zigzag gray line, and two more for the green zigzag.

17. In order to make my drawing fairly accurate, I drew a short horizontal line at the top of the zigzag line and another at the bottom. Then I created a three-step Blend to equally divide the space, as shown in Figure 12.13. Drag down guidelines to the Blend steps, and discard the Blend.

Figure 12.13
Dividing the vertical space, and drawing the top half of the pattern.

18. Continue as you see in Figure 12.13, and draw the symmetrical shapes that make up the top half of the design. When the design is complete, use the Reflect tool to flip it, then join the halves of everything as you did on the upper pattern in Step 13. Save.

There's probably a name for the jagged diamond shape you see on the right of the cup design, but I'll just stick with diamond. To draw the diamond, you have two choices: You can plot a zigzag pattern for a quadrant, then clone and reflect it, or you can draw overlapping rectangles and use the Union Xtra to create massive shapes. I like the zigzag quadrant, myself. Look at Figure 12.14 to see the difference between the two methods, and take your pick of methods to draw the diamond. You can decide whether to use stroke width or more zigzag rectangles for some of the paths in the design.

The finished cup pattern should look similar to Figure 12.15. Don't worry if it doesn't; it's just a drawing. Admittedly, the diamond pattern gets tedious.

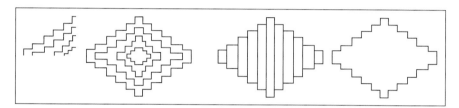

Figure 12.14

Alternate ways to draw the diamond shape: Draw a quadrant and clone pieces (far left and middle left), or draw several rectangles and use the Union Xtra (middle right and far right).

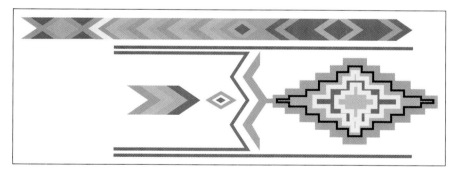

Figure 12.15

The cup pattern in the flat.

Making the Cup 3D

Okay, now you'll use the Envelope feature to get the design into three dimensions:

1. Start by creating a clone of the design you made in Steps 1 through 19 in the previous section so you'll have a parachute in case something goes terribly awry. Then place it on the desktop, out of your way.

2. Center the design in the cup, and align the top of the dart design with the same part of the design on the cup's rim. Your design should hang out just about equally on both sides of the cup in the photo. Select the Rectangle Envelope from its drop-down menu. With the design selected, click the Apply Envelope button.

3. Drag a selection box encompassing all three points on the left side of the Envelope. Then select any one of the points and drag the side of the Envelope in to where it meets the side of the cup. Adjust the horizontal control handle on the top-left point until the artwork matches the curve of the cup lip. Then adjust the horizontal handle on the bottom-left point.

4. Select the right side points on the Envelope and adjust them in as you did on the left side. It may take some fiddling to get the curves just right. If you get it all loused up, or you're frustrated, remove the art from the Envelope and start over. Don't adjust the handles in the middle of the sides—that tends to do strange things to your artwork when you're working on a cylindrical object such as this. Turn on the Envelope Map if you want to view tighter precision.

5. When you're finished with the Envelope procedure, save the drawing. The artwork should look very similar to Figure 12.16.

Figure 12.16
The design has been Enveloped onto the cup.

The first thing you will notice is that the drawing doesn't quite fit the cup. Depending on the task at hand, this may be quite acceptable. On the other hand, if your drawing will be printed on high-quality presses and scrutinized by people who demand attention to detail—well then, this just won't work. You won't go all the way here, but I'll get you started.

6. Click the Release button in the Envelope toolbar.

7. The objects that were Enveloped are now released and are just as if you had drawn them in place. Now it's a relatively easy matter to adjust the points to fit where they are critical. This process only takes a few minutes, and the difference is quite noticeable. Compare Figure 12.17 to the first-cut image in Figure 12.16.

Figure 12.17
The tweaked design on the cup.

The Problem with Envelopes

The Envelope feature is a real time-saver, and I use it often, but it can do some strange things to your art. For instance, zoom in to about 1000% to the area shown in Figure 12.17 and look at the dart shapes. Depending on their location within the Envelope, some points have been deleted to be replaced by rounded curves. In other spots, points have been added. You might assume that this would happen while the art is being tortured by the control handles, so just be aware that it happens. If you are making something as critical as a logo, then take the extra time to zoom in and clean everything up. You've still saved hours of struggling to get perspective and warp into your drawing.

The Cup Body

Next, you will treat the body or front wall of the cup as a single shape with a gradient fill.

Begin by making the line art visible and cloning the various shapes and lines necessary to isolate the cup front. Hide anything that's in your way:

1. Create a new layer named Cup Face, and move it beneath the Cup Design layer.

2. In order to get the gradient perfectly matched to the photo, you have to do a little cheating. Draw a rectangle completely across the cup from edge to edge. Open the Fill Inspector and select a basic graduated fill. If you've still got the photo layer locked, unlock it now.

3. Choose the Eyedropper tool, and select a sample from the shadow area in the finger hole of the handle. Drag the sample to the Color Mixer panel, and click the Add To Swatches button. If you want to name the color, go ahead; otherwise accept the RGB numbers and click Add.

4. Drag a swatch of that color onto the far-left color well in the Fills panel. Conversely, you can click the color well box—the color box will open with all named colors in it, and you can choose the color there.

5. Select colors with the Eyedropper tool across the surface of the cup, and place the newly sampled colors in positions relative to the photo. If you're doing a good job, the rectangle will become invisible except for its lack of texture. And, that's what you're looking for, so move those color swatches around until you can't see the rectangle any longer.

6. When you have your color ramp built, go to the Styles panel and select New from the triangle menu. Name the style Front of Cup. Then, select the shape that you drew for the face of the cup and apply the Front of Cup style to it. You'll smile because you will notice that only the texture has left the cup if your gradient fill was done well. Discard the rectangle.

The Handle

The handle will create a few more problems because of the compound curves involved. Creating the handle will also be difficult because of the slight nuances in color and the way the gradients shift and meld into one another. To get the easy stuff out of the way, start by creating a new layer named Specular Highlights.

1. Using the Ellipse tool, draw the large highlight on the top of the handle, the three little ones where the bottom of the handle meets the cup, the one on the rim, and the two on the inside of the cup's back wall. Place them all on the Specular Highlights layer and lock the layer.

2. Create an outline for the entire handle shape. It will have a gradient fill that goes from a middle gray to a light gray to a darker gray at the bottom. Choose the colors directly from the photo with the Eyedropper tool. Add them to your Swatches panel as you go.

I created a shape that runs across the top, down the back, and through the middle of the handle that will be used as the end result of a Blend. Look closely at Figure 12.18. The left side (Keyline view) of the figure shows where the shapes break and the types of Blends I made. You can see the results on the right side (Preview view). I added the handle on the far left of the figure for clarity. The handle in the middle right image shows the areas that are darker than the handle (more or less shadow areas).

However, give the shape that defines the left edge of the handle the same color fill as you have set for the middle of the handle. Then clone that shape and move the larger areas inward as seen in the keyline drawing on the left. Give this clone the darker shadow color. When it Blends into the lighter color, it almost disappears into the main color. The colors are so close in value that it makes the Blend in one step—causing banding that could show, so change the Blend steps to at least four in the Object Inspector.

Note: Depending on the size of the ultimate printed piece, one step for the Blend might be just enough. Do test prints to see if banding is evident in the Blend. If you can see banding when you print from a laser or ink jet printer, you quite possibly will see it when your drawing comes off an offset press.

Figure 12.18
The handle in keyline (top) and
preview (bottom) views, showing
how the handle is developed.

The Rim

Next, create the cup's rim:

1. Notice how the color changes as light travels around the cup's rim in
    the photo. The rim is darker in the middle than in the foreground or
    back lip, so a gradient fill is in order. Create a new layer named Rim.

2. Create the rim by tracing or adapting paths and drawing the thickness
    of the wall. Use a gradient fill of a light gray in the back, a fairly dark
    gray in the middle, and a light one again in the front. Create a sliver of
    highlight that goes under the specular highlight on the front lip. Save.

The Inside Wall

Okay, I confess. The inside of the cup is tougher than the handle. The problem
you have to overcome is a tonal gradation from top to bottom and from left to
right. That's tough in vector terms. Our gradients go only in one direction. But
FreeHand lets us blend graduated fills, and there's the answer.

In the center of the cup wall, draw a rectangle about half a pica wide (6 points,
maybe an eighth of an inch—it's not critical) and the height of the wall from
the coffee to the rim.

1. Start by moving the rectangle to just above the rim. Move it to the left
    until it just splits the cusp of the inside rim. Make a clone of the rect-
    angle and Shift+drag it to about a third of the way across the cup.
    Clone the second rectangle and move it the other third of the way.

Figure 12.19

Preparing the tricky inside wall.

Then, clone that and drag it across to the other rim. You should have an arrangement similar to that shown in Figure 12.19. I have added gradient fills and emphasized the tones in the rectangles for clarity.

2. Now, select the rectangle on the left, open the Fills Inspector, and choose Basic Gradient Fill. Set the angle wheel to 90°. Using the Eyedropper tool, select a color from the darkest shadow area on the wall directly beneath the rectangle. Drag that color to the left color well in the Fills ramp. Then pick a color just above it, midway to the top, and place that color swatch in the middle of the ramp. Repeat this action at the top of the wall. Save.

3. Repeat Step 2 for the other three rectangles, selecting colors from beneath their position on the cup, and save again. Make sure that each rectangle gets the same number of colors in the Fills ramp.

4. Select all four rectangles and choose Modify|Combine|Blend. You will have a very close approximation of the left-to-right, up-to-down color blending. Save, and hide the group.

5. Create a new layer named Inside Wall.

6. Trace the wall area. (Continue the shape behind the flow of coffee.) Don't worry about the bubbles or the shadow behind the coffee flow. Draw the line inside the rim art so you won't have to worry about color leaks. Draw the bottom of the wall as it meets the coffee, just below the coffee line. When you draw the coffee, you'll draw above this layer.

7. Choose View|Show All to bring back the Blend. Adjust the height and width so it covers the inside wall shape completely, and cut it to the Clipboard. Select the wall outline and do a Paste Inside.

8. Move the Inside Wall layer beneath the Rim layer. Save.

You'll save the coffee for last, but the cup should look like what you see in Figure 12.20. I did the cup wall in two sections to make it easier for you to see how the drawing will "work" when it's done.

Figure 12.20
The finished cup.

Trim the Rim

If you really want to get detailed, you can clone the rim and create a combination highlight and shadow for the rim. Just split the rim on the inside where it meets the coffee, and hide the inside remnant. Select the outer path and delete the two end points that lie alongside the coffee. Select Show All, select both paths, and use the Expand Path Xtra to give them both a width of 0.5 points. Then give each of them a gradient fill that creates the right kind of shadow or highlight for the part of the rim it occupies. See Figure 12.21 for a keyline visual explanation of this exercise.

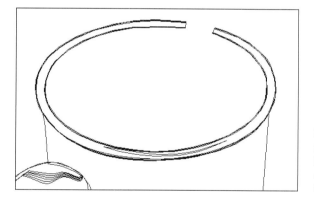

Figure 12.21
Expanded paths filled with highlight and shadow colors add depth. This keyline view shows the construction involved.

The Espresso Pot

Now you will tackle the aluminum features of the pot. It won't take long, and then you can finish off with the fun stuff—the coffee. You'll use the same techniques for selecting colors and creating shapes to fill with Blends or gradients.

Start with yet another new layer and name it Coffeepot.

Starting at the bottom and working your way up is the way to go for two reasons: First, this method provides logic to your workflow (you always know what you're going to do next). Second, whatever you draw goes on top of the last thing you drew. Therefore, you'll overlap parts of the drawing, which cuts down on the amount of paper or color leak from misregistration of the line work. So, start at the very bottom of the pot and draw the triangular shape.

Working your way from the right side of the photo to the left, it should take about half an hour to 45 minutes to create the rectangular color model (as you did for the inside wall)—make it a style, then draw the shape and apply the style. Notice particularly the way the zigzag multi-level lid gets handled. Each face of the lid (and sides) is a different filled shape. The three lid pieces have gradients that use very tight color arrangements at the ends of the gradients in order to create the smooth transition. The angles range from 12° to 14° for this particular photo.

Take a little time on the inside of the spout. The colors there are pretty neat, and will really make the coffee pop. Save often. For the record, I ended up with 14 different styles, and, I think, about 18 or 19 shapes. Some shapes are filled with a solid color. The finished product is shown in Figure 12.22.

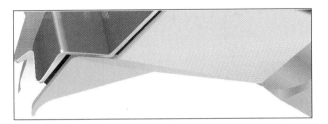

Figure 12.22
The finished espresso pot.

Coffee Comes in Two Flavors

Now you will make the coffee being poured, and the coffee in the cup. You'll take them one at a time, again, starting at the bottom. You will draw each of the distinct color areas of the coffee. Then in some cases you will create blends from those colored areas and in other instances let the color float on top of the blended areas.

You can get started by saving your document in case you haven't lately. (Look for the asterisk after the file name in the document window, or the full-strength logo in the menu bar. If you see those, you haven't saved.) Zoom in so the entire coffee experience fills your screen.

1. Create three new layers. Name them Cup Coffee, Bubbles, and The Pour. Select the Cup Coffee layer and choose the Pen tool. Look for the five major color areas in the coffee within the cup. You will notice a dark shadow area near the bottom, where you're looking through the most coffee. There's a sort of gray highlight on top of those shadows, which is a reflection of the inside cup wall. And then there are three shades of coffee (as we see through less and less of the coffee), ending with a light tan or root beer color as the liquid hits the wall of the cup.

2. Now that you know where the color breaks are, select colors from those areas and add them to your Swatches panel.

3. Draw an encompassing area that will go beneath everything. Give it the next-to-the-lightest color. Hide the shape.

4. Draw the lightest area (the root beer color) where it joins the cup and melds into the middle area. Group all the shapes you draw and hide them.

5. Draw the dark coffee areas (not the darkest shadows), group them, and hide them.

6. Draw the dark shadow areas, but not the pour portion. Save that for a later step.

7. Draw the highlight areas last, and group them.

8. Choose Show All from the View menu and see what you have. Figure 12.23 shows a keyline view of the color breaks and blends I created in my drawing.

Figure 12.23
A keyline view showing the color breaks and blending in the coffee area.

9. Ick! Looks pretty bad, but take one section at a time and clone it, then use the Inset Path Xtra with a setting of around -1.5 points. Give the new object the fill of the middle coffee color (the one that lies under all the rest). Hide it, select the original, and bring it to the front. Select show All, and Blend the two objects.

10. Step 9 will take time and patience. When you're done, your artwork will look something like Figure 12.24. The bottom edge looks rough, but you'll be placing it beneath the Rim layer, so it gets covered nicely. Save.

Figure 12.24
Coffee in the cup.

Bursting Bubbles

Everyone knows what bubbles look like, but drawing them is a real challenge. You almost need to draw them on a bubble-by-bubble basis. Sounds like fun, huh? Well, you can get around it by creating a few, turning them into Graphic Hose elements, and splattering them around the cup. Then, release them from their symbols and tweak them as necessary.

Basically, the photo contains four bubbles. The largest bubbles lie along the outside of the cup, and are more a study in line art than in fills. Notice that the highlight for most of the bubbles is on the bottom as well as on the top. The bubbles are lightest at the top, then they get dark abruptly in an arc in the bottom third, then they get really dark. You will see two highlights, the large one on the front surface of the bubble, and a smaller one on the back of the bubble. For some odd reason, elliptical dark accents show up at the top, which is evidently a reflection of the bottom of the bubble sitting on the surface. All in all, this part of the project is going to be a bear.

1. Start by clicking the Bubbles layer in the Layers panel, and drawing a circle on the layer with the Ellipse tool. Most of the bubbles have a medium- to light-gray outline, which must be around 0.5 point or smaller. Anything larger will not work.

2. As you can see in Figure 12.25, you can pop your bubble in many ways. Every one of these bubbles was taken directly from the drawing. Most require a Paste Inside, and most of those are circles of the same size but different color. The highlights are what really make the bubbles pop, so to speak. Even the dark bubbles deserve a Specular highlight.

Figure 12.25
The bubbles take on many configurations, depending on where they are. Drawing them calls for a lot of experimentation.

3. Look closely at the photo, and place bubbles where they belong. Notice how their stacking order works. Build the bubble rows from the back, near the cup wall, to the front or open area. Stay away from Lens fills if you can. Lens fills would probably work, but with all that's going on in this drawing, a few Lens fills could choke the printer.

The Pour

We're nearing the end of the project, where you'll finally get down to the coffee coming out of the pot. When you draw in the manner described in this book, you draw what you see, so it's a simple matter to trace the shapes and give them the same color fill as the photo. Try to develop a pattern of working so nothing gets left out.

You'll start by drawing the bottom part of the liquid as it hits the coffee in the cup:

1. You will see a dark brown spot on the left, and a reddish-brown area to the back and right. Draw them and Blend them together.

2. Draw the lightning bolt shadow that runs down the middle of the pour. Notice that you can draw two elliptical shapes toward the top and join them with the rest of the shape to create a compound path, letting the background color come through. That saves drawing the shapes and trying to match the background color—especially if it is a gradient or Blend.

3. Fill the lightning bolt shadow with a Blend, ending with the reddish-brown teardrop shape at the bottom. Save.

4. Tackle the two-piece shadow accent on the bottom right. Make the larger area a reddish orange and the darker accents gradient fills of dark brown to dark red.

5. Draw the other accents on the top-left of the pour, and notice that near the pot itself, some of the outer edges of the coffee pick up a gray outline from the coffeepot. You can get by with a 0.5-point line, but I drew shapes and filled them.

6. Draw the bottom background of the coffee. Fill it with a gradient fill of light tan to a dark tan at the very bottom. These shadings are very subtle. Try to mimic the photo as much as possible.

7. Now draw the upper pour body; it has a darker tone to it.

8. Draw the large reddish section of coffee still in the pot. The liquid consists of a gradient of very dark reddish-brown to that beautiful orange-tan as it leaves the pot.

9. Add the shadow at the bottom of the spout. Save.

10. Draw the pure white highlights across the bottom of the lip, and hide them, then draw the orangish shape in back of it. Save again. The drawing should look very similar to Figure 12.26.

The Finishing Touches

The scene looked a little bland, so I hid the background and traced the shadows from the photo. I gave them a Darken Lens fill of about 35%. Then I set some type in Johann Sparkling ITC. The finished drawing is shown in Figure 12.27, and in the color section of the book. You may disagree with my color choices, but something drew me to these two colors for a background gradient. Blue and maroon—or is it brown?

Figure 12.26
The Pour. It looks like you can see through it.

Figure 12.27
The finished rendering of Pocono Espresso.

That's it. The coffee's done. You're done. Print it out and stick it on the refrigerator with the other projects from the book. Nice work!

PROJECT The Bottomless Cup of Espresso— Make Mine SWF Flavored

This project is a little bonus activity for you. You can make an easy Flash animation from the photorealistic artwork in short order.

Save the document you created in the previous project with a new name, and discard any extra pages you may have produced as you worked.

1. Create a new layer and name it Flow.

2. Select the lightning bolt accent from the pour and also select the dark red spot on the lower right of the pour, plus the ice cream cone shape on the top left.

3. Move those objects to the Flow layer, and save.

4. Now drag the separator bar in the Layers panel above all the layers except Flow, which is at the top of the list. Everything will go to the background except the items on Flow.

5. Select the lightning bolt graphic. If you did as I did and built a compound path, use the Split Xtra to break the shape up. Delete the two holes (if you had any in the shape). Then clone the shape and use the Reflect tool to flip the shape horizontally. Hold the mouse button down until you have the clone aligned on top of the original and at the same angle.

6. Tweak the clone until it's exactly on top of the original, and not hanging off the pour anywhere. Then select both original and clone and create a Blend. If you want to take it easy, change the number of steps in the Blend to 12; otherwise, stick with the default 25 steps. Save.

7. Select the Animate|Release To Layers Xtra, and save again.

8. Now select all the other objects on the Flow layer. Click on the first of the new layers added when you did the Animate Xtra.

9. Clone the objects and move them up a little, and click the second layer. You are creating an animation based on layers already in sequence.

10. Continue with the process: Clone, shift, assign to next layer. Keep going until you have made assignments to every layer. Save often.

11. Now go to Control|Movie Settings and set up the panel as shown in Figure 12.28.

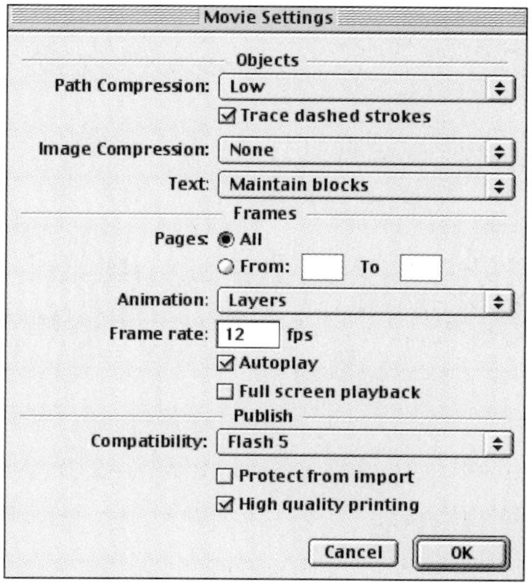

Figure 12.28
The Movie Settings for the Coffee Movie.

12. Click OK, then select Control|Test Movie. Hold tight—it takes a few seconds, maybe longer to render. At times my Mac seems to hang, and then everything takes off and finishes.

13. The coffee should be pouring out of the spout now. If you want to save the movie, choose Control|Export Movie. The file size is under 80KB.

Naturally, you could get carried away and have bubbles moving and popping and the ripples in the cup moving around—without too much work at all. If you come up with something good, email it to me at **rockwell@nidus-corp.com**.

Moving On

In this chapter, you've learned that just because you haven't done something before isn't evidence that you can't do it at all. Most of the time, you only need the incentive to try. A teacher once told me that *"trying is an excuse for not doing."* Many times that saying has come back to haunt me and give me the nudge I need to *do* something.

You learned that one photo can be used at least four different ways: from a black-and-white drawing, to a stylized drawing, to a realistic rendering, to a Web movie. If you followed through, you must have gained a lot of confidence. Good job! The next chapter is yours. I hope you come back to this book from time to time for a little refresher course. Please visit Ian Kelleigh's site (**www.FreeHandSource.com**) for new tips and tricks for working with FreeHand, and mine (**www.nidus-corp.com/books.html**) for samples of FreeHand illustrations and addendums to this book.

Index

3D effects. *See also* 3D Rotation Xtra; Envelopes; Perspective Grid.
    coffee cup project, 305–307
    for the Web, 181
    precomputer methods, 180–181
3D Rotation Xtra
    description, 182
    Easy mode, 182–184
    Expert mode, 184–185
    joystick metaphor, 182–183
    projects, 185–187
    Rotate From location, 182–183
    rotating objects, 182–183
    viewpoint, 184–185
4-process color, 56–57

A

Abstract shapes, 39
Action project, 136–137
ActionScript, 273
Add Points Xtra
    closed paths, 35–36
    dividing a line equally, 39
    modifying a path, 39
    project, 41–52
Aerosol can project, 198–206
Aerosol spray effect, 285–289
Airplane project, 136–137
Aligning text, 215–216
Animation. *See also* Flash support.
    backgrounds, 282–284
    blend steps, 282
    creating, 270–273

    speed, 277
    walking fly, 280
Auto-expanding text blocks, 213–214
Axonometric projections, 144–145, 146–147

B

Backgrounds, animation, 282–284
Bézier curves, 41–52
Bitmapped images
    distortions, 180
    Flow Inside Path command, 217
    flowing text around objects, 217
    Run Around Selection command, 217
Bleed area, 11
Blend Xtra, 74–76
Blends. *See also* Contour gradients; Gradient fills.
    animation, 282
    definition, 74
    Flow Inside Path command, 217
    flowing text around objects, 217
    Run Around Selection command, 217
Blends, projects
    cone, 78–79
    cube, 77–78
    power saw, 90–97
    rose, 83–86
    sphere, 79–81
Bologna sandwich project, 161–164
Border project, 129–135
Bounding boxes, 170
Broccoli project, 111–116
Brush and ink technique, example, 51–52

Brush feature. *See also* Brushes; Cloning; Duplicating; Graphic Hose feature.
    description, 122
    gradient fills, 123
    new features, 18–19
    perspective, 133–134
    spraying objects, 123
    stretching objects, 123
    vs. clones, 122
    vs. Graphic Hose, 122–123
    vs. symbols, 122
Brush feature, projects
    airplane, 136–137
    cartoon action, 136–137
    decorative border, 129–135
    eagle, 137–140
    glass tab, 124–129
Brush strokes
    applying to paths, 18–19
    stylizing line drawings, 297–300
Brushes
    altering, 123
    applying, examples, 132
    creating, examples, 127–129, 131–132, 135–136
    custom brush colors, 301
    organic, creating, 135–136
    vector-based. *See* Brush feature.
Bubbles, drawing, 314
Bulleted lists, 215
Butt cap, 35

C

Car drawing project, 63–72
Cartoon action project, 136–137
Cat tasties package project, 245–252
Cherries project, 107–111
Child Pages. *See also* Master Pages.
    changing, 22
    creating, 241
    definition, 240
    modifying layout of, 241
    releasing from Master Pages, 241

Circles, drawing, 46, 88
Clipboard icon, 199
Cloning. *See also* Brush feature; Duplicating; Graphic Hose feature.
    project, 41–52
    vs. Brush feature, 122
Closed paths
    creating, 38
    definition, 34
CMYK color, 56–58
Coffee bag project, 116–120
Coffee cup and pot projects
    drawing, 294–316
    Flash animation, 316–318
Color boxes, new features, 26
Color fills. *See* Blends; Contour gradients; Gradient fills.
Color libraries, 60–61
Color Mixer panel, 62–63
Color transitions. *See* Blends; Contour gradients; Gradient fills.
Coloring drawings, 300–301
Colors
    4-process, 56–57
    abrupt changes, 96
    choosing from existing images. *See* Eyedropper Xtra.
    choosing from libraries, 60–61
    CMYK, 56–58
    creating, 62–63
    custom brushes, 301
    displaying on monitors, 56
    dragging and dropping. *See* Eyedropper Xtra.
    duotones, 57
    exporting, 61
    fluorescents, 57
    HLS, 59
    hue, 59
    lightness, 59
    maximum number of, 61
    naming, 63
    Pantone Matching System. *See* PMS colors.
    PMS, converting to, 65
    PMS, uses for, 57
    process, 56–57

project, 63–72
RGB, 58–59
saturation, 59
shade, 63
spot, 57–58
tint, 63
Web-safe, 60
Commands
Convert To Symbol, 105, 109
Copy To Symbol, 105, 109
Flow Inside Path, 217, 219
frequently used, 260
Paste Inside, 151
Run Around Selection, 217, 219
Commenting your work, 275
Compound paths, creating, 40
Compressing images, Flash, 276–277
Cone projects
blends, 78–79
Contour gradients, 89
gradient fills, 81–82
Contour gradients
description, 82
example, 77
new features, 19–20
vs. Gradient Mesh, 83
Contour gradients, projects
cone, 89
cube, 86–88
power saw, 90–97
rose, 83–86
sphere, 89
Convert To Symbol command, 105, 109
Copy As Path button, 199
Copy To Symbol command, 105, 109
Copying and pasting Envelopes, 199
Copying objects. *See* Brush feature; Cloning; Duplicating; Graphic Hose feature.
Corner handles on points
dragging to fit curves, 47
dragging too far, 48
extraneous, removing, 44
overextended, 48
project, 41–52

Correct Direction Xtra, 40
Cows
aerosol can project, 198–206
newsletter project, 222–232, 234–238
paperback book project, 190–196
rude cows movie, 278–290
Create button, 199
Creating
animation, 270–273
brushes, examples, 127–129, 131–132, 135–136
Child Pages, 241
closed paths, 38
colors, 62–63
documents, 11
Flash movies, 273–277
Master Pages, 240
SWF files, 276
symbols, 100
Cube projects
blends, 77–78
Contour gradients, 86–88
gradient fills, 81
Cursor distance, setting, 45
Custom brushes, color, 301
Custom Views, 10, 41–52
Cylinder, wrapping around
description, 196–198
project, 198–206

D

Dashed lines, exporting to Flash, 276–277
Decorative border project, 129–135
Default pages. *See also* Master Pages.
vs. templates, 14
Deleting
portions of drawings, 278
presets, 199
sections of paths, 153
symbols, 101
Depth, example, 126–127
Desktop
Custom Views, 10
fitting pages, 9

graphics and file size, 7
navigating, 9
preview modes, 9
size, 7
viewing pages, 9
Digital cameras, 41
Dimetric projections, 147–148
Discretionary hyphen, inserting, 212
Distortions. *See also* 3D Rotation Xtra; Envelopes;
Perspective Grid.
bitmapped images, 180
Fisheye Lens Xtra, 193
Divide Xtra, 37
Documents
creating, 11
symbols, global modification, 101–102
unsaved document indicator, 28
Drawings
circles, 46, 88
compound curves, 308
deleting portions of, 278
exporting, resulting crop size, 7
for Web pages. *See* Web production.
line, 294–297
sharp corners, 301
Drawings, projects
3D effect, 305–307
bubbles, 314
car, 63–72
coffee cup and pot, 294–318
coloring the drawing, 300–301
compound curves, 308
gradient fill, 307–310
hands, 49–52
line drawings, 294–297
photorealism, 302–305
pouring liquid, 314–315
stylized brush strokes, 297–300
Dreamweaver support, 289–290
Duotone color, 57
Duplicate pages. *See also* Master Pages; Templates.
definition, 239
vs. Master Pages, 242–243

Duplicating. *See also* Brush feature; Cloning;
Graphic Hose feature.
grids, 160, 170
objects, 102
Perspective Grid, 159, 160

E

Eagle project, 137–140
Easy mode, 3D Rotation Xtra, 182–184
Ellipse tool, 41–52
Ellipses, major and minor axes, 70
Em dash, inserting, 212
Em space, inserting, 212
En dash, inserting, 212
En space, inserting, 212
End-of-column character, inserting, 212
End-of-line character, inserting, 212
English Garden logo project, 129–135
Envelopes
3D effect, 305–307
bitmaps in, 119
Clipboard icon, 199
Copy As Path button, 199
copying and pasting, 199
Create button, 199
deleting presets, 199
description, 187–188
distortion effects, 188
editing text, 211
flat distortions, 190–196
Map icon, 199
photorealism, 302–305
projects, aerosol can, 198–206
projects, paperback book, 190–196
Release icon, 199
Remove icon, 199
removing from an object, 199
saving as preset, 199
showing/hiding the Envelope map, 199
text effects, 188–190
toolbar, 199
unexpected results, 307
vs. Perspective Grid, 194

wrapping around a cylinder, description,
196–198
wrapping around a cylinder, project, 198–206
Examples. *See* Projects.
Expand Stroke Xtra
definition, 38
project, 41–52
Expert mode, 3D Rotation Xtra, 184–185
Exporting
color, 61
dashed lines to Flash, 276–277
drawings, resulting crop size, 7
graphics to Flash, 275–277, 289
symbols, 102, 116
vector graphics for the Web, 28
Eyedropper Xtra
dragging and dropping colors, 61–62, 67, 111
on locked layers, 42

F

File formats, Web production, 255
File Info dialog box, new features, 27
Fills. *See* Blends; Contour gradients; Gradient fills.
Fisheye Lens Xtra
flat distortions, 193
text along a path, 220
Fixed-size text blocks, 213–214
Flash support
ActionScript, 273
animation speed, 277
assigning actions, 274–275
commenting your work, 275
dashed lines, 276–277
editing text, 277
Full Screen action, 274
Go To action, 273–274
image compression, 276–277
importing FreeHand graphics, 275–277, 289
Load Movie action, 274
Movie Settings panel, 276–277
movies, creating, 273–277
movies, playing frame by frame, 277–278
movies, testing, 277–278

new features, 27–28, 255–256
Note section, 275
path compression, 276–277
Play and Stop action, 274
Print action, 274
project, 278–290
Start/Stop Drag action, 274
SWF files, creating, 276
Tell Target action, 274
Unload Movie action, 274
Flat distortions project, 190–196
Flow Inside Path command, 217, 219
Fluorescent color, 57
Fly animation, 280
Fonts, defining, 216–217
Formatting text, 210–212
Fractal shapes, 40
Fractalize Xtra, 40
FreeHand Source, Web site, 7, 87
Full Screen action, 274

G

Glass tab project, 124–129
Go To action, 273–274
Gradient fills. *See also* Blends; Contour gradients.
abrupt color changes, 96
blending, 309–310
Brush feature, 123
definition, 74
description, 76–77
Linear, 76–77
Logarithmic, 76–77
Radial, 76–77
Gradient fills, projects
coffee cup, 307–308
cone, 81–82
cube, 81
sphere, 82
Gradient Mesh tool *vs.* Contour gradients, 83
Graduated fills. *See* Gradient fills.
Graphic Hose feature. *See also* Brush feature;
Cloning; Duplicating.
description, 102–103
vs. Brush feature, 122–123

Graphic Hose feature, projects
    broccoli, 111–116
    cherries, 107–111
    coffee bag, 116–120
    peas in a pod, 103–107
Graphics. *See also* Inline graphics; Objects; Symbols.
    and file size, 7
    exporting to Flash, 275–277, 289
    repeating. *See* Brush feature; Cloning;
        Duplicating; Graphic Hose feature.
    text inside, 218
    text surrounding, 217–218
Grids
    alignment, 159
    applying, 11
    changing, 11
    duplicating, 160, 170
    lines, hiding, 161, 166
    mousing, 158
    names won't select correctly, 169
Grouping symbols, 101
Groups, flowing text around, 217
Guidelines, displaying, 12

H

Hand tool, new features, 25
Handles. *See* Corner handles.
Hands, drawing, 49–52
HLS color, 59
HTML
    editing, 258
    files, 258
    pages, publishing, 256–258
    source code, viewing, 257
Hue, 59
Hyphen, inserting, 212

I

Image compression, Flash, 276–277
Images. *See* Graphics; Objects; Symbols.
Importing
    into Flash, 275–277, 289

    symbols, 102, 116
    text. *See* Text, importing into FreeHand.
Inline graphics, 222, 226, 231–232
Inset Path Xtra, 38–39
Insetting paths, 38–39
International Press Telecommunications Council
    Protocol, 27
Intersect Xtra, 37–38
Intersecting shapes, 37–38
Isometric projections, 144, 147–148

J

Join tool, 41–52
Joins
    definition, 34–35
    project, 41–52
    selecting, 38

K

Kelleigh, Ian, 7, 87, 155, 242, 278
Keyboard shortcuts, 4–5

L

Labels. *See* Text.
Layers
    hiding, 67
    Master Pages, 243
    project, 41–52
    Web production, 254, 256–257
Learmont, Ralph, 242
Library panel, new features, 21
Lightness, 59
Line drawings. *See* Drawings.
Line weight
    default, 35
    selecting, 38
Lines. *See* Paths.
Links
    creating, 255
    overlapping, 256–257

selecting, 20–21
troubleshooting, 256–257
Load Movie action, 274
Logos
English Garden, 129–135
newsletter, 224–225
star, 248

M

Macintosh OS X compatibility, 18, 28–29
Main toolbar, 6
Major axes, ellipses, 70
Map icon, 199
Master Pages. *See also* Child Pages; Duplicate pages;
Templates.
background color, 241
creating, 240
definition, 11–12
layers, 243
new features, 22
page numbering, 241–242
vs. duplicate pages, 242–243
vs. templates, 242–243
Web navigation buttons, 257
Minor axes, ellipses, 70
Misregistrations (printing), correcting, 243–245
Mist effect, 285–289
Modifying symbols, 100–101
Mom's Diner sign project, 169–177
Monitors
displaying color, 56
working with two, 26
Morphing shapes, 74–76
Mouse overs, 280–282
Movie Settings panel, 276–277
Movies, Flash
creating, 273–277
playing frame by frame, 277–278
testing, 277–278
Moving objects, setting cursor distance, 45
Multiple pages, 8
Multiview projections, 144–146

N

Naming colors, 63
Navigation
desktop, 9
Web, buttons on a Master Page, 257
Web, Navigation panel, 20–21, 255
Navigation panel, 20–21, 255
New features
Brush feature, 18–19
Color boxes, 26
Contour gradients, 19–20
File Info dialog box, 27
Flash integration, 27–28
Hand tool, 25
International Press Telecommunications
Council Protocol, 27
Library panel, 21
Macintosh OS X compatibility, 18, 28–29
Master Pages, 22
Navigation panel, 20–21
Pen tool, 22–24
Print Area feature, 28
Smart Cursor pointers, 24–25
Subselect tool, 25
symbol libraries, 21
symbols, editing, 26
unsaved document indicator, 28
News media, cataloging files for, 27
Nonbreaking space, inserting, 212
Note section, 275

O

Objects. *See also* Graphics; Symbols.
3D. *See* 3D effects.
converting to symbols, 105, 109
copying to symbols, 105, 109
finding center of, 117
grouping/ungrouping on layers, 165
movement, setting cursor distance, 45
on Perspective Grid. *See* Perspective grid,
applying objects.
repeating. *See* Brush feature; Graphic Hose
feature.

spacing equally, 75
spraying. *See* Brush feature.
stretching, 123
Web, overlapping, 257
Oblique projections, 144–145
Organic brushes, 135–136
Orthographic projections, 144–145
Outsetting paths, 38–39
Overlapping
    links, 256–257
    shapes, 36
    Web objects, 257

P

Page defaults, setting
    default pages *vs.* templates, 14
    in panels, 13
    on documents, 13
    saving, 14
Page numbering
    Master Pages, 241–242
    renumbering pages, 8, 22
Pages
    fitting to desktop, 9
    master. *See* Master Pages.
    multiple, 8
    printing, size and orientation, 8
    renumbering, 8, 22
    viewing, 9–10
Paperback book project, 190–196
Paragraph marks, displaying, 212
Paste Inside command, 151
Paste inside project, 41–52
Path compression, Flash, 276–277
Path direction
    changing, 34–35
    reversing, 40
    setting, 40
Path shapes
    abstract, 39
    cookie-cutter cutouts, 36–37
    fractal, 40

intersections, 37–38
morphing, 74–76
overlapping, 36
separating, 37
transitions. *See* Blends.
Path Xtras. *See* Xtras, for paths.
Paths
    aligning, 68
    applying brush strokes, 18–19
    closed, 34
    closing, 38
    compound, creating, 40
    cookie-cutter cutouts, 36–37
    definition, 34
    deleting sections of, 153
    displaying, 34
    dividing a line equally, 39
    end caps, 34–35, 38
    insetting/outsetting, 38–39
    Joins, 34–35
    joins, selecting, 38
    line weight, default, 35
    line weight, selecting, 38
    points, adding, 35–36, 39
    points, removing, 39
    roughening, 39
    simplifying, 39
    start point, determining, 46
    stroking, 34
    transparency effects, 37
Peas-in-a-pod project, 103–107
Pen tool
    new features, 22–24
    project, 41–52
Perspective Grid
    definition, 156–157
    example, 133–134
    grid alignment, 159
    grid lines, hiding, 161, 166
    grid names won't select correctly, 169
    grids, duplicating, 160, 170
    mousing, 158
    text along a path, 220
    text editing on, 211
    vs. Envelopes, 194

Perspective Grid, applying objects
  bounding boxes, 170
  changing dimensions, 160
  duplicating, 159, 160
  flopping, 160
  point of view, moving, 159
  removing, 161
  rules for, 157–158
  selecting objects, 171
  text, 161
  to horizontal grid, 159
  to vertical grid, 158
  vanishing points, arranging, 159
Perspective Grid, projects
  bologna sandwich, 161–164
  CD jewel case, 148–156
  Mom's Diner sign, 169–177
  table setting, 164–169
Perspective projections
  axonometric, 144–145, 146–147
  dimetric, 147–148
  isometric, 144, 147–148
  multiview, 144–146
  oblique, 144–145
  orthographic, 144–145
  perspective, 145
  trimetric, 147–148
Photorealism, 302–305
Photos inside type characters project, 246–247
Pictures. *See* Graphics; Objects; Symbols.
Play and Stop action, 274
Plug-ins. *See* Xtras.
PMS colors
  converting to, 65
  uses for, 57
Point of view, moving, 159
Points
  adding, 35–36, 39
  removing, 39
Power saw project
  blends, 90–97
  Contour gradients, 90–97
Preview modes, 9
Print action, 274

Print Area feature, new features, 28
Printing
  misregistrations, correcting, 243–245
  pages, size and orientation, 8
  trapping, description, 243–245
  trapping, project, 245–252
Printing, projects
  cat tasties package, 245–252
  photos inside type characters, 246–247
  star logo, 248
  text on a path, 249–250
  trapping, 245–252
Process color, 56–57
Projection methods. *See* Perspective projections.
Projects
  3D effects, 185–187
  3D Rotation Xtra, 185–187
  aerosol can, 198–206
  airplane, 136–137
  blends. *See* Blends, projects.
  bologna sandwich, 161–164
  broccoli, 111–116
  Brush feature. *See* Brush feature, projects.
  car drawing, 63–72
  cartoon action, 136–137
  cherries, 107–111
  coffee bag, 116–120
  color usage, 63–72
  cones, blends, 78–79
  Contour gradients. *See* Contour gradients, projects.
  decorative border, 129–135
  eagle, 137–140
  English Garden logo, 129–135
  Envelopes, 190–196
  Flash movie, 278–290
  flat distortions, 190–196
  glass tab, 124–129
  gradient fills. *See* Gradient fills, projects.
  Graphic Hose feature. *See* Graphic Hose feature, projects.
  hacksaw, 41–52
  logos, 129–135, 248
  Mom's Diner sign, 169–177
  paperback book, 190–196

paths, 41–52

peas in a pod, 103–107

power saw, 90–97

printing. *See* Printing, projects.

rose, 83–86

rude cows movie, 278–290

solar paddle wheel, 185–187

star logo, 248

table setting, 164–169

text. *See* Text, projects.

wrapping around a cylinder, 198–206

Projects, cones

Contour gradients, 89

gradient fills, 81–82

Projects, cubes

blends, 77–78

Contour gradients, 86–88

gradient fills, 81

Projects, spheres

blends, 79–81

Contour gradients, 89

gradient fills, 82

Punch Xtra, 36–37

R

Rasterizing vector art, 83

Release icon, 199

Remove icon, 199

Renumbering pages, 8, 22

Repeating objects. *See* Brush feature; Cloning; Duplicating; Graphic Hose feature.

Replacing symbols, 101

Reverse Direction Xtra, 40

RGB color, 58–59

Rose project, 83–86

Rotate From location, 182–183

Rotating objects in 3D. *See* 3D Rotation Xtra.

Roughen Xtra, 39

Roughening paths, 39

Round cap, 35

Rude cows movie, 278–290

Run Around Selection command, 217, 219

Run-ins, 218

Runarounds, 217–218, 231–232

S

Saturation, 59

Separating shapes, 37

Shading backgrounds, example, 125–126

Shading color, 63

Shadows, example, 126–127

Shapes

abstract, 39

cookie-cutter cutouts, 36–37

fractal, 40

intersections, 37–38

morphing, 74–76

overlapping, 36

separating, 37

transitions. *See* Blends.

Simplify Xtra, 39

Simplifying paths, 39

Slomski, Michael, 242

Smart Cursor pointers, new features, 24–25

Snapping to toolbars, 10

Solar paddle wheel project, 185–187

Source code (HTML), viewing, 257

Spaces, displaying, 212

Sphere projects

blends, 79–81

Contour gradients, 89

gradient fills, 82

Split tool, 41–52

Spot colors

definition, 57–58

printing, 243–245

Square cap, 35

Star logo project, 248

Start/Stop Drag action, 274

Stroke transitions. *See* Blends.

Stroking paths, 34

Subselect tool, new features, 25

SWF files, creating, 276

Symbol libraries, new features, 21

Symbols panel. *See* Library panel.

Symbols, regular. *See also* Brush feature; Graphic Hose feature; Graphics; Objects.

converting from objects, 105, 109

copying from objects, 105, 109

creating, 100

definition, 100

deleting, 101

duplicating, 102

editing, new features, 26

exporting, 102, 116

global document modification, 101–102

grouping, 101

importing, 102, 116

modifying, 100–101

replacing, 101

spraying as random patterns. *See* Graphic Hose feature.

squishing, 122

stroking along a path. *See* Brush feature.

uses for, 101–102

T

Table setting project, 164–169

Tables

    description, 232–234

    project, 234–238

    Web production, 254, 256–257

Tabs

    displaying, 212

    project, 231–232

    setting, 213–216

Tear-off tabs, toolbars, 10–11

Tell Target action, 274

Templates. *See also* Duplicate pages; Master Pages.

    definition, 239

    vs. default pages, 14

    vs. Master Pages, 242–243

Text

    animating, 270–273

    bulleted lists, 215

    disappearing, 221

    editing in Flash, 277

    Envelopes, 188–190

    expanding to fill space, 231

    flat distortions, 188–190

    Flow Inside Path command, 217, 219

    fonts, defining, 216–217

    formatting, 210–212

importing into Freehand, 210–213

in an Envelope, editing, 211

in tables. *See* Tables.

inline graphics, 222, 226, 231–232

inside graphic objects, 218

on the Perspective Grid, editing, 211

Run Around Selection command, 217, 219

run-ins, 218

runarounds, 217–218, 231–232

stylized highlights, 225

surrounding graphic objects, 217–218

tabs, 231–232

upside down, 219

Word Udders, 231

Text blocks

    aligning text, 215–216

    discretionary hyphen, inserting, 212

    em dash, inserting, 212

    em space, inserting, 212

    en dash, inserting, 212

    en space, inserting, 212

    end-of-column character, inserting, 212

    end-of-line character, inserting, 212

    fixed-size *vs.* auto-expanding, 213–214

    invisibles, displaying, 212

    nonbreaking space, inserting, 212

    paragraph marks, displaying, 212

    spaces, displaying, 212

    tabs, displaying, 212

    tabs, setting, 213–216

    Text Ruler, 213–216

    thin space, inserting, 212

    word wrap, 213, 215–216

    Wrapping Tab, 215–216

Text Inspector, 216–217

Text Ruler, 213–216

Text, on paths

    attaching, 218–221

    cat tasties project, 249–250

    moving, 225

    newsletter project, 231–232

    special effects, 230

    spirals, 229

Text, projects
  aerosol can, 198–206
  cat tasties, 249–250
  inline graphics, 231–232
  logos, 134–135, 224–225
  newsletter, 222–232, 234–238
  paperback book, 190–196
  printing text on a path, 249–250
  runarounds, 231–232
  tables, 231–232, 234–238
  tabs, 231–232
  wrapping text around a cylinder, 198–206
Thin space, inserting, 212
Tinting color, 63
Toolbars
  default arrangements, 6
  Envelope, 199
  floating panels, 10–11
  Main, 6
  snapping to, 10
  tear-off tabs, 10–11
  Tools Panel, 10
  top, 10
Tools. *See also* Brush feature; Graphic Hose feature;
  Print Area feature; Xtras.
  Ellipse, 41–52
  Gradient Mesh *vs.* Contour gradients, 83
  Hand, 25
  Join, 41–52
  Pen, 22–24, 41–52
  Split, 41–52
  Subselect, 25
Tools Panel, 10
Top toolbar, 10
Transitions. *See* Blends; Contour gradients; Gradient
  fills.
Transparency effects, 37
Trapping
  description, 243–245
  project, 245–252
Trimetric projections, 147–148
Troubleshooting
  disappearing text, 221
  Envelopes, unexpected results, 307

  links go to wrong target, 256
  upside down text, 219
Type. *See* Text.

U

Union Xtra
  definition, 36
  project, 41–52
Unload Movie action, 274
Unsaved document indicator, 28

V

Vanishing points, arranging, 159
Vector graphics
  exporting for the Web, 28
  rasterizing, 83
Vector-based brushes. *See* Brush feature.
Viewpoint, in 3D Rotation Xtra, 184–185

W

Web production
  3D effects, 181
  animation, creating, 270–273
  exporting vector graphics for, 28
  file formats, 255
  Flash support. *See* Flash support.
  HTML files, 258
  HTML pages, publishing, 256–258
  HTML, editing, 258
  HTML, viewing source code, 257
  layers, 254, 256–257
  links, creating, 255
  links, overlapping, 256–257
  links, selecting, 20–21
  navigation, 20–21
  navigation buttons on a Master Page, 257
  Navigation Panel, 255
  objects, overlapping, 257
  page size, 263
  tables, 254, 256–257

Web production, projects
    fireworks site, 262–270
    simple site, 258–262
Web-safe colors, 60
Word Udders, 231
Word wrap, 213, 215–216
Wrapping around a cylinder
    description, 196–198
    project, 198–206
Wrapping Tab, 215–216

X

Xtras. *See also* Tools.
    3D effects. *See* 3D Rotation Xtra; Envelopes.
    Blend, 74–76
    definition, 7
    Fisheye Lens, flat distortions, 193
    Fisheye Lens, text along a path, 220
    PageNumbering 1.1, 242
    Smart Cursor status, 25
    Trap, 244–245
    Web site, 7
Xtras, 3D Rotation
    description, 182
    Easy mode, 182–184
    Expert mode, 184–185
    joystick metaphor, 182–183
    projects, 185–187
    Rotate From location, 182–183
    rotating objects, 182–183

    text along a path, 220
    viewpoint, 184–185
Xtras, Eyedropper
    dragging and dropping colors, 61–62, 67, 111
    on locked layers, 42
Xtras, for paths
    Add Points, closed paths, 35–36
    Add Points, dividing a line equally, 39
    Add Points, modifying a path, 39
    Add Points, project, 41–52
    Correct Direction, 40
    Divide, 37
    Expand Stroke, definition, 38
    Expand Stroke, project, 41–52
    Fractalize, 40
    Inset Path, 38–39
    Intersect, 37–38
    Punch, 36–37
    Reverse Direction, 40
    Roughen, 39
    Simplify, 39
    Union, definition, 36
    Union, project, 41–52

Z

Zero point, setting, 12

Expand your creative skills with these Creative Professionals Press titles

Flash 5® f/x & Design
by Bill Sanders
Media: CD-ROM

ISBN #: 1-57610-816-3
$49.99 U.S., $74.99 CAN.

Beginning with the core concepts and tools of Flash 5, this book explores ways to create attractively effective Flash movies. Not an art or design lesson, *Flash™ 5 fx & Design* shows the reader how to use Flash 5 tools to create lively animations and designs using one's own artistic talents, tastes, and imagination. It covers the basics, but it also goes beyond into a solid introduction of ActionScript, adding Flash 5 animation to QuickTime Movies, and even importing external data. Each Flash 5 element is supported by step-by-step examples and projects guiding the reader through the finite details of Flash 5's powerful set of possibilities. The accompanying CD-ROM contains 50 projects in both FLA and SWF files, allowing readers to see the finished results plus examine the projects and examples in the book to better understand how to apply the techniques to one's own work. Attention to detail such as mixing color schemes, crucial ActionScripting, the use of the new panels for precision placement and scaling, plus other Flash 5 innovations make this title a must-have book for the Flash designer and developer.

Fireworks® 4 f/x & Design
by Joyce J. Evans
Media: 2 CD-ROMs

ISBN #: 1-57610-996-8
$49.99 U.S., $74.99 CAN.

Fireworks® 4 f/x & Design teaches how to use some of the more advanced aspects of an image editor. Readers will obtain knowledge needed to produce professional level images, buttons, animations, and graphical interfaces for the Web. This guide goes beyond explaining the functions of Fireworks by showing how to produce usable elements that can be effectively incorporated into a professional Web site. This book includes two CD-ROMs containing trial versions of Dreamweaver®, Flash®, and FreeHand®; over 12,000 comping images; plus many other extras.

Dreamweaver® 4 f/x & Design
by Laurie Ulrich
Media: CD-ROM

ISBN #: 1-57610-789-2
$49.99 U.S., $74.99 CAN.

Dreamweaver® 4 f/x & Design improves, enriches, and builds upon the reader's current Dreamweaver skills. Emphasis is made on use of text, graphics, color, and special effects including sound, animated GIF files, and Flash movies in the book's chapters. Quick tips are given to format and position Web page content through HTML. With real-world applications, this book will strengthen Dreamweaver skills and improve Web page design. The CD-ROM included with this book contains HTML files created in the book's projects and numerous multimedia elements including sounds, animated GIFs, and Flash movies.

Integrating Flash™, Fireworks® and FreeHand® f/x & Design
by Joyce J. Evans
Media: CD-ROM

ISBN #: 1-58880-163-2
$49.99 U.S., $77.99 CAN.

Integrating Flash™, Fireworks® and FreeHand® f/x & Design teaches how to bring together Macromedia's popular Web-design tools into one logical workflow. This book will allow you to become comfortable using the complete Macromedia environment to develop professional-level Web pages with interactivity. An accompanying CD-ROM includes movies demonstrating techniques discussed in the book, clip art demo with 500 pieces, demo plug-ins, and standalone third-party applications.

Flash Forward with Coriolis Books

Flash™ 5 Visual Insight

Authors: Sherry London and Dan London

Audience: Novice to Intermediate Flash™ users

- Fundamentals of Flash™ 5 through a graphically oriented format.
- Projects showing the full range of the product's capabilities.
- Color section illustrating features of Flash™.
- Teaches Flash™ tools and their options, then guides readers to create their own movies.

Flash™ ActionScript f/x and Design

Author: Bill Sanders

Audience: Intermediate to Advanced Flash™ users

- Combines major concepts to show how to create more elaborate, elegant, and outstanding Flash™ 5 movies
- Teaches strategies to integrate ActionScript into Flash™ movies producing desired effects.
- Shows basic algorithms for creating movies not possible without ActionScript.

Flash™ 5 f/x and Design

Author: Bill Sanders

Audience: Intermediate to Advanced Flash™ users

- Newest features of Flash™, with case studies and tutorials.
- Contains advanced topics, including how to use data from external sources, text files, HTML pages, or servers.
- CD-ROM with 50 Flash™ 5 movies in FLA and SWF formats, and trial versions of Flash™, Dreamweaver®, Fireworks®, and FreeHand®.

Flash™ 5 Cartoons and Games f/x and Design

Authors: Bill Turner, James Robertson, and Richard Bazley

Audience: Intermediate to Advanced Flash™ users

- Reveals very beneficial Flash code and authoring source files.
- Learn cartooning with the use of lip-synching with Magpie Pro® and storyboarding in Flash™.
- CD-ROM includes demo versions of Flash™, SmartSound®, Magpie Pro®, and complete authoring files for animation and games, plus numerous games.

Flash™ is the leading vector technology for designing high-impact, low-bandwidth Web sites that deliver motion, sound, interactivity, and graphics. Vector-based Flash™ content downloads faster, is scalable, and boasts higher quality than other graphic formats. The Web experience becomes more attractive and compelling than ever before through the use of Flash™.

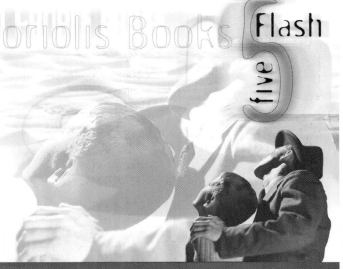

©2001 The Coriolis Group, LLC All Rights Reserved. SS

Visit us at creative.coriolis.com
Available at book and computer stores worldwide.

What's on the CD-ROM

The *FreeHand 10 f/x & Design*'s companion CD-ROM contains elements specifically selected to enhance the usefulness of this book, including:

- A 30-day trial version of Macromedia FreeHand 10. It is a fully-functioning demo that you can use to complete all the projects in this book—including saving and printing files
- A 30-day trial version of Macromedia Flash 5. This demo is also fully functional
- All necessary files to complete the projects in this book, including reference photos and partially started drawings
- A library of electronic symbols to be used in electronic schematic drawings
- An isometric grid and scale for isometric drawings
- A portfolio of hand reference photos you can use in your own work
- A library of 147 new PANTONE colors
- Two different methods of creating automatic page numbering to Master Pages (Mac only)

Note: To complete the projects in this book, you will need:

- Macromedia FreeHand 10
- Adobe Type Manager Version 4 or later with Type-1 fonts (recommended)
- Netscape Navigator or Microsoft Internet Explorer, both version 4 or later (recommended)

System Requirements

Software

- **Windows:** Windows 98, NT4, 2000, ME, or later
- **Macintosh:** Power Mac Mac OS 8.6 or later, including OS X (FreeHand 10 is the first drawing program to operate natively in OS X)

Hardware

- **Windows:** 133MHz processor is the minimum required
- **Macintosh:** G3 or G4 PowerPC Macintosh processor is the minimum required
- 64MB of available RAM is the minimum required
- Requires a minimum of 70MB of available hard disk space
- Requires a minimum 256-color, 800×600 resolution monitor, (1024×768, millions of colors recommended)
- PostScript Level 2-compatible printer or higher